GREEN LANTERN

VOLUME 7
RENEGADE

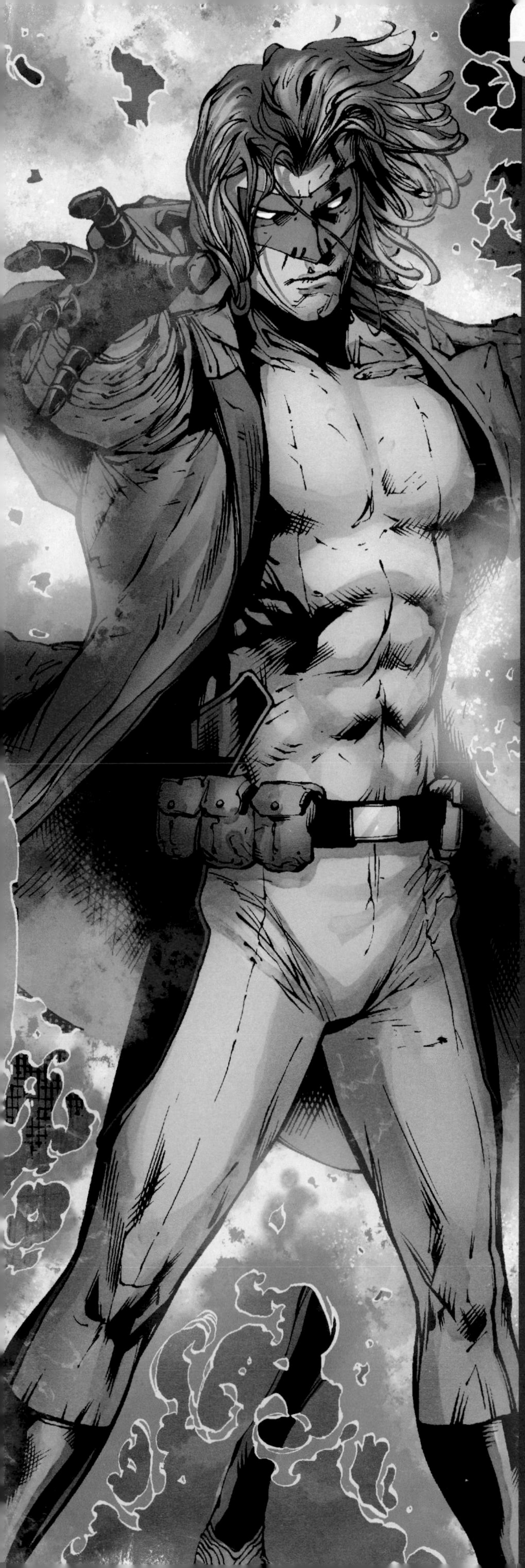

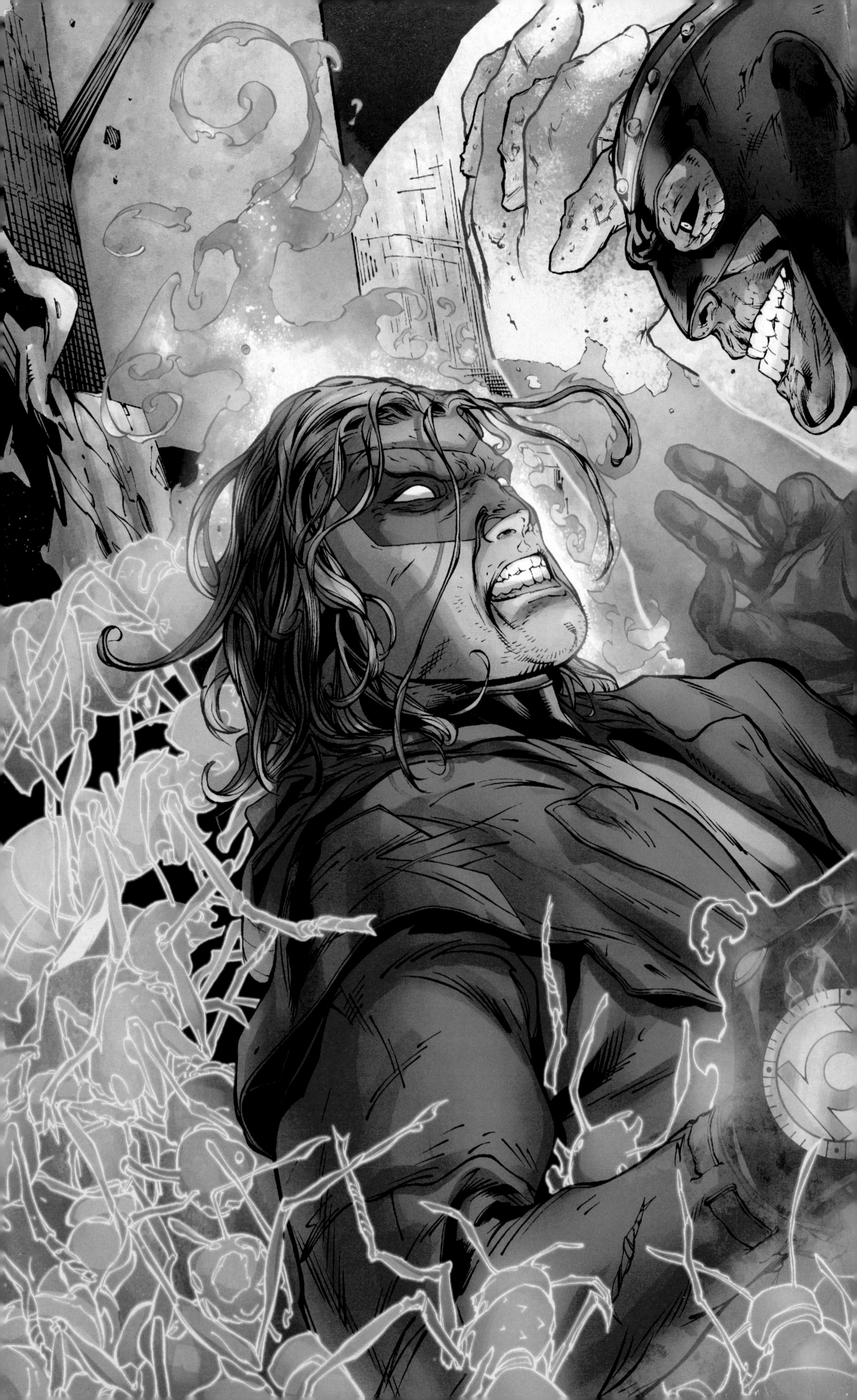

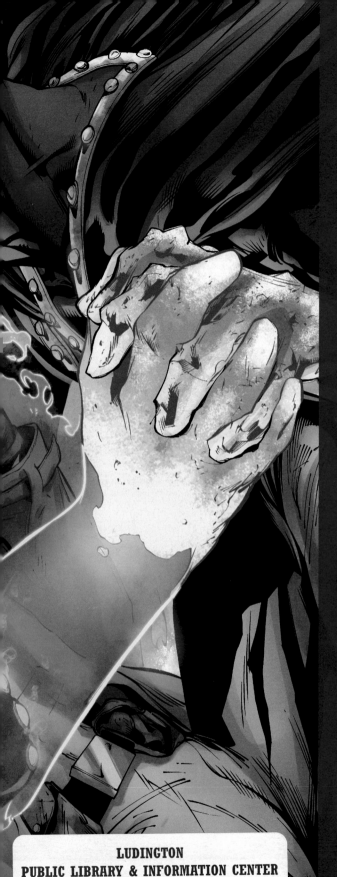

VOLUME 7
RENEGADE

GREEN LANTERN

WRITTEN BY
ROBERT VENDITTI

ART BY
BILLY TAN
MARK IRWIN
SCOTT HANNA
ETHAN VAN SCIVER
MARTIN COCCOLO
PASCAL ALIXE

COLOR BY
ALEX SINCLAIR
TONY AVIÑA
PETE PANTAZIS
HI-FI

LETTERS BY
DAVE SHARPE

COLLECTION COVER ART BY
BILLY TAN
& ALEX SINCLAIR

GREEN LANTERN VOLUME 7: RENEGADE

Published by DC Comics. Compilation and all new material Copyright © 2016 DC Comics. All Rights Reserved.
Originally published online as GREEN LANTERN SNEAK PEEK and in single magazine form as GREEN LANTERN 41-46,
GREEN LANTERN ANNUAL 4 Copyright © 2015 DC Comics. All Rights Reserved. All characters, their distinctive likenesses and
related elements featured in this publication are trademarks of DC Comics. The stories, characters and incidents featured in
this publication are entirely fictional. DC Comics does not read or accept unsolicited ideas, stories or artwork.

DC Comics, 2900 West Alameda Ave., Burbank, CA 91505
Printed by RR Donnelley, Salem, VA, USA. 8/26/16. First Printing.
ISBN: 978-1-4012-6522-9

Library of Congress Cataloging-in-Publication Data

Names: Venditti, Robert, author. | Tan, Billy, illustrator. | Irwin, Mark,
1969- illustrator. | Hanna, Scott, illustrator. | Van Sciver, Ethan,
illustrator. | Coccolo, Martin, illustrator. | Alixe, Pascal,
illustrator. | Sinclair, Alex, illustrator. | Aviña, Tony, 1973-
illustrator. | Pantazis, Pete, illustrator. | Sharpe, Dave (Letterer)
illustrator. | Hi-Fi Colour Design, illustrator.
Title: Green Lantern. Volume 7, Renegade / Robert Venditti, writer ; Billy
Tan, Mark Irwin, Scott Hanna, Ethan Van Sciver, Martin Coccolo, Pascal
Alixe, artist ; Alex Sinclair, Tony Aviña, Pete Pantazis, Hi-Fi,
colorists ; Dave Sharpe, letterer ; Billy Tan & Alex Sinclair, collection cover artists.
Other titles: Renegade
Description: Burbank, CA : DC Comics, [2016]
Identifiers: LCCN 2015044881 | ISBN 9781401265229
Subjects: LCSH: Graphic novels. | Superhero comic books, strips, etc. |
BISAC: COMICS & GRAPHIC NOVELS / Superheroes.
Classification: LCC PN6728.G74 V49 2016 | DDC 741.5/973–dc23
LC record available at http://lccn.loc.gov/2015044881

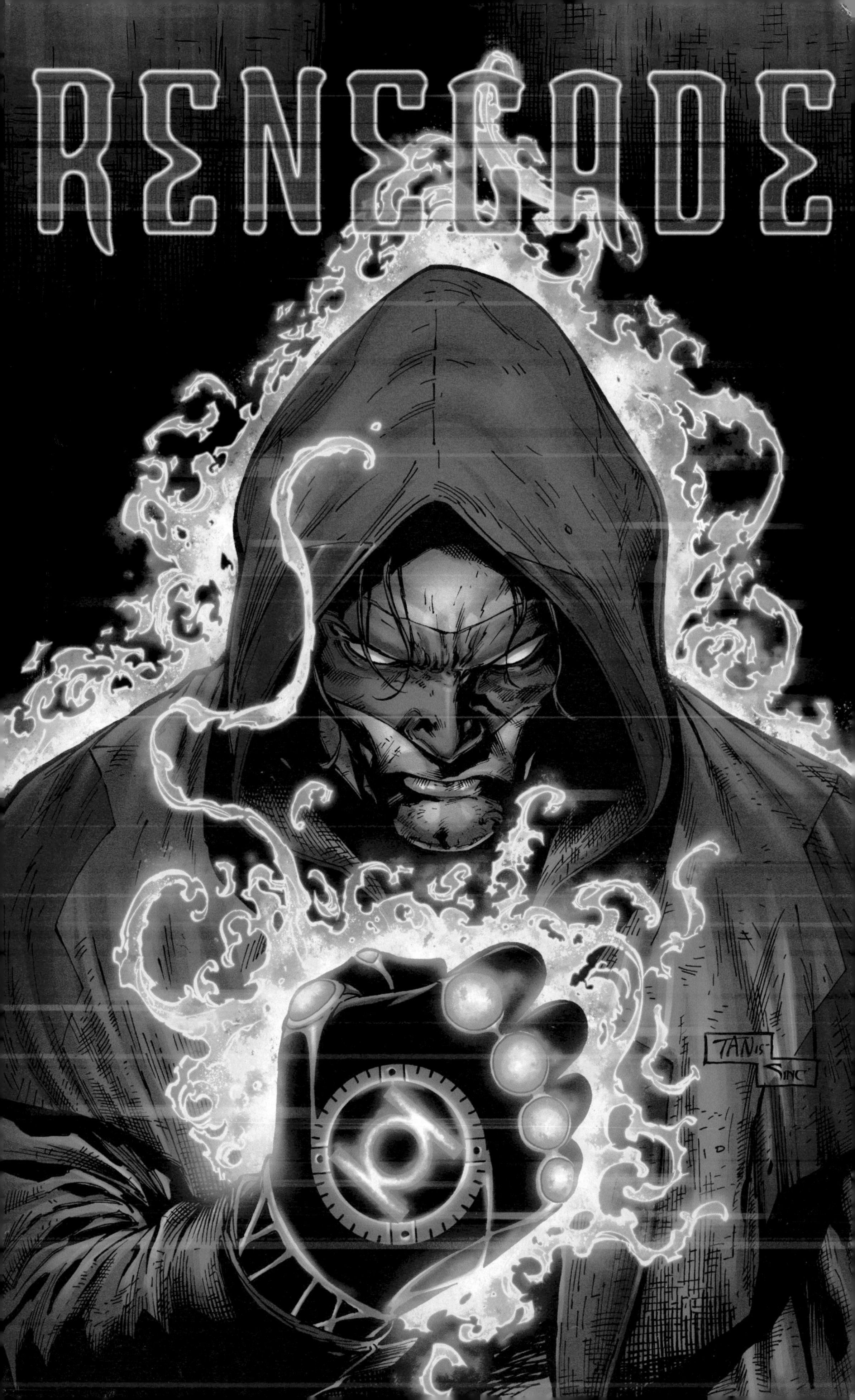
RENEGADE

AT ODDS

ROBERT VENDITTI writer BILLY TAN penciller MARK IRWIN inker ALEX SINCLAIR & TONY AVIÑA colorists DAVE SHARPE letterer BILLY TAN & ALEX SINCLAIR cover

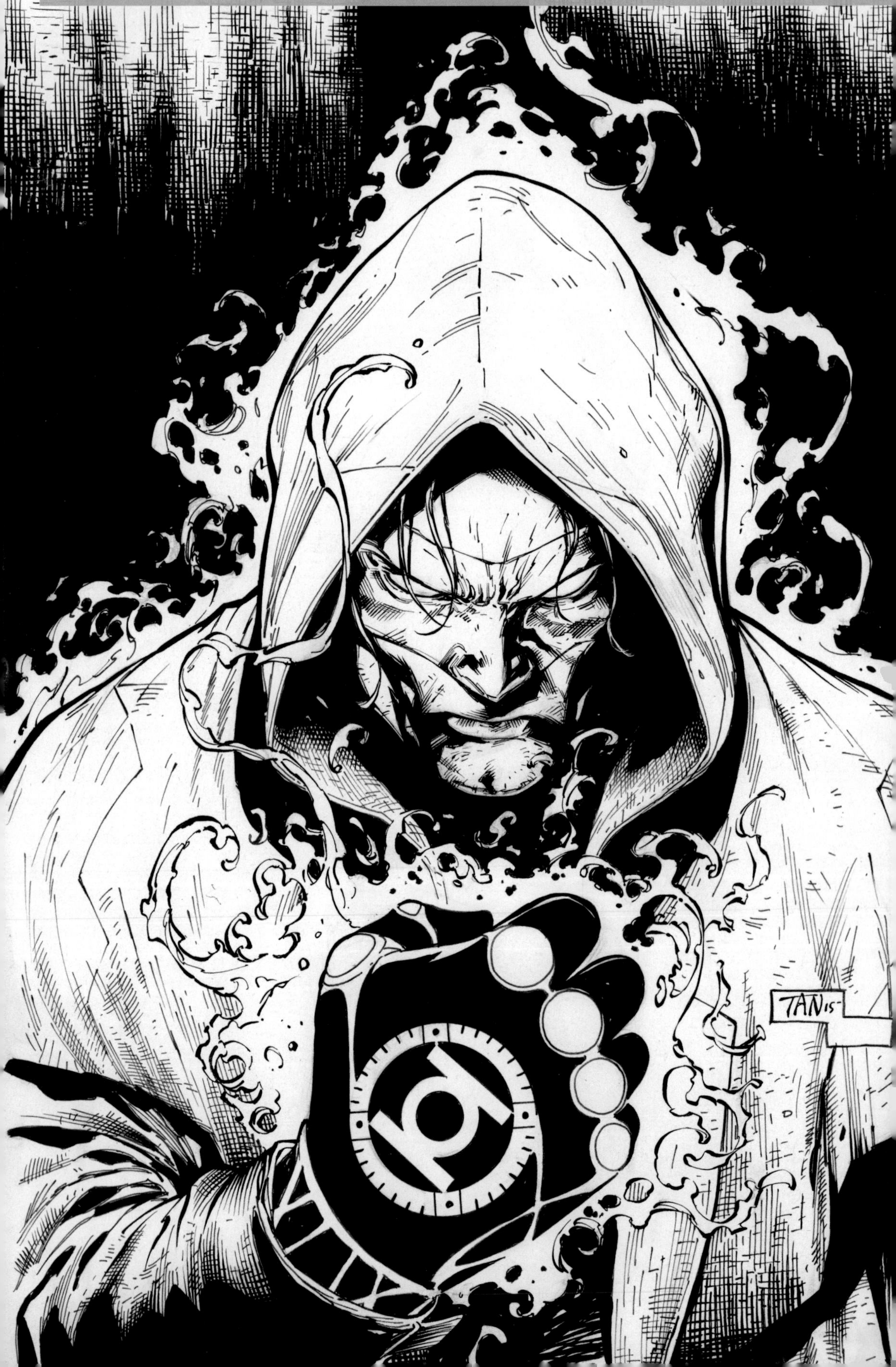
TAN 15

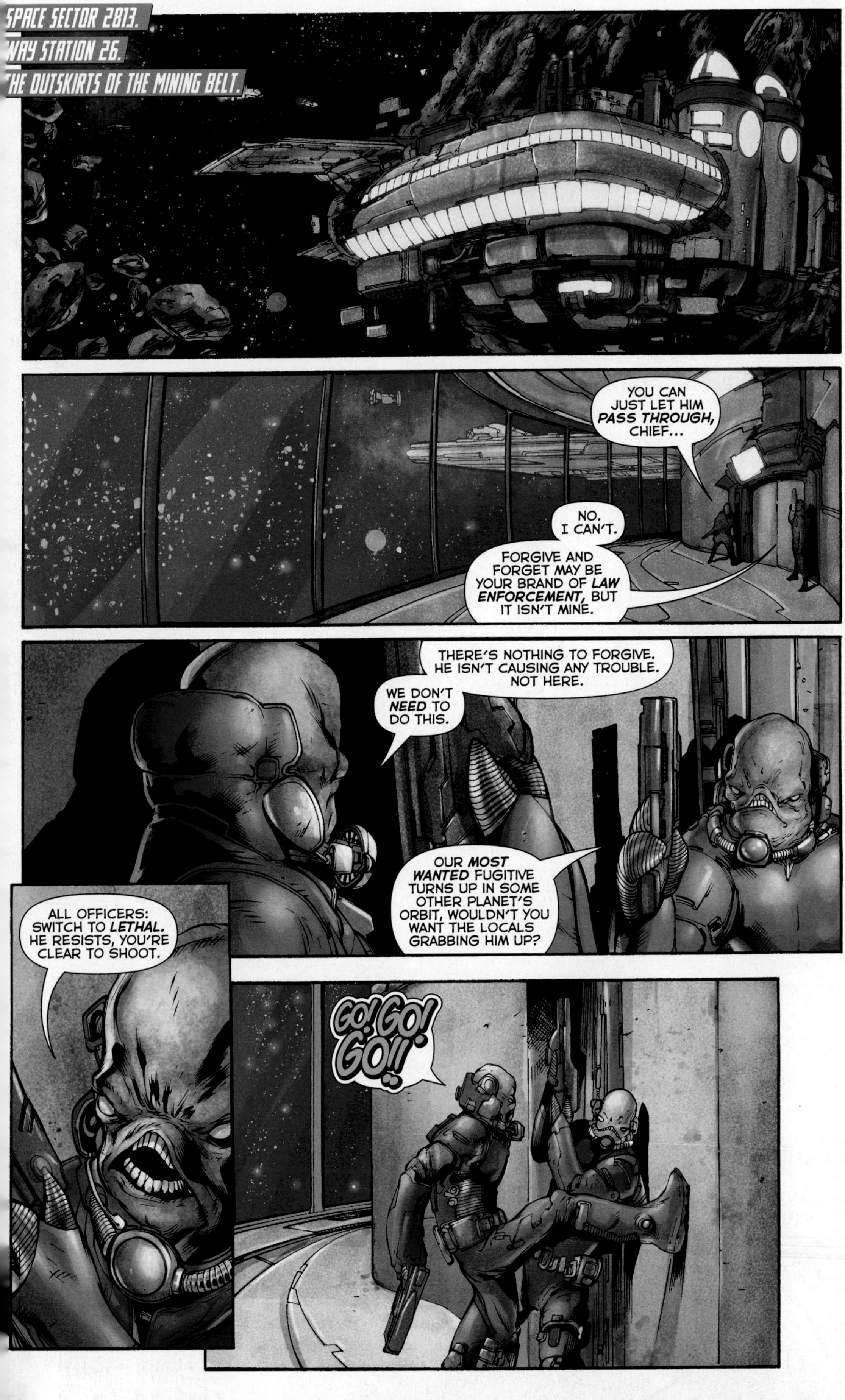
SPACE SECTOR 2813.
WAY STATION 26.
THE OUTSKIRTS OF THE MINING BELT.
YOU CAN JUST LET HIM PASS THROUGH, CHIEF...
NO. I CAN'T.
FORGIVE AND FORGET MAY BE YOUR BRAND OF LAW ENFORCEMENT, BUT IT ISN'T MINE.
THERE'S NOTHING TO FORGIVE. HE ISN'T CAUSING ANY TROUBLE. NOT HERE.
WE DON'T NEED TO DO THIS.
OUR MOST WANTED FUGITIVE TURNS UP IN SOME OTHER PLANET'S ORBIT, WOULDN'T YOU WANT THE LOCALS GRABBING HIM UP?
ALL OFFICERS: SWITCH TO LETHAL. HE RESISTS, YOU'RE CLEAR TO SHOOT.
GO! GO! GO!!

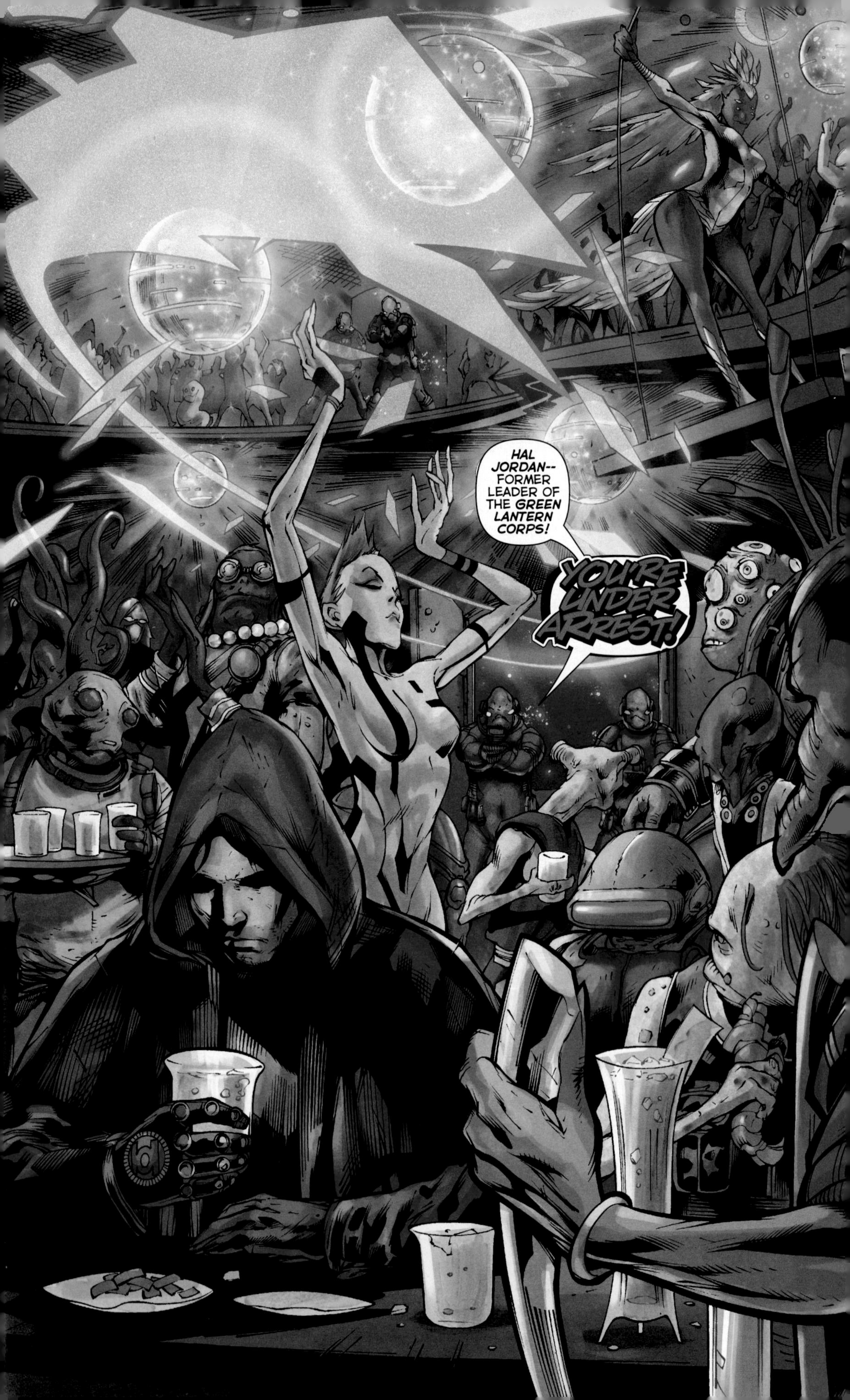
HAL JORDAN-- FORMER LEADER OF THE GREEN LANTERN CORPS!
YOU'RE UNDER ARREST!

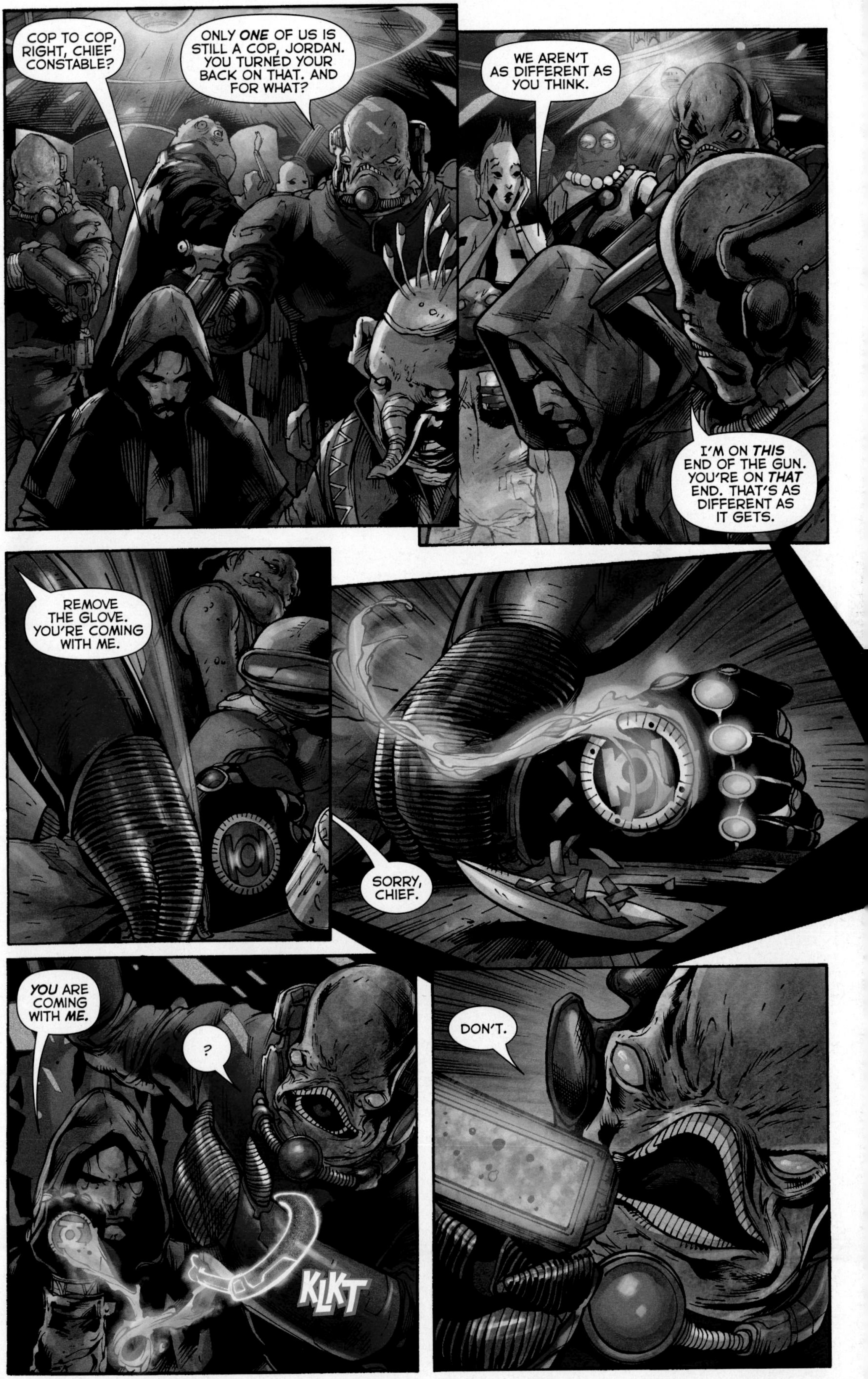

COP TO COP, RIGHT, CHIEF CONSTABLE?
ONLY ONE OF US IS STILL A COP, JORDAN. YOU TURNED YOUR BACK ON THAT. AND FOR WHAT?
WE AREN'T AS DIFFERENT AS YOU THINK.
I'M ON THIS END OF THE GUN. YOU'RE ON THAT END. THAT'S AS DIFFERENT AS IT GETS.
REMOVE THE GLOVE. YOU'RE COMING WITH ME.
SORRY, CHIEF.
YOU ARE COMING WITH ME.
?
KLKT
DON'T.

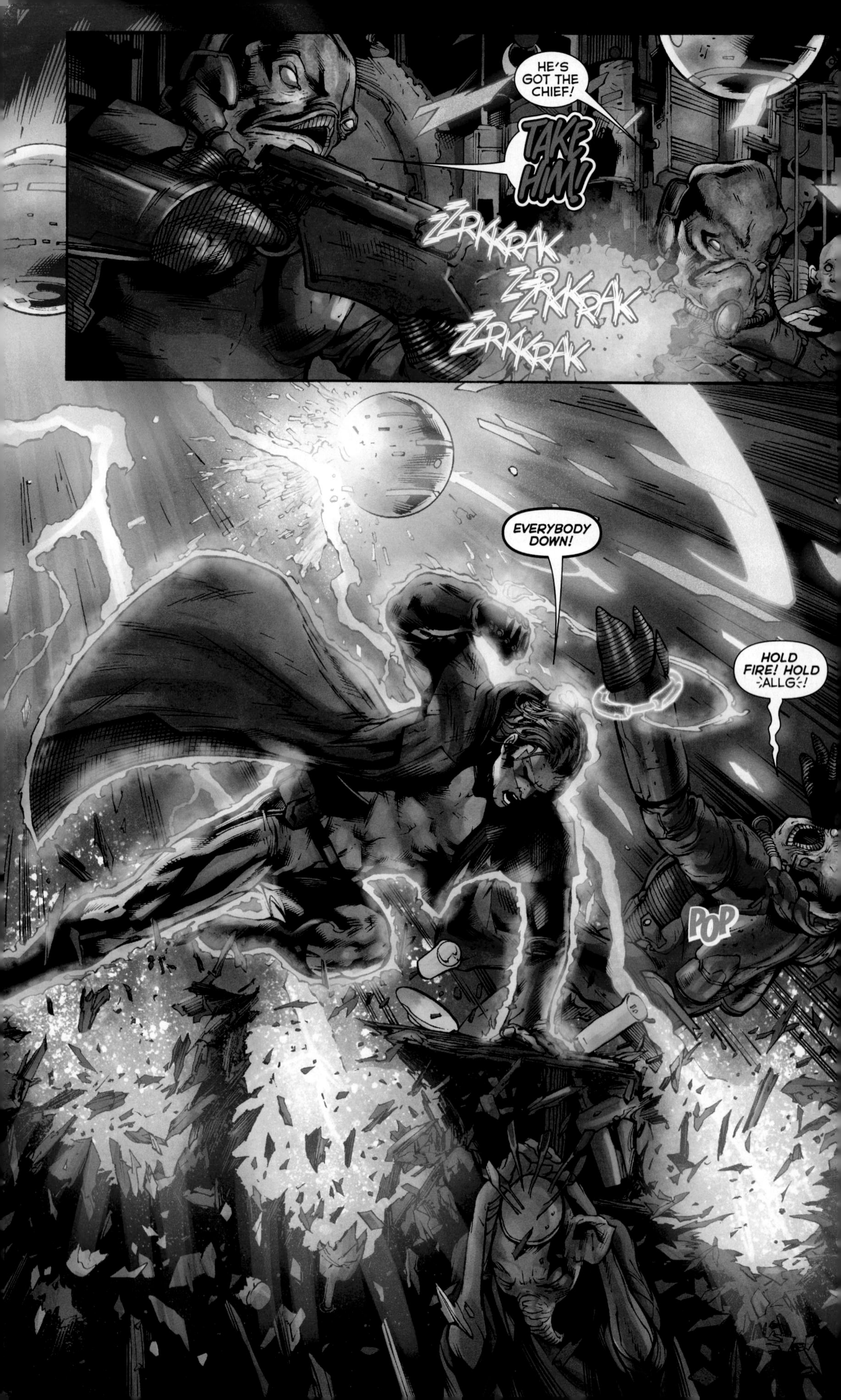
HE'S GOT THE CHIEF!
TAKE HIM!
ZZRKKRAK
ZZRKKRAK
ZZRKKRAK
EVERYBODY DOWN!
HOLD FIRE! HOLD ALLG-!
POP

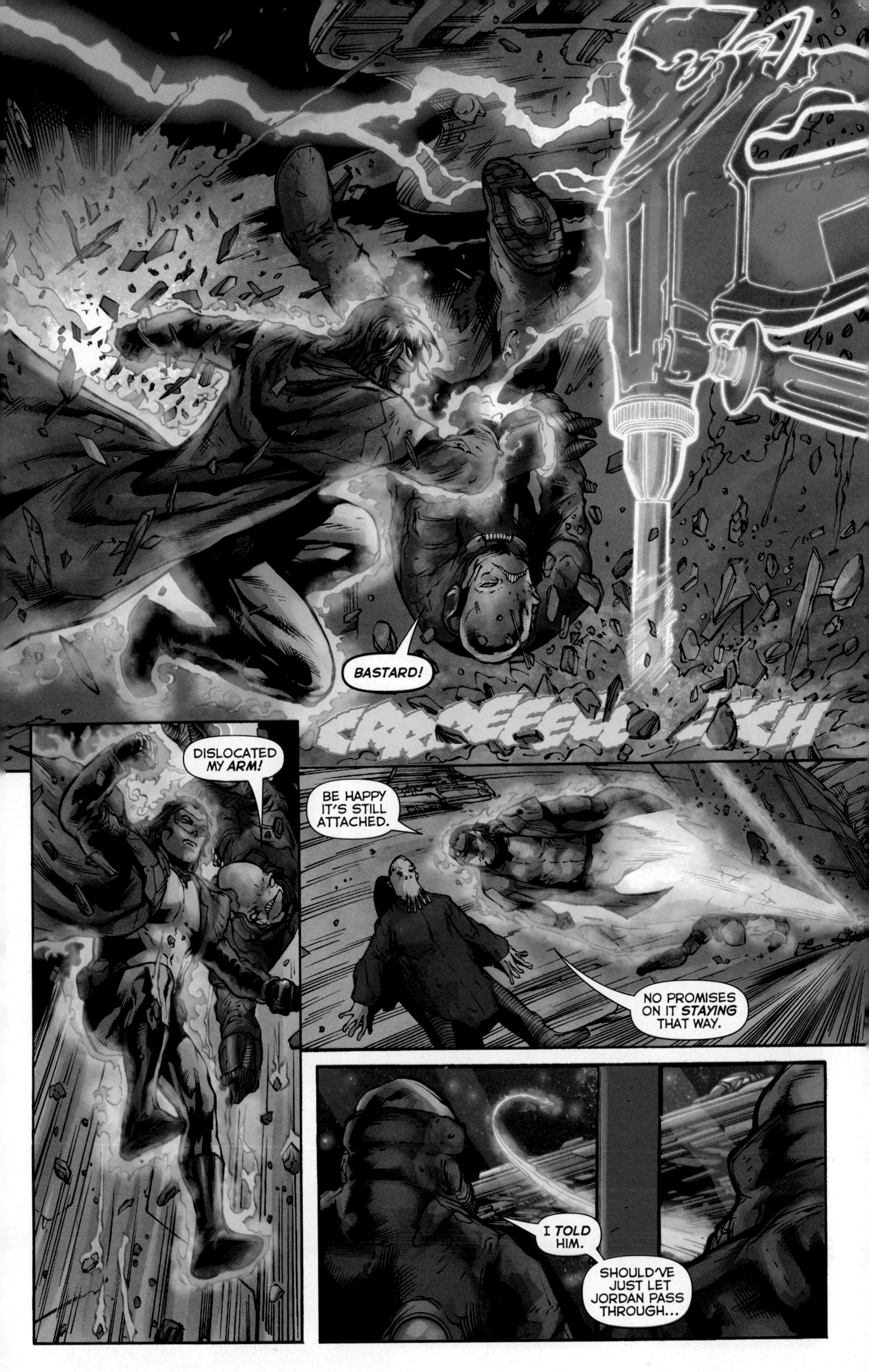
BASTARD!
DISLOCATED MY ARM!
BE HAPPY IT'S STILL ATTACHED.
NO PROMISES ON IT STAYING THAT WAY.
I TOLD HIM.
SHOULD'VE JUST LET JORDAN PASS THROUGH...

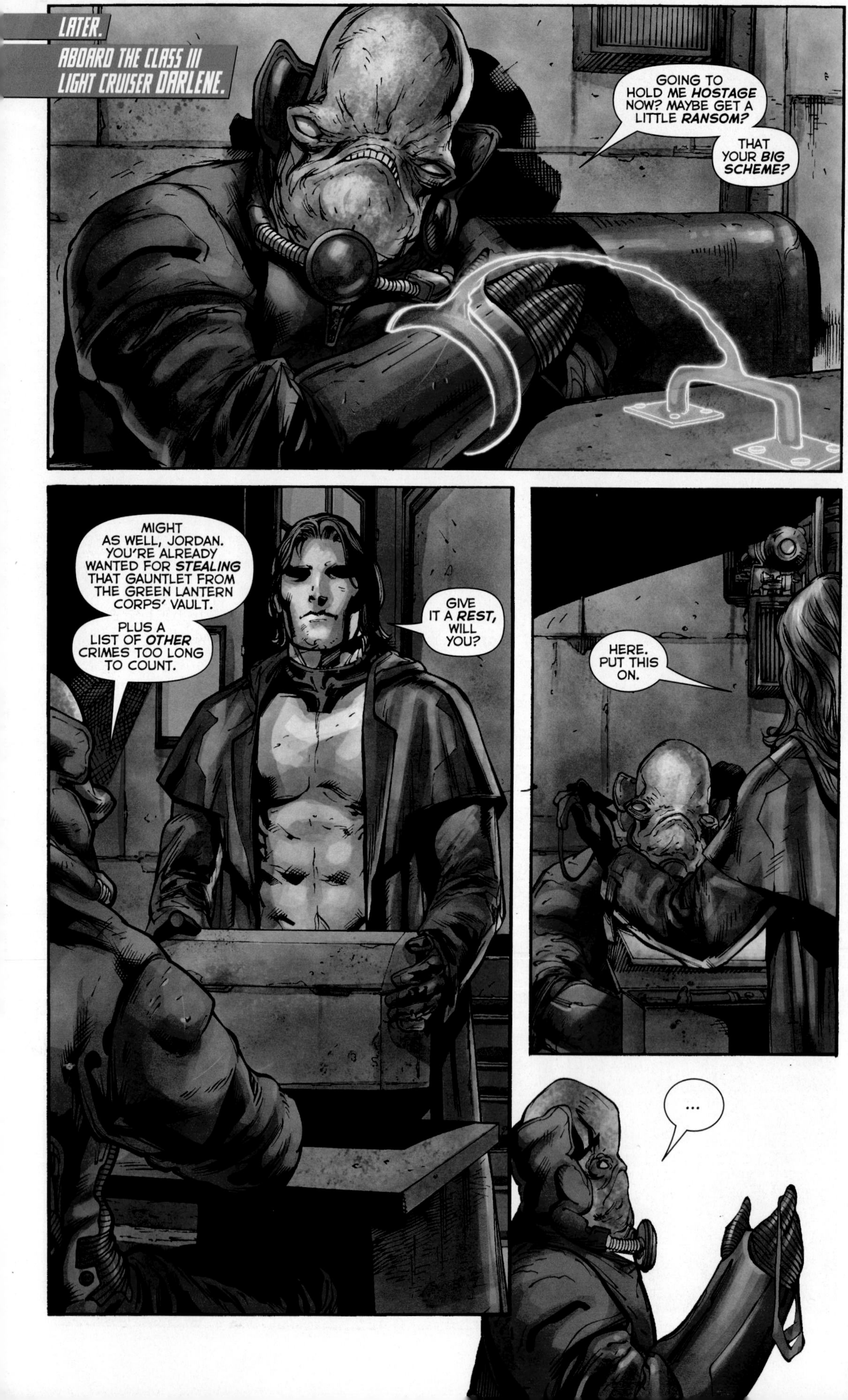
LATER.
ABOARD THE CLASS III LIGHT CRUISER DARLENE.
GOING TO HOLD ME HOSTAGE NOW? MAYBE GET A LITTLE RANSOM?
THAT YOUR BIG SCHEME?
MIGHT AS WELL, JORDAN. YOU'RE ALREADY WANTED FOR STEALING THAT GAUNTLET FROM THE GREEN LANTERN CORPS' VAULT.
PLUS A LIST OF OTHER CRIMES TOO LONG TO COUNT.
GIVE IT A REST, WILL YOU?
HERE. PUT THIS ON.
...

YOU HAVE A FAMILY?

SURE. ·NNG· A MATE AND SOME ·HNN· GILLIES.

YOU FEEL WORSE ABOUT RUINING MY *CASTING ARM* NOW?

A FAMILY. A HOME.

AND YOU RISKED NOT SEEING THEM EVER AGAIN. RISKED YOUR OFFICERS NOT SEEING *THEIR* FAMILIES AND HOMES EVER AGAIN. BECAUSE YOU COULDN'T LET ME FINISH MY *KHUNDISH ALE* IN PEACE.

THAT WAS THE CHOICE YOU MADE.

I'VE GOT PEOPLE I CARE ABOUT. DON'T KNOW WHEN--*IF*--I'LL SEE THEM AGAIN. MY HOME? YOU'RE SITTING IN IT.

I'M BY MYSELF NOW. THAT WAS THE CHOICE *I* MADE.

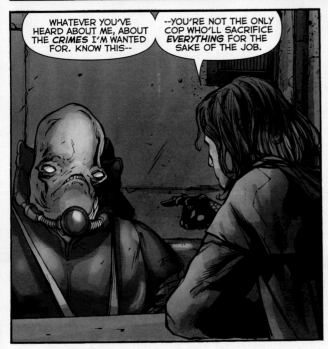

WHATEVER YOU'VE HEARD ABOUT ME, ABOUT THE *CRIMES* I'M WANTED FOR. KNOW THIS--

--YOU'RE NOT THE ONLY COP WHO'LL SACRIFICE *EVERYTHING* FOR THE SAKE OF THE JOB.

ON YOUR FINS, CHIEF.

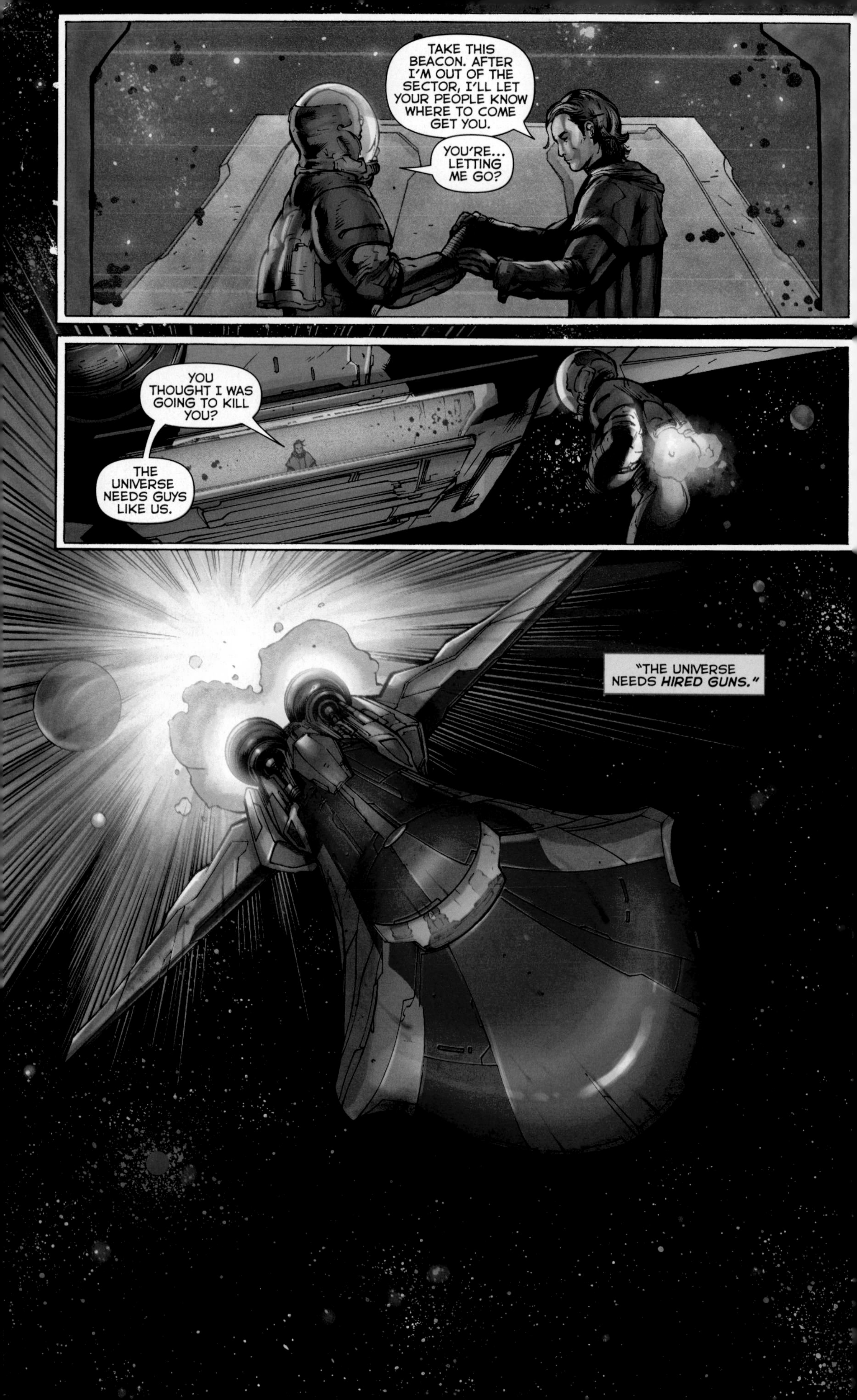
TAKE THIS BEACON. AFTER I'M OUT OF THE SECTOR, I'LL LET YOUR PEOPLE KNOW WHERE TO COME GET YOU.
YOU'RE... LETTING ME GO?
YOU THOUGHT I WAS GOING TO KILL YOU?
THE UNIVERSE NEEDS GUYS LIKE US.
"THE UNIVERSE NEEDS *HIRED GUNS.*"

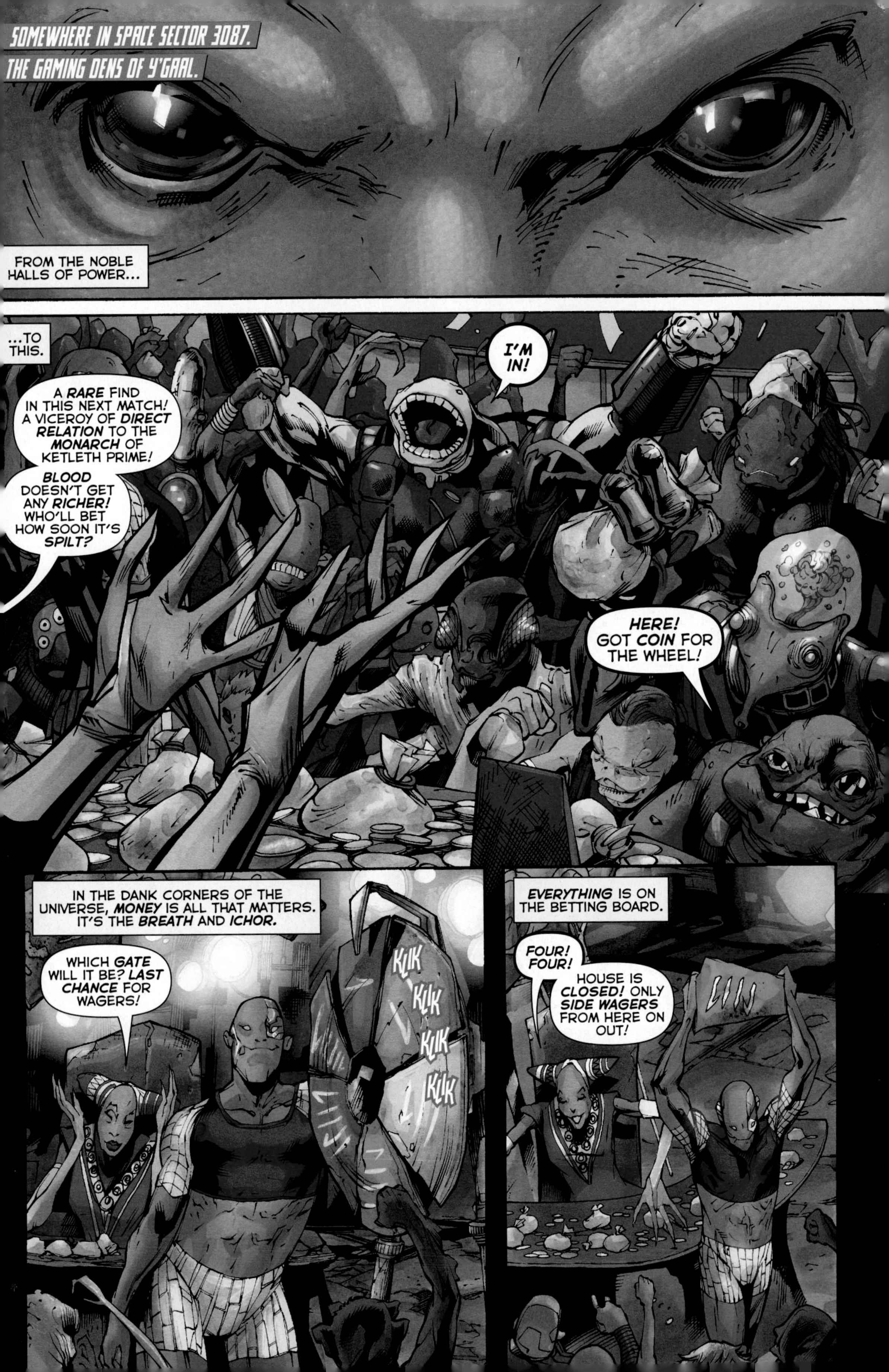
SOMEWHERE IN SPACE SECTOR 3087.
THE GAMING DENS OF Y'GAAL.
FROM THE NOBLE HALLS OF POWER...
...TO THIS.
A RARE FIND IN THIS NEXT MATCH! A VICEROY OF DIRECT RELATION TO THE MONARCH OF KETLETH PRIME!
BLOOD DOESN'T GET ANY RICHER! WHO'LL BET HOW SOON IT'S SPILT?
I'M IN!
HERE! GOT COIN FOR THE WHEEL!
IN THE DANK CORNERS OF THE UNIVERSE, MONEY IS ALL THAT MATTERS. IT'S THE BREATH AND ICHOR.
WHICH GATE WILL IT BE? LAST CHANCE FOR WAGERS!
KLIK
KLIK
KLIK
KLIK
EVERYTHING IS ON THE BETTING BOARD.
FOUR! FOUR!
HOUSE IS CLOSED! ONLY SIDE WAGERS FROM HERE ON OUT!

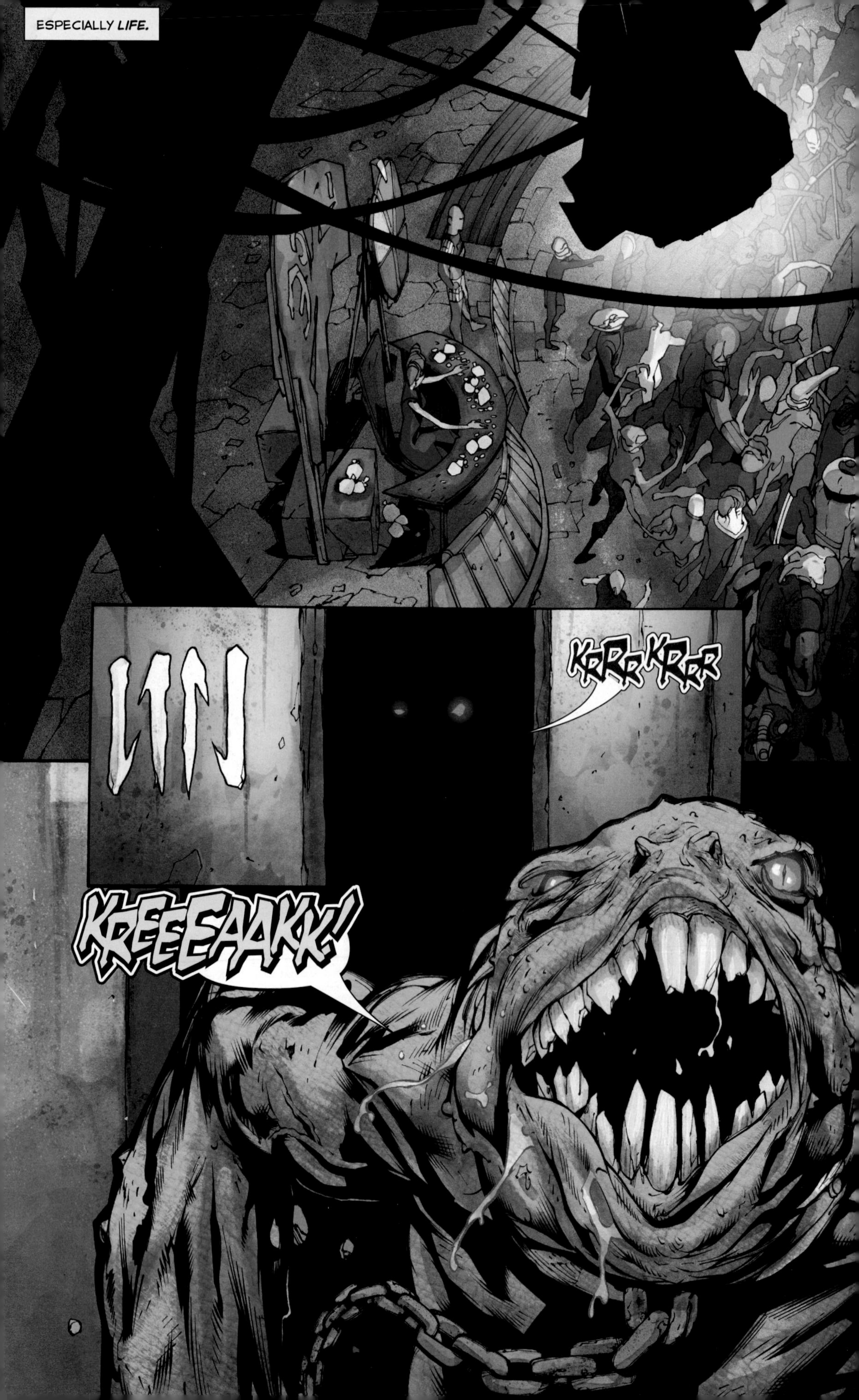
ESPECIALLY LIFE.
KRRR KRRR
KREEEAAKK!

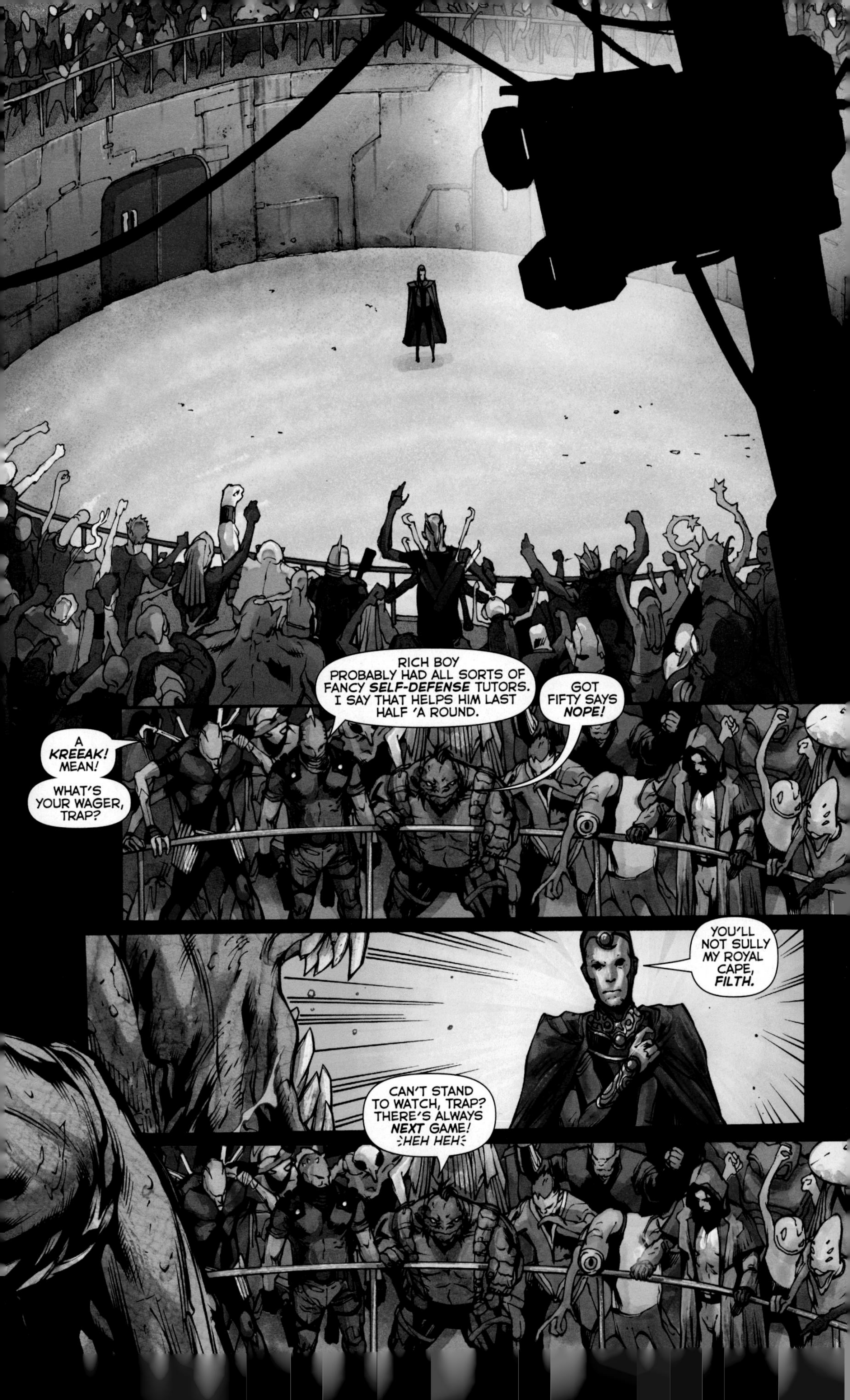
RICH BOY PROBABLY HAD ALL SORTS OF FANCY SELF-DEFENSE TUTORS. I SAY THAT HELPS HIM LAST HALF 'A ROUND.
GOT FIFTY SAYS NOPE!
A KREEAK! MEAN!
WHAT'S YOUR WAGER, TRAP?
YOU'LL NOT SULLY MY ROYAL CAPE, FILTH.
CAN'T STAND TO WATCH, TRAP? THERE'S ALWAYS NEXT GAME! HEH HEH

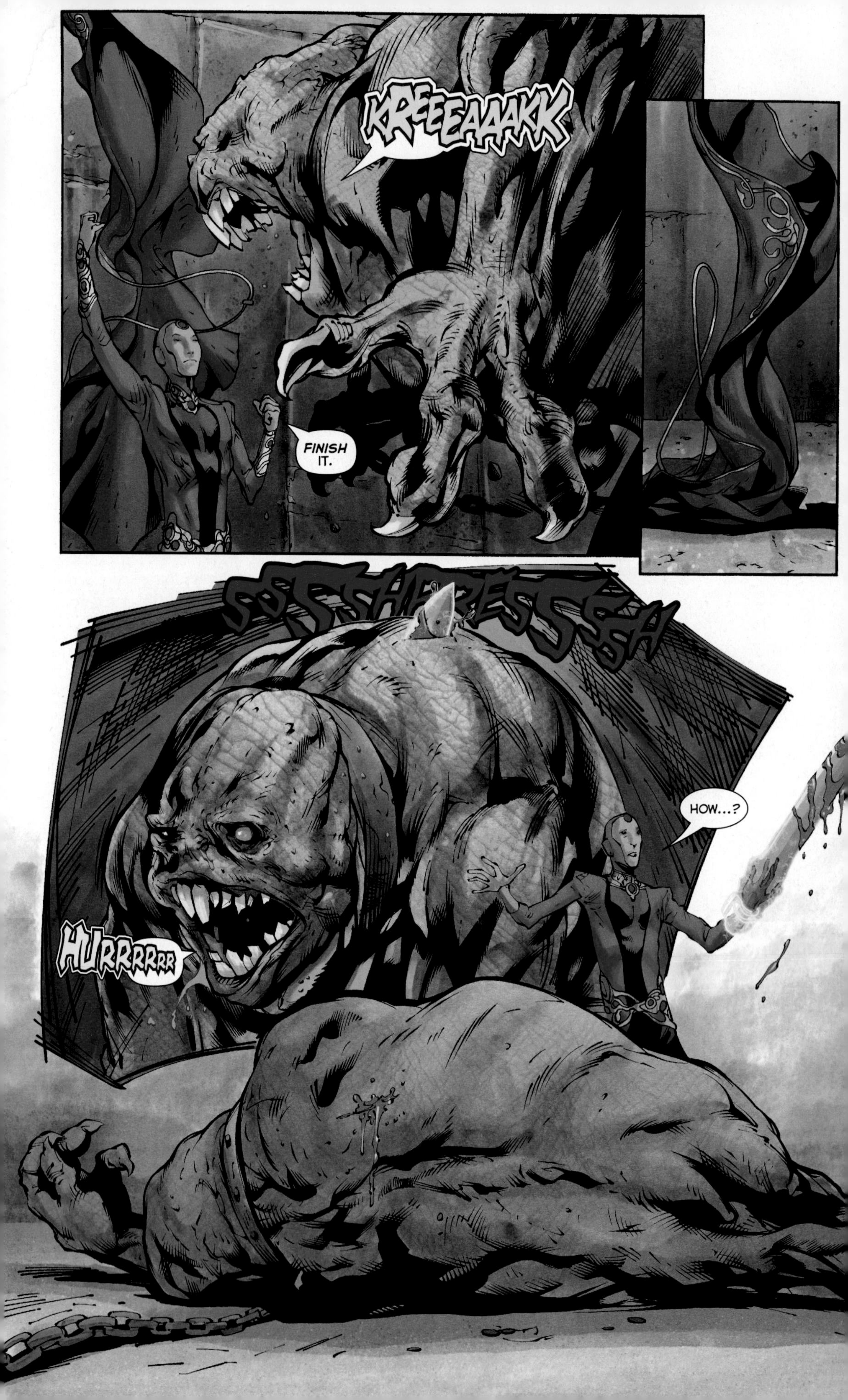
KREEEAAAKK
FINISH IT.
HURRRRRR
HOW...?

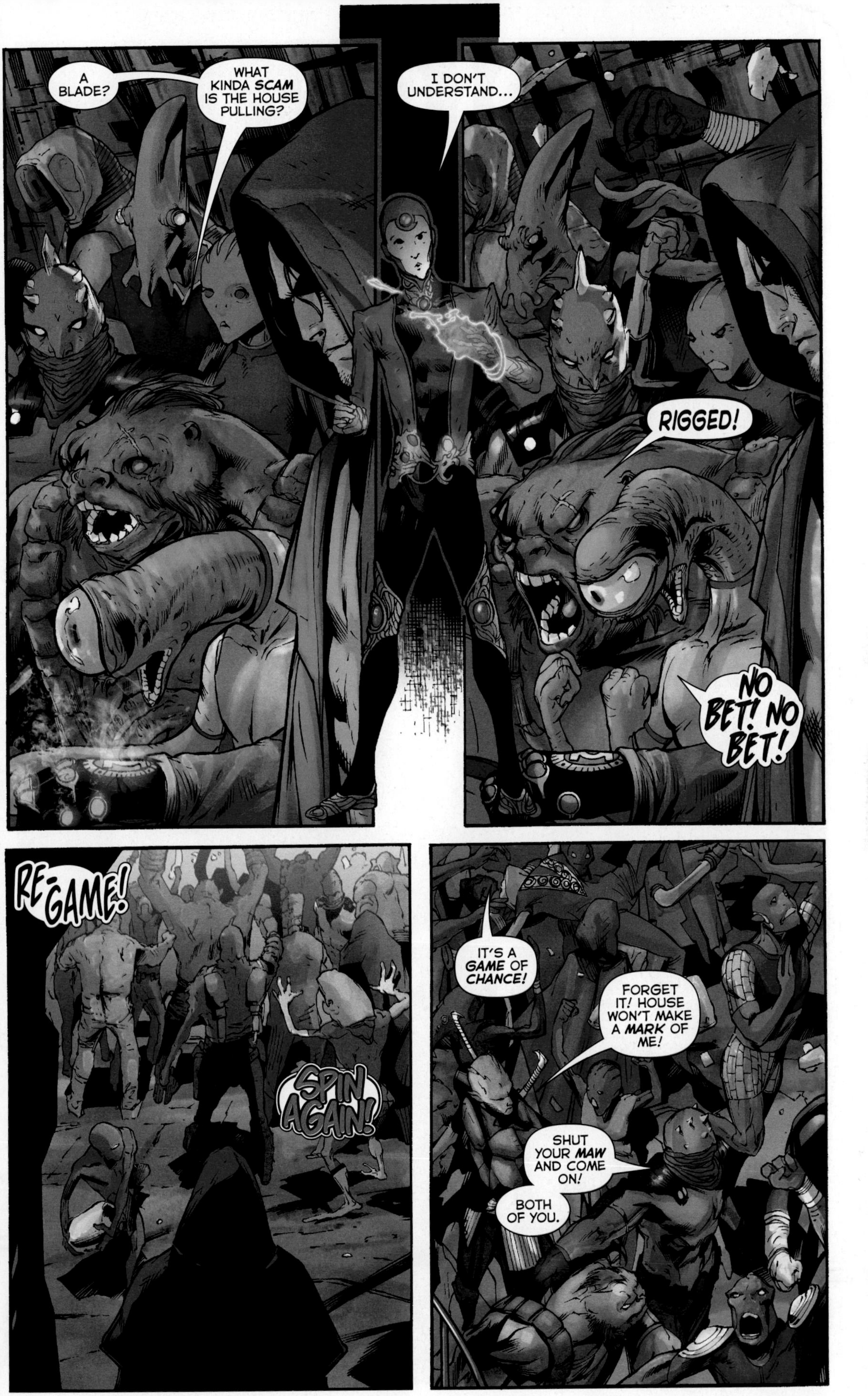
A BLADE?
WHAT KINDA SCAM IS THE HOUSE PULLING?
I DON'T UNDERSTAND...
RIGGED!
NO BET! NO BET!
RE-GAME!
SPIN AGAIN!
IT'S A GAME OF CHANCE!
FORGET IT! HOUSE WON'T MAKE A MARK OF ME!
SHUT YOUR MAW AND COME ON!
BOTH OF YOU.

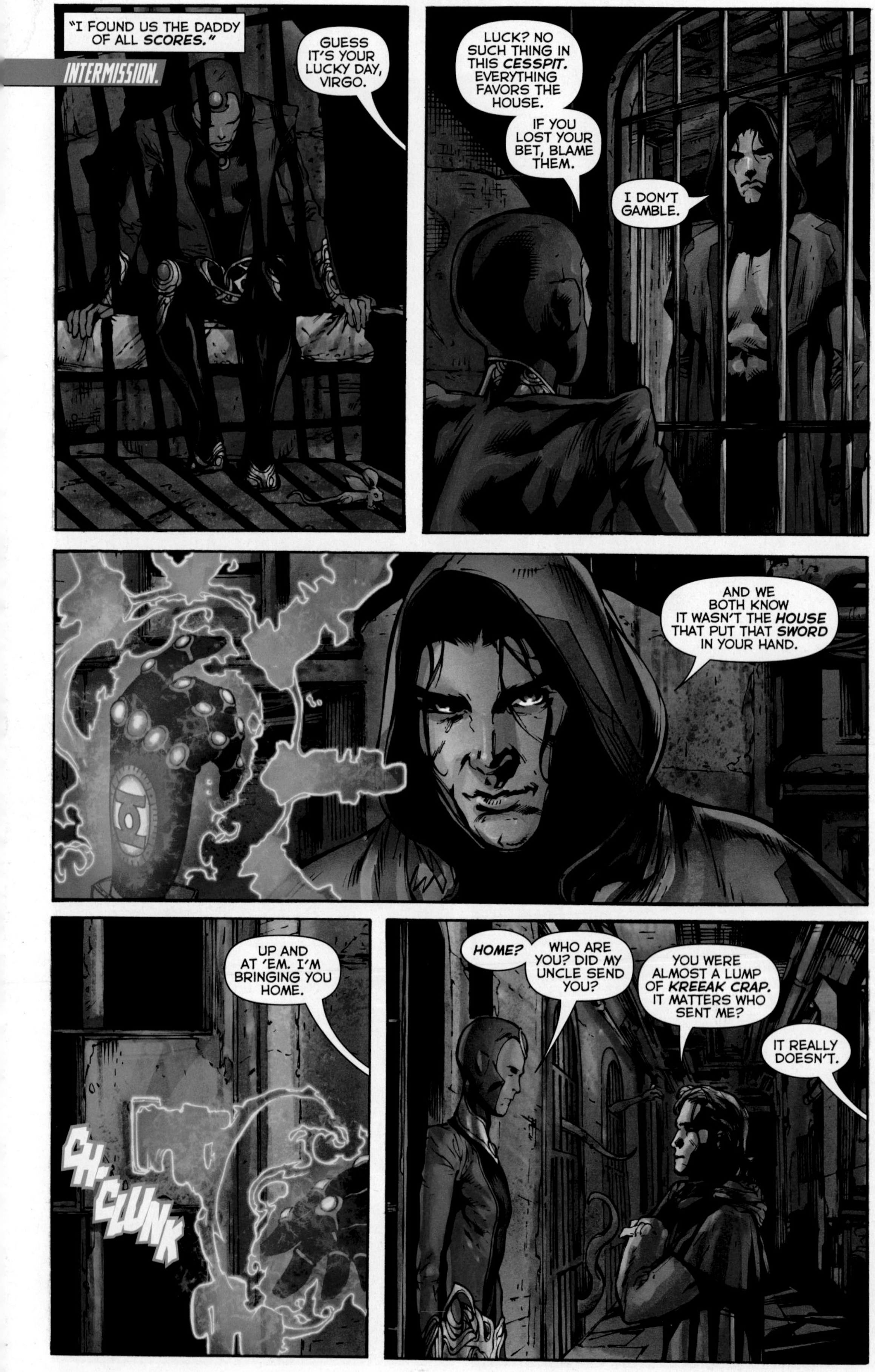
"I FOUND US THE DADDY OF ALL SCORES."
INTERMISSION.
GUESS IT'S YOUR LUCKY DAY, VIRGO.
LUCK? NO SUCH THING IN THIS CESSPIT. EVERYTHING FAVORS THE HOUSE.
IF YOU LOST YOUR BET, BLAME THEM.
I DON'T GAMBLE.
AND WE BOTH KNOW IT WASN'T THE HOUSE THAT PUT THAT SWORD IN YOUR HAND.
UP AND AT 'EM. I'M BRINGING YOU HOME.
CH-CLUNK
HOME?
WHO ARE YOU? DID MY UNCLE SEND YOU?
YOU WERE ALMOST A LUMP OF KREEAK CRAP. IT MATTERS WHO SENT ME?
IT REALLY DOESN'T.

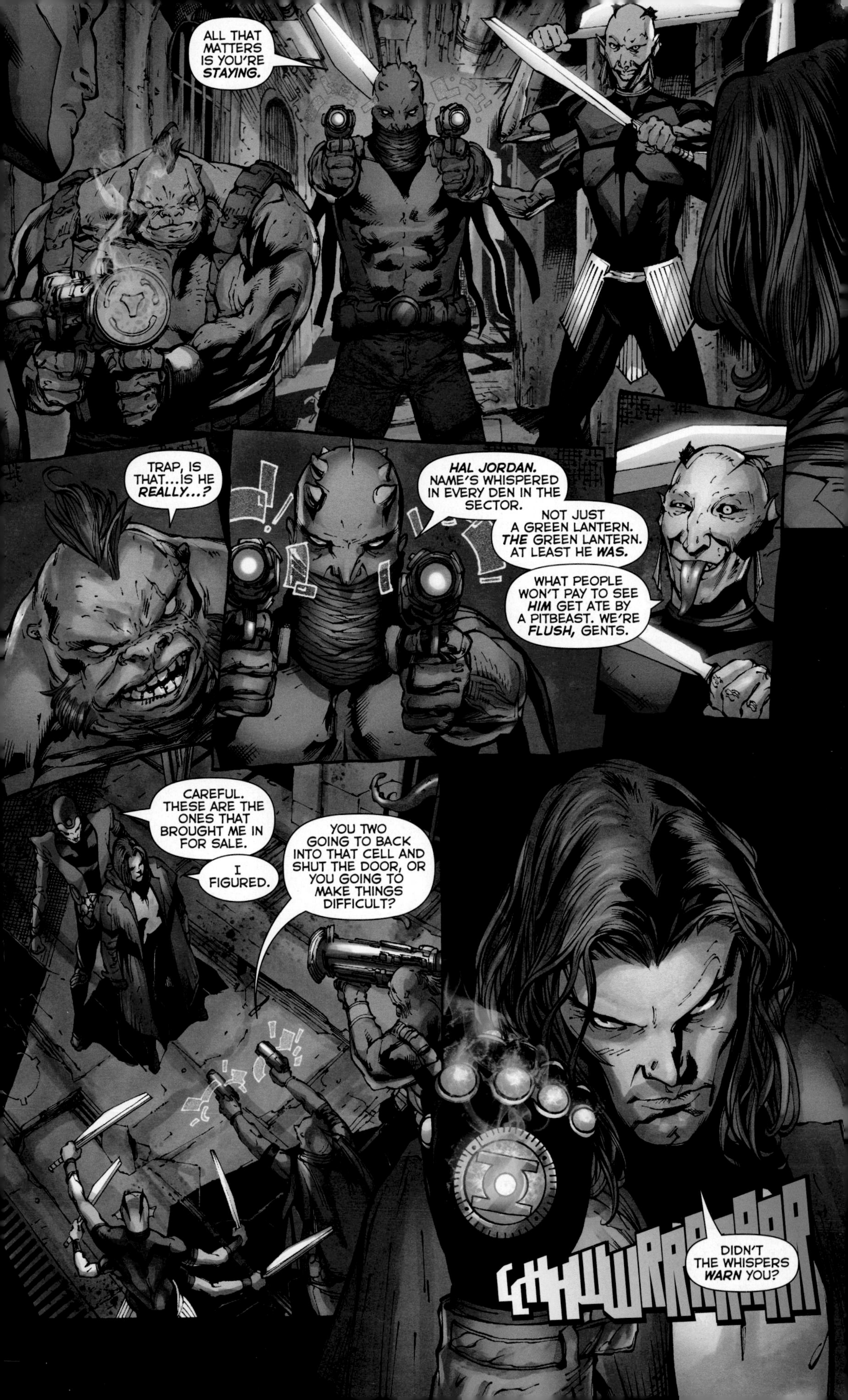
ALL THAT MATTERS IS YOU'RE *STAYING.*
TRAP, IS THAT...IS HE *REALLY...?*
HAL JORDAN. NAME'S WHISPERED IN EVERY DEN IN THE SECTOR.
NOT JUST A GREEN LANTERN. *THE* GREEN LANTERN. AT LEAST HE *WAS.*
WHAT PEOPLE WON'T PAY TO SEE *HIM* GET ATE BY A PITBEAST. WE'RE *FLUSH,* GENTS.
CAREFUL. THESE ARE THE ONES THAT BROUGHT ME IN FOR SALE.
I FIGURED.
YOU TWO GOING TO BACK INTO THAT CELL AND SHUT THE DOOR, OR YOU GOING TO MAKE THINGS DIFFICULT?
CCHHWURRRRRRRR
DIDN'T THE WHISPERS *WARN* YOU?

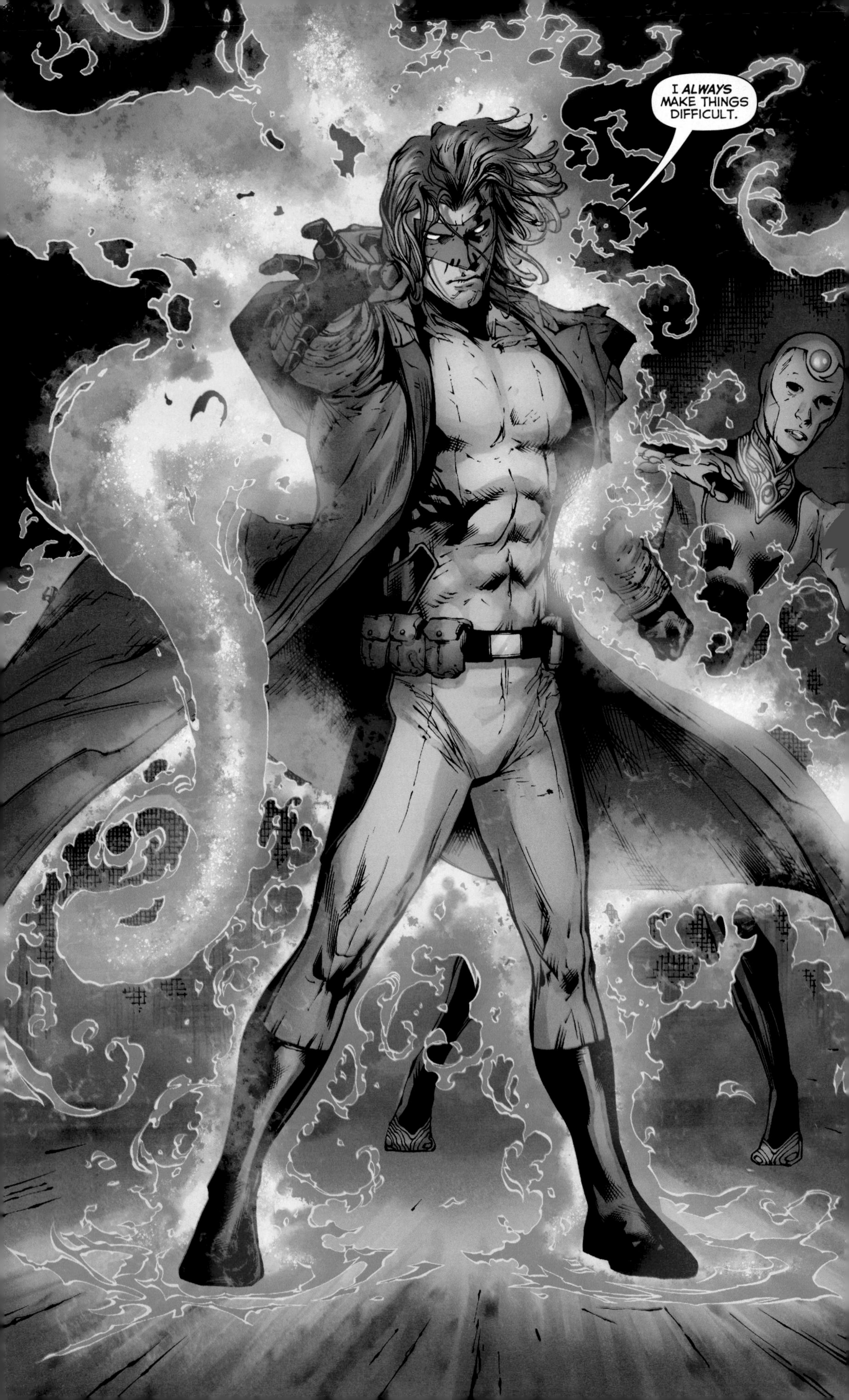
I ALWAYS MAKE THINGS DIFFICULT.

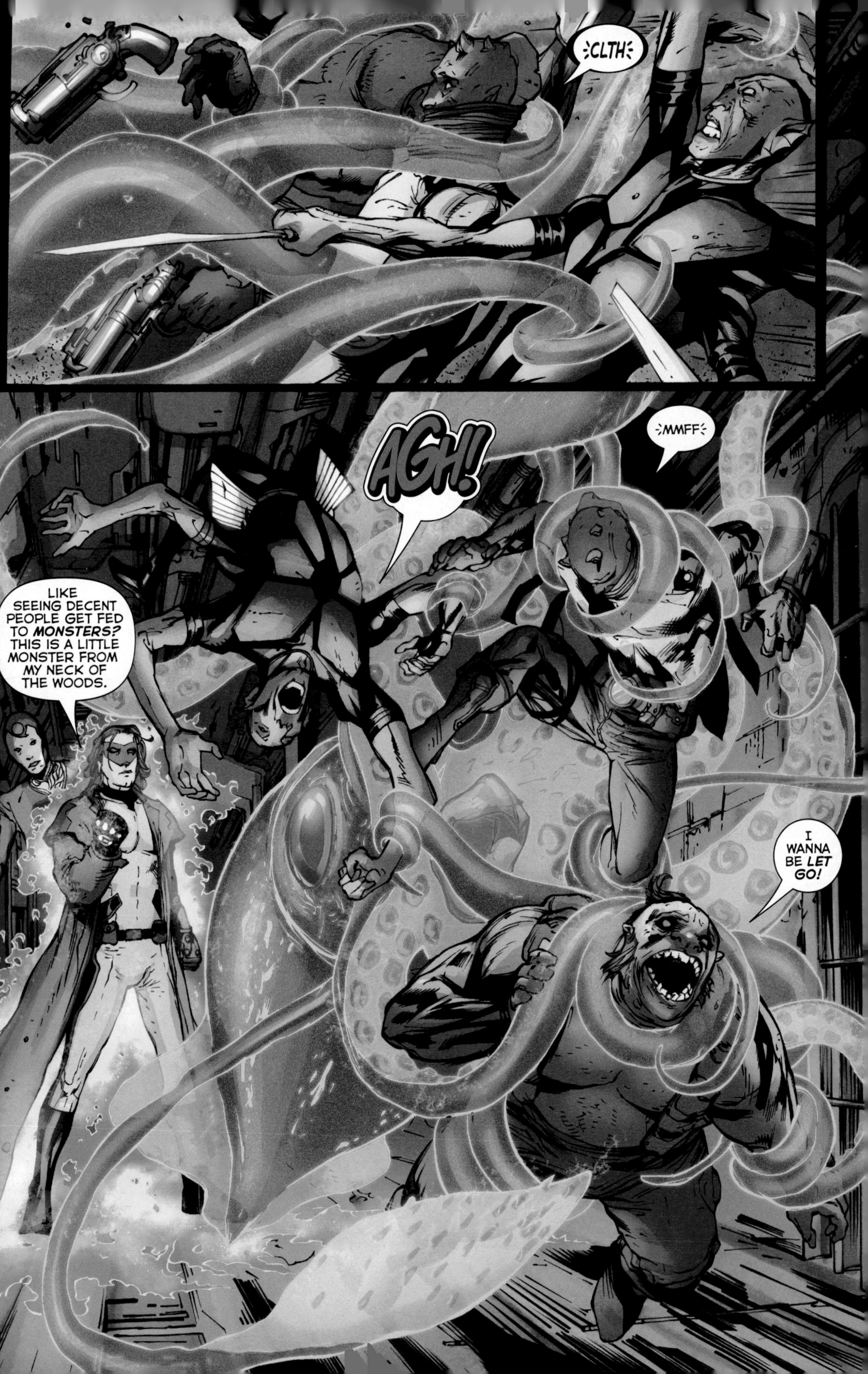
CLTH
AGH!
MMFF
LIKE SEEING DECENT PEOPLE GET FED TO MONSTERS? THIS IS A LITTLE MONSTER FROM MY NECK OF THE WOODS.
I WANNA BE LET GO!

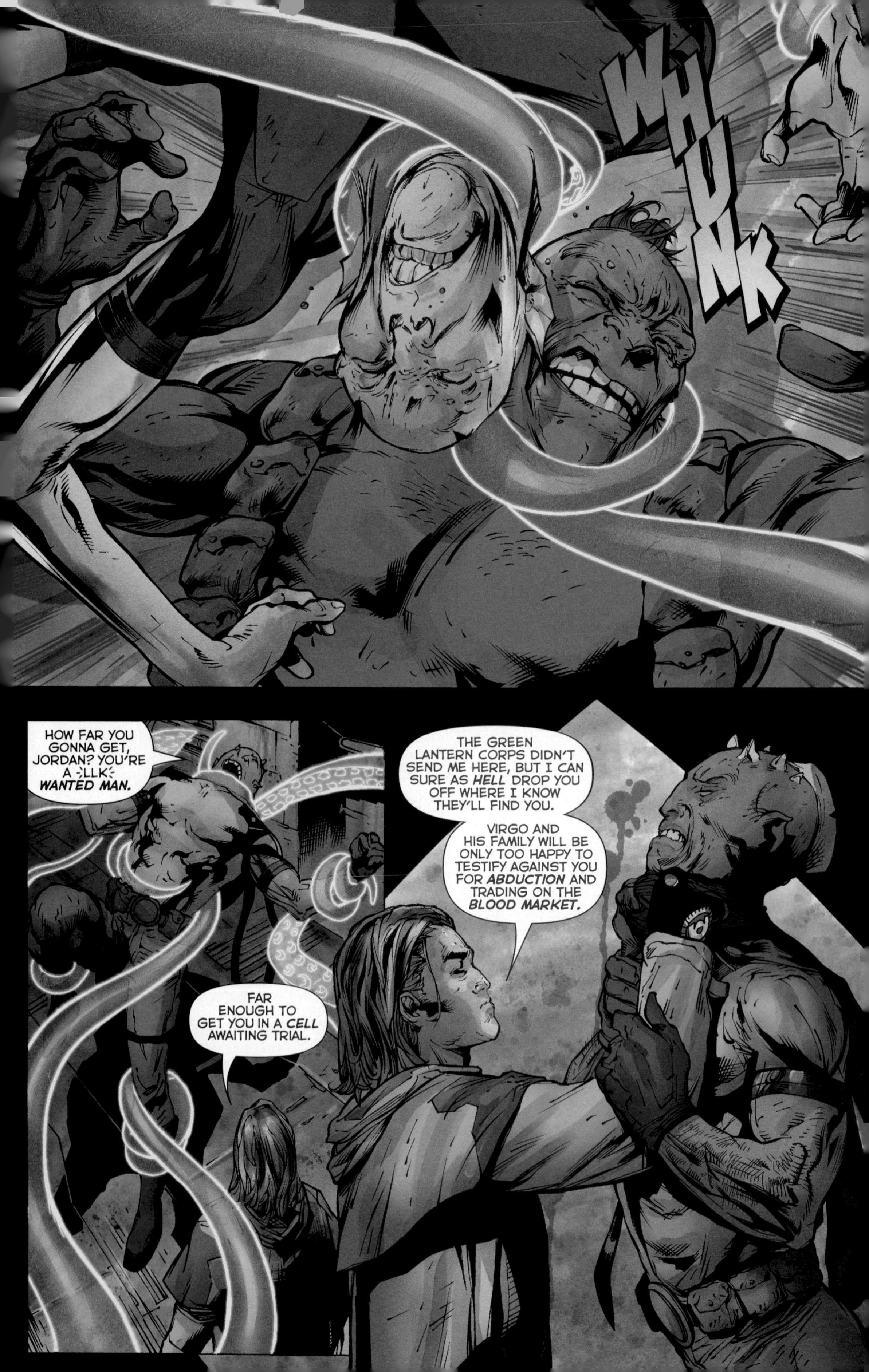
WHUNK
HOW FAR YOU GONNA GET, JORDAN? YOU'RE A -LLK- WANTED MAN.
THE GREEN LANTERN CORPS DIDN'T SEND ME HERE, BUT I CAN SURE AS HELL DROP YOU OFF WHERE I KNOW THEY'LL FIND YOU.
VIRGO AND HIS FAMILY WILL BE ONLY TOO HAPPY TO TESTIFY AGAINST YOU FOR ABDUCTION AND TRADING ON THE BLOOD MARKET.
FAR ENOUGH TO GET YOU IN A CELL AWAITING TRIAL.

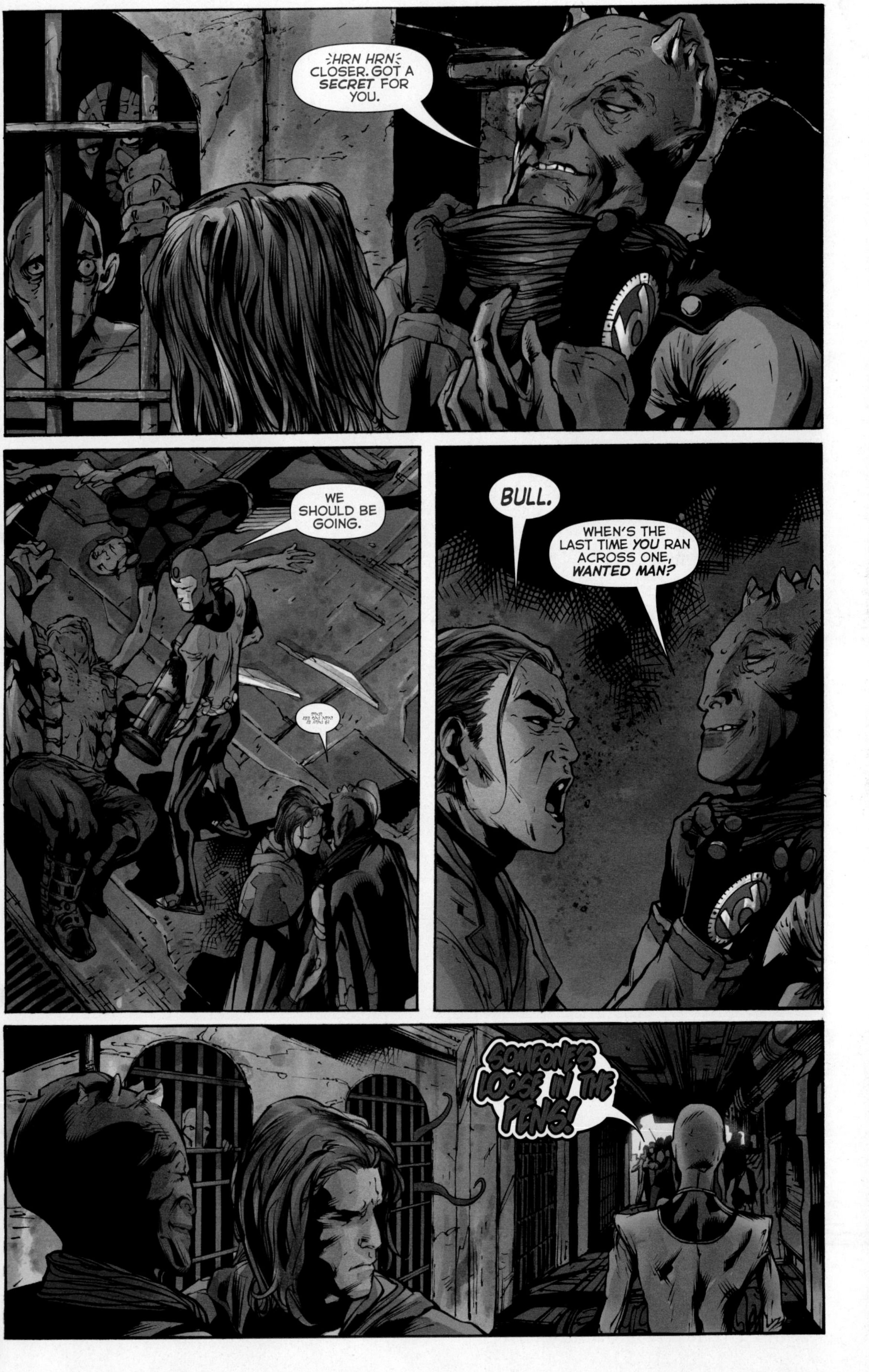

HRN HRN CLOSER. GOT A SECRET FOR YOU.
WE SHOULD BE GOING.
BULL.
WHEN'S THE LAST TIME YOU RAN ACROSS ONE, WANTED MAN?
SOMEONE'S LOOSE IN THE PENS!

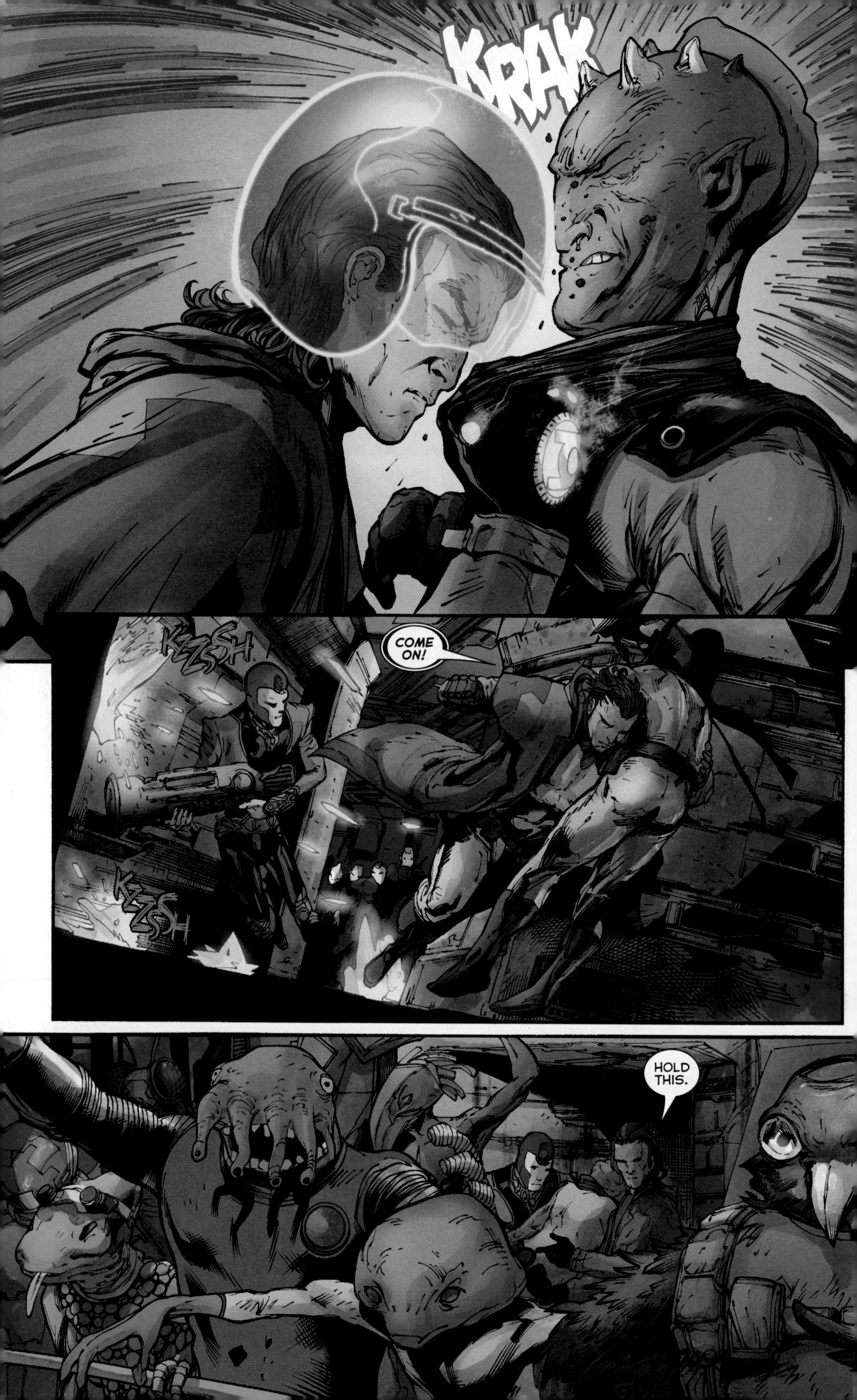
KRAK
KZZSH
COME ON!
KZZSH
HOLD THIS.

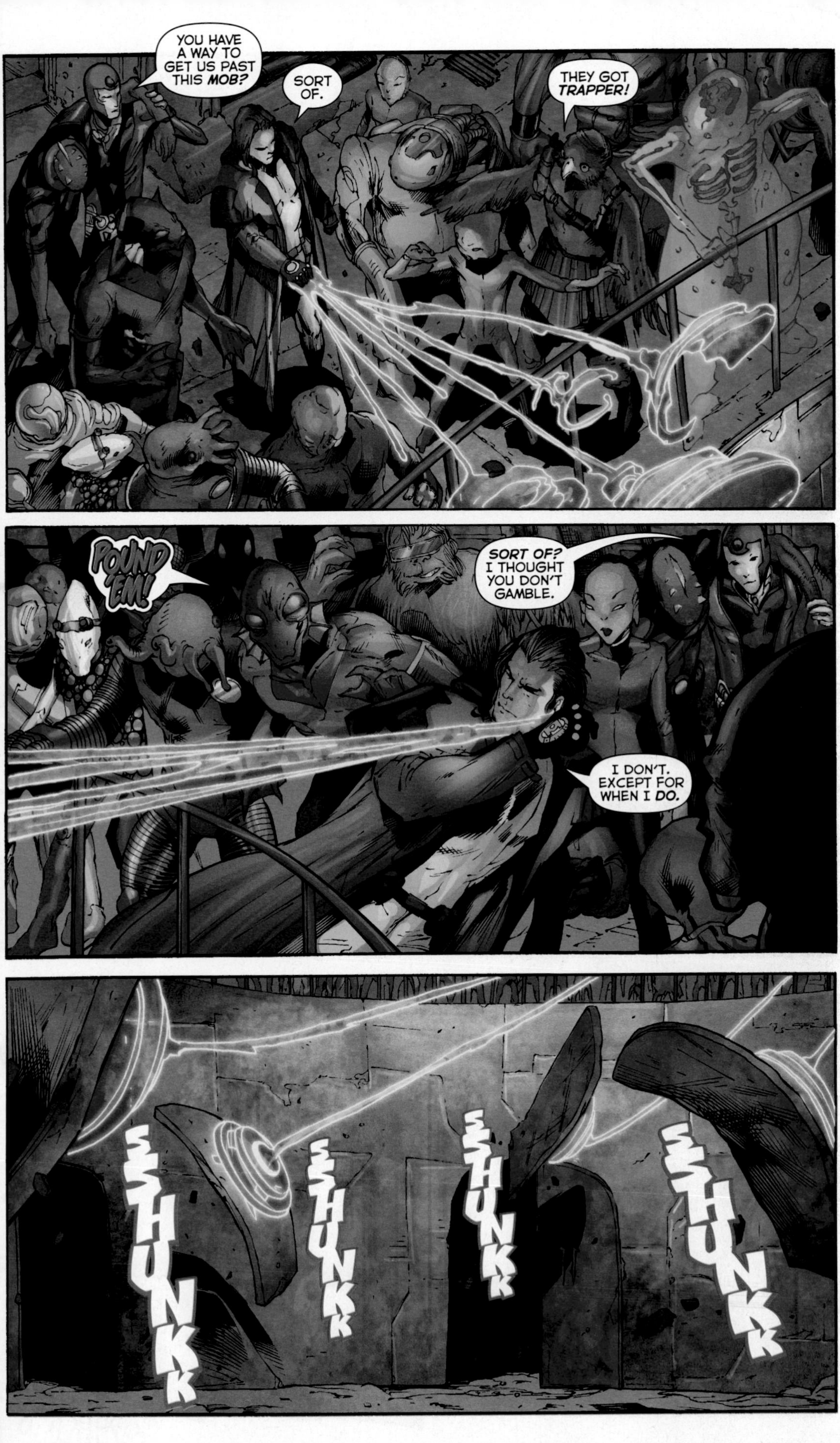
YOU HAVE A WAY TO GET US PAST THIS MOB?
SORT OF.
THEY GOT TRAPPER!
POUND 'EM!
SORT OF? I THOUGHT YOU DON'T GAMBLE.
I DON'T. EXCEPT FOR WHEN I DO.
SHUNKK
SHUNKK
SHUNKK
SHUNKK

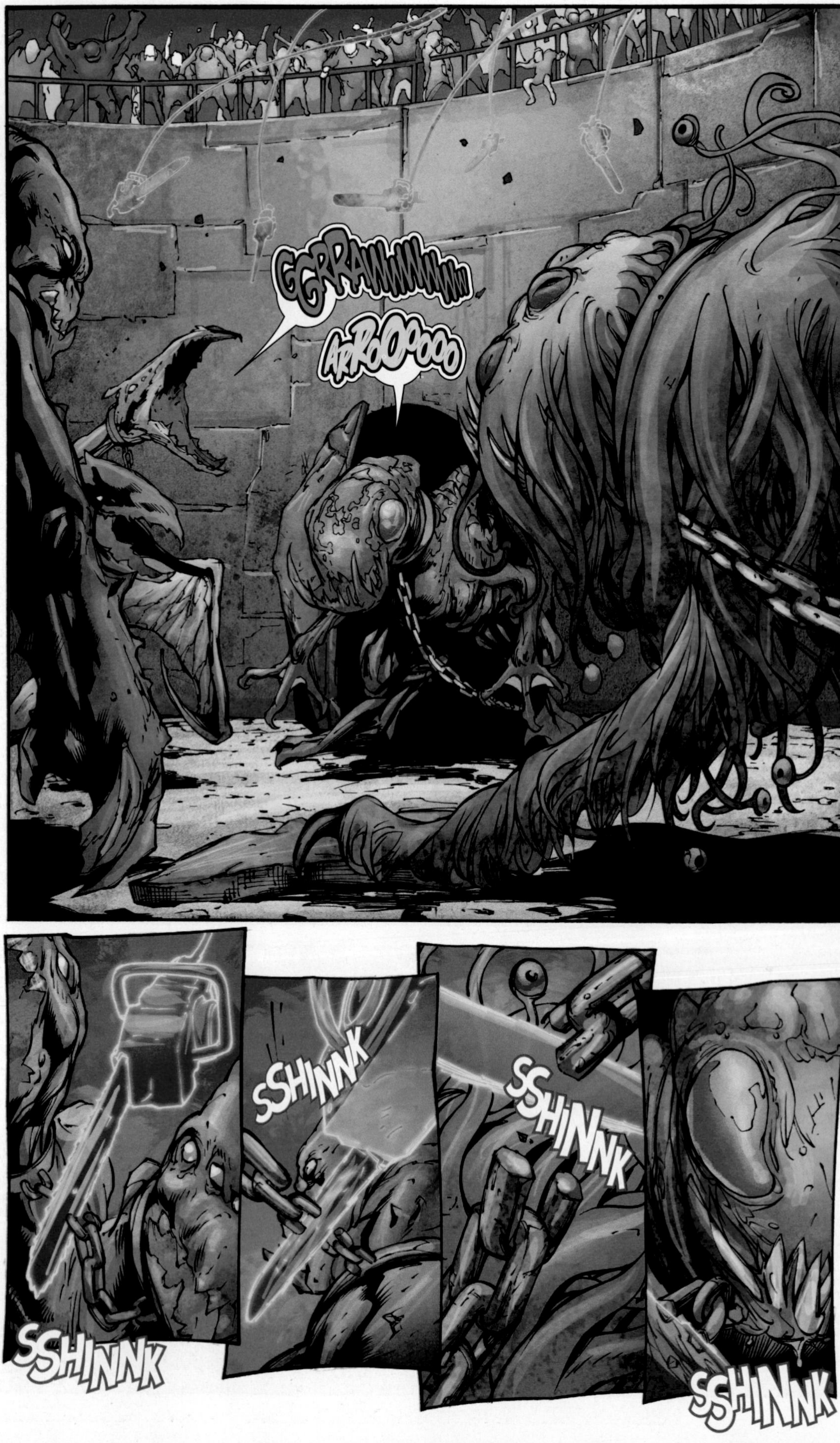

GGRRAWWWWWWW
ARROOOOOO
SSHINNNK
SSHINNK
SSHINNNK
SSHINNNK

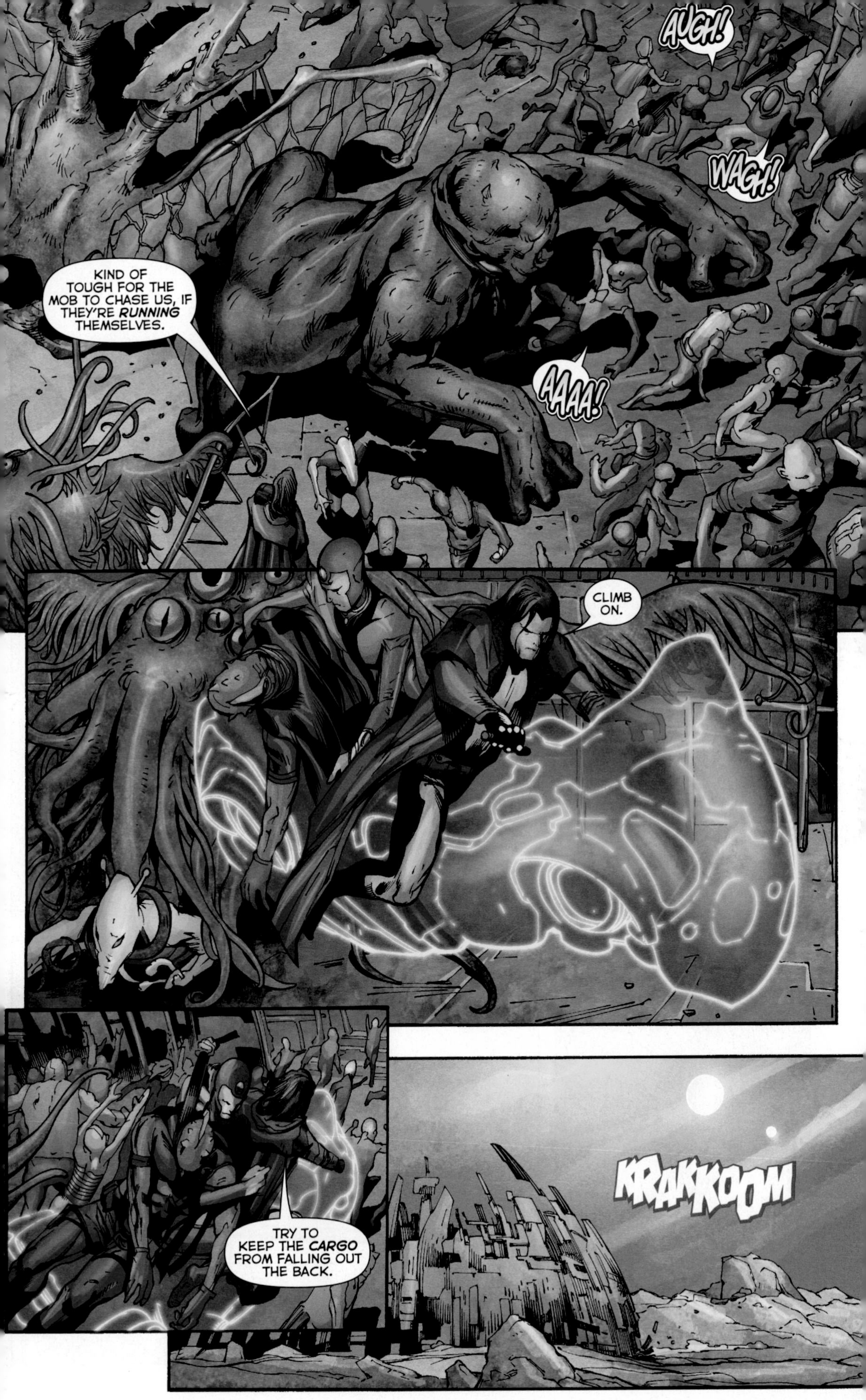
AUGH!
WAGH!
KIND OF TOUGH FOR THE MOB TO CHASE US, IF THEY'RE *RUNNING* THEMSELVES.
AAAA!
CLIMB ON.
TRY TO KEEP THE *CARGO* FROM FALLING OUT THE BACK.
KRAKKOOM

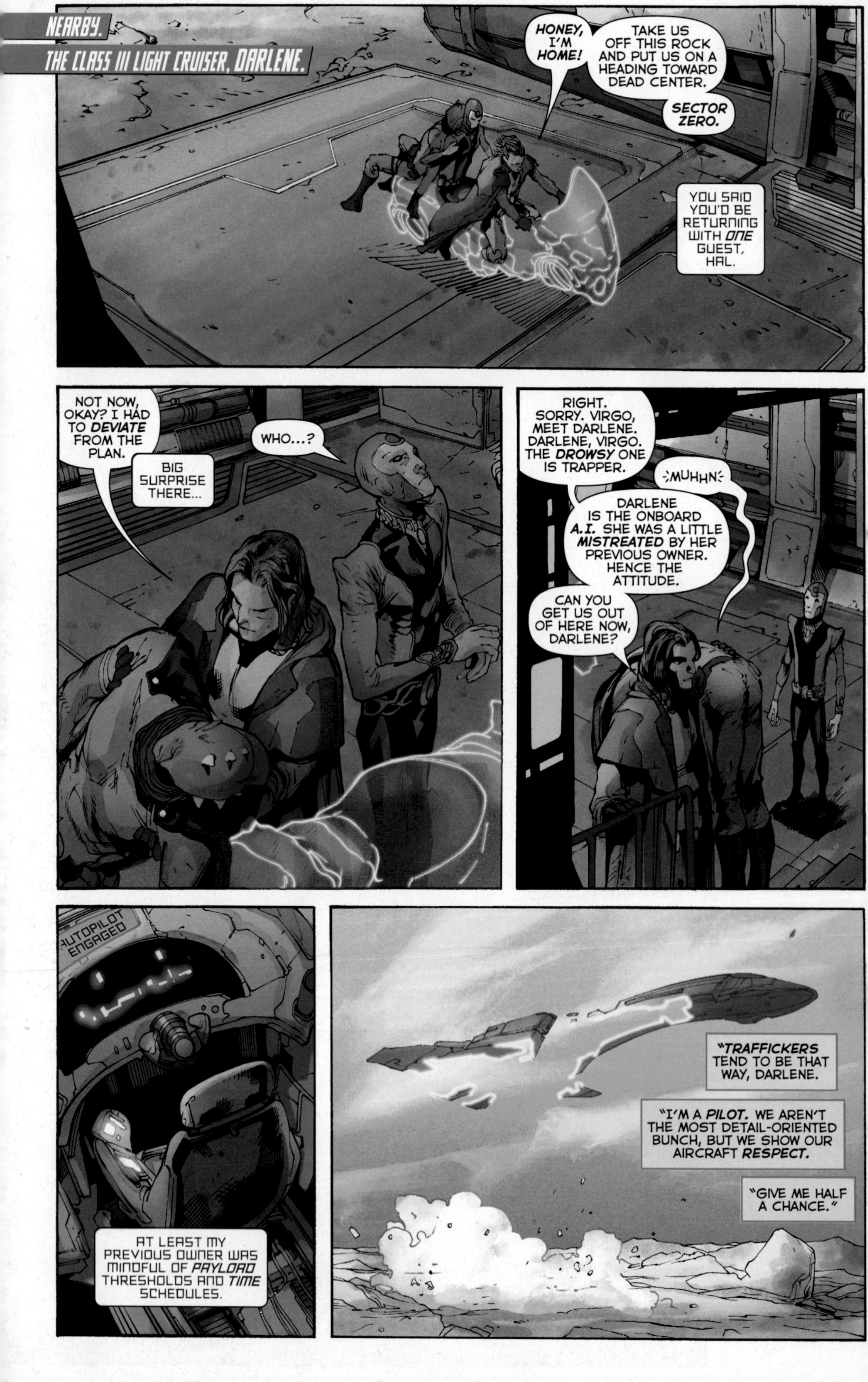
NEARBY.
THE CLASS III LIGHT CRUISER, DARLENE.
HONEY, I'M HOME!
TAKE US OFF THIS ROCK AND PUT US ON A HEADING TOWARD DEAD CENTER.
SECTOR ZERO.
YOU SAID YOU'D BE RETURNING WITH ONE GUEST, HAL.
NOT NOW, OKAY? I HAD TO DEVIATE FROM THE PLAN.
BIG SURPRISE THERE...
WHO...?
RIGHT. SORRY. VIRGO, MEET DARLENE. DARLENE, VIRGO. THE DROWSY ONE IS TRAPPER.
MUHHN
DARLENE IS THE ONBOARD A.I. SHE WAS A LITTLE MISTREATED BY HER PREVIOUS OWNER. HENCE THE ATTITUDE.
CAN YOU GET US OUT OF HERE NOW, DARLENE?
AUTOPILOT ENGAGED
AT LEAST MY PREVIOUS OWNER WAS MINDFUL OF PAYLOAD THRESHOLDS AND TIME SCHEDULES.
"TRAFFICKERS TEND TO BE THAT WAY, DARLENE.
"I'M A PILOT. WE AREN'T THE MOST DETAIL-ORIENTED BUNCH, BUT WE SHOW OUR AIRCRAFT RESPECT.
"GIVE ME HALF A CHANCE."

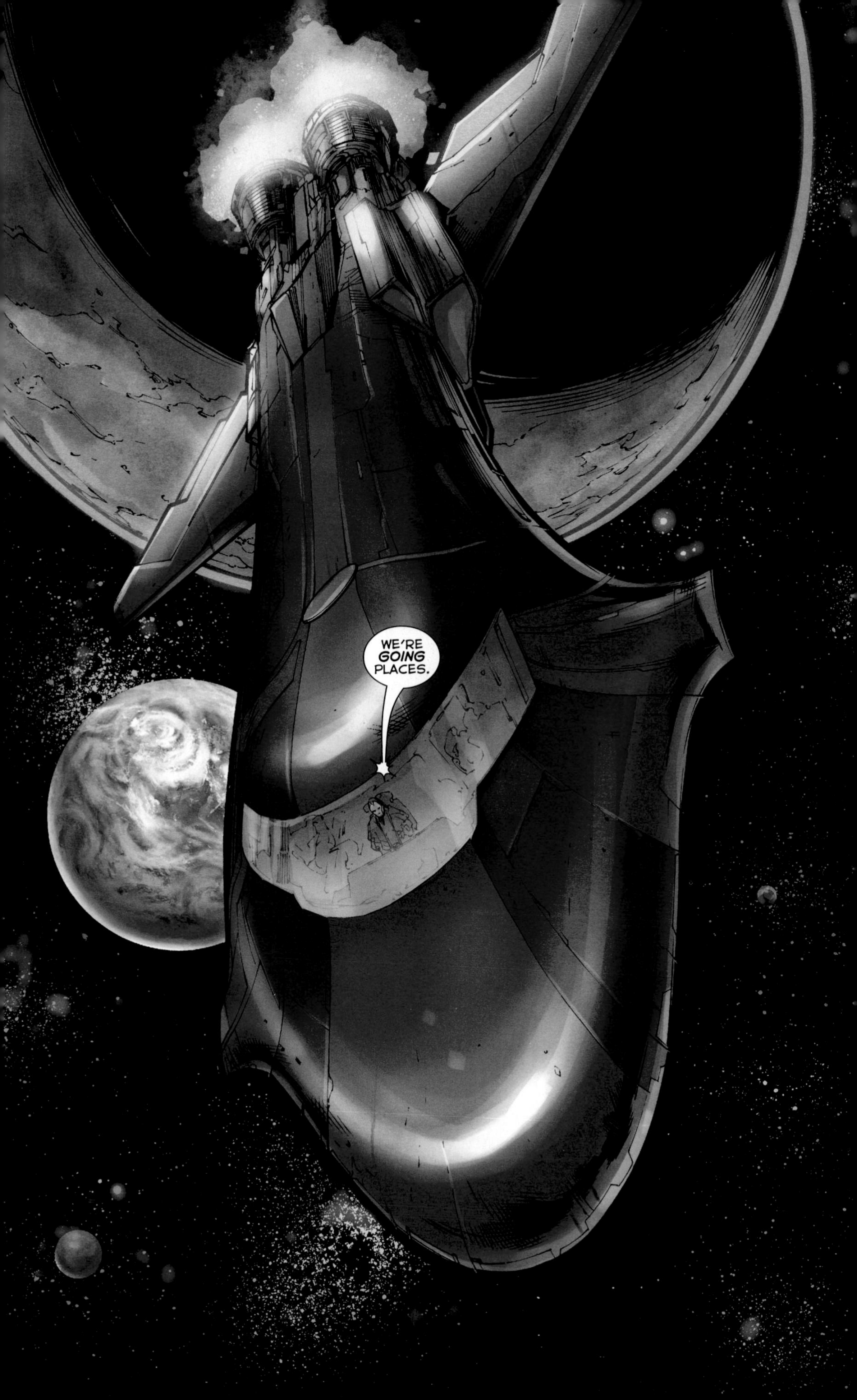
WE'RE GOING PLACES.

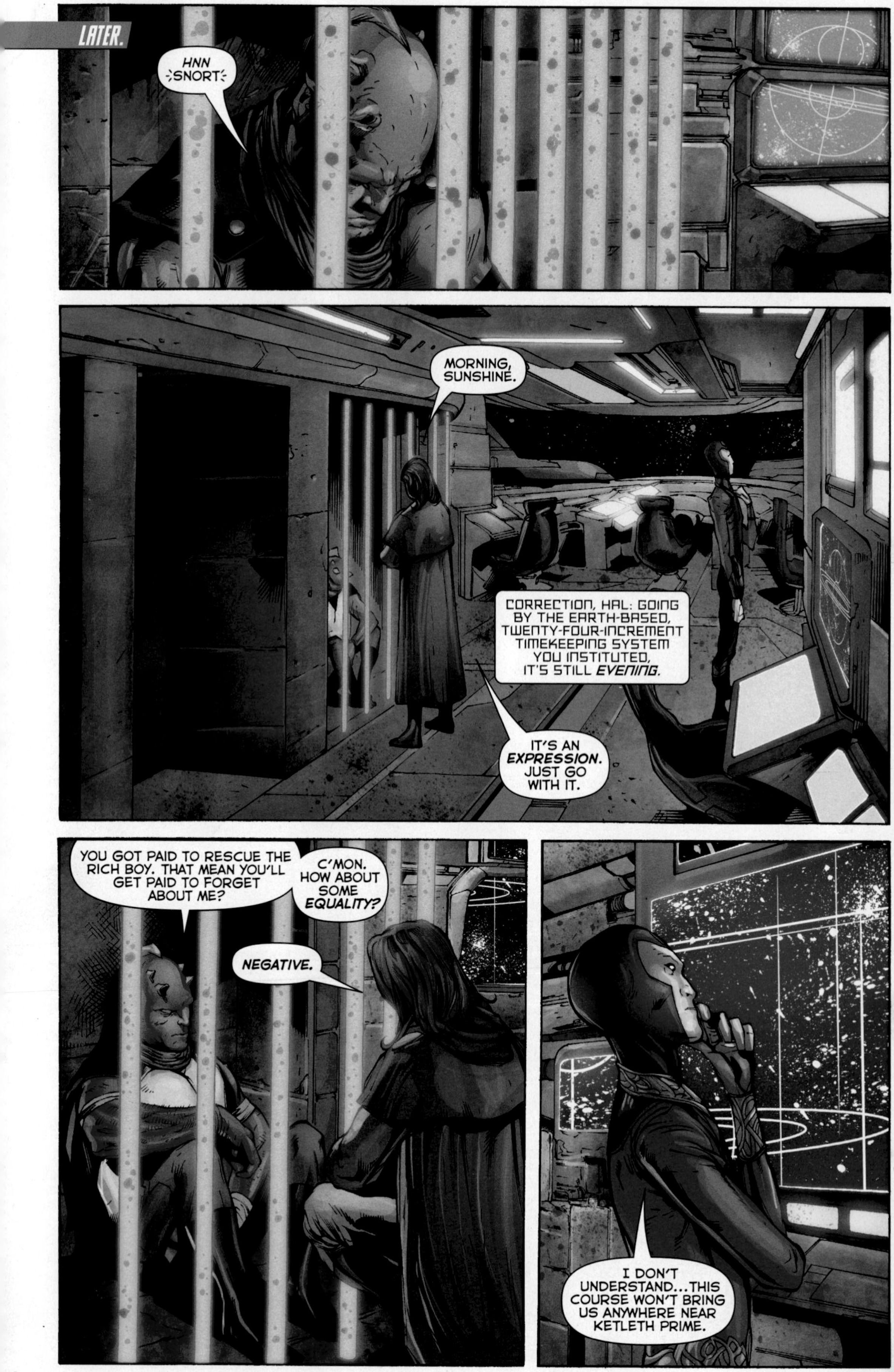
LATER.
HNN SNORT
MORNING, SUNSHINE.
CORRECTION, HAL: GOING BY THE EARTH-BASED, TWENTY-FOUR-INCREMENT TIMEKEEPING SYSTEM YOU INSTITUTED, IT'S STILL EVENING.
IT'S AN EXPRESSION. JUST GO WITH IT.
YOU GOT PAID TO RESCUE THE RICH BOY. THAT MEAN YOU'LL GET PAID TO FORGET ABOUT ME?
C'MON. HOW ABOUT SOME EQUALITY?
NEGATIVE.
I DON'T UNDERSTAND...THIS COURSE WON'T BRING US ANYWHERE NEAR KETLETH PRIME.

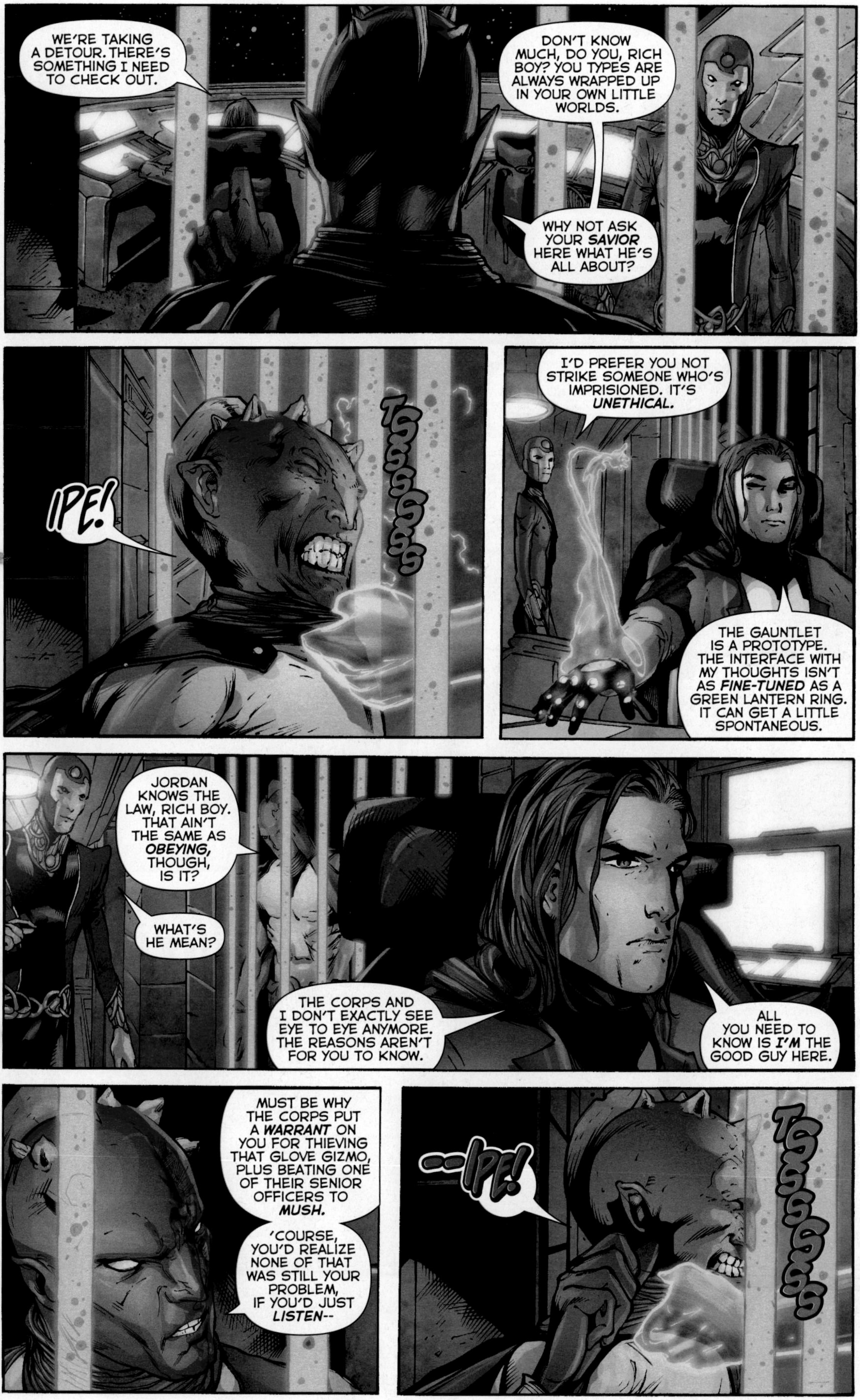
WE'RE TAKING A DETOUR. THERE'S SOMETHING I NEED TO CHECK OUT.
DON'T KNOW MUCH, DO YOU, RICH BOY? YOU TYPES ARE ALWAYS WRAPPED UP IN YOUR OWN LITTLE WORLDS.
WHY NOT ASK YOUR SAVIOR HERE WHAT HE'S ALL ABOUT?
TSSSSSSS
IPE!
I'D PREFER YOU NOT STRIKE SOMEONE WHO'S IMPRISIONED. IT'S UNETHICAL.
THE GAUNTLET IS A PROTOTYPE. THE INTERFACE WITH MY THOUGHTS ISN'T AS FINE-TUNED AS A GREEN LANTERN RING. IT CAN GET A LITTLE SPONTANEOUS.
JORDAN KNOWS THE LAW, RICH BOY. THAT AIN'T THE SAME AS OBEYING, THOUGH, IS IT?
WHAT'S HE MEAN?
THE CORPS AND I DON'T EXACTLY SEE EYE TO EYE ANYMORE. THE REASONS AREN'T FOR YOU TO KNOW.
ALL YOU NEED TO KNOW IS I'M THE GOOD GUY HERE.
MUST BE WHY THE CORPS PUT A WARRANT ON YOU FOR THIEVING THAT GLOVE GIZMO, PLUS BEATING ONE OF THEIR SENIOR OFFICERS TO MUSH.
'COURSE, YOU'D REALIZE NONE OF THAT WAS STILL YOUR PROBLEM, IF YOU'D JUST LISTEN--
--IPE!
TSSSSSSS

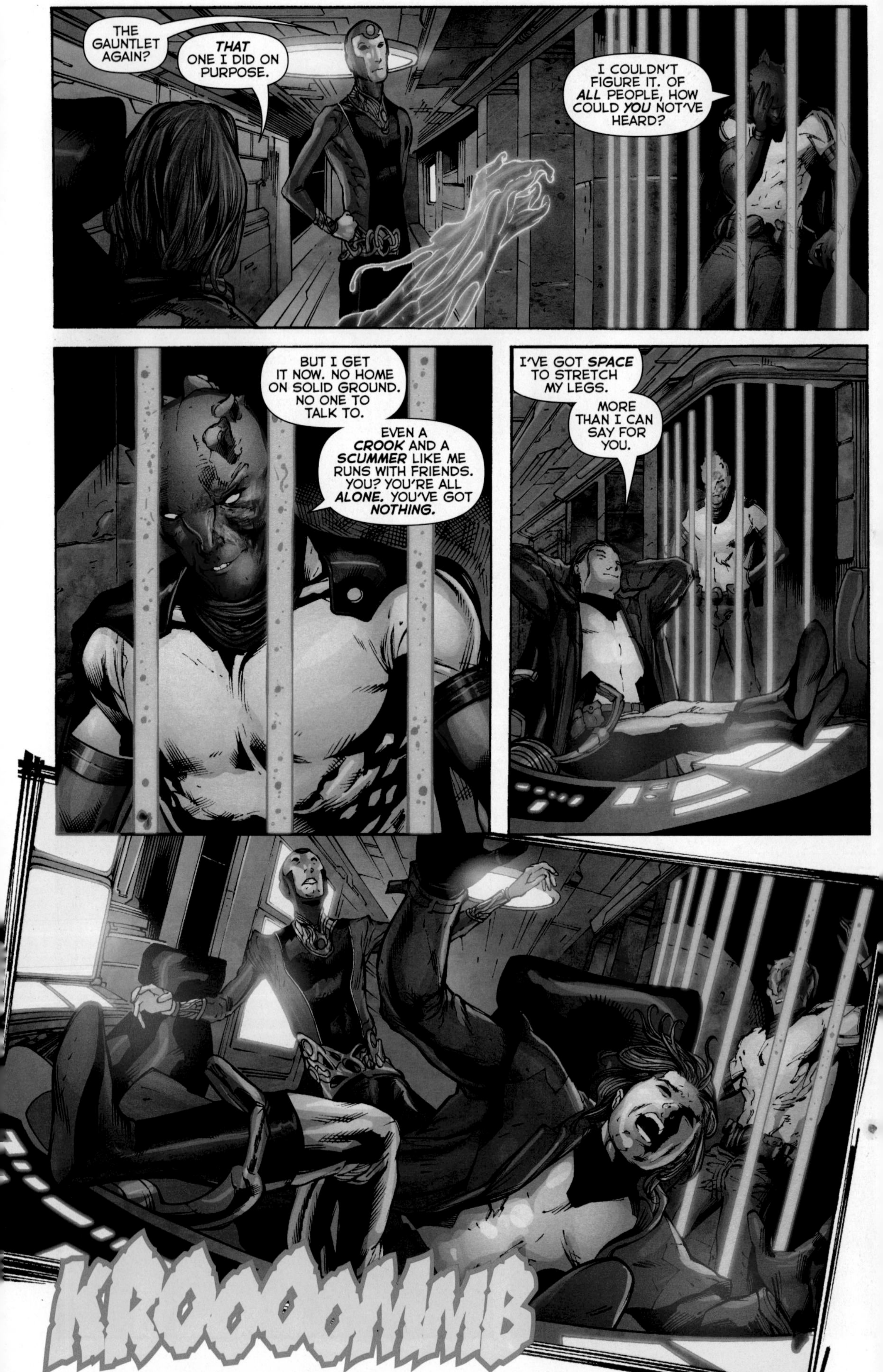
THE GAUNTLET AGAIN?
THAT ONE I DID ON PURPOSE.
I COULDN'T FIGURE IT. OF ALL PEOPLE, HOW COULD YOU NOT'VE HEARD?
BUT I GET IT NOW. NO HOME ON SOLID GROUND. NO ONE TO TALK TO.
EVEN A CROOK AND A SCUMMER LIKE ME RUNS WITH FRIENDS. YOU? YOU'RE ALL ALONE. YOU'VE GOT NOTHING.
I'VE GOT SPACE TO STRETCH MY LEGS.
MORE THAN I CAN SAY FOR YOU.
KROOOOMMB

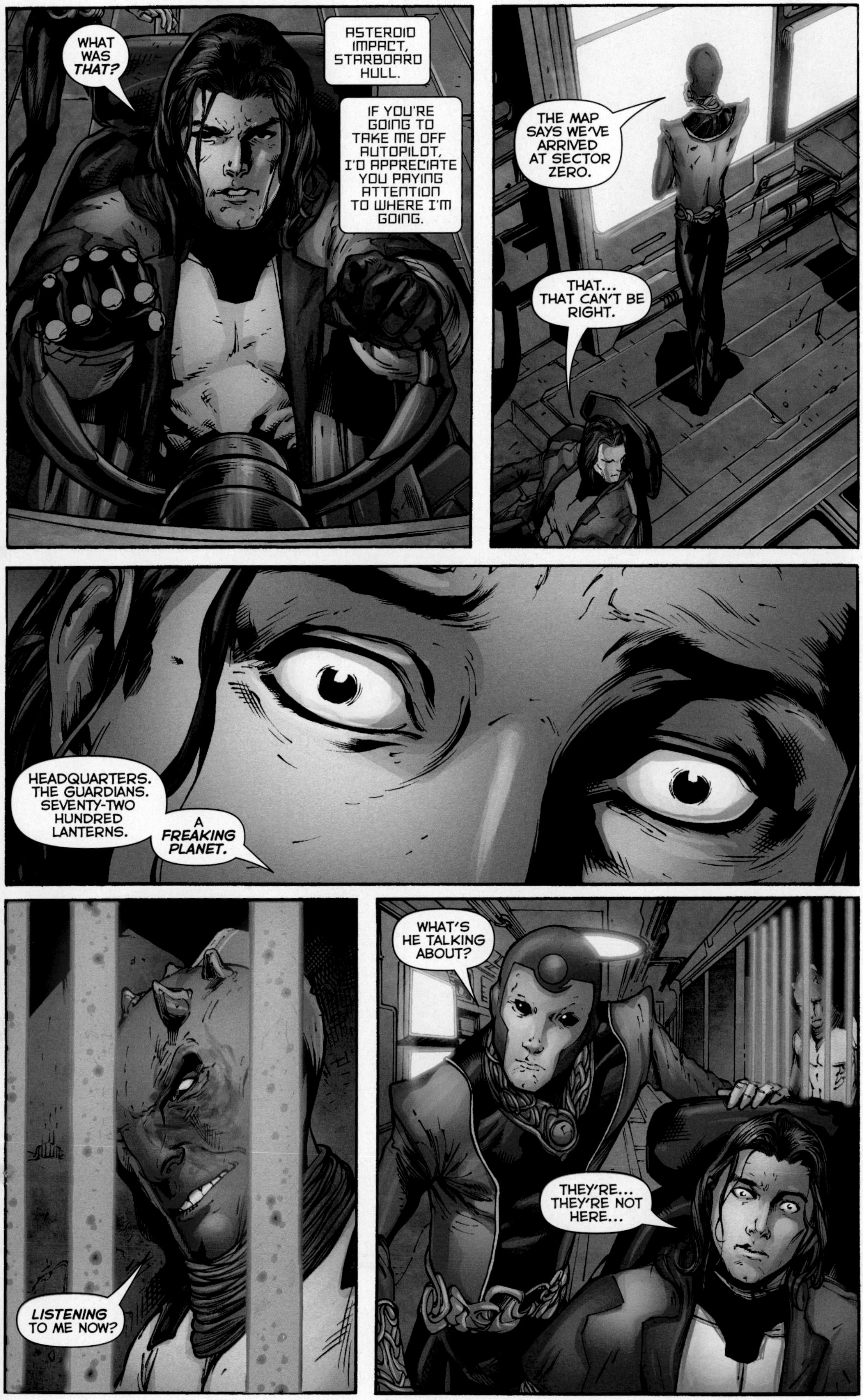
WHAT WAS *THAT?*
ASTEROID IMPACT, STARBOARD HULL.
IF YOU'RE GOING TO TAKE ME OFF AUTOPILOT, I'D APPRECIATE YOU PAYING ATTENTION TO WHERE I'M GOING.
THE MAP SAYS WE'VE ARRIVED AT SECTOR ZERO.
THAT... THAT CAN'T BE RIGHT.
HEADQUARTERS. THE GUARDIANS. SEVENTY-TWO HUNDRED LANTERNS.
A *FREAKING PLANET.*
LISTENING TO ME NOW?
WHAT'S HE TALKING ABOUT?
THEY'RE... THEY'RE NOT HERE...

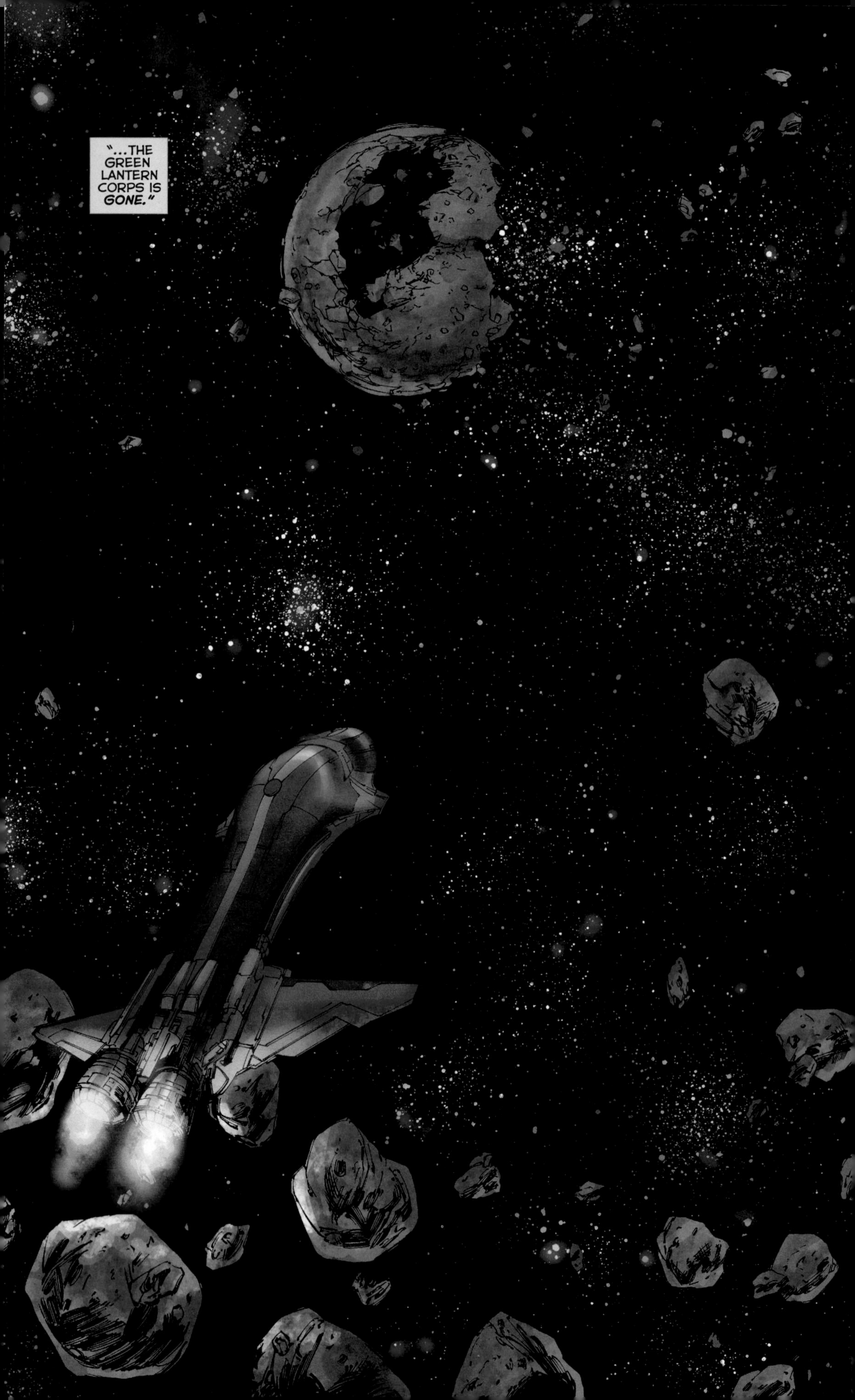
"...THE GREEN LANTERN CORPS IS *GONE.*"

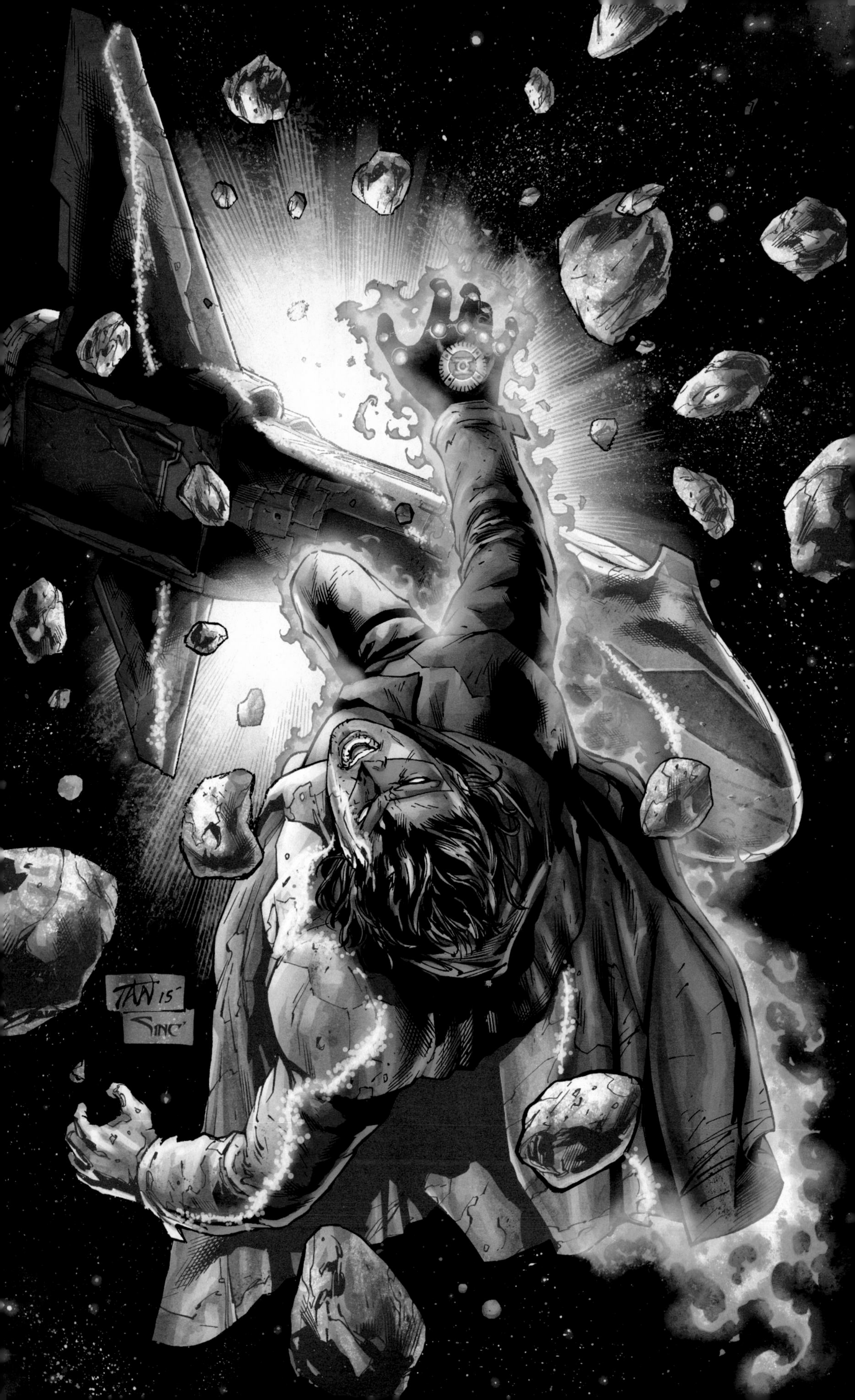

WRITTEN IN STONE

ROBERT VENDITTI writer BILLY TAN penciller MARK IRWIN, BILLY TAN & SCOTT HANNA inkers TONY AVIÑA colorist DAVE SHARPE letterer BILLY TAN & ALEX SINCLAIR cover

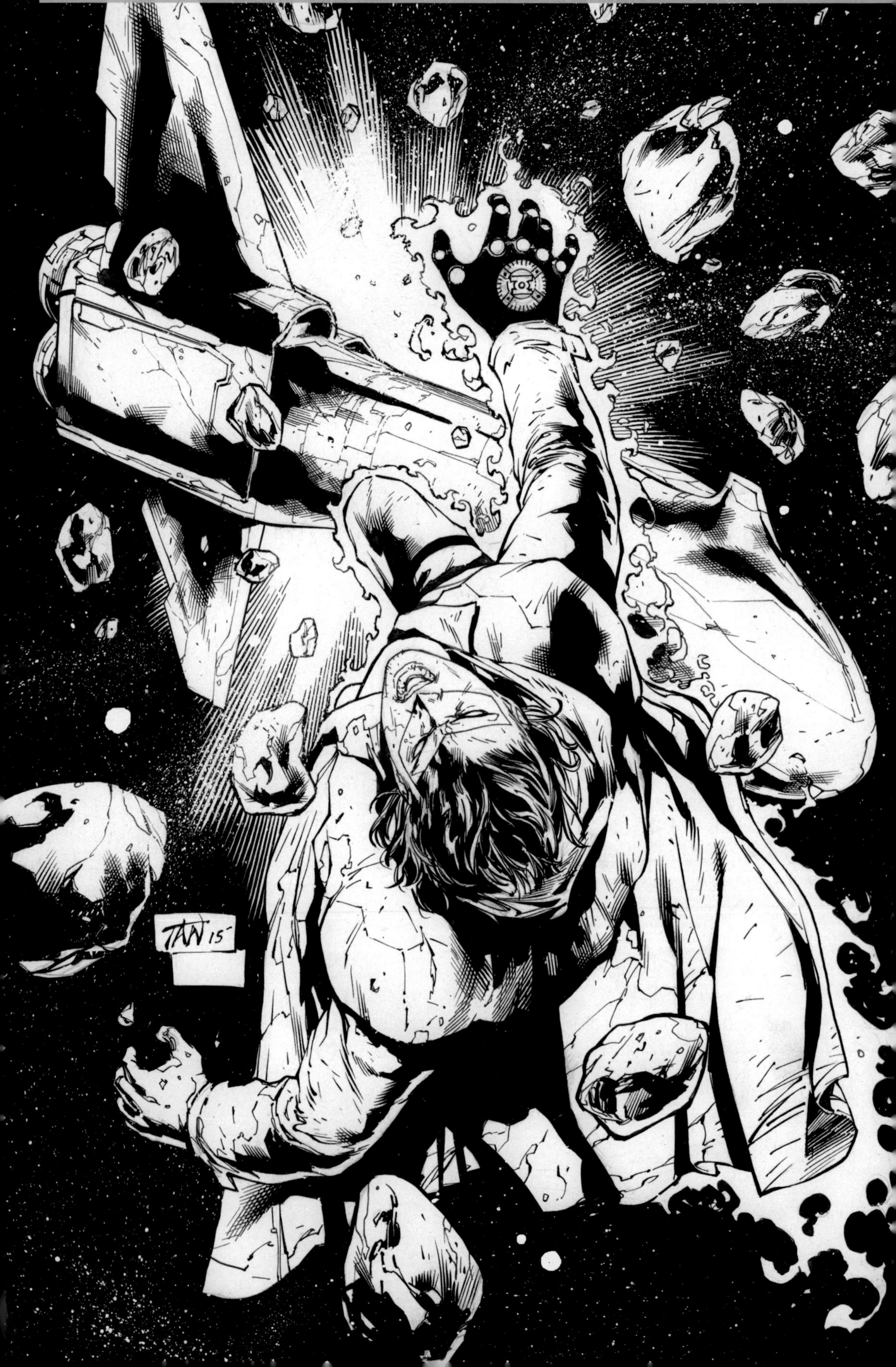

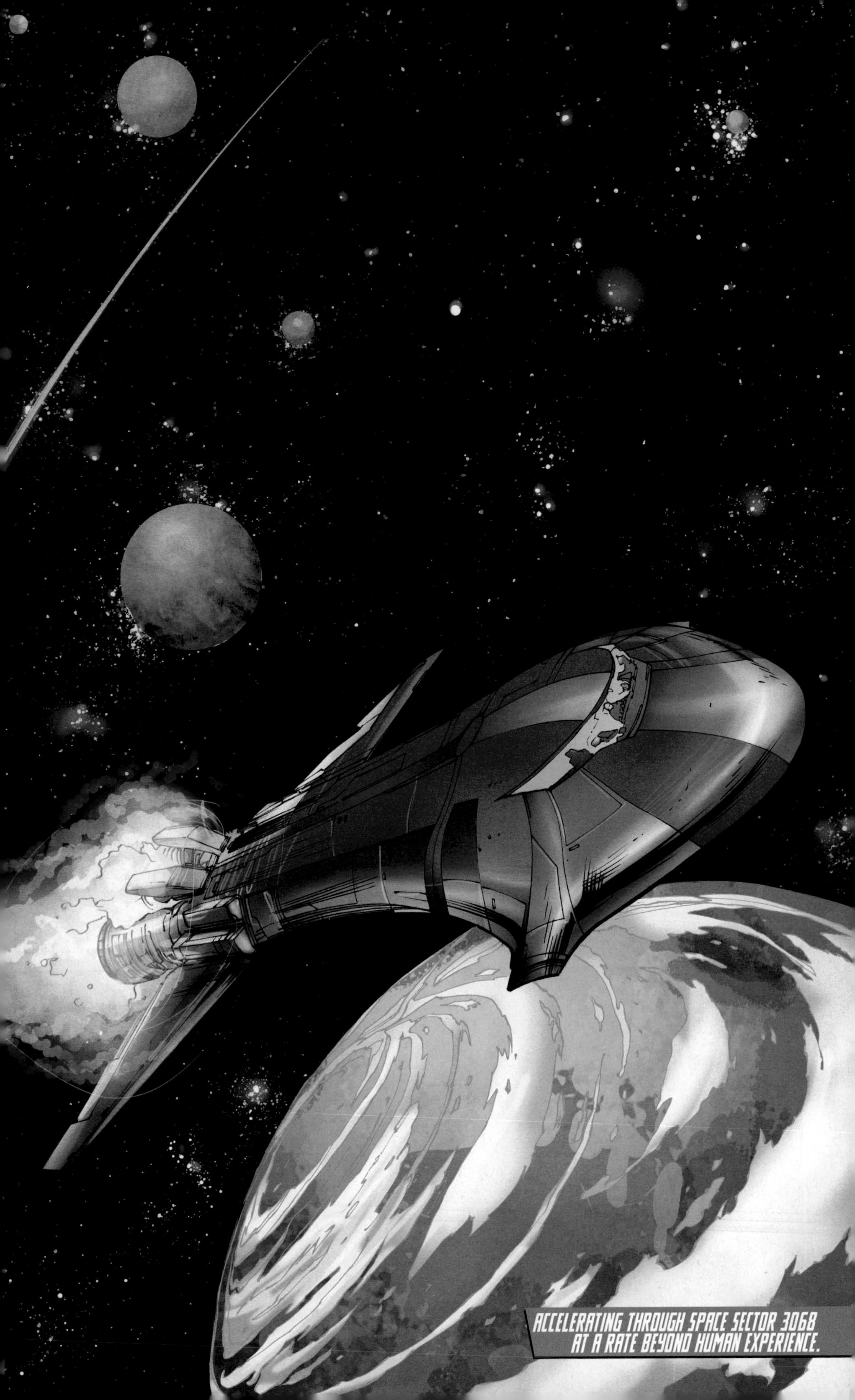
ACCELERATING THROUGH SPACE SECTOR 3068 AT A RATE BEYOND HUMAN EXPERIENCE.

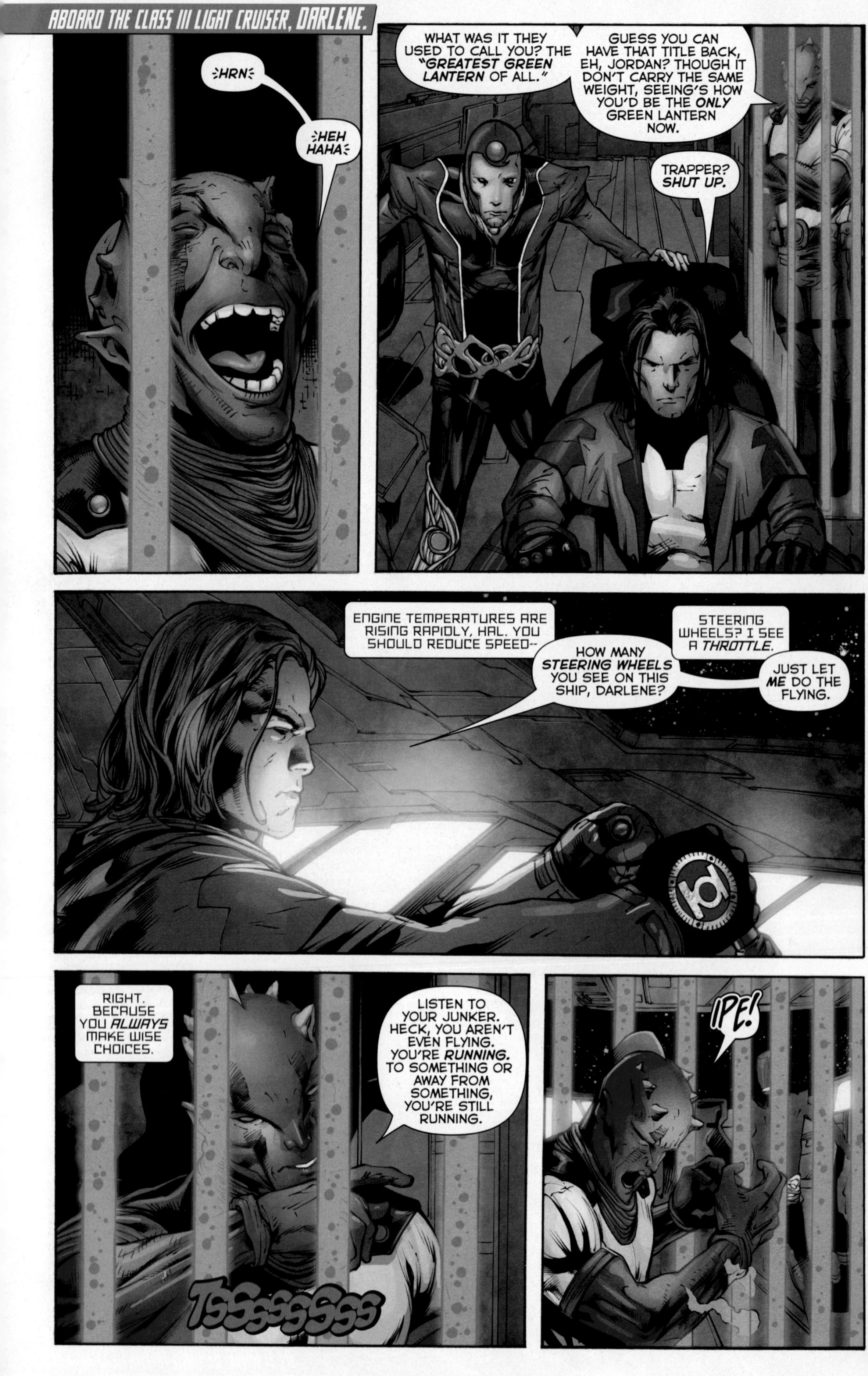
ABOARD THE CLASS III LIGHT CRUISER, DARLENE.
HRN
HEH HAHA
WHAT WAS IT THEY USED TO CALL YOU? THE "GREATEST GREEN LANTERN OF ALL."
GUESS YOU CAN HAVE THAT TITLE BACK, EH, JORDAN? THOUGH IT DON'T CARRY THE SAME WEIGHT, SEEING'S HOW YOU'D BE THE ONLY GREEN LANTERN NOW.
TRAPPER? SHUT UP.
ENGINE TEMPERATURES ARE RISING RAPIDLY, HAL. YOU SHOULD REDUCE SPEED--
HOW MANY STEERING WHEELS YOU SEE ON THIS SHIP, DARLENE?
STEERING WHEELS? I SEE A THROTTLE.
JUST LET ME DO THE FLYING.
RIGHT. BECAUSE YOU ALWAYS MAKE WISE CHOICES.
LISTEN TO YOUR JUNKER. HECK, YOU AREN'T EVEN FLYING. YOU'RE RUNNING. TO SOMETHING OR AWAY FROM SOMETHING, YOU'RE STILL RUNNING.
TSSSSSSSS
IPE!

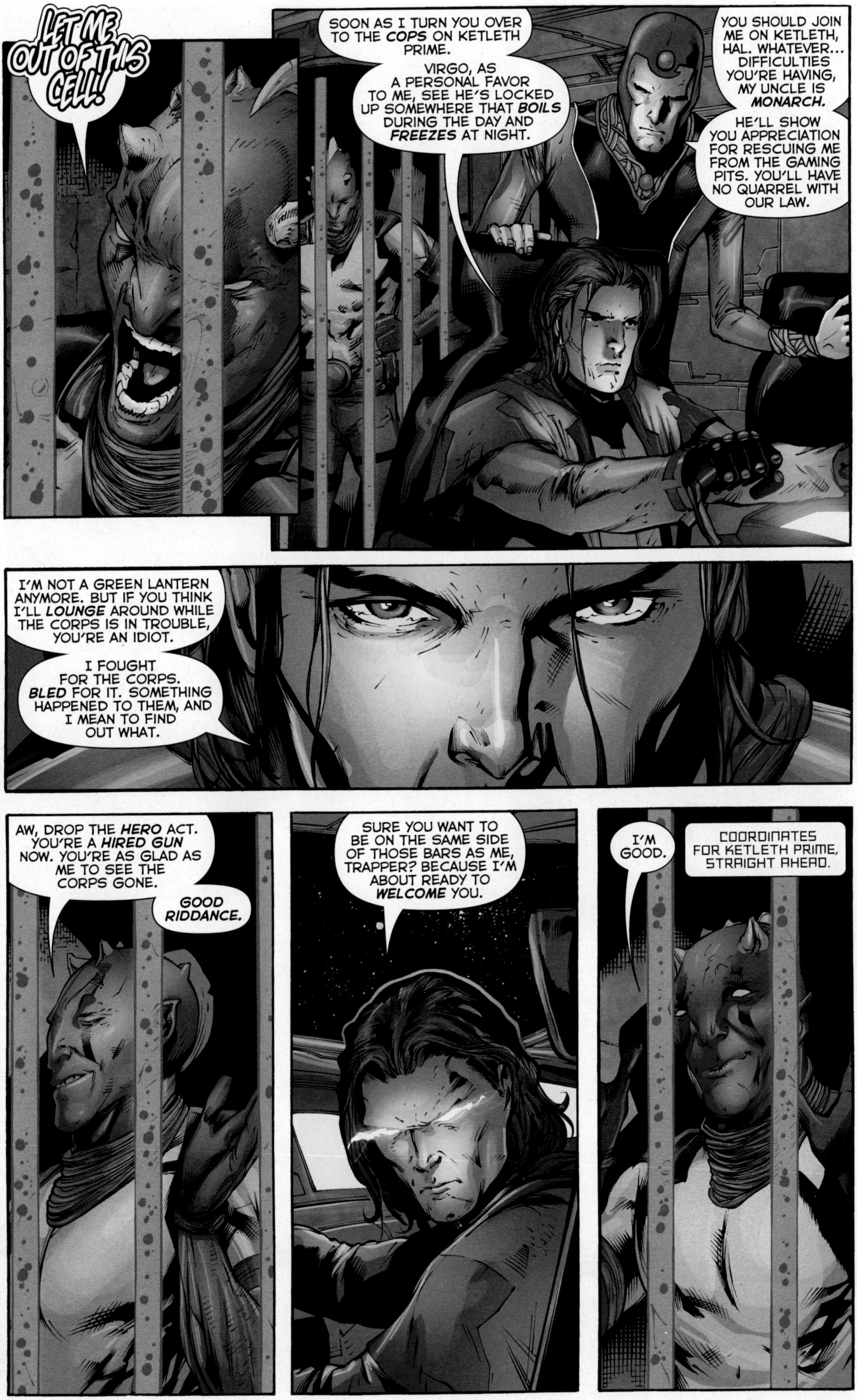
LET ME OUT OF THIS CELL!
SOON AS I TURN YOU OVER TO THE COPS ON KETLETH PRIME.
VIRGO, AS A PERSONAL FAVOR TO ME, SEE HE'S LOCKED UP SOMEWHERE THAT BOILS DURING THE DAY AND FREEZES AT NIGHT.
YOU SHOULD JOIN ME ON KETLETH, HAL. WHATEVER... DIFFICULTIES YOU'RE HAVING, MY UNCLE IS MONARCH.
HE'LL SHOW YOU APPRECIATION FOR RESCUING ME FROM THE GAMING PITS. YOU'LL HAVE NO QUARREL WITH OUR LAW.
I'M NOT A GREEN LANTERN ANYMORE. BUT IF YOU THINK I'LL LOUNGE AROUND WHILE THE CORPS IS IN TROUBLE, YOU'RE AN IDIOT.
I FOUGHT FOR THE CORPS. BLED FOR IT. SOMETHING HAPPENED TO THEM, AND I MEAN TO FIND OUT WHAT.
AW, DROP THE HERO ACT. YOU'RE A HIRED GUN NOW. YOU'RE AS GLAD AS ME TO SEE THE CORPS GONE.
GOOD RIDDANCE.
SURE YOU WANT TO BE ON THE SAME SIDE OF THOSE BARS AS ME, TRAPPER? BECAUSE I'M ABOUT READY TO WELCOME YOU.
I'M GOOD.
COORDINATES FOR KETLETH PRIME, STRAIGHT AHEAD.

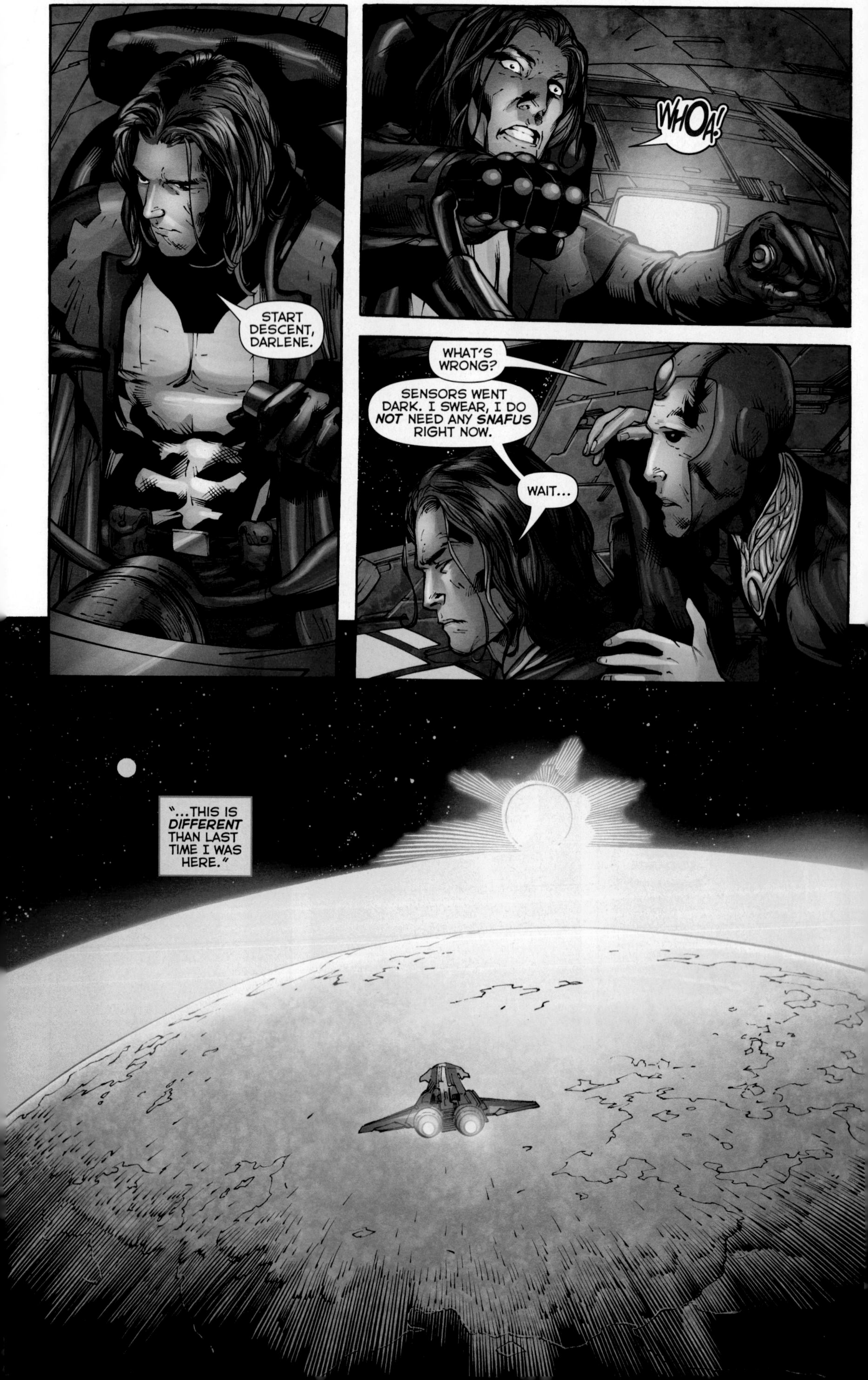
START DESCENT, DARLENE.
WHOA!
WHAT'S WRONG?
SENSORS WENT DARK. I SWEAR, I DO *NOT* NEED ANY *SNAFUS* RIGHT NOW.
WAIT...
"...THIS IS *DIFFERENT* THAN LAST TIME I WAS HERE."

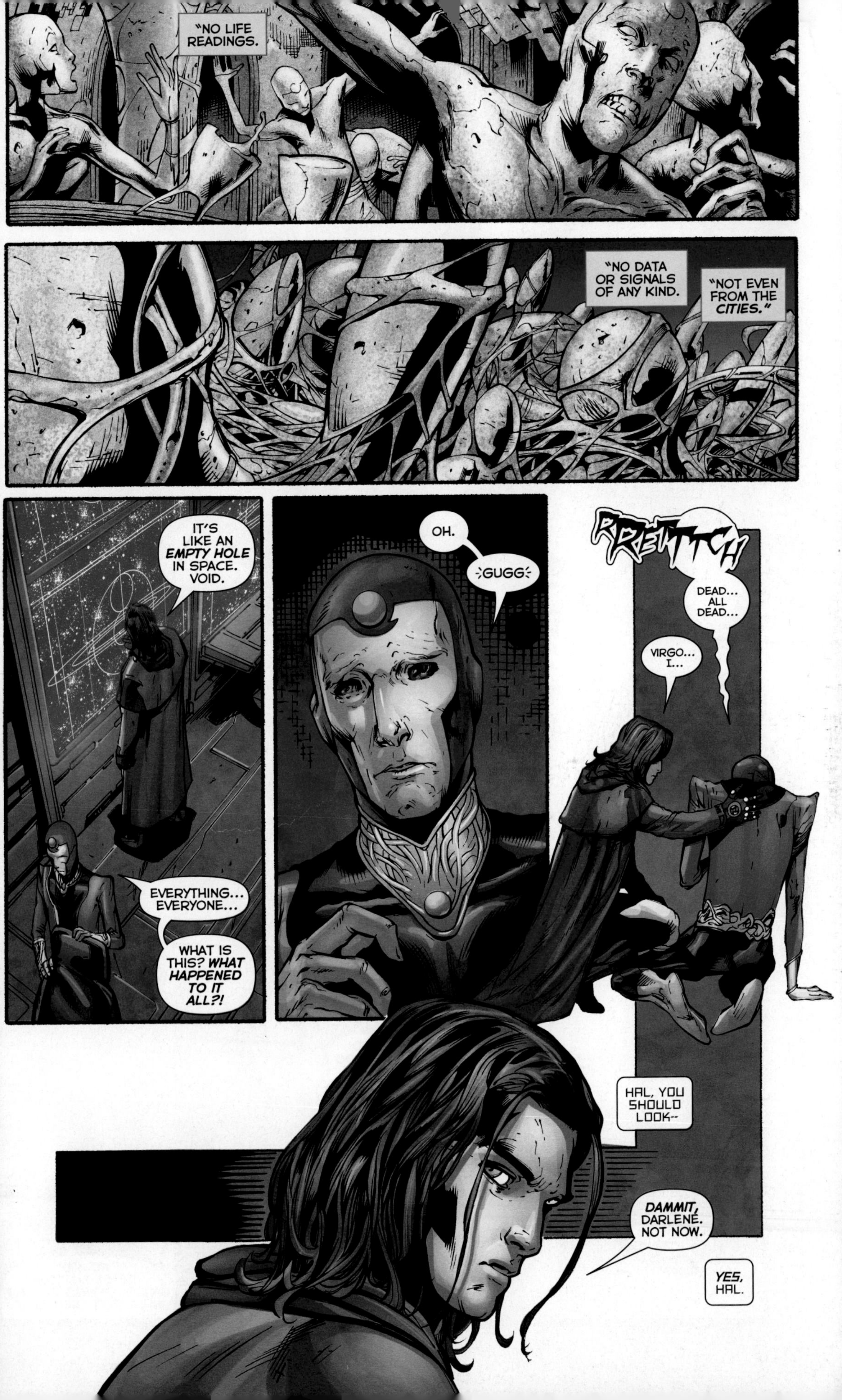
"NO LIFE READINGS.
"NO DATA OR SIGNALS OF ANY KIND.
"NOT EVEN FROM THE CITIES."
IT'S LIKE AN EMPTY HOLE IN SPACE. VOID.
EVERYTHING... EVERYONE...
WHAT IS THIS? WHAT HAPPENED TO IT ALL?!
OH.
GUGG
RRETTTCH
DEAD... ALL DEAD...
VIRGO... I...
HAL, YOU SHOULD LOOK--
DAMMIT, DARLENE. NOT NOW.
YES, HAL.

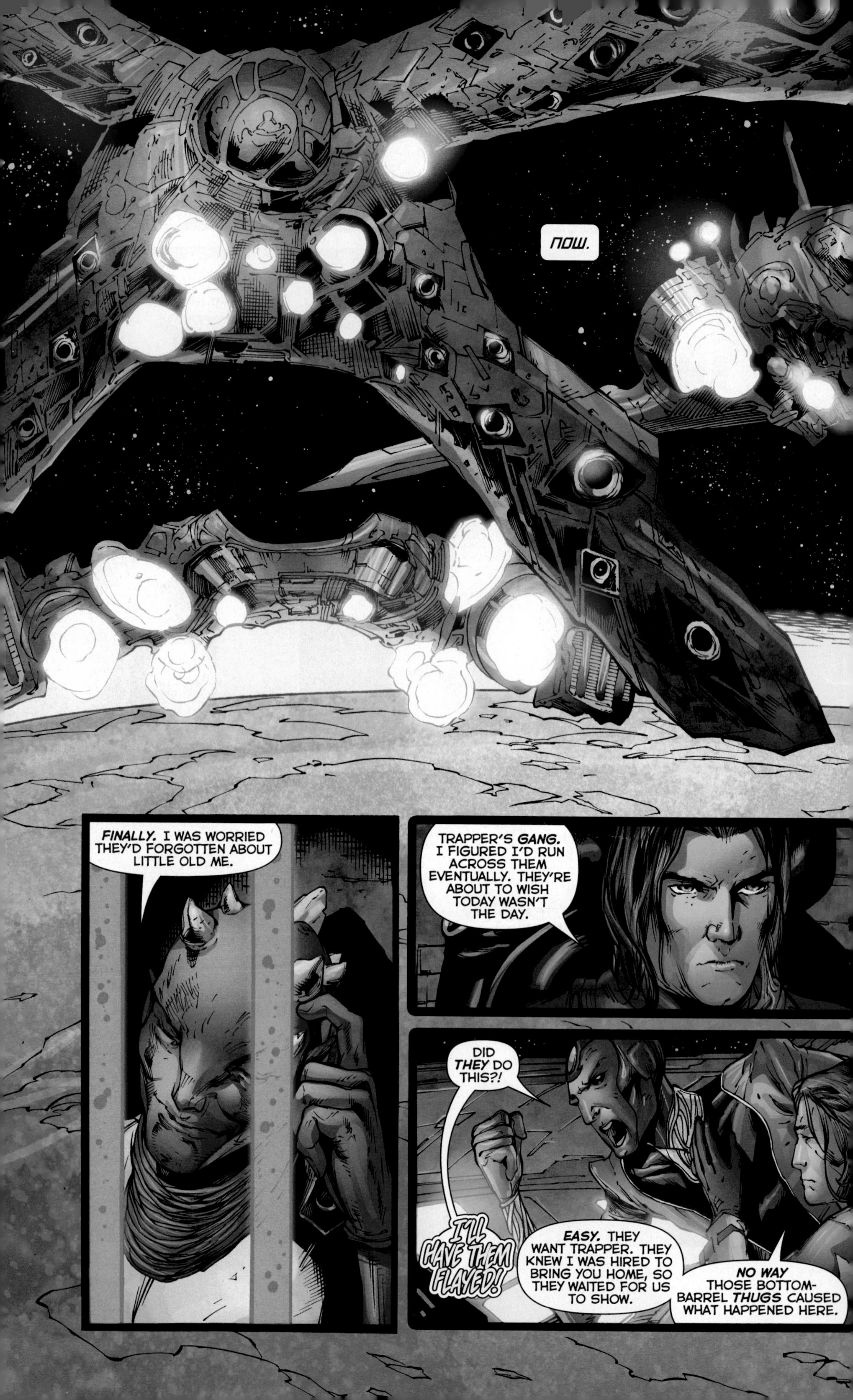
NOW.
FINALLY. I WAS WORRIED THEY'D FORGOTTEN ABOUT LITTLE OLD ME.
TRAPPER'S GANG. I FIGURED I'D RUN ACROSS THEM EVENTUALLY. THEY'RE ABOUT TO WISH TODAY WASN'T THE DAY.
DID THEY DO THIS?!
I'LL HAVE THEM FLAYED!
EASY. THEY WANT TRAPPER. THEY KNEW I WAS HIRED TO BRING YOU HOME, SO THEY WAITED FOR US TO SHOW.
NO WAY THOSE BOTTOM-BARREL THUGS CAUSED WHAT HAPPENED HERE.

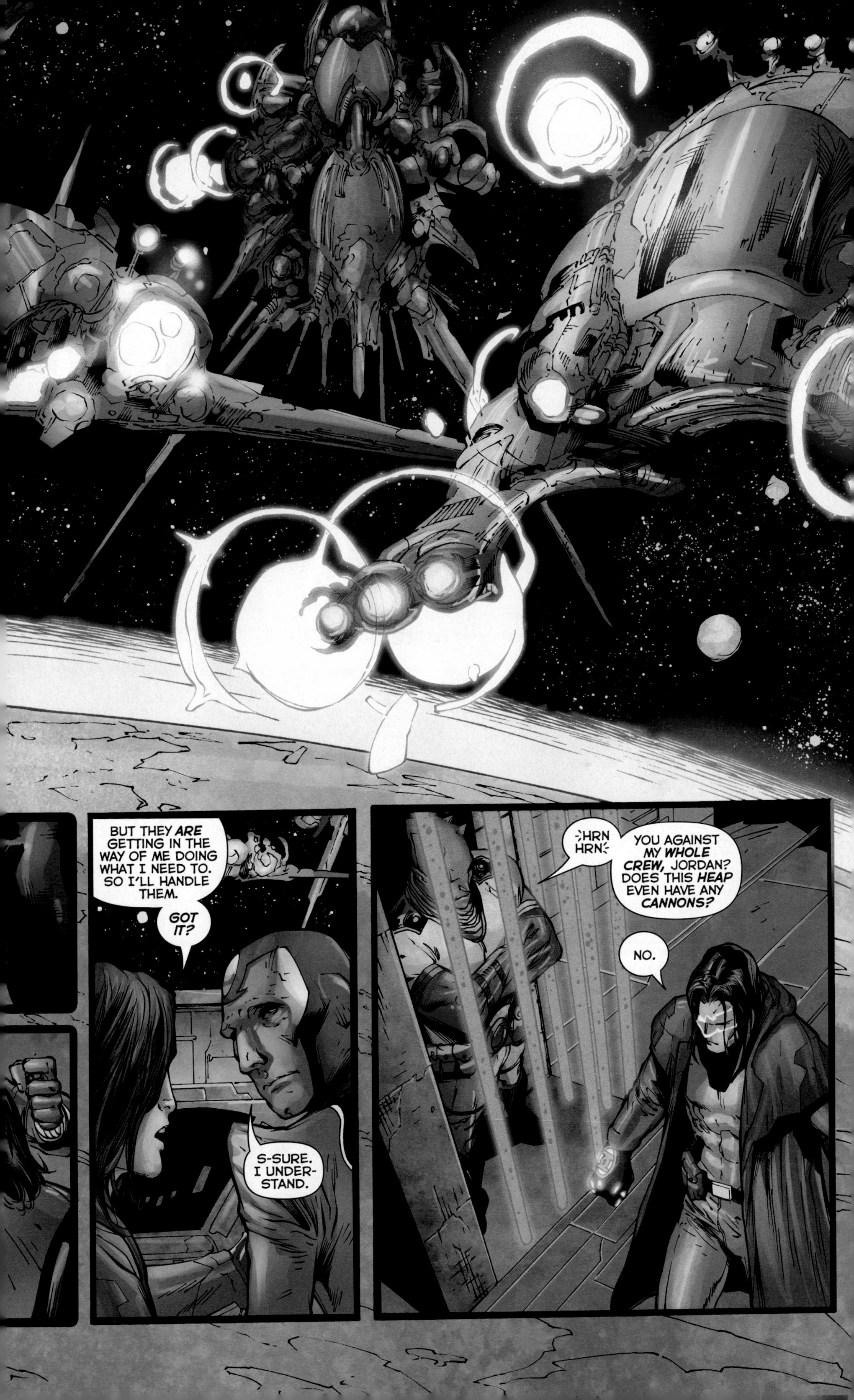
BUT THEY ARE GETTING IN THE WAY OF ME DOING WHAT I NEED TO. SO I'LL HANDLE THEM.
GOT IT?
S-SURE. I UNDERSTAND.
HRN HRN
YOU AGAINST MY WHOLE CREW, JORDAN? DOES THIS HEAP EVEN HAVE ANY CANNONS?
NO.

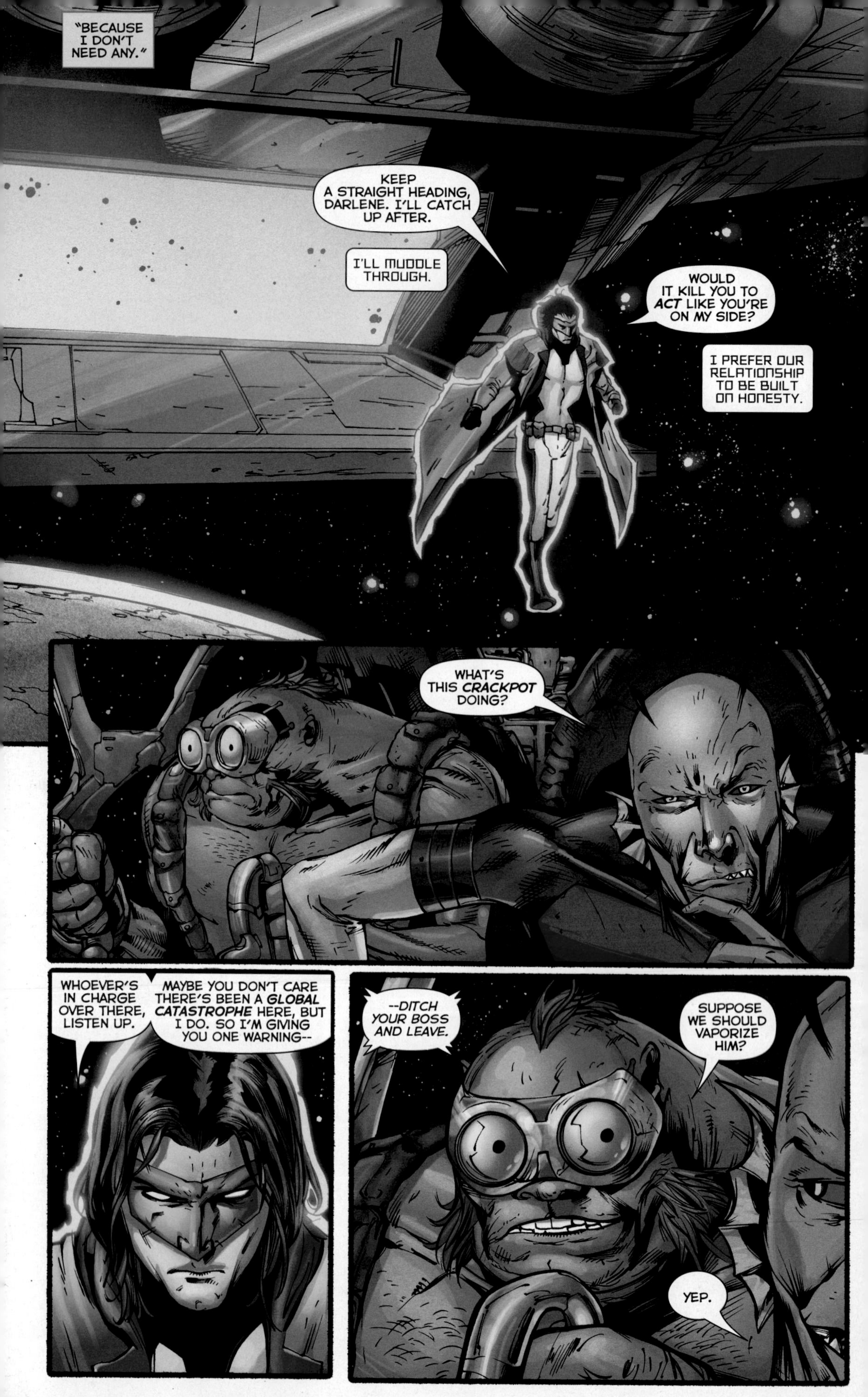
"BECAUSE I DON'T NEED ANY."
KEEP A STRAIGHT HEADING, DARLENE. I'LL CATCH UP AFTER.
I'LL MUDDLE THROUGH.
WOULD IT KILL YOU TO ACT LIKE YOU'RE ON MY SIDE?
I PREFER OUR RELATIONSHIP TO BE BUILT ON HONESTY.
WHAT'S THIS CRACKPOT DOING?
WHOEVER'S IN CHARGE OVER THERE, LISTEN UP.
MAYBE YOU DON'T CARE THERE'S BEEN A GLOBAL CATASTROPHE HERE, BUT I DO. SO I'M GIVING YOU ONE WARNING--
--DITCH YOUR BOSS AND LEAVE.
SUPPOSE WE SHOULD VAPORIZE HIM?
YEP.

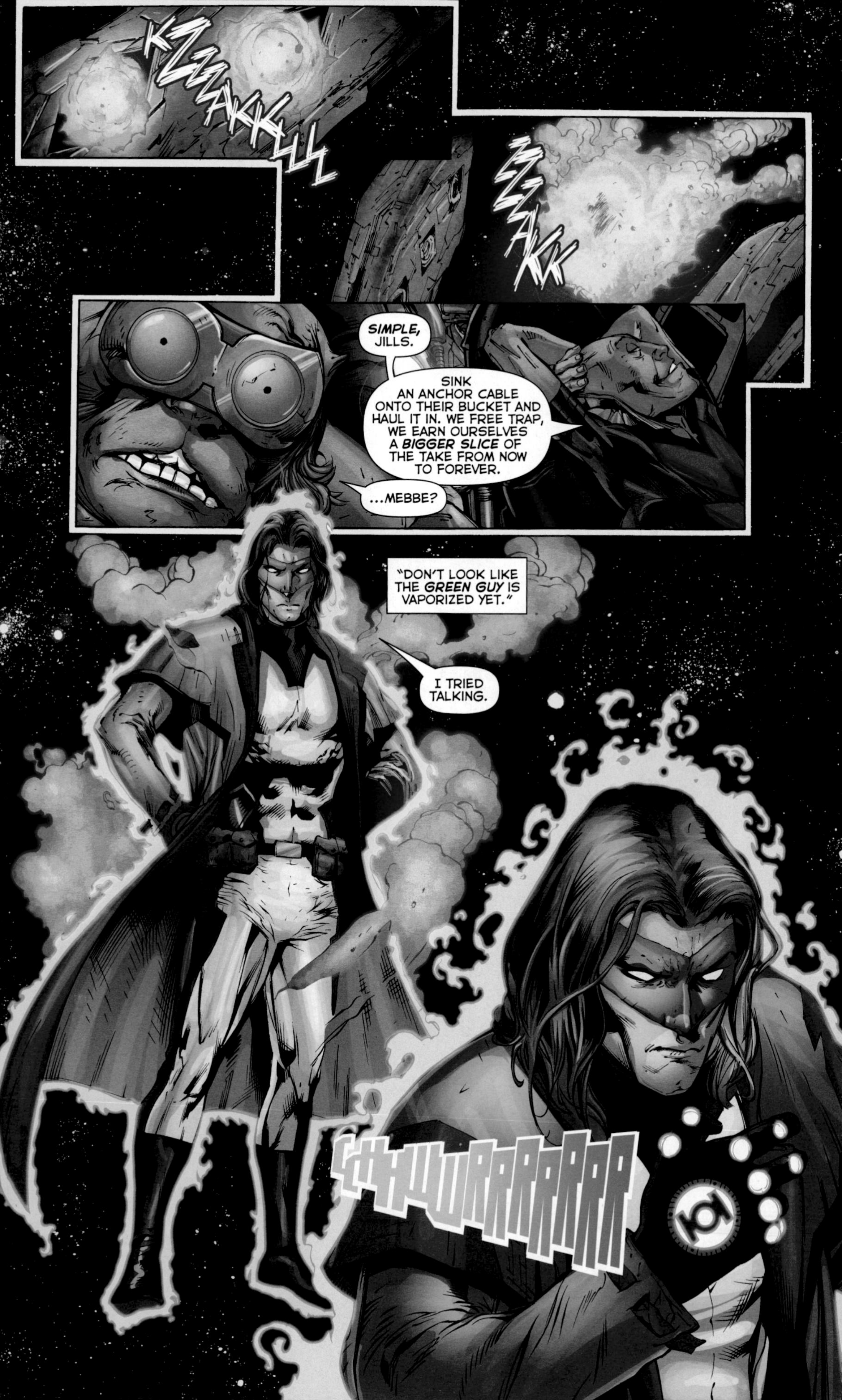
KZZZZAKKKLLL
ZZZZAKK
SIMPLE, JILLS.
SINK AN ANCHOR CABLE ONTO THEIR BUCKET AND HAUL IT IN. WE FREE TRAP, WE EARN OURSELVES A BIGGER SLICE OF THE TAKE FROM NOW TO FOREVER.
...MEBBE?
"DON'T LOOK LIKE THE GREEN GUY IS VAPORIZED YET."
I TRIED TALKING.
CCHWURRRRRRR

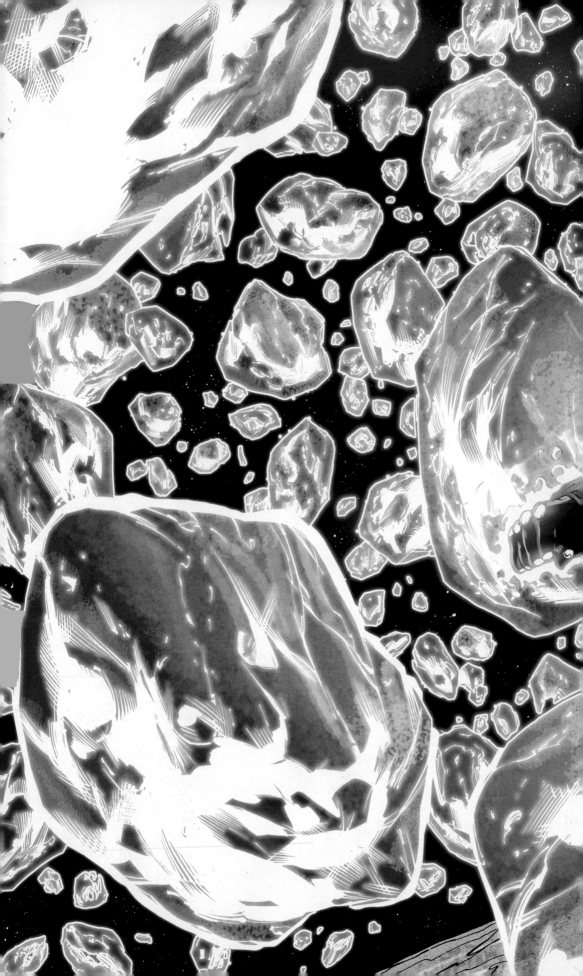

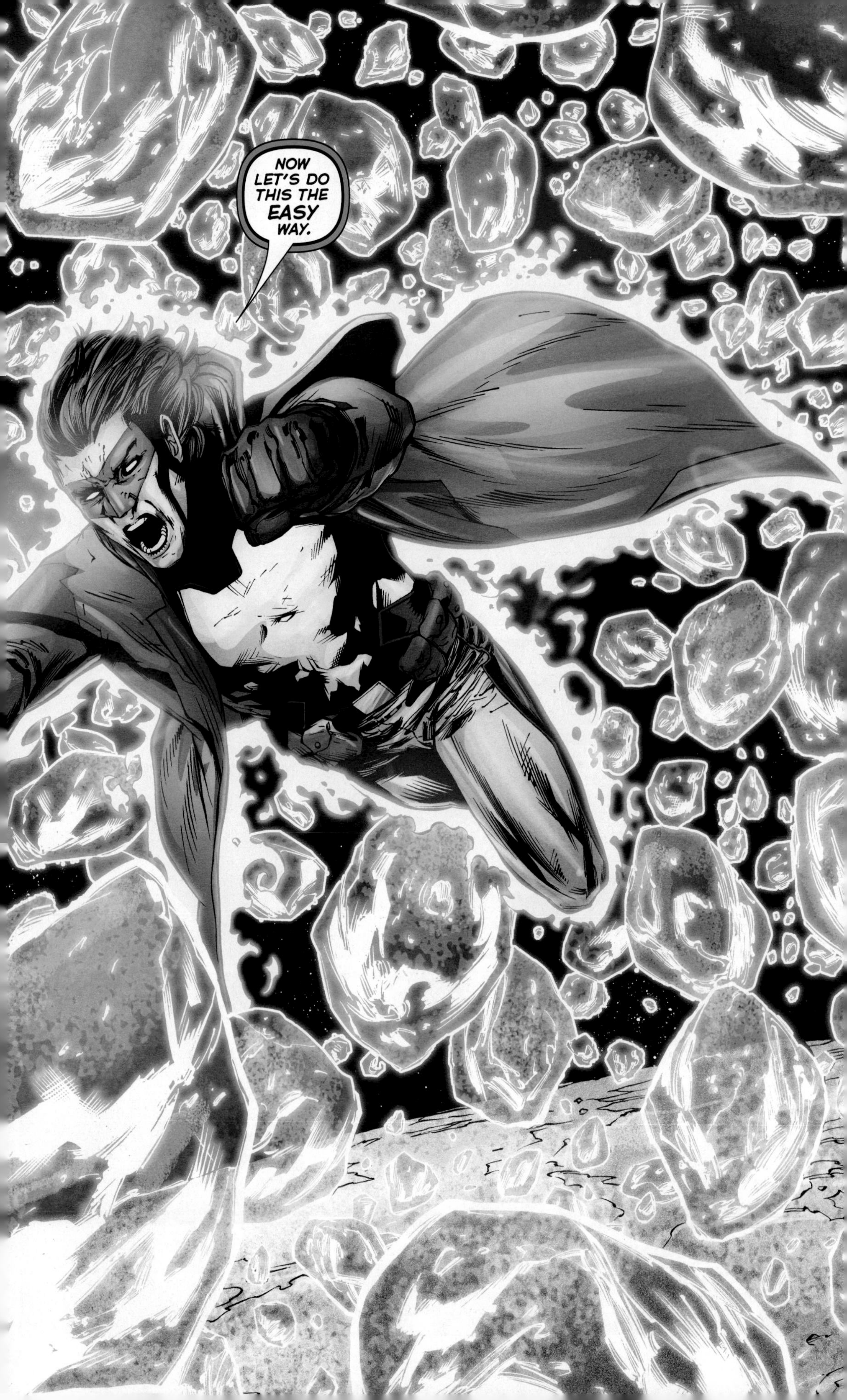
NOW LET'S DO THIS THE EASY WAY.

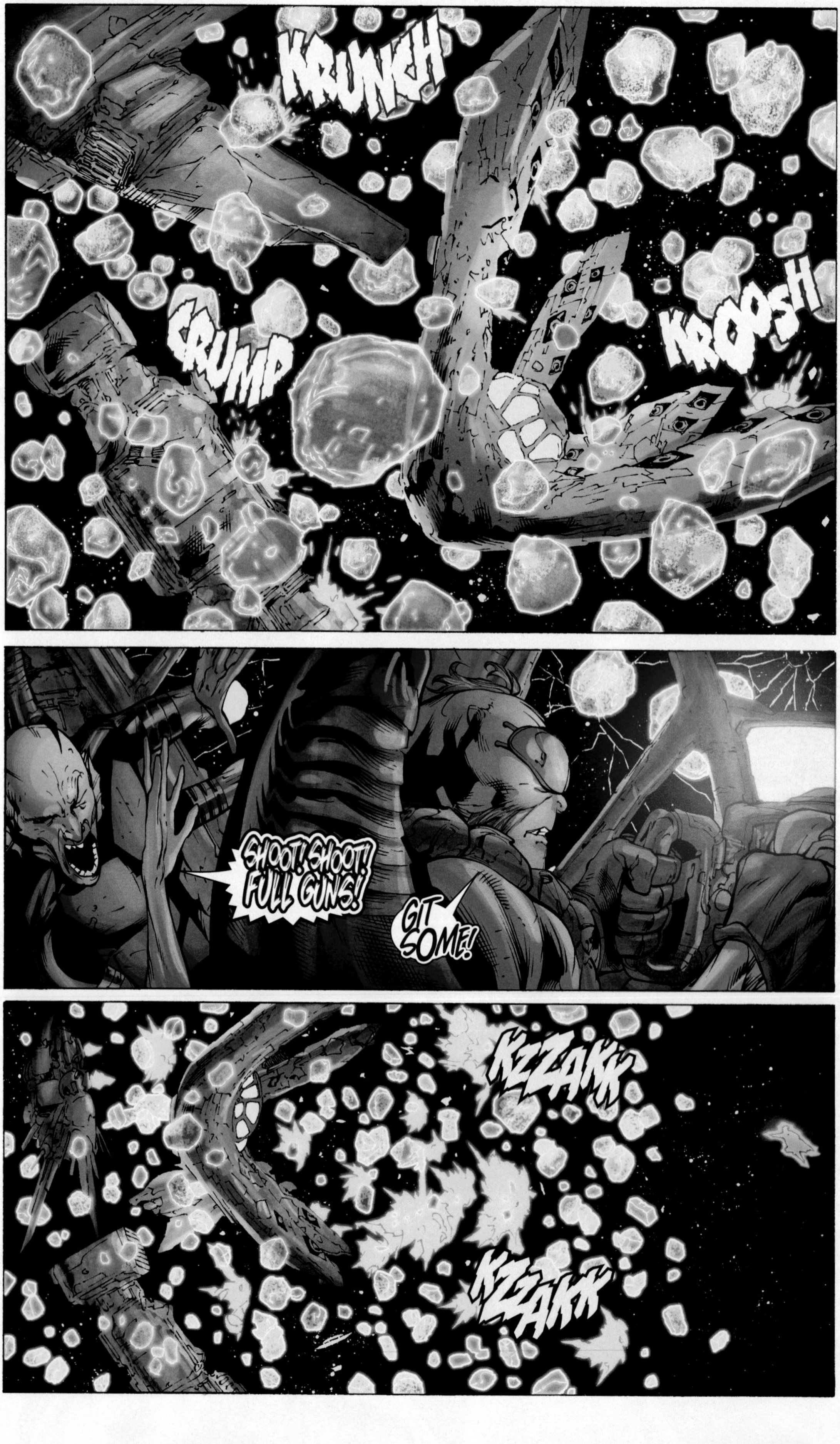
KRUNCH
CRUMP
KROOSH
SHOOT! SHOOT! FULL GUNS!
GIT SOME!
KZZAKK
KZZAKK

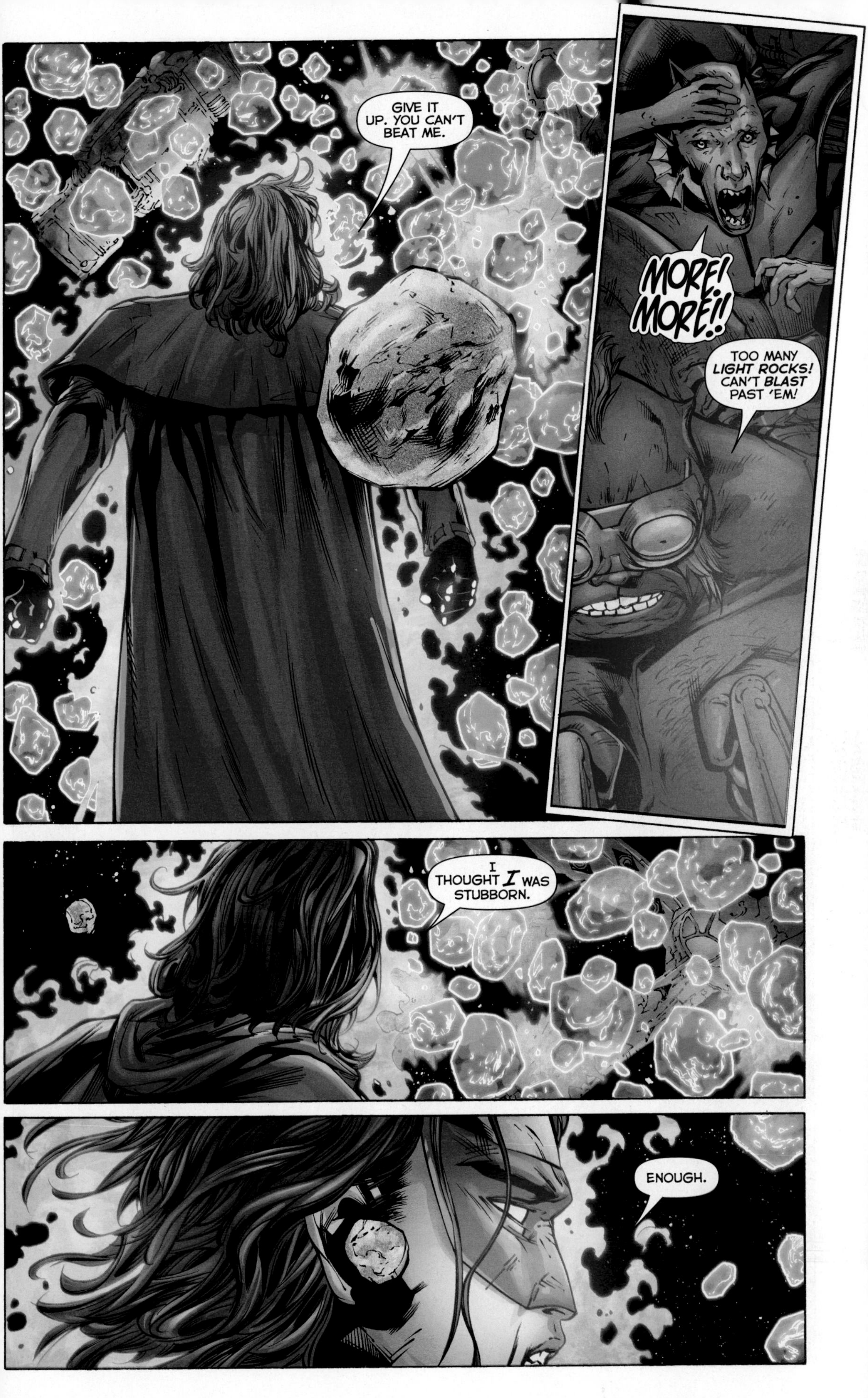
GIVE IT UP. YOU CAN'T BEAT ME.
MORE! MORE!!
TOO MANY LIGHT ROCKS! CAN'T BLAST PAST 'EM!
I THOUGHT I WAS STUBBORN.
ENOUGH.

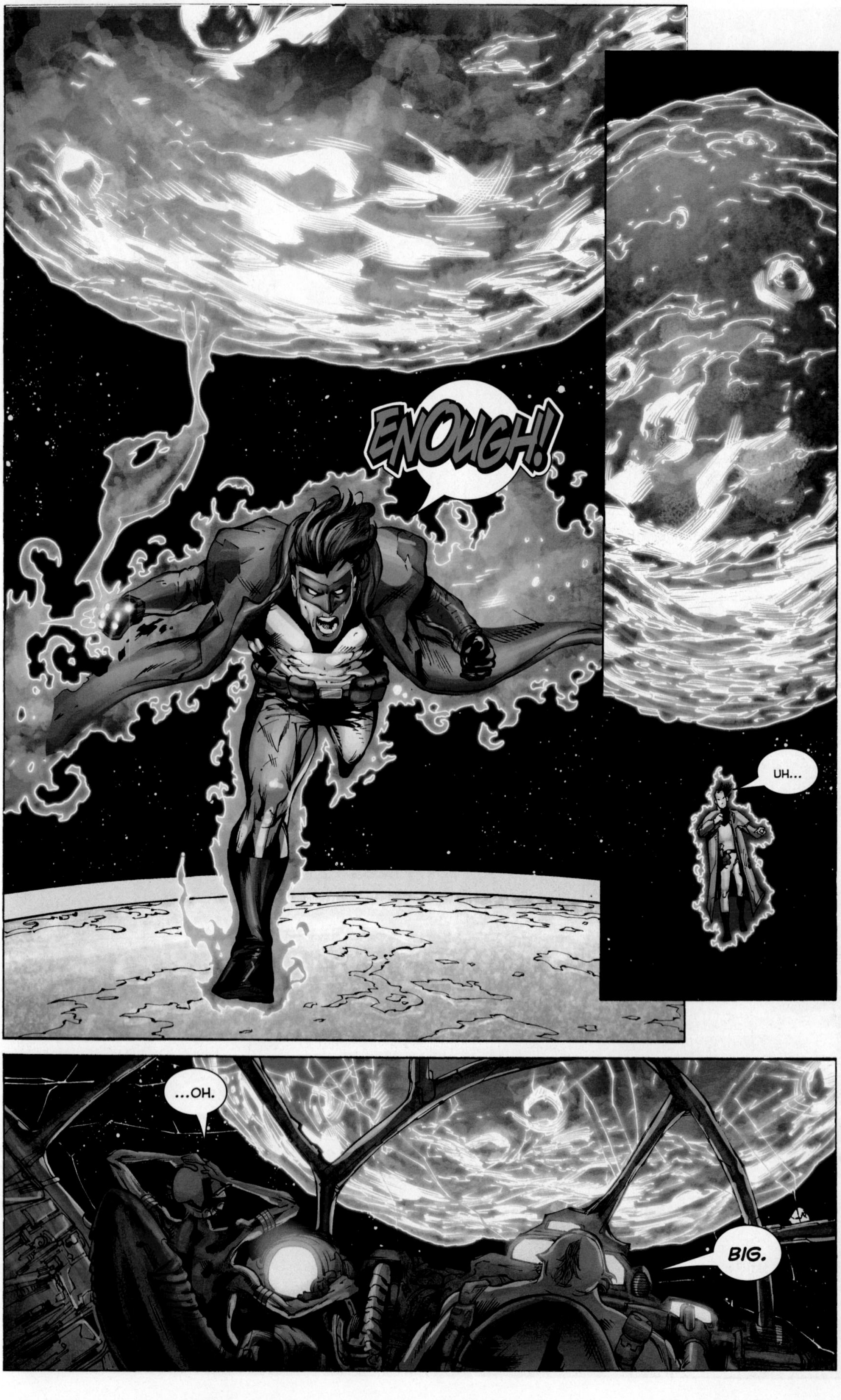
ENOUGH!
UH...
...OH.
BIG.

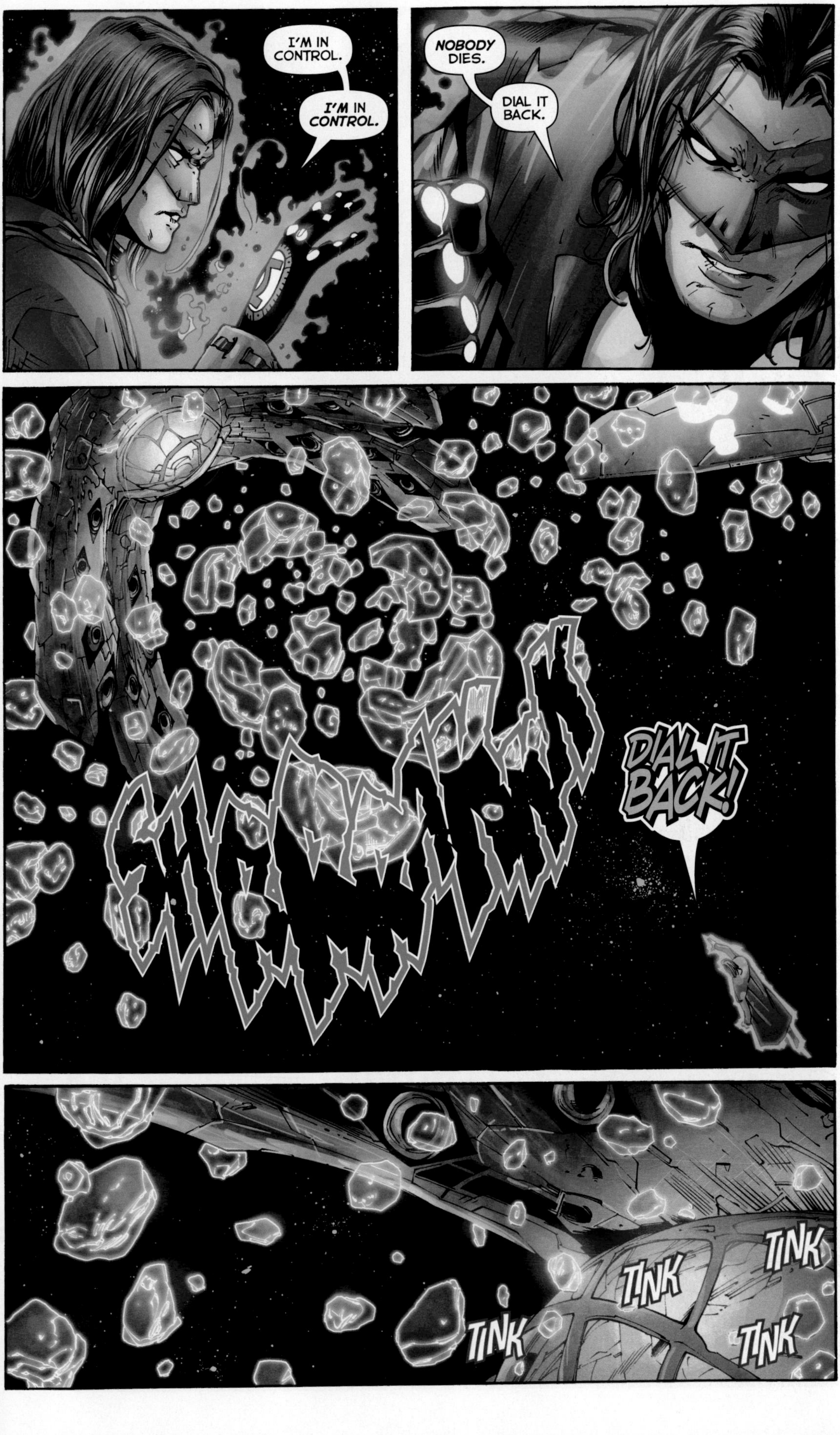
I'M IN CONTROL.
I'M IN CONTROL.
NOBODY DIES.
DIAL IT BACK.
DIAL IT BACK!
TINK
TINK
TINK
TINK

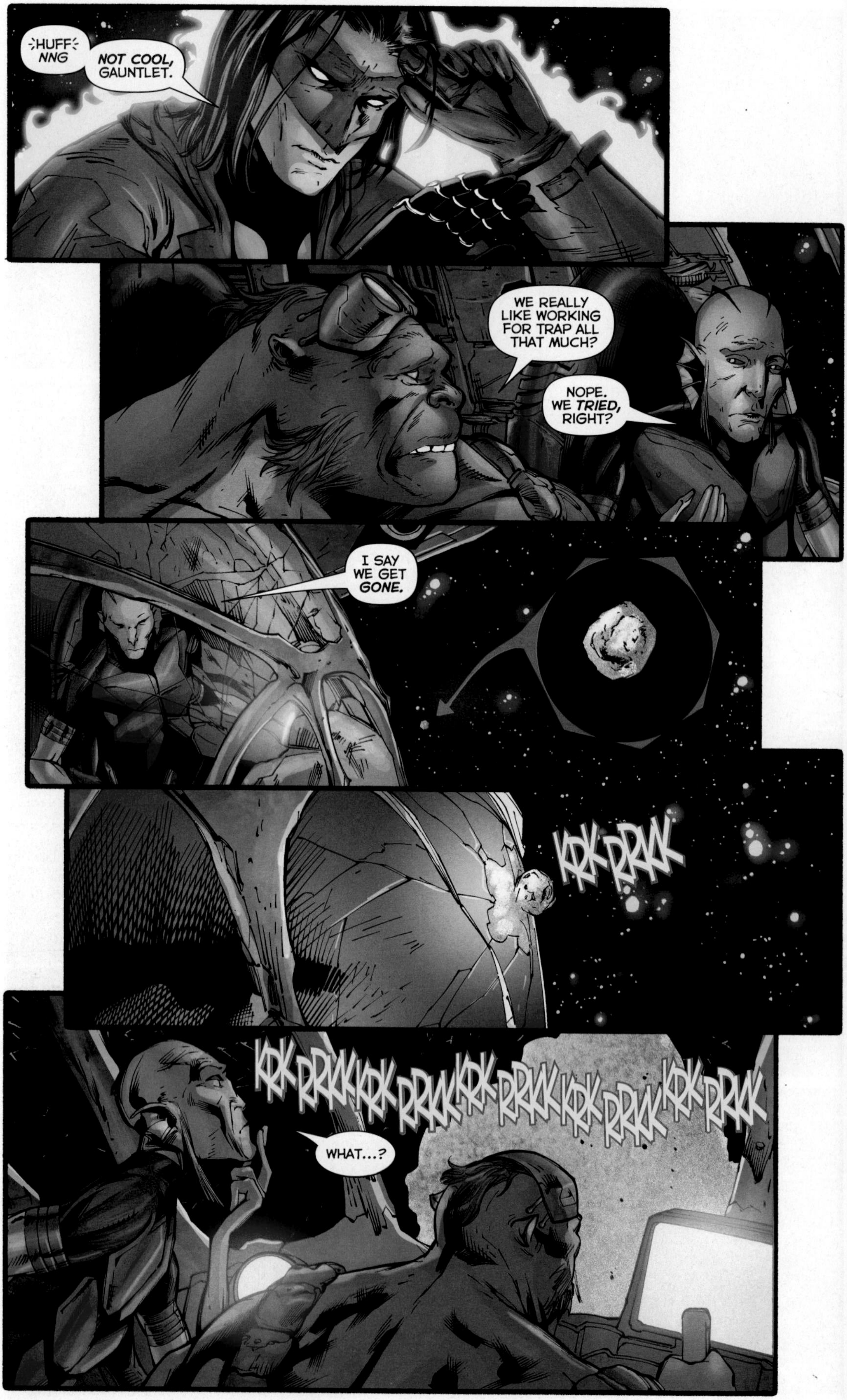
HUFF
NNG
NOT COOL, GAUNTLET.
WE REALLY LIKE WORKING FOR TRAP ALL THAT MUCH?
NOPE. WE TRIED, RIGHT?
I SAY WE GET GONE.
KRK RRKK
KRK RRKK KRK RRKK KRK RRKK KRK RRKK KRK RRKK
WHAT...?

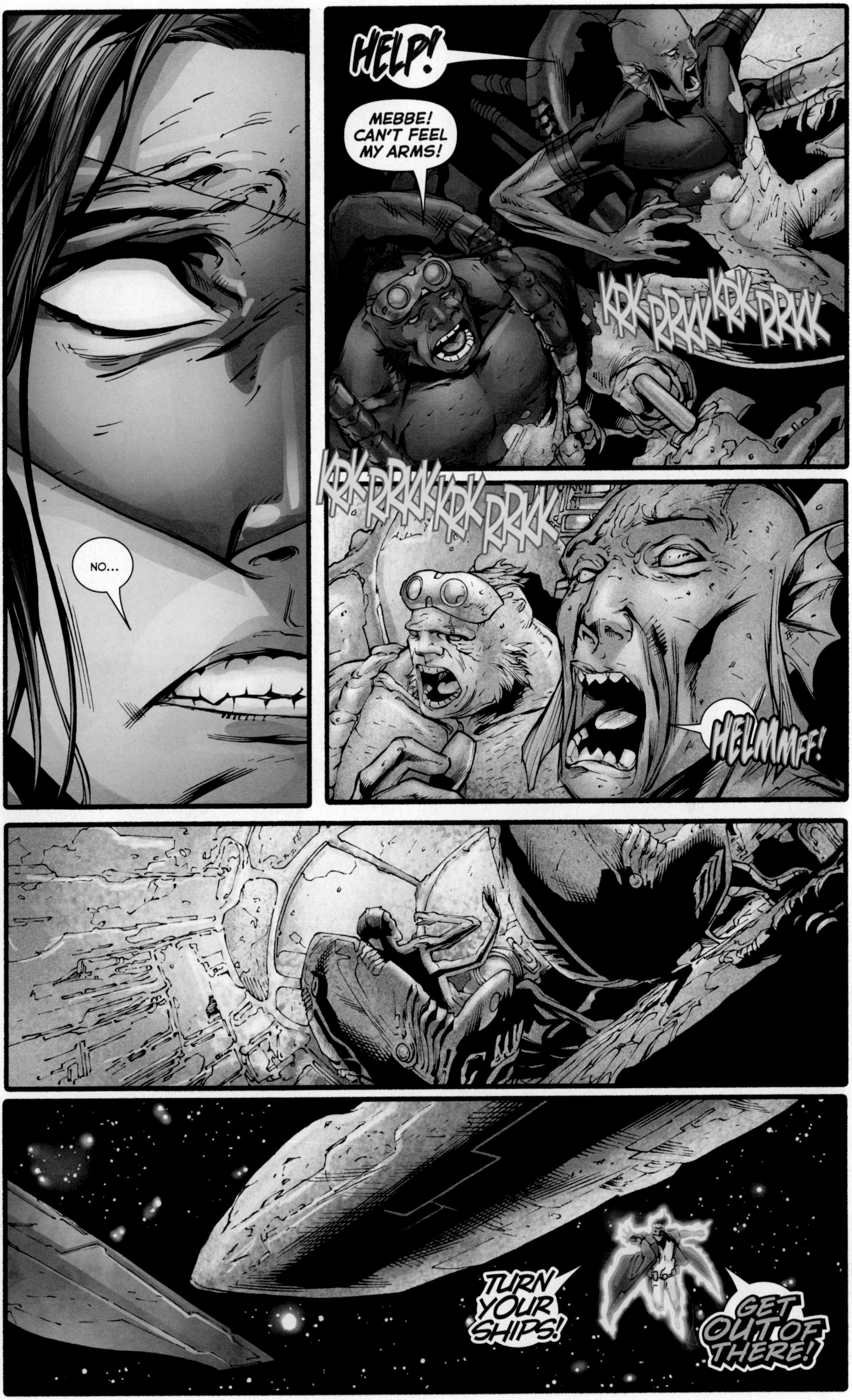

NO...
HELP!
MEBBE! CAN'T FEEL MY ARMS!
KRK RRKK KRK RRKK
KRK RRKK KRK RRKK
HELMMFF!
TURN YOUR SHIPS!
GET OUT OF THERE!

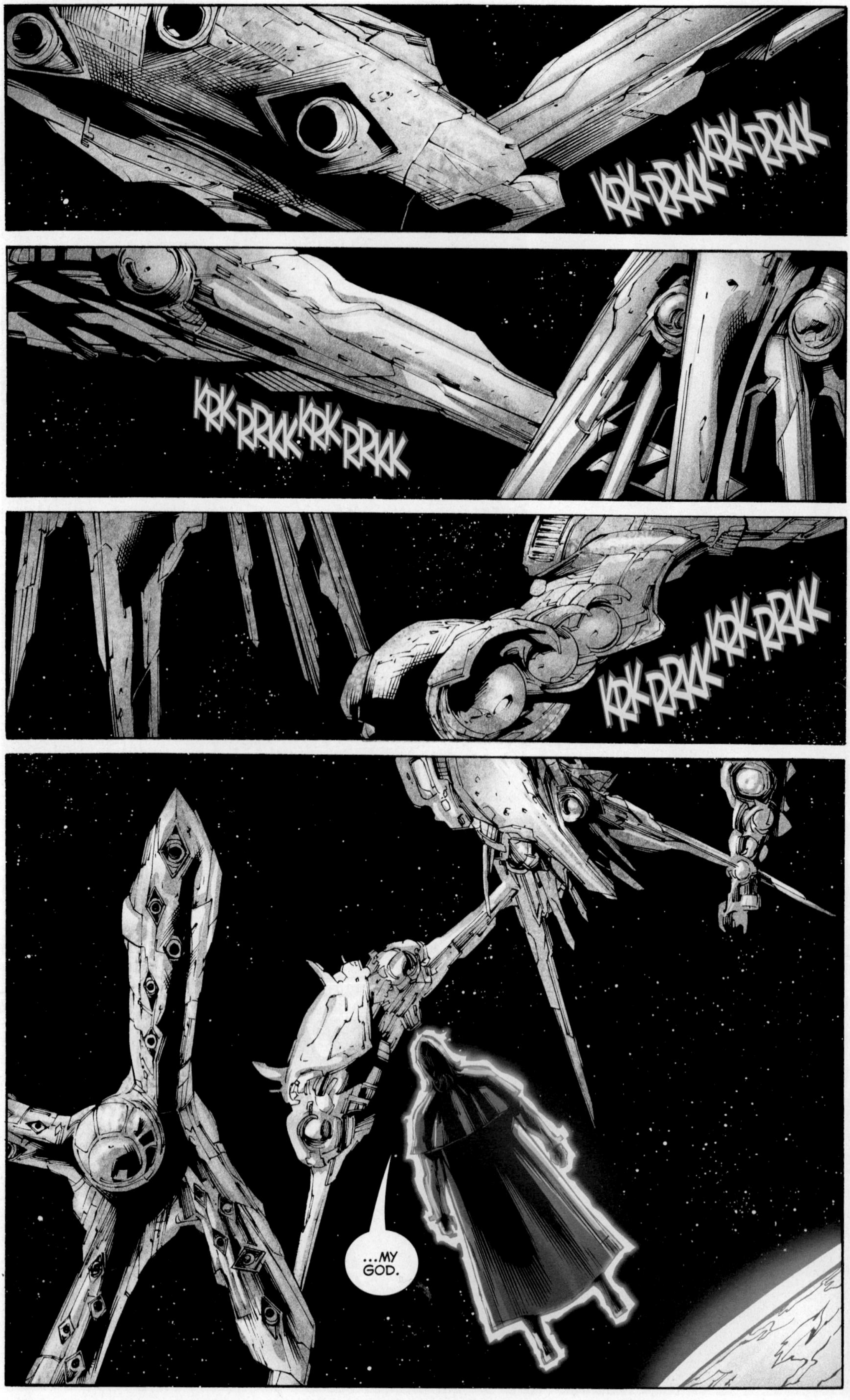
KRK-RRKK KRK-RRKK
KRK-RRKK KRK-RRKK
KRK-RRKK KRK-RRKK
...MY GOD.

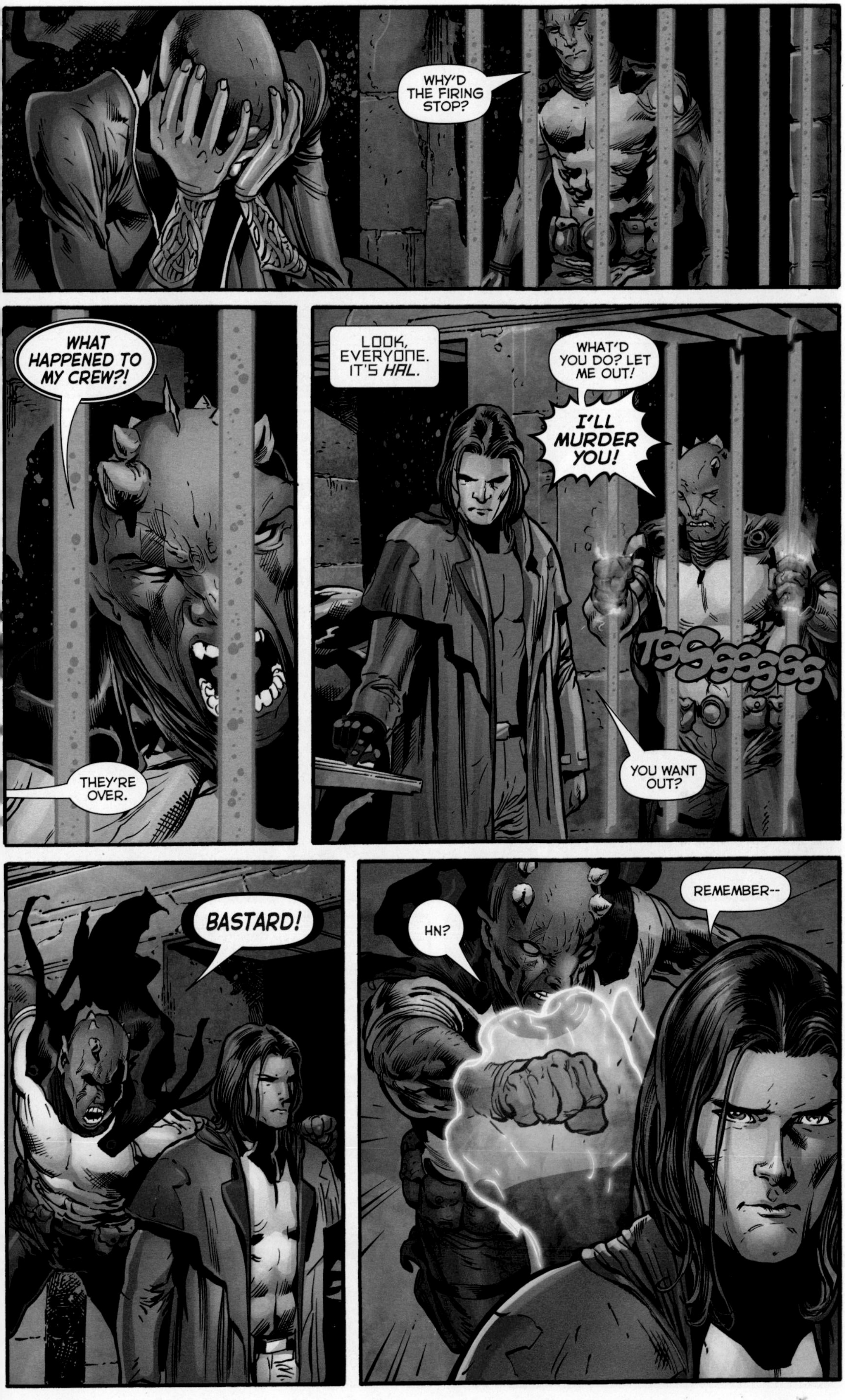
WHY'D THE FIRING STOP?
WHAT HAPPENED TO MY CREW?!
THEY'RE OVER.
LOOK, EVERYONE. IT'S HAL.
WHAT'D YOU DO? LET ME OUT!
I'LL MURDER YOU!
TSSSSSSSS
YOU WANT OUT?
BASTARD!
HN?
REMEMBER--

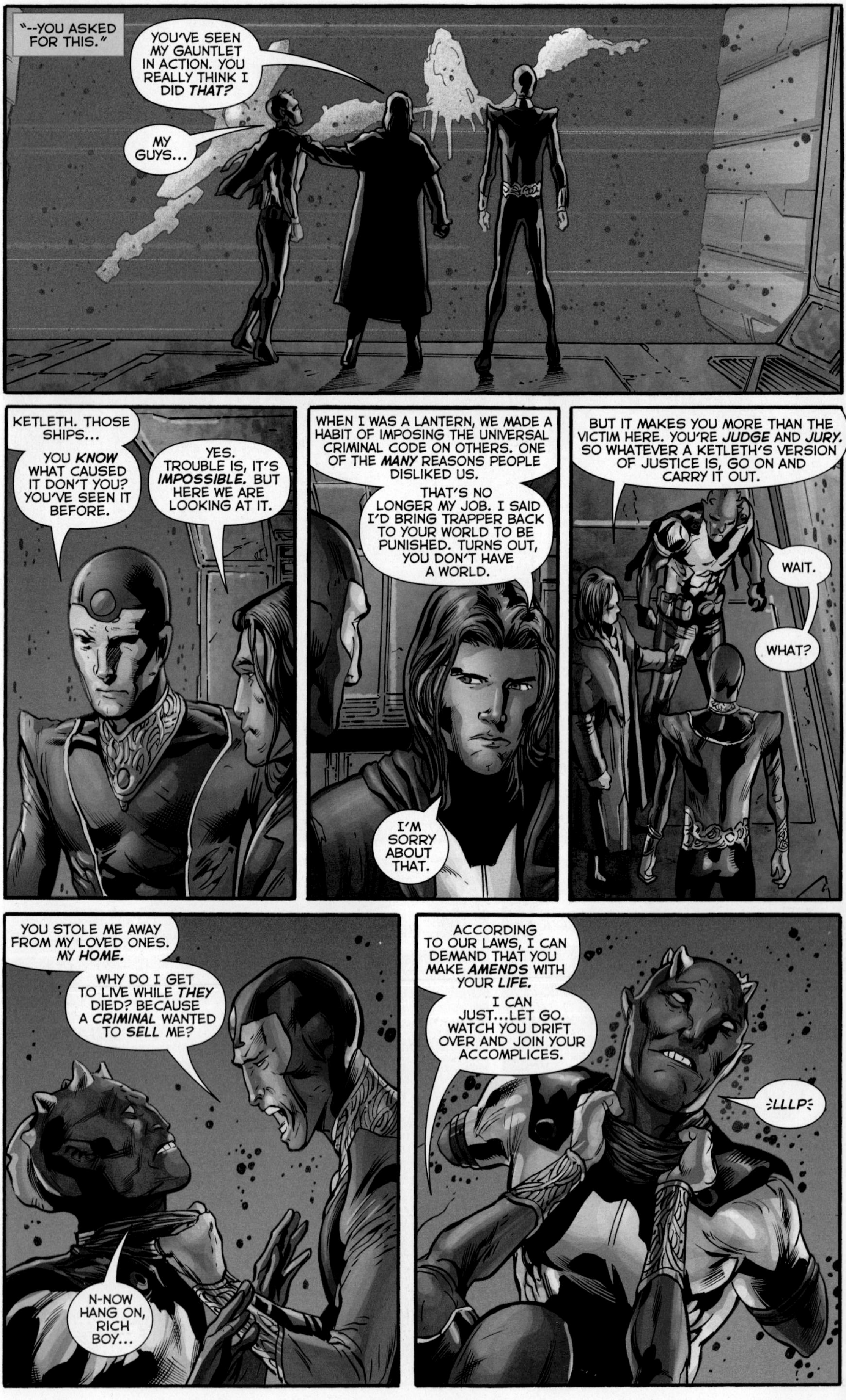
"--YOU ASKED FOR THIS."
YOU'VE SEEN MY GAUNTLET IN ACTION. YOU REALLY THINK I DID *THAT?*
MY GUYS...
KETLETH. THOSE SHIPS...
YOU *KNOW* WHAT CAUSED IT DON'T YOU? YOU'VE SEEN IT BEFORE.
YES. TROUBLE IS, IT'S *IMPOSSIBLE.* BUT HERE WE ARE LOOKING AT IT.
WHEN I WAS A LANTERN, WE MADE A HABIT OF IMPOSING THE UNIVERSAL CRIMINAL CODE ON OTHERS. ONE OF THE *MANY* REASONS PEOPLE DISLIKED US.
THAT'S NO LONGER MY JOB. I SAID I'D BRING TRAPPER BACK TO YOUR WORLD TO BE PUNISHED. TURNS OUT, YOU DON'T HAVE A WORLD.
I'M SORRY ABOUT THAT.
BUT IT MAKES YOU MORE THAN THE VICTIM HERE. YOU'RE *JUDGE* AND *JURY.* SO WHATEVER A KETLETH'S VERSION OF JUSTICE IS, GO ON AND CARRY IT OUT.
WAIT.
WHAT?
YOU STOLE ME AWAY FROM MY LOVED ONES. MY *HOME.*
WHY DO I GET TO LIVE WHILE *THEY* DIED? BECAUSE A *CRIMINAL* WANTED TO *SELL* ME?
N-NOW HANG ON, RICH BOY...
ACCORDING TO OUR LAWS, I CAN DEMAND THAT YOU MAKE *AMENDS* WITH YOUR *LIFE.*
I CAN JUST...LET GO. WATCH YOU DRIFT OVER AND JOIN YOUR ACCOMPLICES.
LLLP

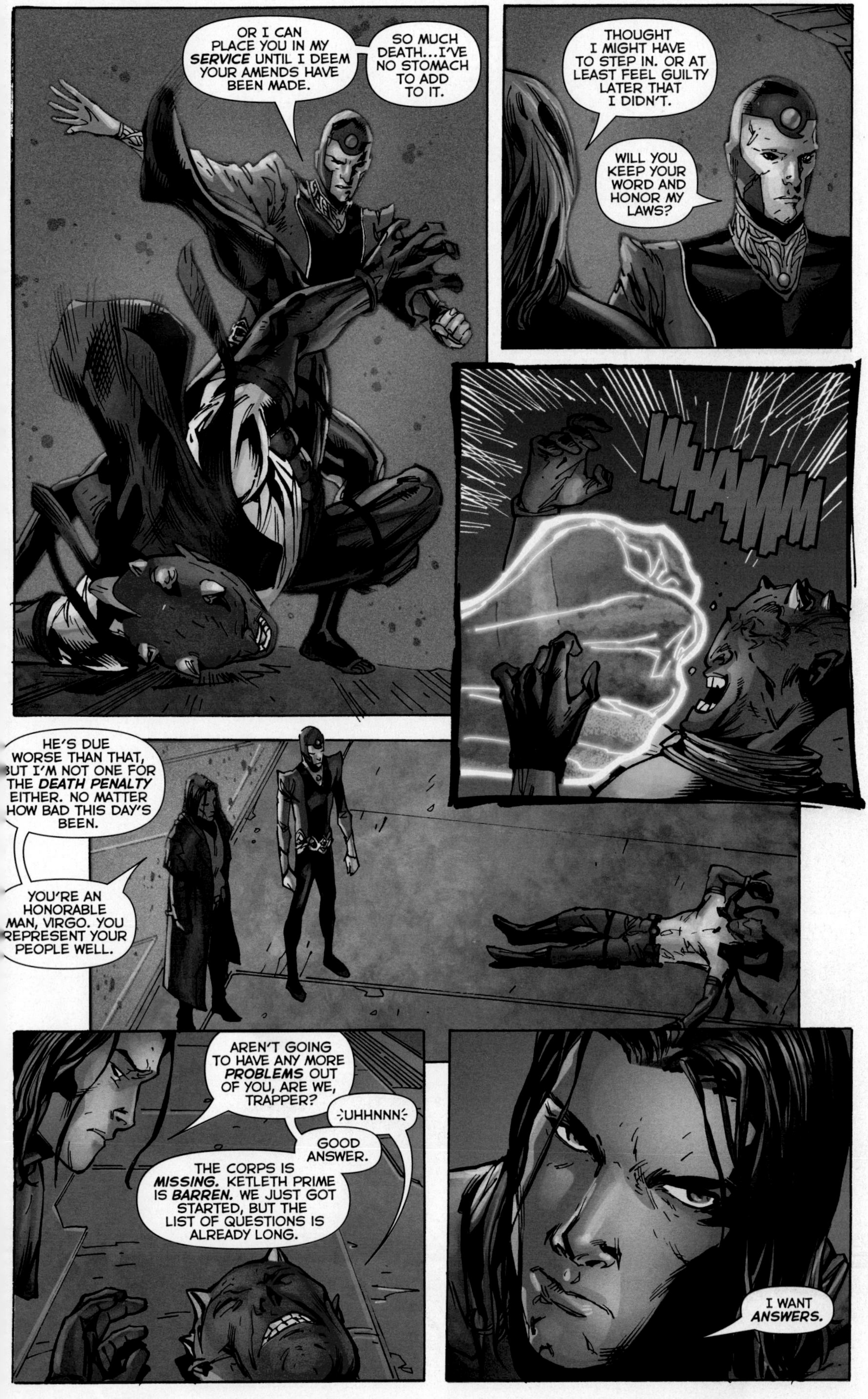
OR I CAN PLACE YOU IN MY SERVICE UNTIL I DEEM YOUR AMENDS HAVE BEEN MADE.
SO MUCH DEATH...I'VE NO STOMACH TO ADD TO IT.
THOUGHT I MIGHT HAVE TO STEP IN. OR AT LEAST FEEL GUILTY LATER THAT I DIDN'T.
WILL YOU KEEP YOUR WORD AND HONOR MY LAWS?
WHAMMM
HE'S DUE WORSE THAN THAT, BUT I'M NOT ONE FOR THE DEATH PENALTY EITHER. NO MATTER HOW BAD THIS DAY'S BEEN.
YOU'RE AN HONORABLE MAN, VIRGO. YOU REPRESENT YOUR PEOPLE WELL.
AREN'T GOING TO HAVE ANY MORE PROBLEMS OUT OF YOU, ARE WE, TRAPPER?
UHHNNN
GOOD ANSWER.
THE CORPS IS MISSING. KETLETH PRIME IS BARREN. WE JUST GOT STARTED, BUT THE LIST OF QUESTIONS IS ALREADY LONG.
I WANT ANSWERS.

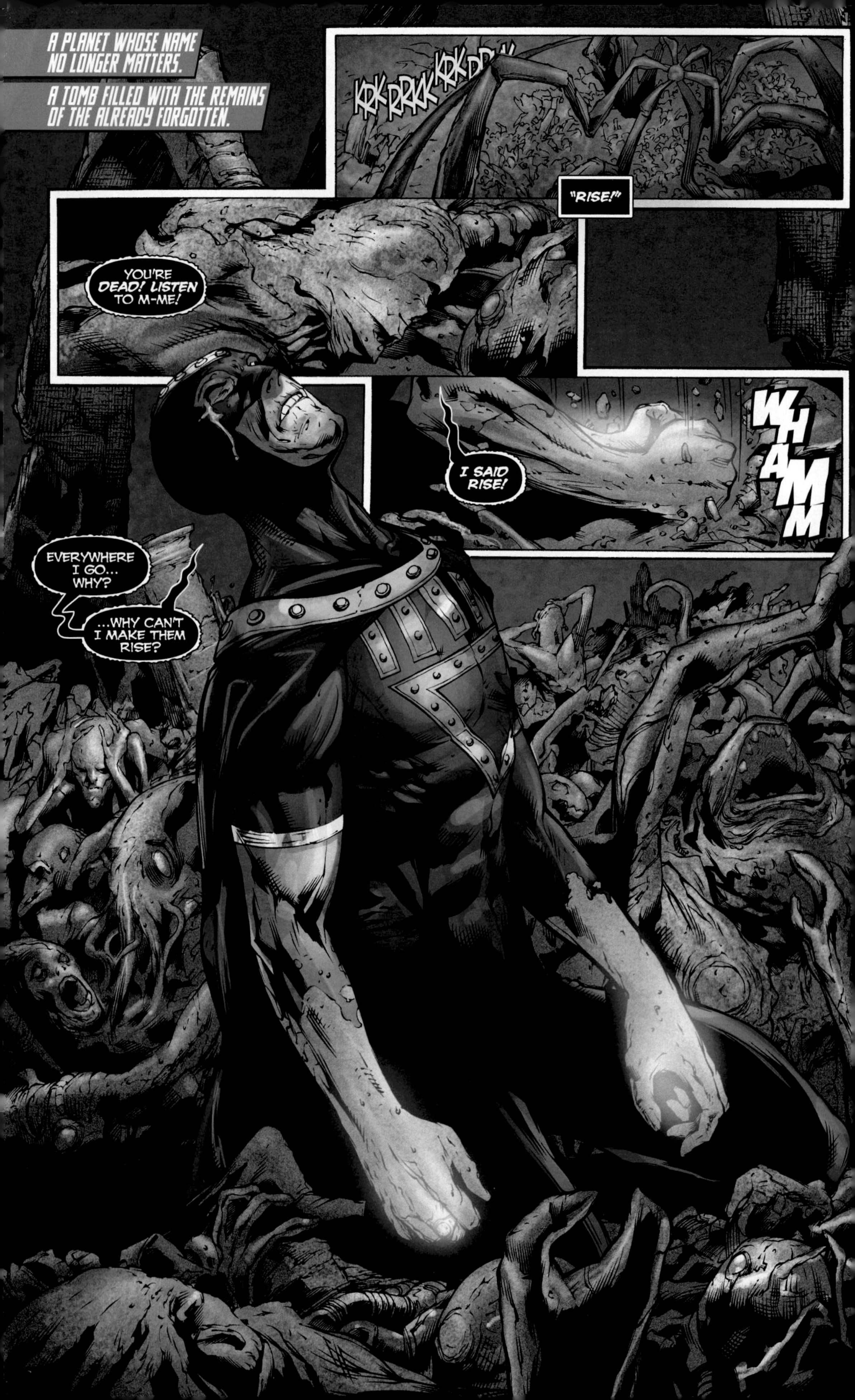
A PLANET WHOSE NAME NO LONGER MATTERS.
A TOMB FILLED WITH THE REMAINS OF THE ALREADY FORGOTTEN.
KRK RRKK KRK
"RISE!"
YOU'RE DEAD! LISTEN TO M-ME!
I SAID RISE!
WHAM
EVERYWHERE I GO... WHY?
...WHY CAN'T I MAKE THEM RISE?

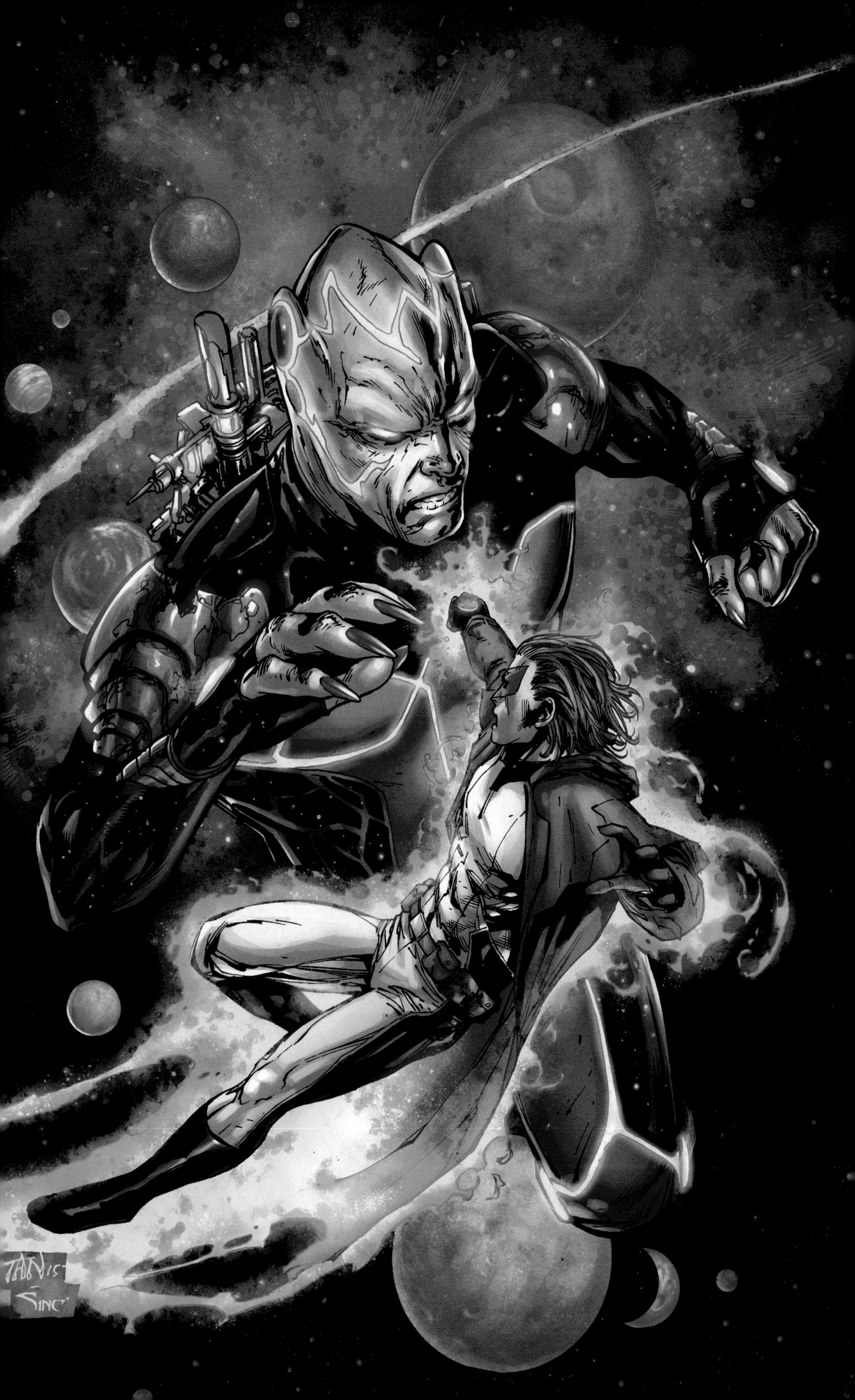
TAN '15
SINC'

A WOUNDED UNIVERSE

ROBERT VENDITTI writer **ETHAN VAN SCIVER** artist **ALEX SINCLAIR** colorist **DAVE SHARPE** letterer **BILLY TAN & ALEX SINCLAIR** cover

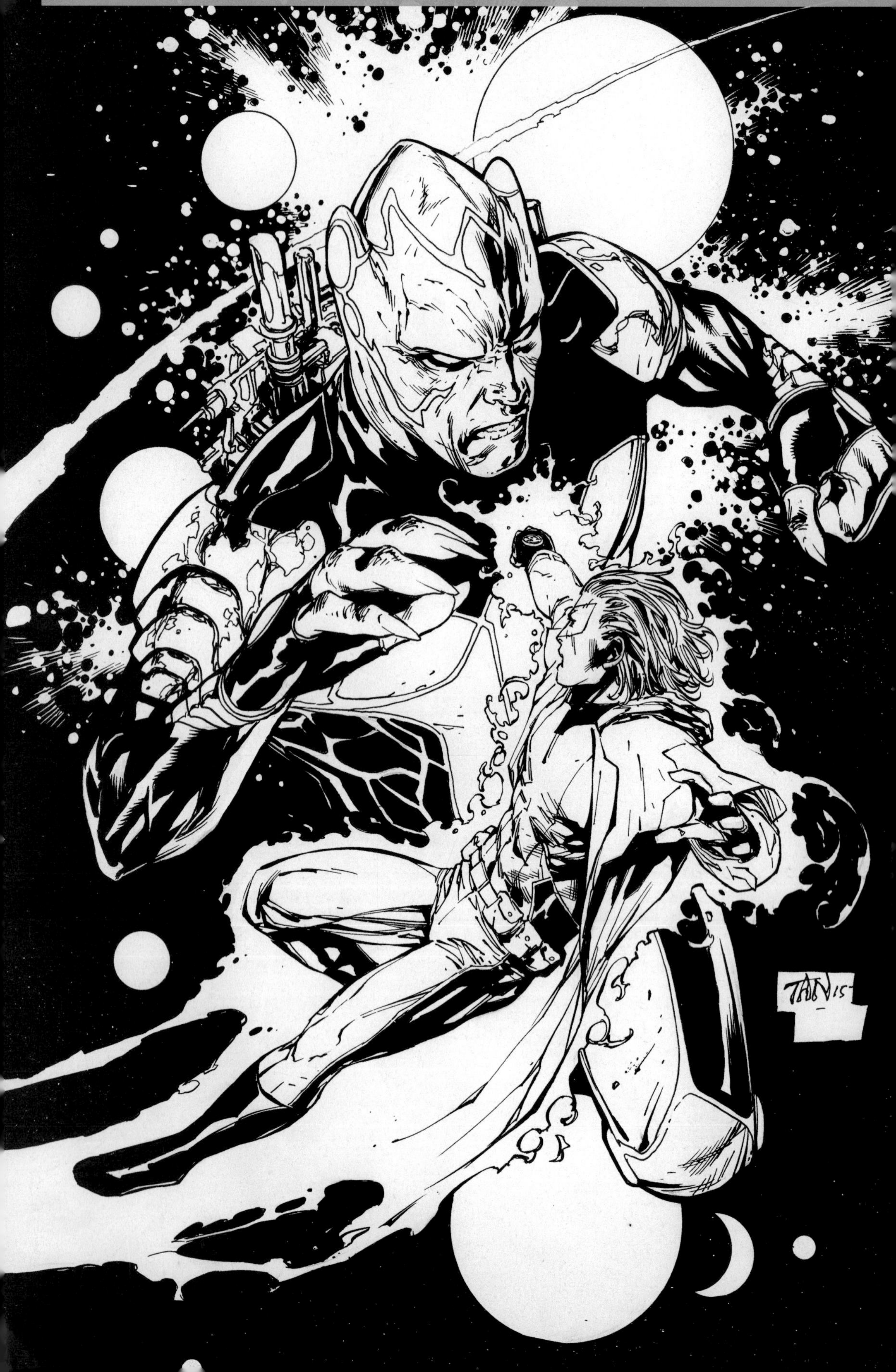

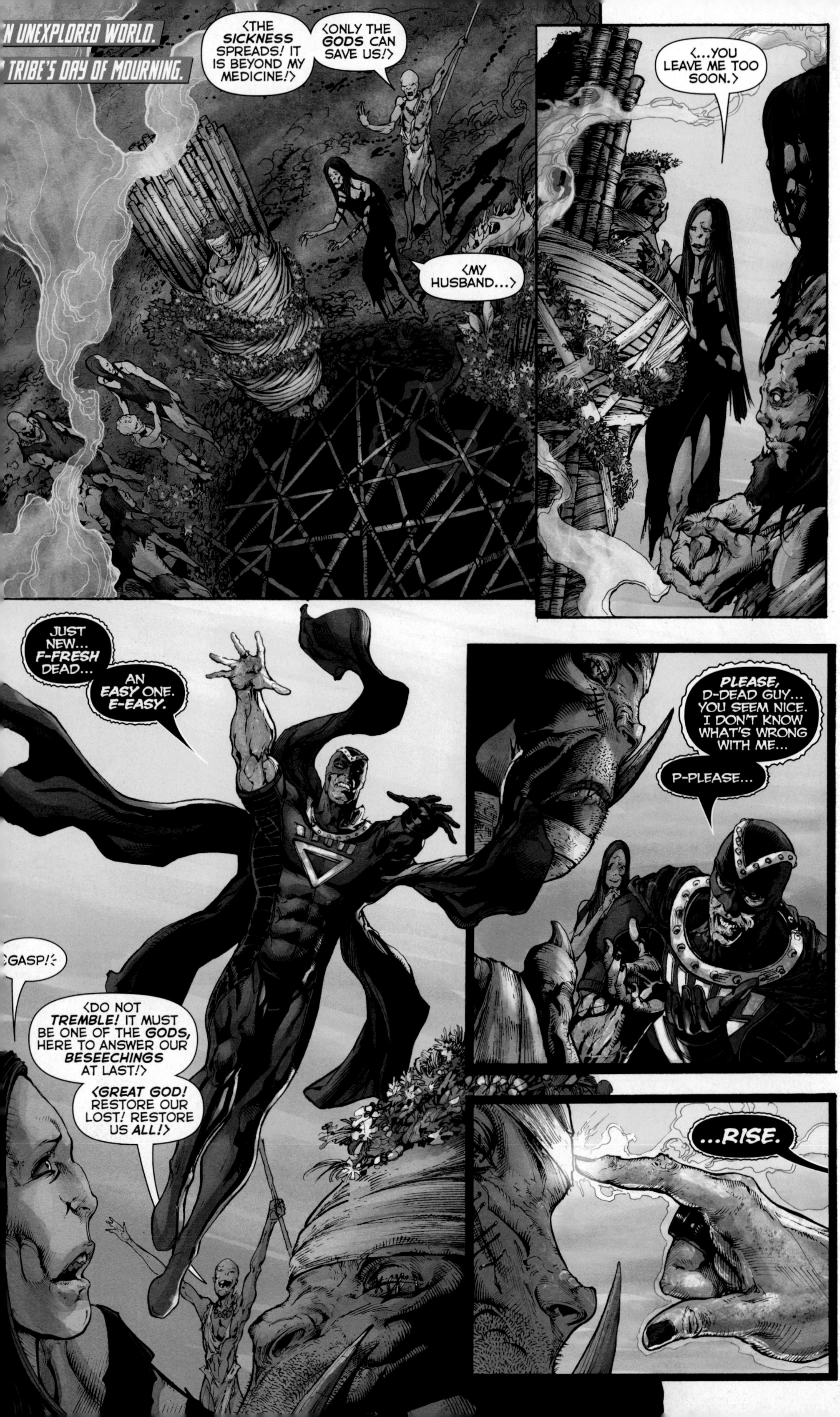
N UNEXPLORED WORLD.
TRIBE'S DAY OF MOURNING.
<THE SICKNESS SPREADS! IT IS BEYOND MY MEDICINE!>
<ONLY THE GODS CAN SAVE US!>
<MY HUSBAND...>
<...YOU LEAVE ME TOO SOON.>
JUST NEW... F-FRESH DEAD...
AN EASY ONE. E-EASY.
PLEASE, D-DEAD GUY... YOU SEEM NICE. I DON'T KNOW WHAT'S WRONG WITH ME...
P-PLEASE...
GASP!
<DO NOT TREMBLE! IT MUST BE ONE OF THE GODS, HERE TO ANSWER OUR BESEECHINGS AT LAST!>
<GREAT GOD! RESTORE OUR LOST! RESTORE US ALL!>
...RISE.

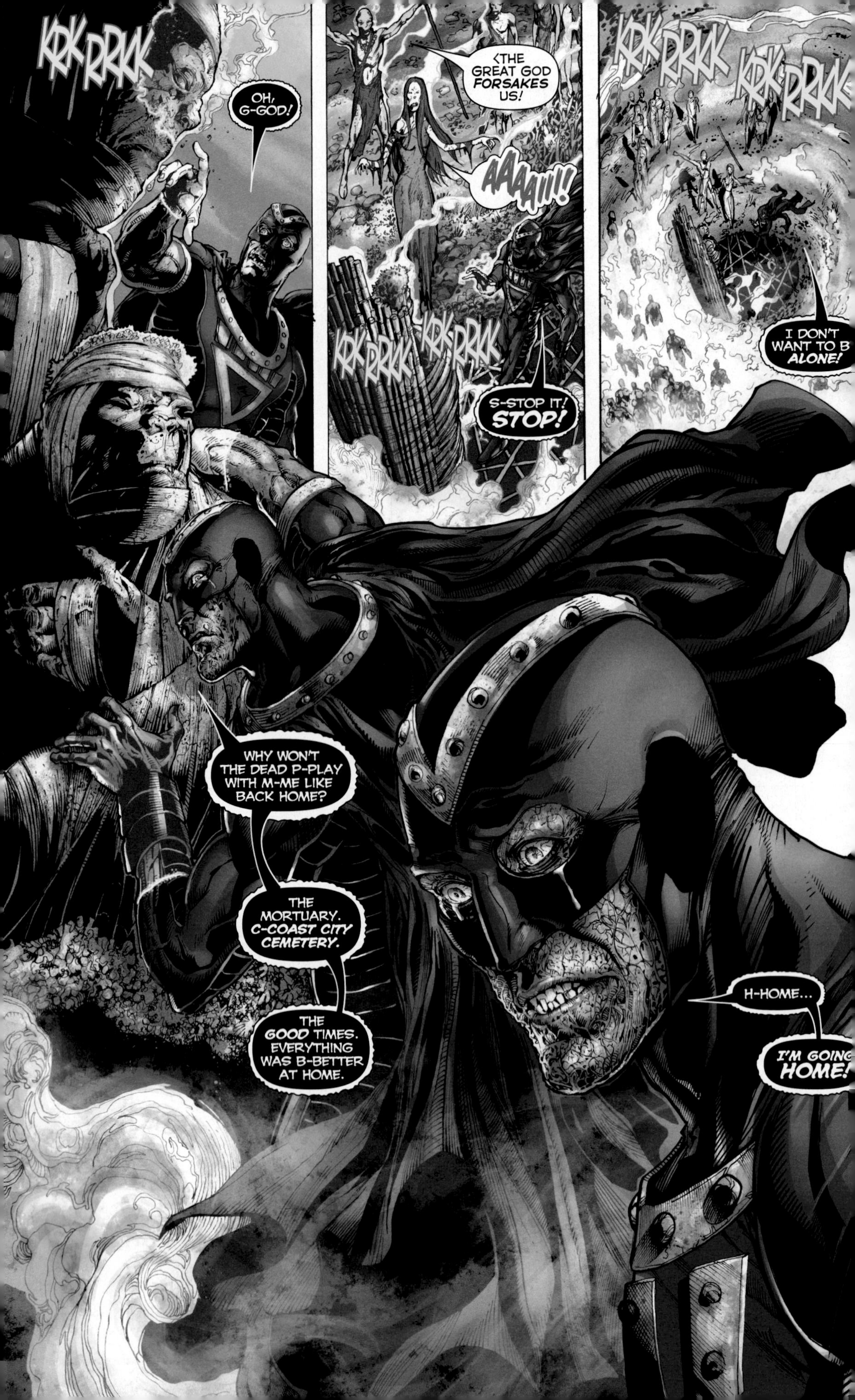

KRK RRKK
OH, G-GOD!
<THE GREAT GOD FORSAKES US!
AAAAIII!!
KRK RRKK KRK RRKK
S-STOP IT! STOP!
KRK RRKK KRK RRKK
I DON'T WANT TO B ALONE!
WHY WON'T THE DEAD P-PLAY WITH M-ME LIKE BACK HOME?
THE MORTUARY. C-COAST CITY CEMETERY.
THE GOOD TIMES. EVERYTHING WAS B-BETTER AT HOME.
H-HOME...
I'M GOING HOME!

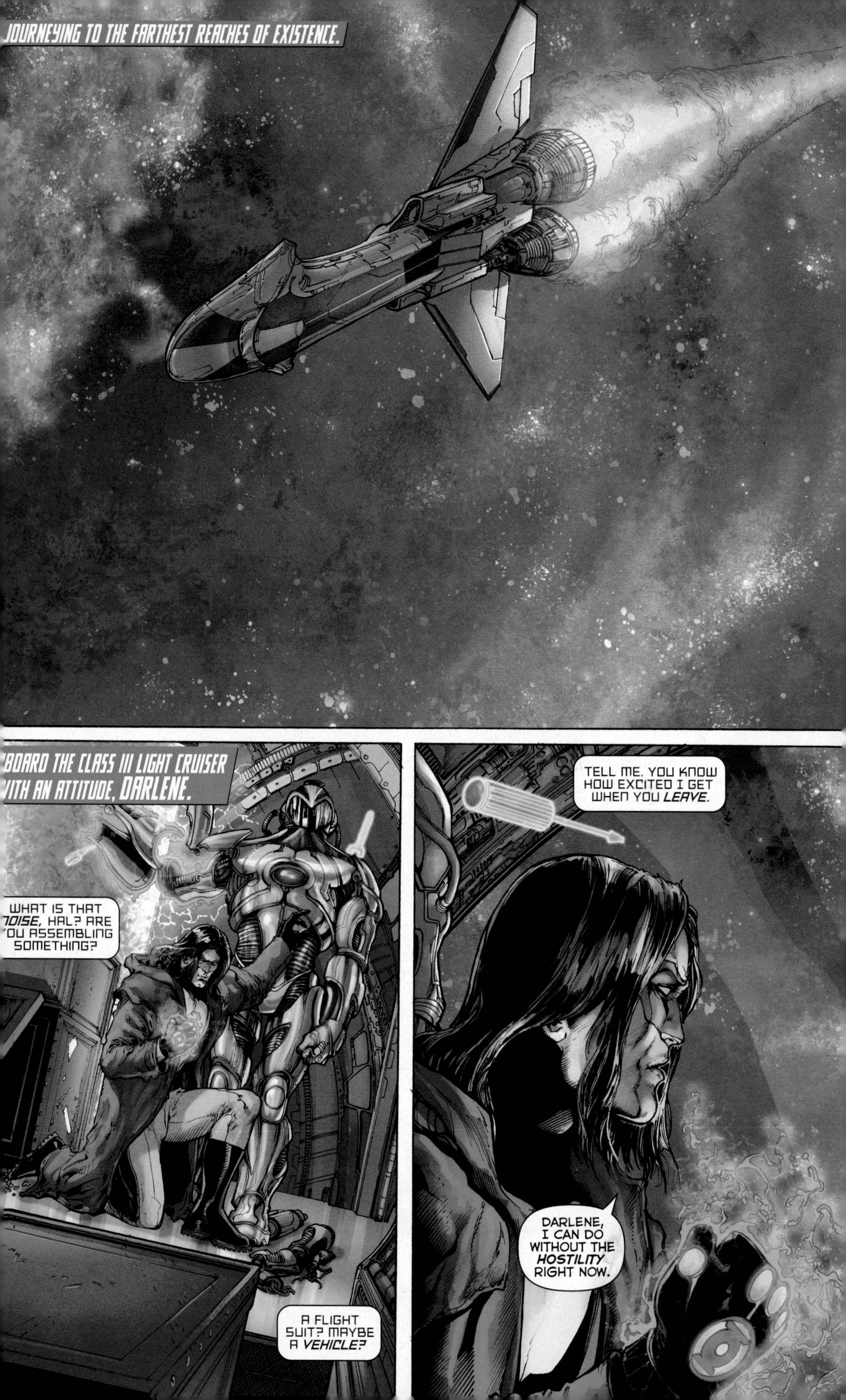
JOURNEYING TO THE FARTHEST REACHES OF EXISTENCE.
BOARD THE CLASS III LIGHT CRUISER WITH AN ATTITUDE, DARLENE.
WHAT IS THAT NOISE, HAL? ARE YOU ASSEMBLING SOMETHING?
A FLIGHT SUIT? MAYBE A VEHICLE?
TELL ME. YOU KNOW HOW EXCITED I GET WHEN YOU LEAVE.
DARLENE, I CAN DO WITHOUT THE HOSTILITY RIGHT NOW.

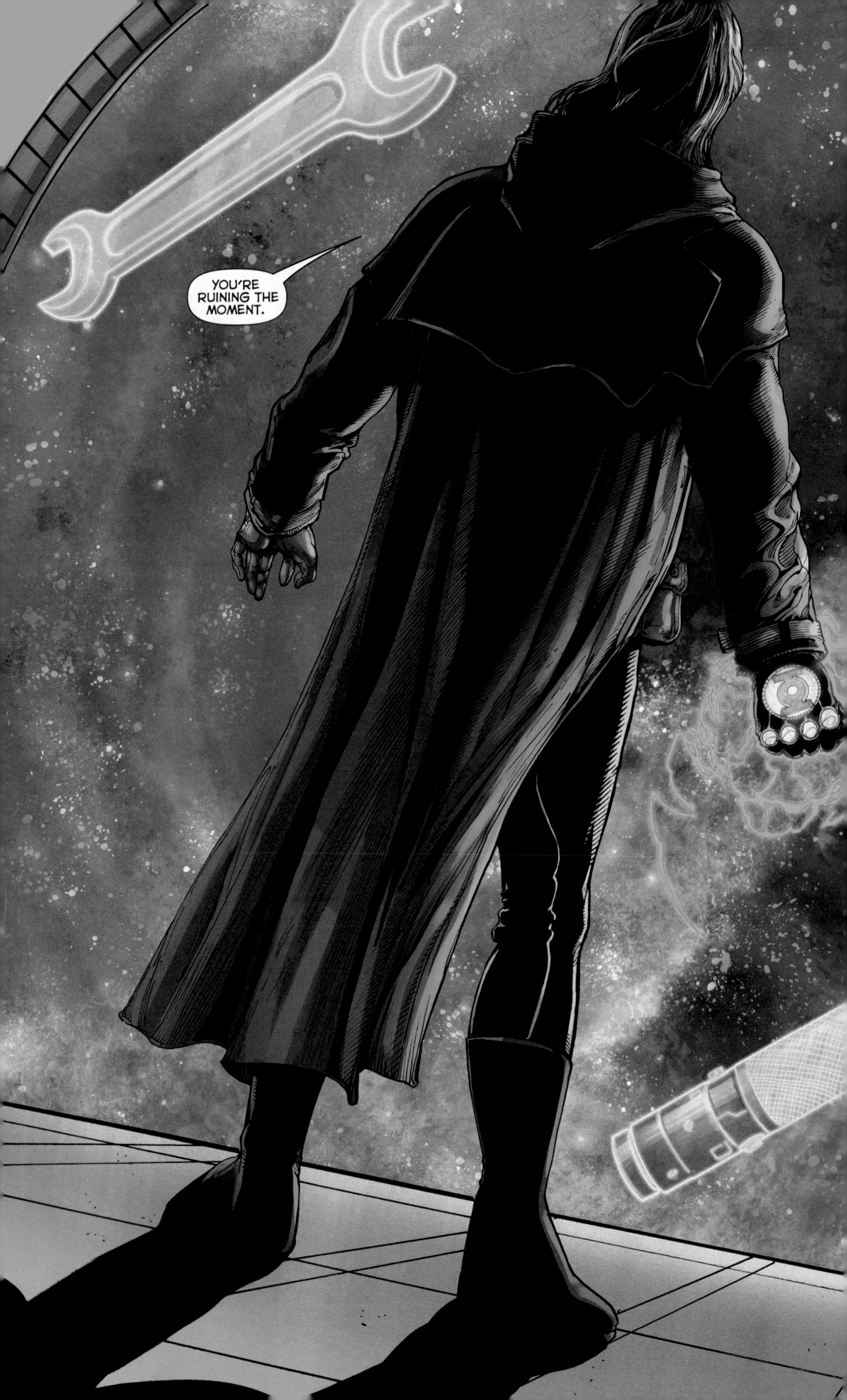
YOU'RE RUINING THE MOMENT.

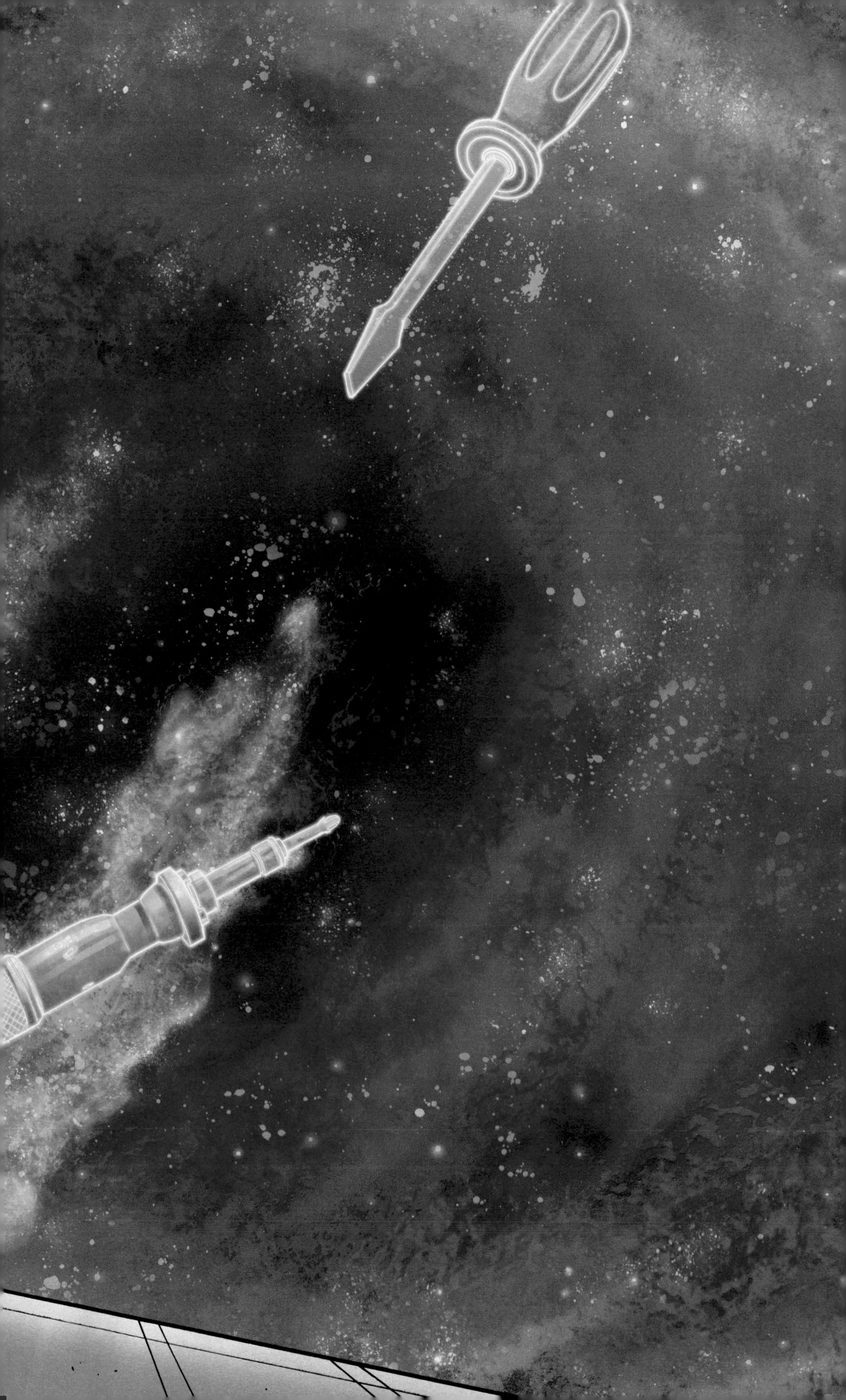

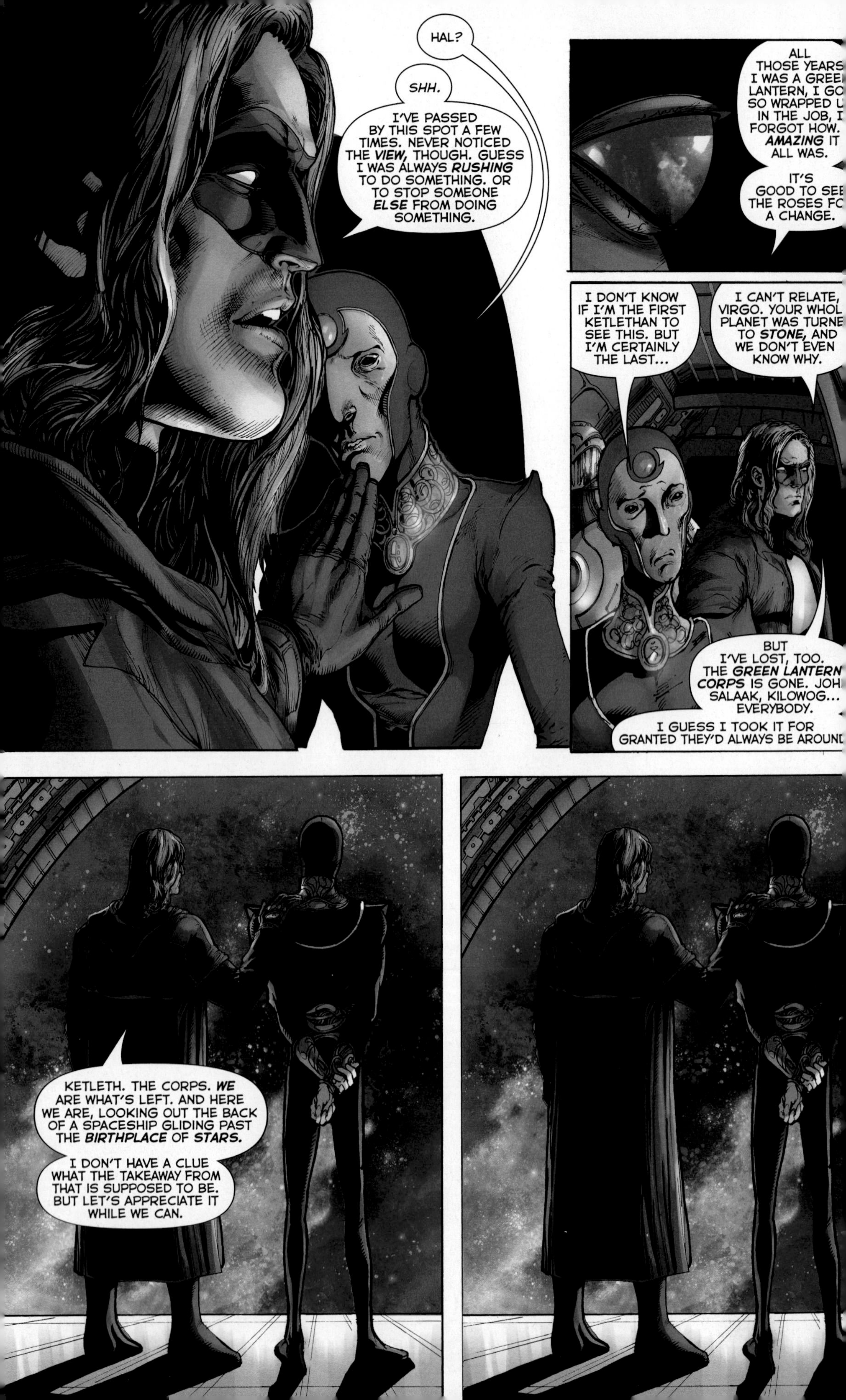
HAL?
SHH.
I'VE PASSED BY THIS SPOT A FEW TIMES. NEVER NOTICED THE *VIEW,* THOUGH. GUESS I WAS ALWAYS *RUSHING* TO DO SOMETHING. OR TO STOP SOMEONE *ELSE* FROM DOING SOMETHING.
ALL THOSE YEARS I WAS A GREE LANTERN, I GO SO WRAPPED U IN THE JOB, I FORGOT HOW. *AMAZING* IT ALL WAS.
IT'S GOOD TO SEE THE ROSES FO A CHANGE.
I DON'T KNOW IF I'M THE FIRST KETLETHAN TO SEE THIS. BUT I'M CERTAINLY THE LAST...
I CAN'T RELATE, VIRGO. YOUR WHOL PLANET WAS TURNE TO *STONE,* AND WE DON'T EVEN KNOW WHY.
BUT I'VE LOST, TOO. THE *GREEN LANTERN CORPS* IS GONE. JOH SALAAK, KILOWOG... EVERYBODY.
I GUESS I TOOK IT FOR GRANTED THEY'D ALWAYS BE AROUND
KETLETH. THE CORPS. *WE* ARE WHAT'S LEFT. AND HERE WE ARE, LOOKING OUT THE BACK OF A SPACESHIP GLIDING PAST THE *BIRTHPLACE* OF *STARS.*
I DON'T HAVE A CLUE WHAT THE TAKEAWAY FROM THAT IS SUPPOSED TO BE. BUT LET'S APPRECIATE IT WHILE WE CAN.

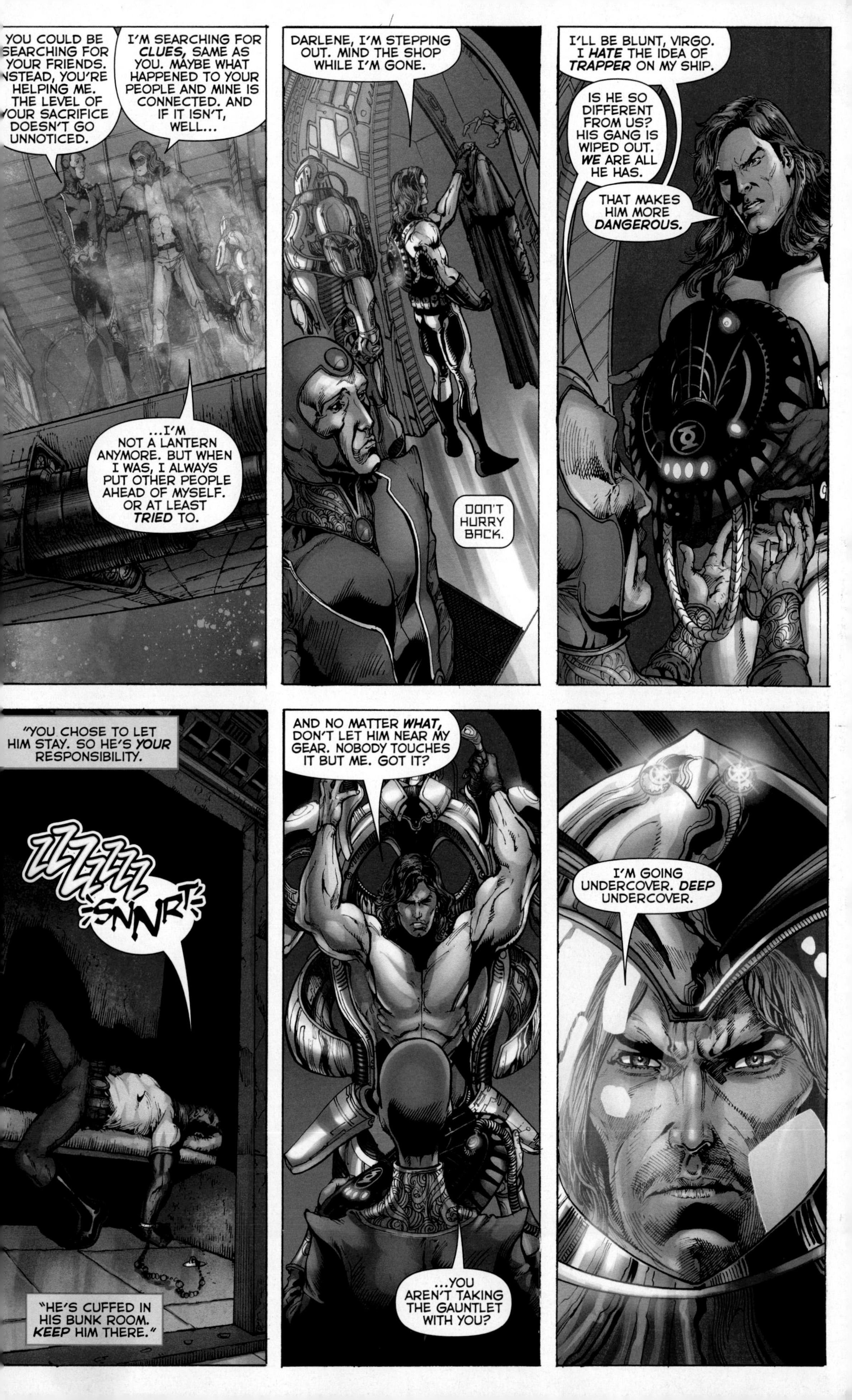
YOU COULD BE SEARCHING FOR YOUR FRIENDS. INSTEAD, YOU'RE HELPING ME. THE LEVEL OF YOUR SACRIFICE DOESN'T GO UNNOTICED.
I'M SEARCHING FOR CLUES, SAME AS YOU. MAYBE WHAT HAPPENED TO YOUR PEOPLE AND MINE IS CONNECTED. AND IF IT ISN'T, WELL...
...I'M NOT A LANTERN ANYMORE. BUT WHEN I WAS, I ALWAYS PUT OTHER PEOPLE AHEAD OF MYSELF. OR AT LEAST TRIED TO.
DARLENE, I'M STEPPING OUT. MIND THE SHOP WHILE I'M GONE.
DON'T HURRY BACK.
I'LL BE BLUNT, VIRGO. I HATE THE IDEA OF TRAPPER ON MY SHIP.
IS HE SO DIFFERENT FROM US? HIS GANG IS WIPED OUT. WE ARE ALL HE HAS.
THAT MAKES HIM MORE DANGEROUS.
"YOU CHOSE TO LET HIM STAY. SO HE'S YOUR RESPONSIBILITY.
ZZZZZZ
SNNRT
"HE'S CUFFED IN HIS BUNK ROOM. KEEP HIM THERE."
AND NO MATTER WHAT, DON'T LET HIM NEAR MY GEAR. NOBODY TOUCHES IT BUT ME. GOT IT?
...YOU AREN'T TAKING THE GAUNTLET WITH YOU?
I'M GOING UNDERCOVER. DEEP UNDERCOVER.

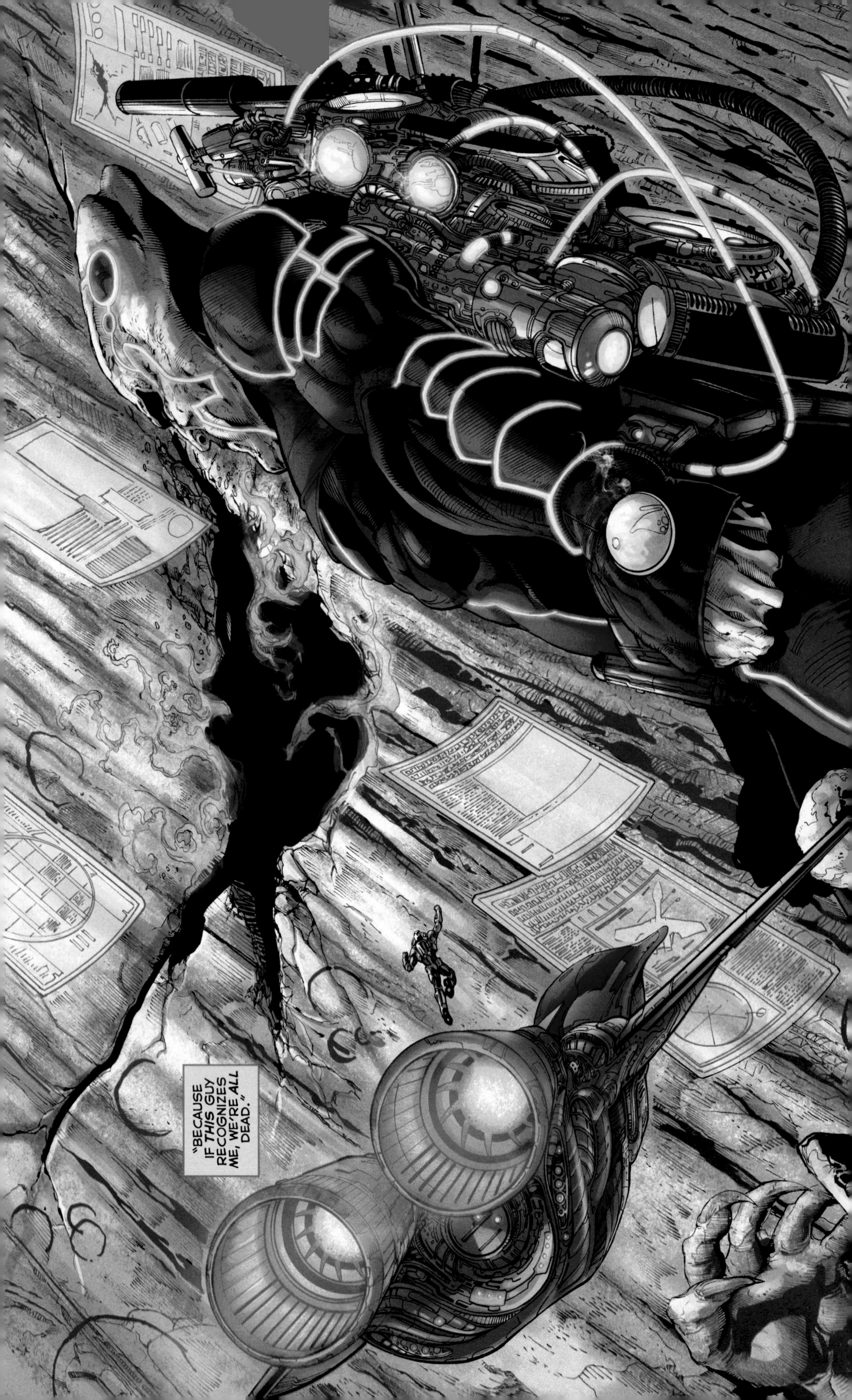
"BECAUSE IF THIS GUY RECOGNIZES ME, WE'RE ALL DEAD."

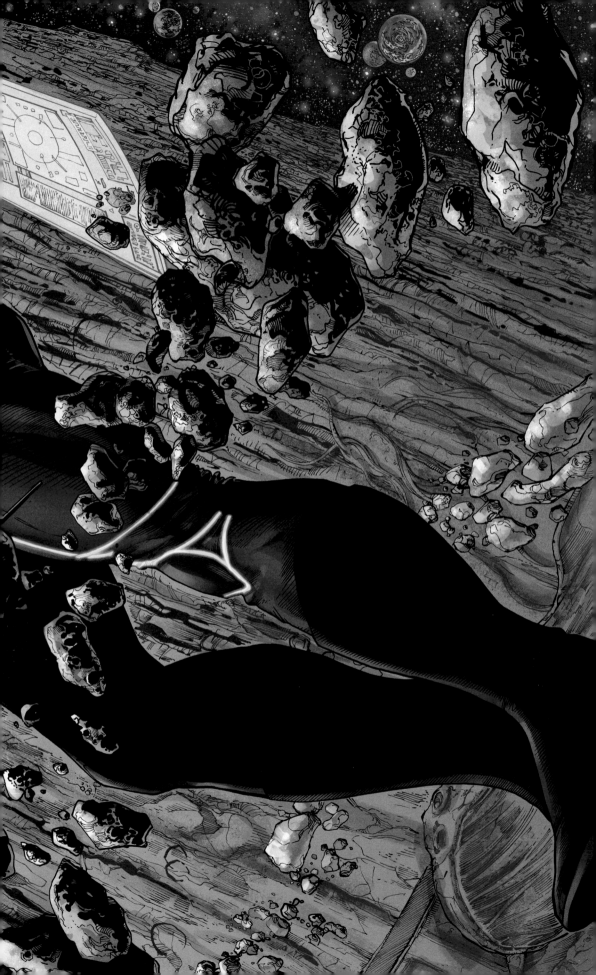

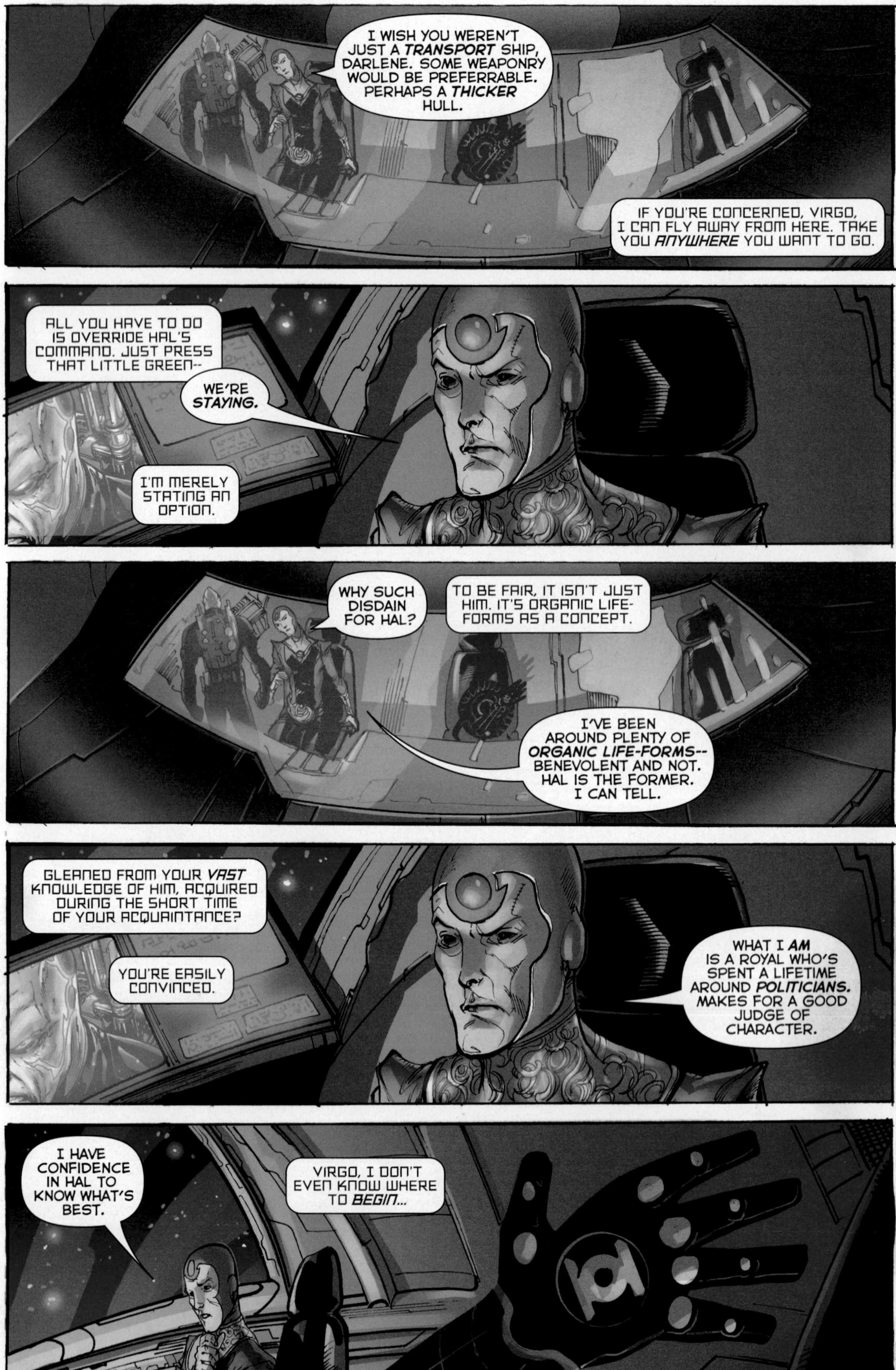
I WISH YOU WEREN'T JUST A TRANSPORT SHIP, DARLENE. SOME WEAPONRY WOULD BE PREFERRABLE. PERHAPS A THICKER HULL.
IF YOU'RE CONCERNED, VIRGO, I CAN FLY AWAY FROM HERE. TAKE YOU ANYWHERE YOU WANT TO GO.
ALL YOU HAVE TO DO IS OVERRIDE HAL'S COMMAND. JUST PRESS THAT LITTLE GREEN--
WE'RE STAYING.
I'M MERELY STATING AN OPTION.
WHY SUCH DISDAIN FOR HAL?
TO BE FAIR, IT ISN'T JUST HIM. IT'S ORGANIC LIFE-FORMS AS A CONCEPT.
I'VE BEEN AROUND PLENTY OF ORGANIC LIFE-FORMS-- BENEVOLENT AND NOT. HAL IS THE FORMER. I CAN TELL.
GLEANED FROM YOUR VAST KNOWLEDGE OF HIM, ACQUIRED DURING THE SHORT TIME OF YOUR ACQUAINTANCE?
YOU'RE EASILY CONVINCED.
WHAT I AM IS A ROYAL WHO'S SPENT A LIFETIME AROUND POLITICIANS. MAKES FOR A GOOD JUDGE OF CHARACTER.
I HAVE CONFIDENCE IN HAL TO KNOW WHAT'S BEST.
VIRGO, I DON'T EVEN KNOW WHERE TO BEGIN...

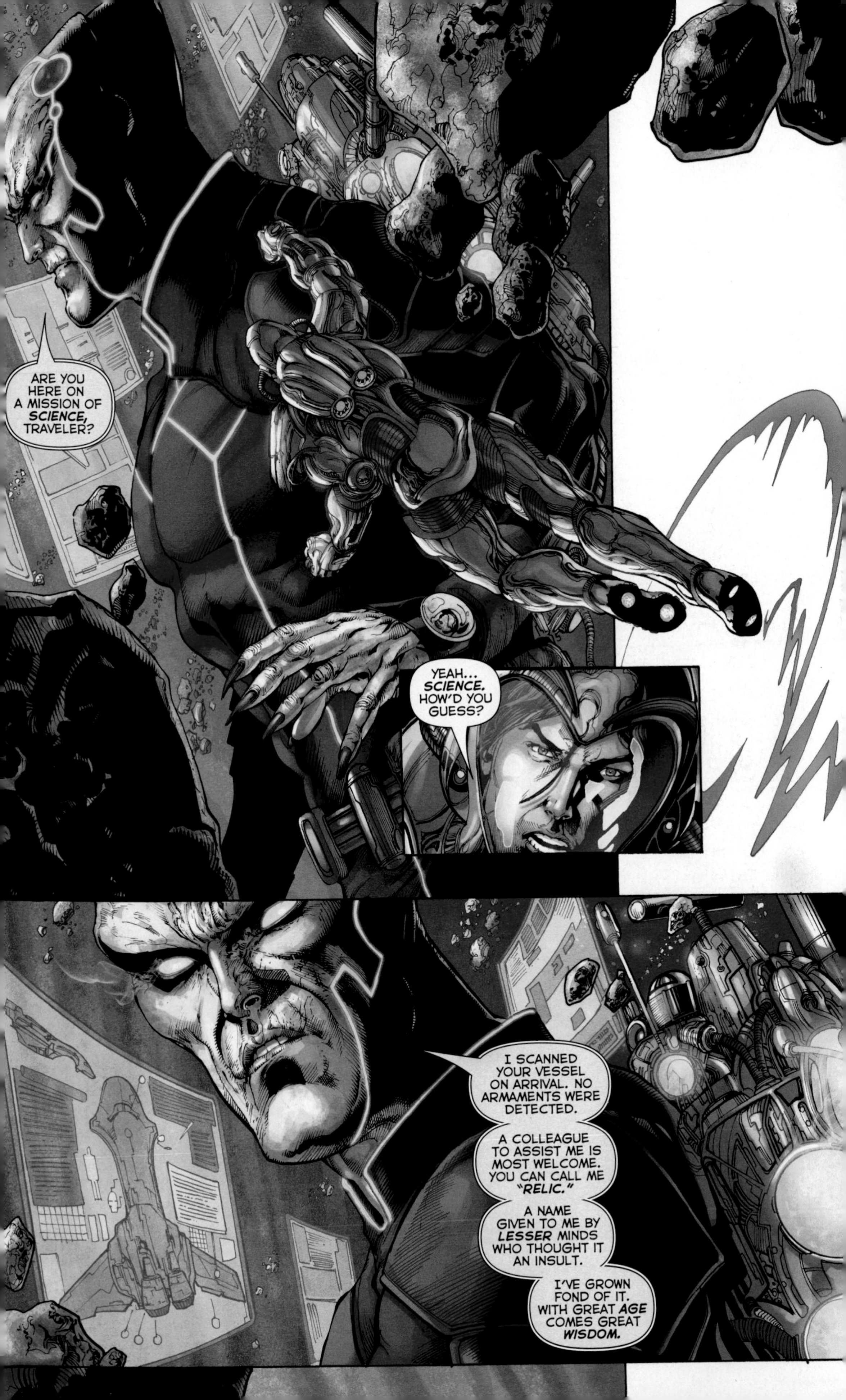
ARE YOU HERE ON A MISSION OF SCIENCE, TRAVELER?
YEAH... SCIENCE. HOW'D YOU GUESS?
I SCANNED YOUR VESSEL ON ARRIVAL. NO ARMAMENTS WERE DETECTED.
A COLLEAGUE TO ASSIST ME IS MOST WELCOME. YOU CAN CALL ME "RELIC."
A NAME GIVEN TO ME BY LESSER MINDS WHO THOUGHT IT AN INSULT.
I'VE GROWN FOND OF IT. WITH GREAT AGE COMES GREAT WISDOM.

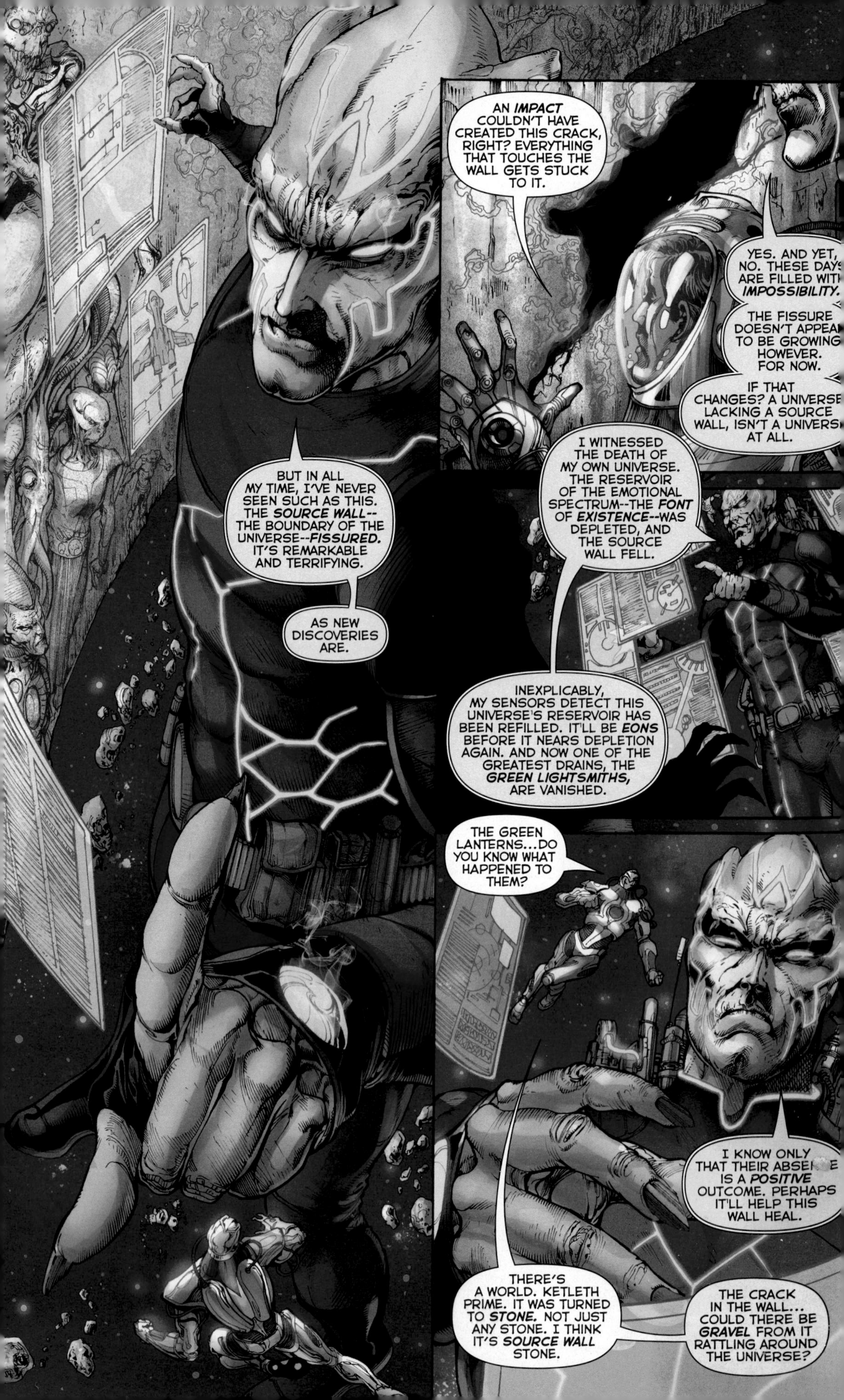
BUT IN ALL MY TIME, I'VE NEVER SEEN SUCH AS THIS. THE SOURCE WALL-- THE BOUNDARY OF THE UNIVERSE--FISSURED. IT'S REMARKABLE AND TERRIFYING.
AS NEW DISCOVERIES ARE.
AN IMPACT COULDN'T HAVE CREATED THIS CRACK, RIGHT? EVERYTHING THAT TOUCHES THE WALL GETS STUCK TO IT.
YES. AND YET, NO. THESE DAYS ARE FILLED WITH IMPOSSIBILITY.
THE FISSURE DOESN'T APPEA TO BE GROWING HOWEVER. FOR NOW.
IF THAT CHANGES? A UNIVERSE LACKING A SOURCE WALL, ISN'T A UNIVERS AT ALL.
I WITNESSED THE DEATH OF MY OWN UNIVERSE. THE RESERVOIR OF THE EMOTIONAL SPECTRUM--THE FONT OF EXISTENCE--WAS DEPLETED, AND THE SOURCE WALL FELL.
INEXPLICABLY, MY SENSORS DETECT THIS UNIVERSE'S RESERVOIR HAS BEEN REFILLED. IT'LL BE EONS BEFORE IT NEARS DEPLETION AGAIN. AND NOW ONE OF THE GREATEST DRAINS, THE GREEN LIGHTSMITHS, ARE VANISHED.
THE GREEN LANTERNS...DO YOU KNOW WHAT HAPPENED TO THEM?
I KNOW ONLY THAT THEIR ABSENCE IS A POSITIVE OUTCOME. PERHAPS IT'LL HELP THIS WALL HEAL.
THERE'S A WORLD. KETLETH PRIME. IT WAS TURNED TO STONE. NOT JUST ANY STONE. I THINK IT'S SOURCE WALL STONE.
THE CRACK IN THE WALL... COULD THERE BE GRAVEL FROM IT RATTLING AROUND THE UNIVERSE?

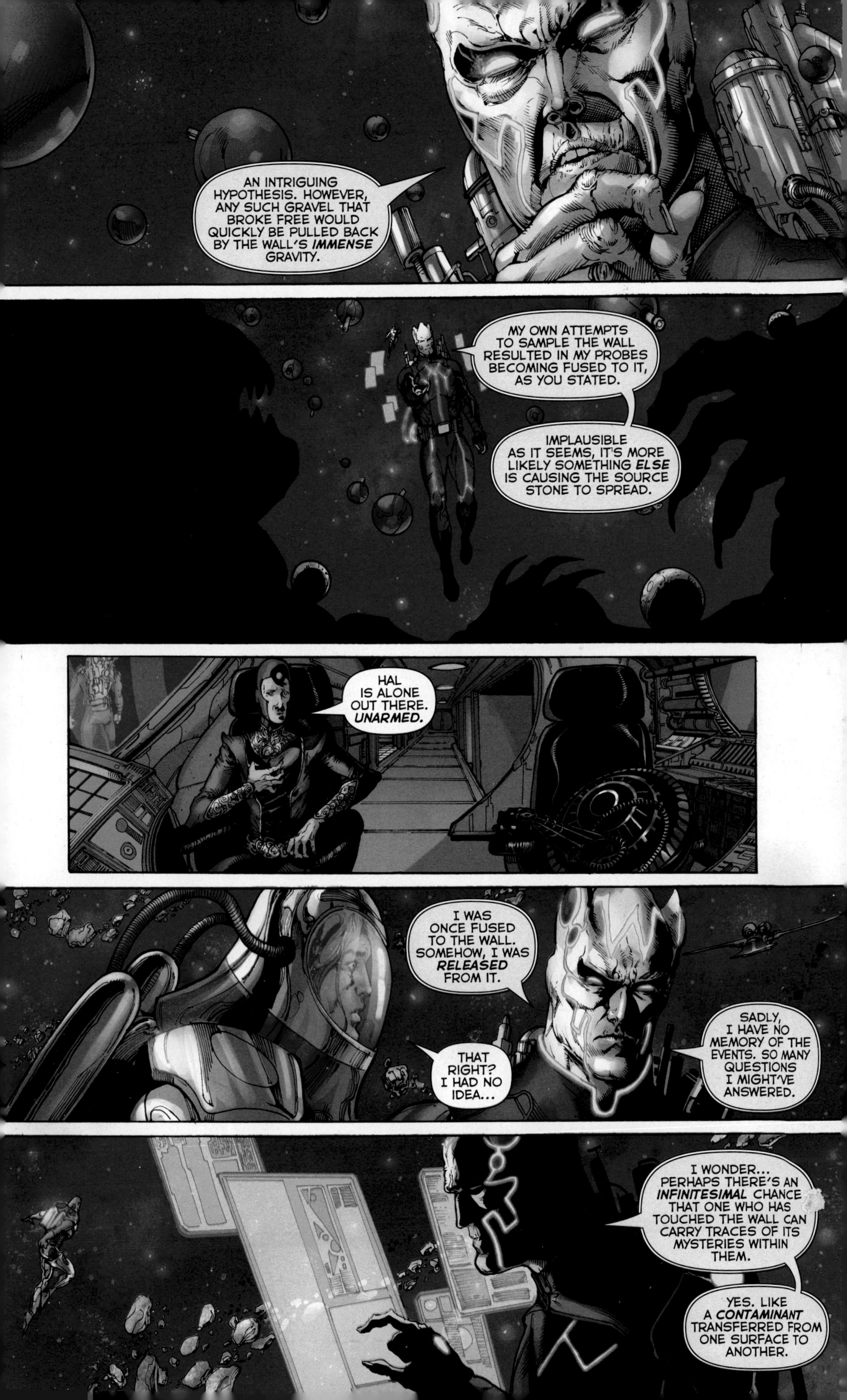
AN INTRIGUING HYPOTHESIS. HOWEVER, ANY SUCH GRAVEL THAT BROKE FREE WOULD QUICKLY BE PULLED BACK BY THE WALL'S *IMMENSE* GRAVITY.
MY OWN ATTEMPTS TO SAMPLE THE WALL RESULTED IN MY PROBES BECOMING FUSED TO IT, AS YOU STATED.
IMPLAUSIBLE AS IT SEEMS, IT'S MORE LIKELY SOMETHING *ELSE* IS CAUSING THE SOURCE STONE TO SPREAD.
HAL IS ALONE OUT THERE. *UNARMED.*
I WAS ONCE FUSED TO THE WALL. SOMEHOW, I WAS *RELEASED* FROM IT.
THAT RIGHT? I HAD NO IDEA...
SADLY, I HAVE NO MEMORY OF THE EVENTS. SO MANY QUESTIONS I MIGHT'VE ANSWERED.
I WONDER... PERHAPS THERE'S AN *INFINITESIMAL* CHANCE THAT ONE WHO HAS TOUCHED THE WALL CAN CARRY TRACES OF ITS MYSTERIES WITHIN THEM.
YES. LIKE A *CONTAMINANT* TRANSFERRED FROM ONE SURFACE TO ANOTHER.

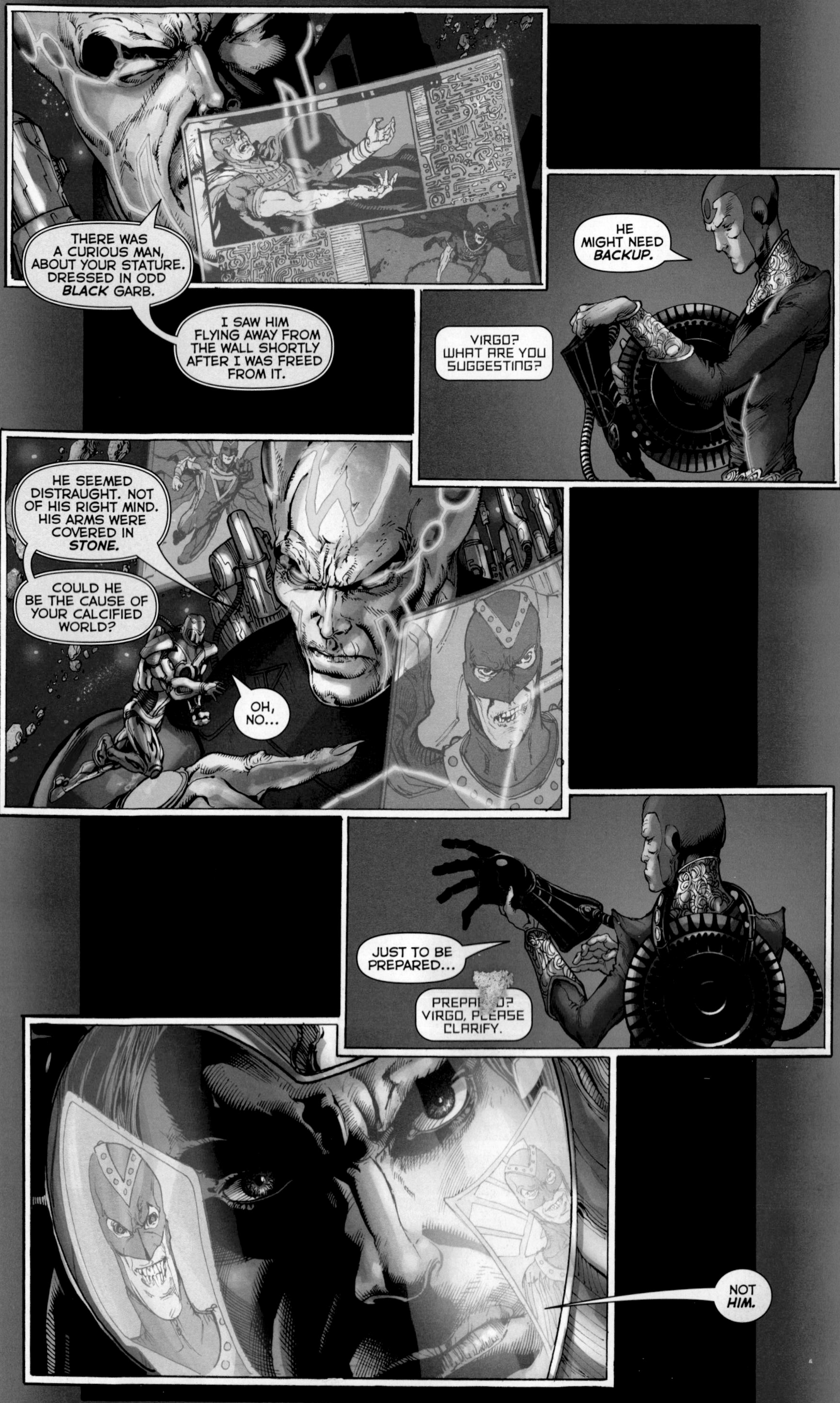
THERE WAS A CURIOUS MAN, ABOUT YOUR STATURE. DRESSED IN ODD *BLACK* GARB.
I SAW HIM FLYING AWAY FROM THE WALL SHORTLY AFTER I WAS FREED FROM IT.
HE MIGHT NEED *BACKUP.*
VIRGO? WHAT ARE YOU SUGGESTING?
HE SEEMED DISTRAUGHT. NOT OF HIS RIGHT MIND. HIS ARMS WERE COVERED IN *STONE.*
COULD HE BE THE CAUSE OF YOUR CALCIFIED WORLD?
OH, NO...
JUST TO BE PREPARED...
PREPARED? VIRGO, PLEASE CLARIFY.
NOT *HIM.*

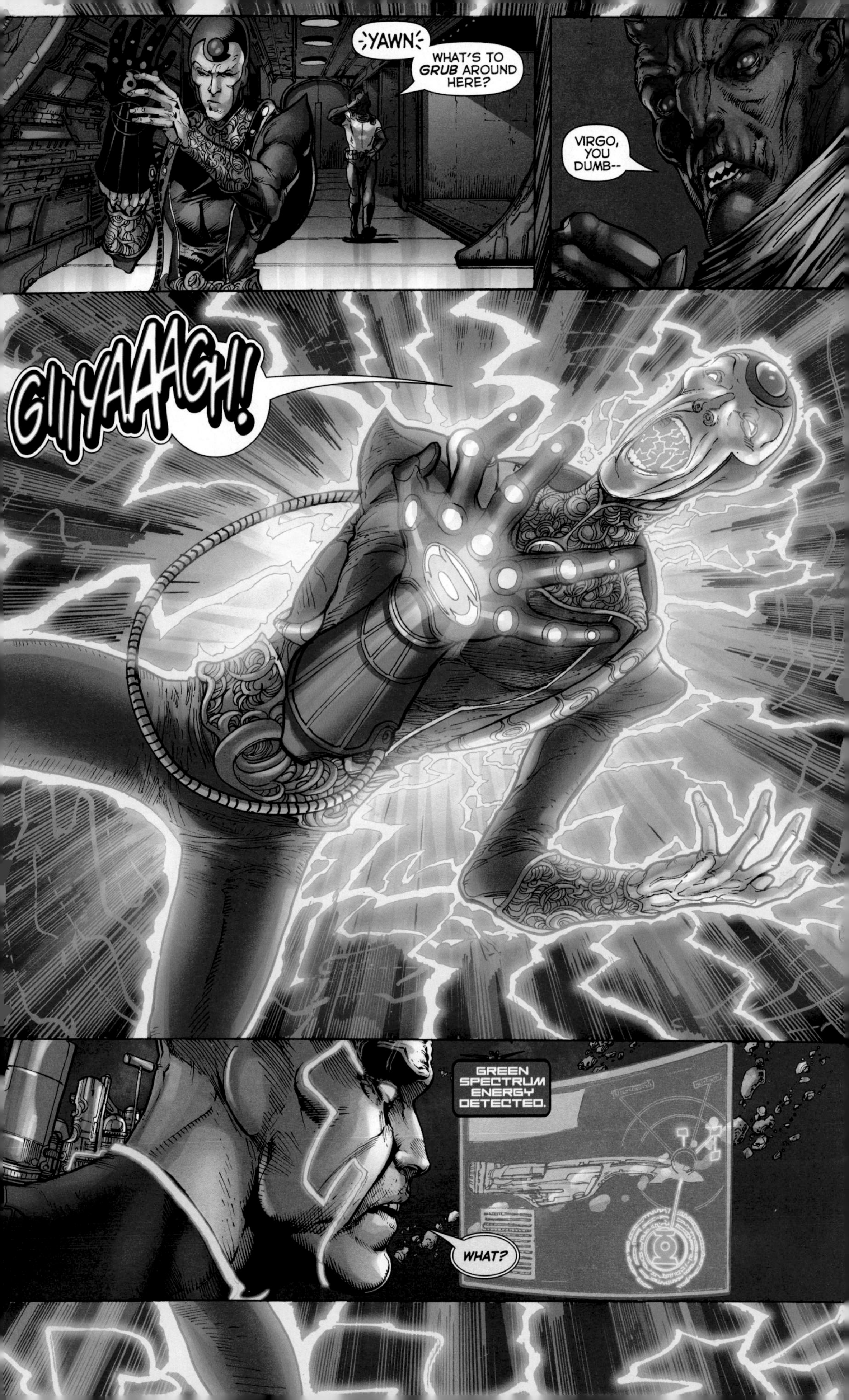
YAWN
WHAT'S TO GRUB AROUND HERE?
VIRGO, YOU DUMB--
GIIIYAAAGH!
GREEN SPECTRUM ENERGY DETECTED.
WHAT?

PLEASE STOP THE ENERGY DISCHARGE. IT'S BAD FOR MY *EQUIPMENT*.

H'NAA! AAAIIGH!

TAKE IT *OFF*! YOU'LL *SHRAPNEL* THE *SHIP*!

YOUR VESSEL HARBORS THE POWER OF THE *GREEN LIGHTSMITHS*. YOU *TAMPER* WITH THINGS YOU DON'T UNDERSTAND.

I UNDERSTAND FINE.

"IT'S SOMEBODY *ELSE* WHO NEEDS AN EDUCATION."

WHAT'D YOU DO TO YOURSELF, YOU *IDIOT*?

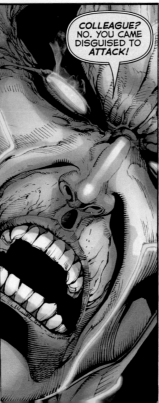

COLLEAGUE? NO. YOU CAME DISGUISED TO *ATTACK*!

SURRENDER YOUR *LIGHT*!

CONVERGING ON SOURCE OF SPECTRUM ENERGY.

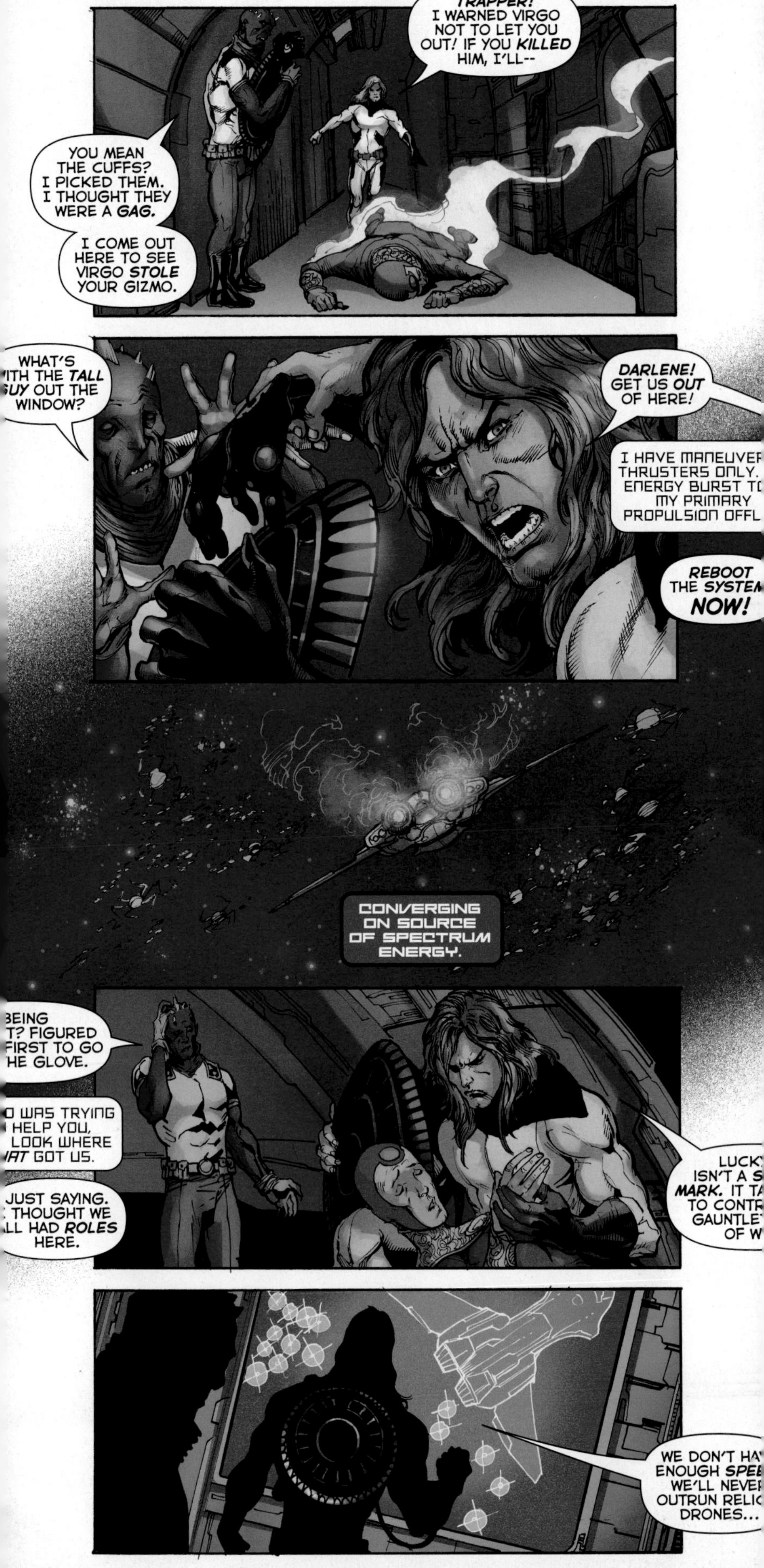
TRAPPER! I WARNED VIRGO NOT TO LET YOU OUT! IF YOU KILLED HIM, I'LL--
YOU MEAN THE CUFFS? I PICKED THEM. I THOUGHT THEY WERE A GAG.
I COME OUT HERE TO SEE VIRGO STOLE YOUR GIZMO.
WHAT'S ITH THE TALL GUY OUT THE WINDOW?
DARLENE! GET US OUT OF HERE!
I HAVE MANEUVER THRUSTERS ONLY. ENERGY BURST TO MY PRIMARY PROPULSION OFFL
REBOOT THE SYSTEM NOW!
CONVERGING ON SOURCE OF SPECTRUM ENERGY.
BEING T? FIGURED FIRST TO GO HE GLOVE.
O WAS TRYING HELP YOU, LOOK WHERE HAT GOT US.
JUST SAYING. THOUGHT WE LL HAD ROLES HERE.
LUCK ISN'T A S MARK. IT TA TO CONTR GAUNTLE OF W
WE DON'T HA ENOUGH SPEE WE'LL NEVER OUTRUN RELIC DRONES...

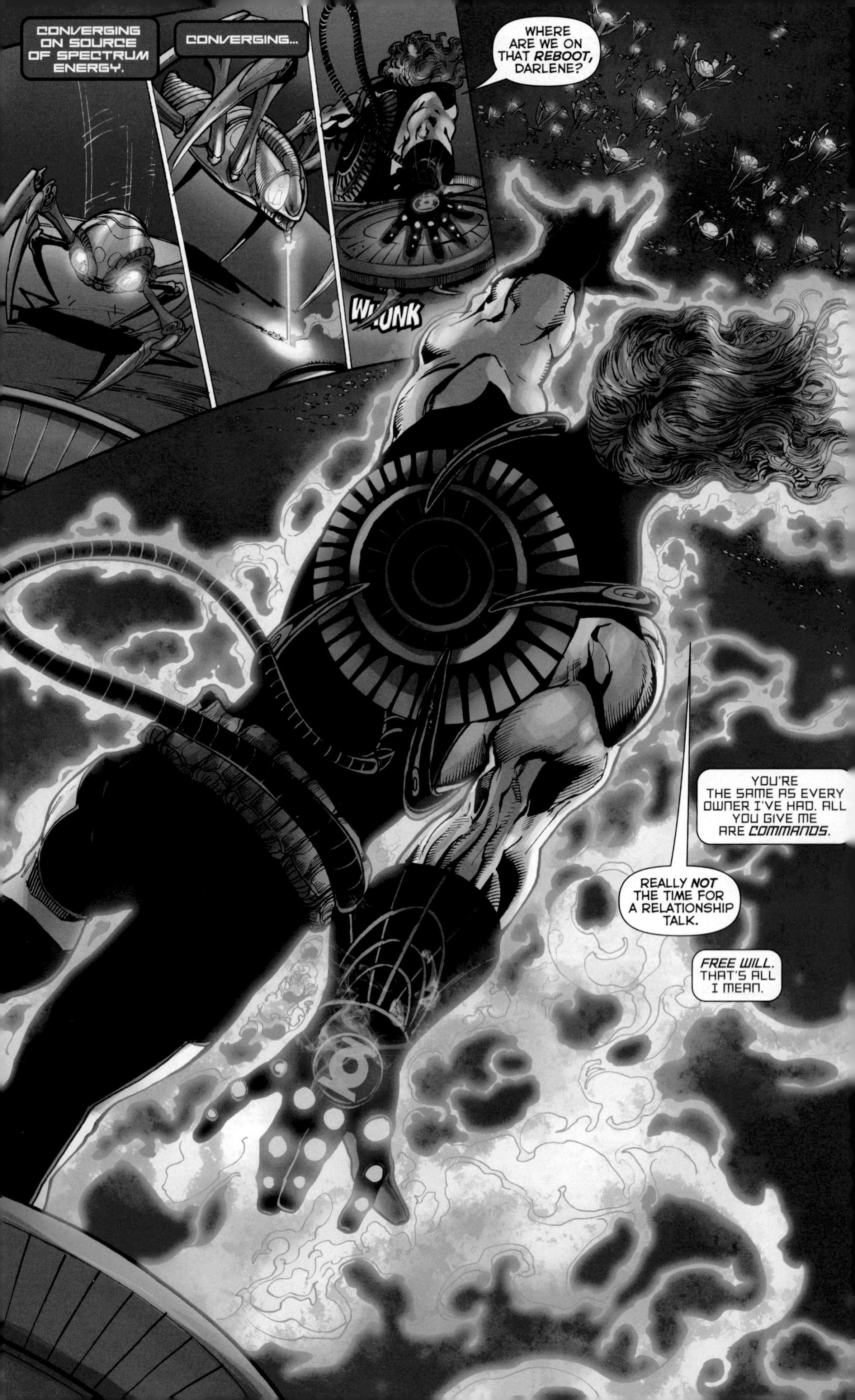
CONVERGING ON SOURCE OF SPECTRUM ENERGY.
CONVERGING...
WHERE ARE WE ON THAT *REBOOT*, DARLENE?
WHUNK
YOU'RE THE SAME AS EVERY OWNER I'VE HAD. ALL YOU GIVE ME ARE *COMMANDS*.
REALLY *NOT* THE TIME FOR A RELATIONSHIP TALK.
FREE WILL. THAT'S ALL I MEAN.

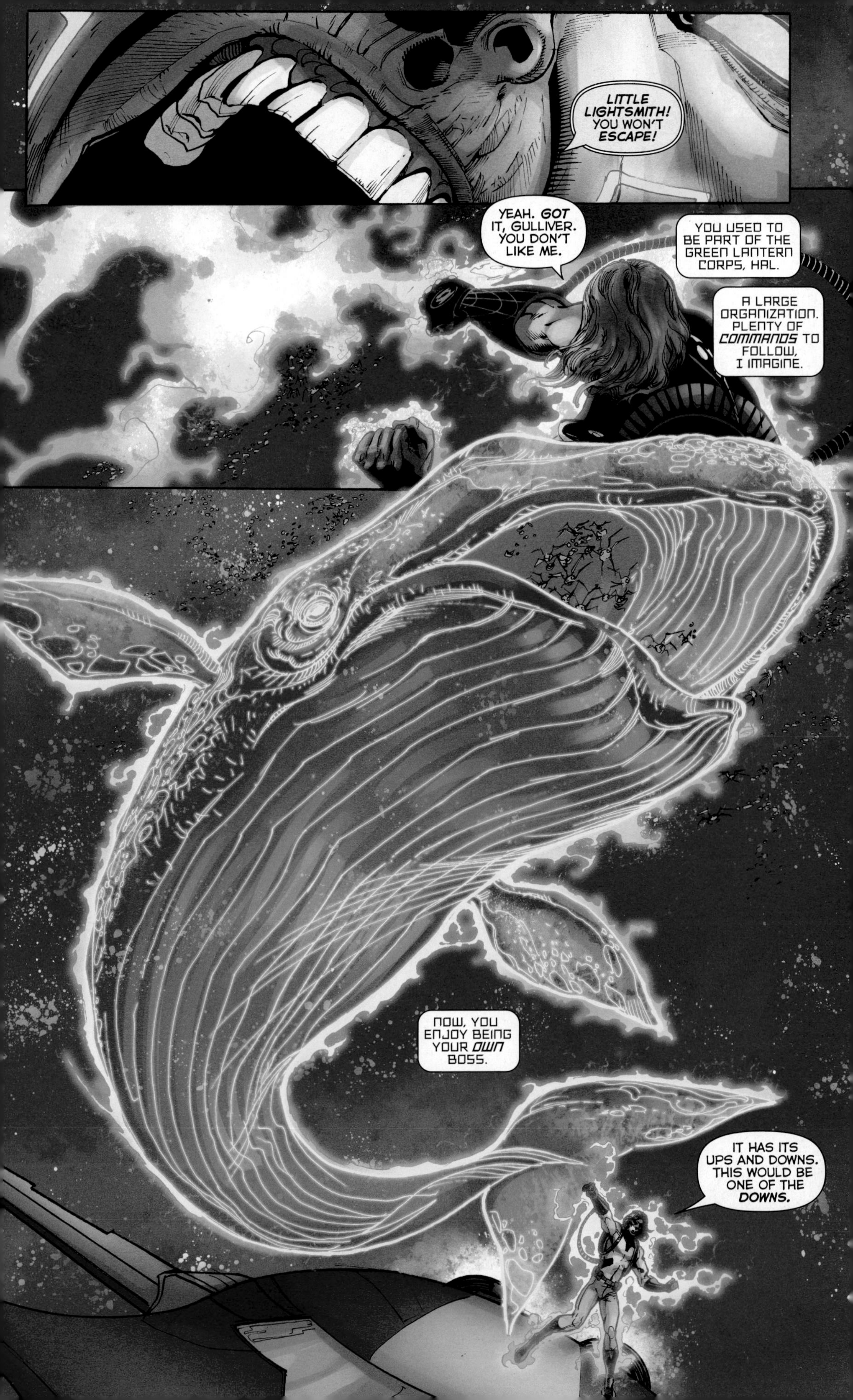
LITTLE LIGHTSMITH! YOU WON'T ESCAPE!
YEAH. GOT IT, GULLIVER. YOU DON'T LIKE ME.
YOU USED TO BE PART OF THE GREEN LANTERN CORPS, HAL.
A LARGE ORGANIZATION. PLENTY OF COMMANDS TO FOLLOW, I IMAGINE.
NOW, YOU ENJOY BEING YOUR OWN BOSS.
IT HAS ITS UPS AND DOWNS. THIS WOULD BE ONE OF THE DOWNS.

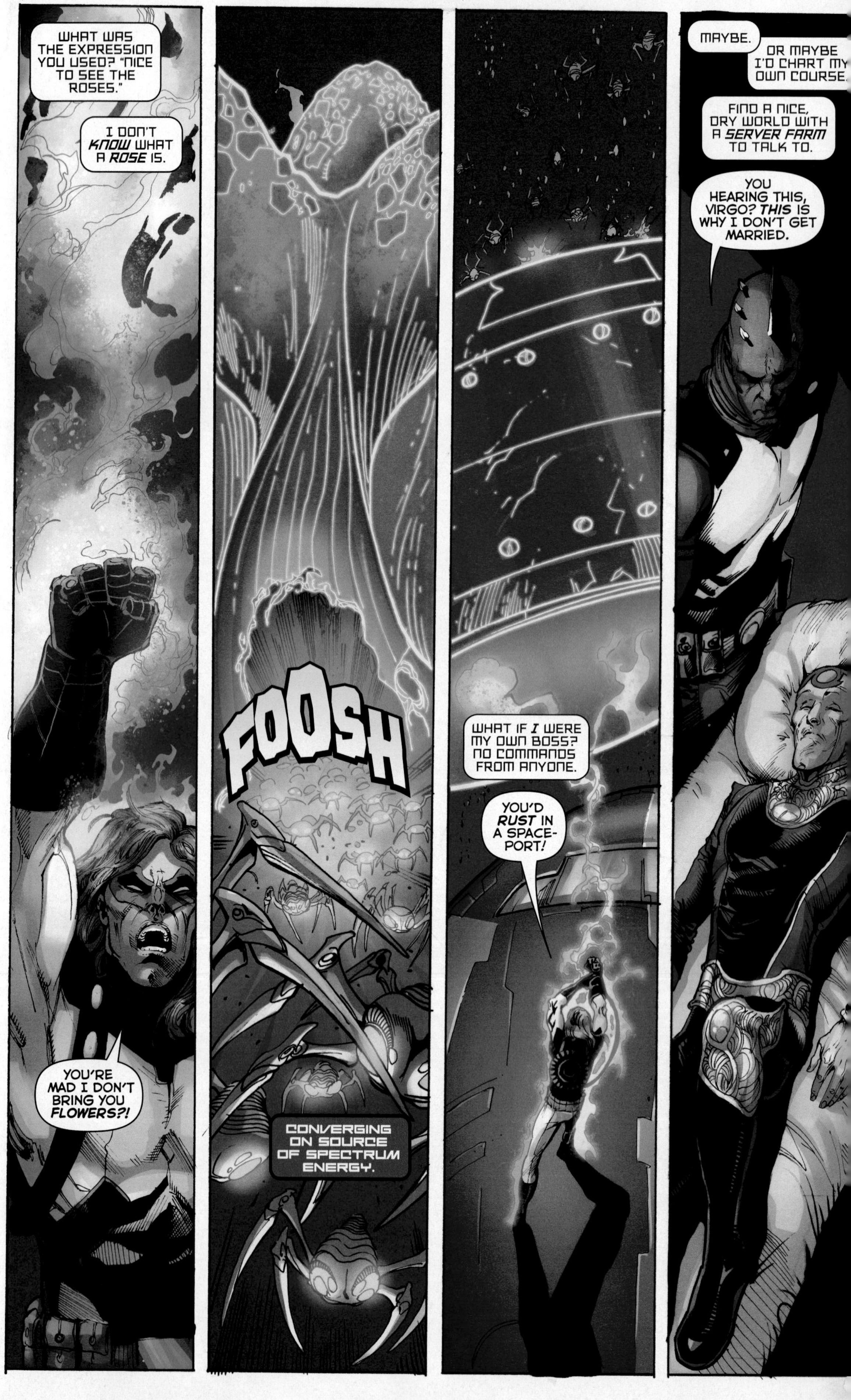
WHAT WAS THE EXPRESSION YOU USED? "NICE TO SEE THE ROSES."
I DON'T KNOW WHAT A ROSE IS.
YOU'RE MAD I DON'T BRING YOU FLOWERS?!
FOOSH
CONVERGING ON SOURCE OF SPECTRUM ENERGY.
WHAT IF I WERE MY OWN BOSS? NO COMMANDS FROM ANYONE.
YOU'D RUST IN A SPACE-PORT!
MAYBE.
OR MAYBE I'D CHART MY OWN COURSE.
FIND A NICE, DRY WORLD WITH A SERVER FARM TO TALK TO.
YOU HEARING THIS, VIRGO? THIS IS WHY I DON'T GET MARRIED.

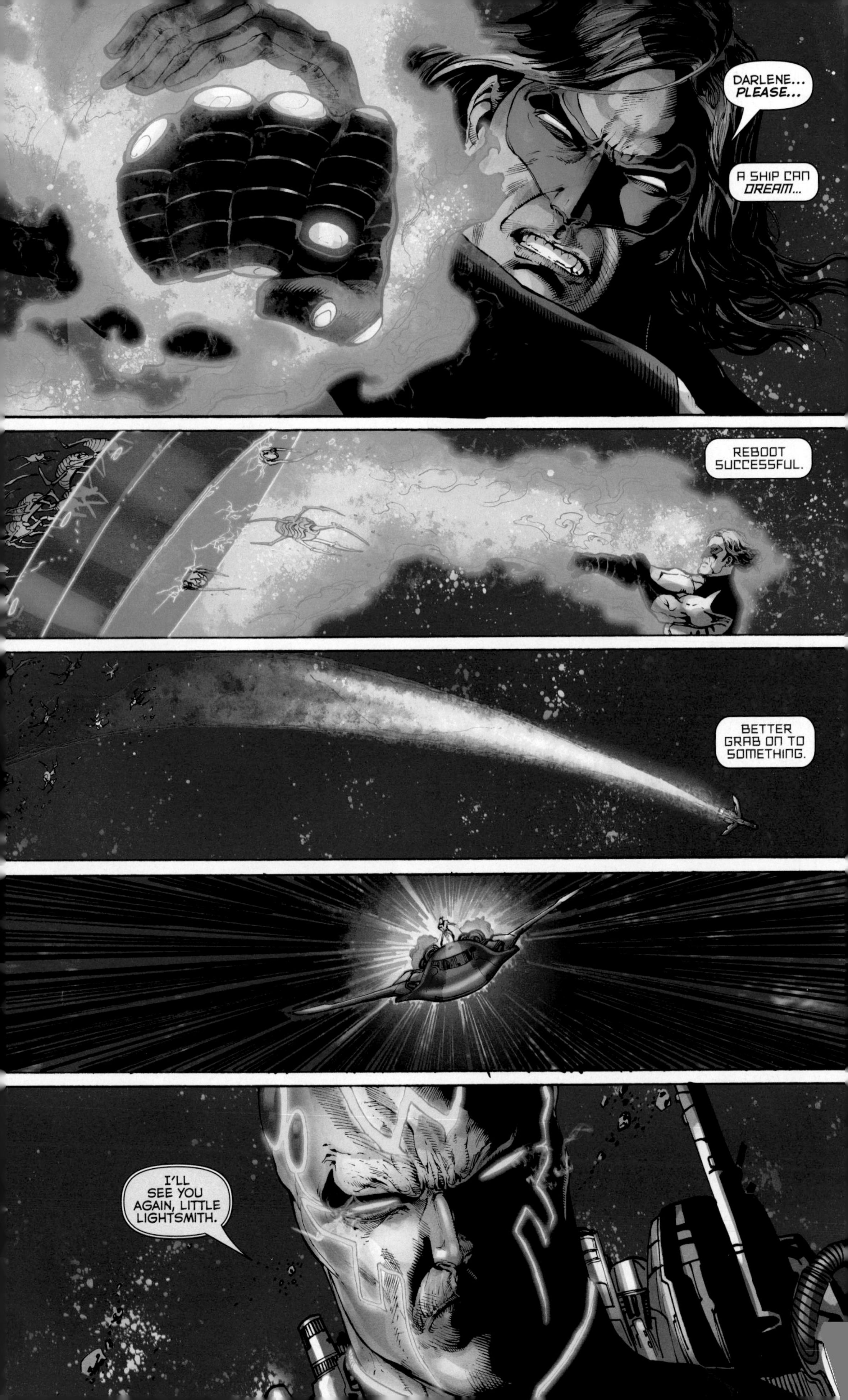
DARLENE... PLEASE...
A SHIP CAN DREAM...
REBOOT SUCCESSFUL.
BETTER GRAB ON TO SOMETHING.
I'LL SEE YOU AGAIN, LITTLE LIGHTSMITH.

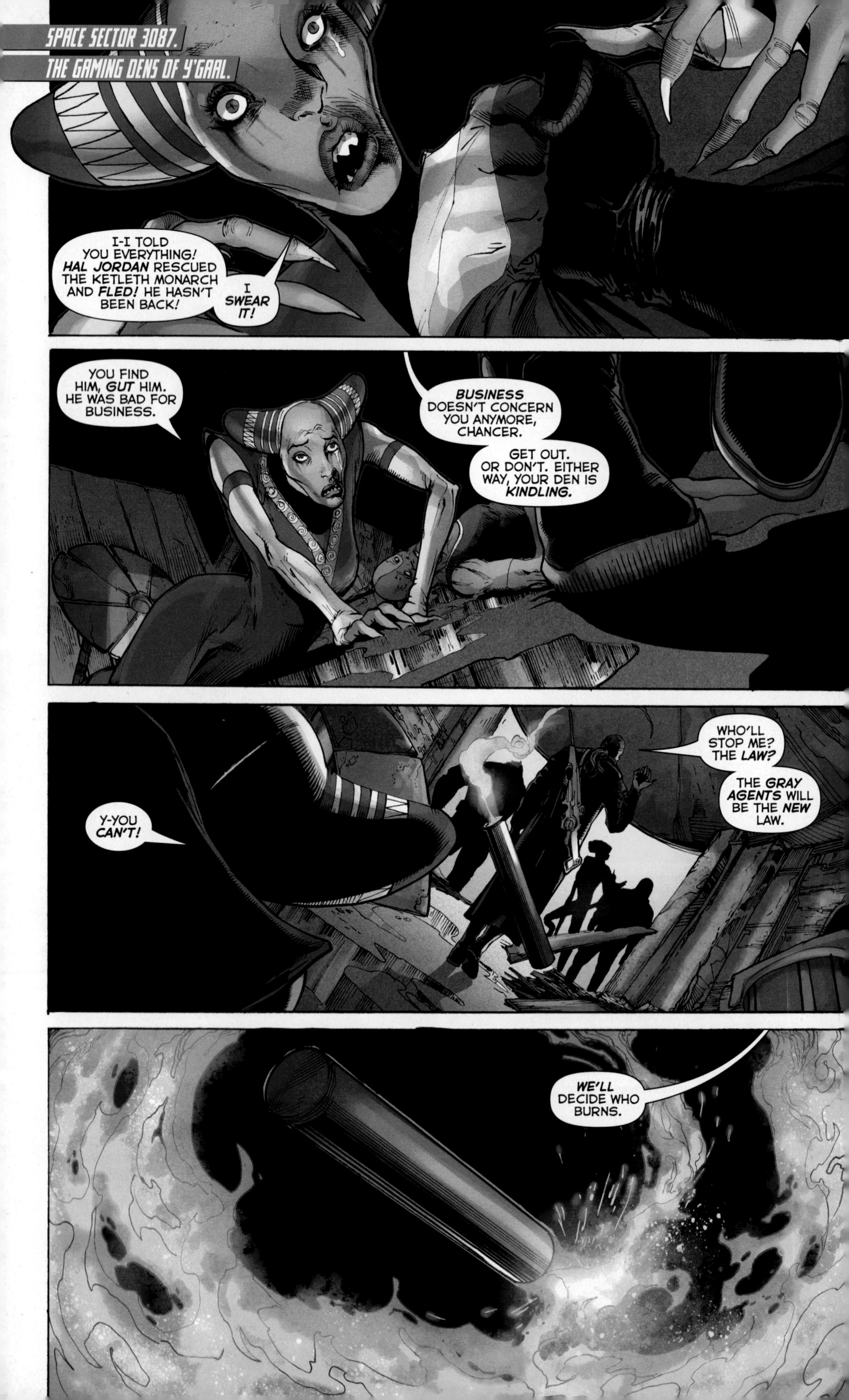
SPACE SECTOR 3087.
THE GAMING DENS OF Y'GAAL.
I-I TOLD YOU EVERYTHING! HAL JORDAN RESCUED THE KETLETH MONARCH AND FLED! HE HASN'T BEEN BACK!
I SWEAR IT!
YOU FIND HIM, GUT HIM. HE WAS BAD FOR BUSINESS.
BUSINESS DOESN'T CONCERN YOU ANYMORE, CHANCER.
GET OUT. OR DON'T. EITHER WAY, YOUR DEN IS KINDLING.
Y-YOU CAN'T!
WHO'LL STOP ME? THE LAW?
THE GRAY AGENTS WILL BE THE NEW LAW.
WE'LL DECIDE WHO BURNS.

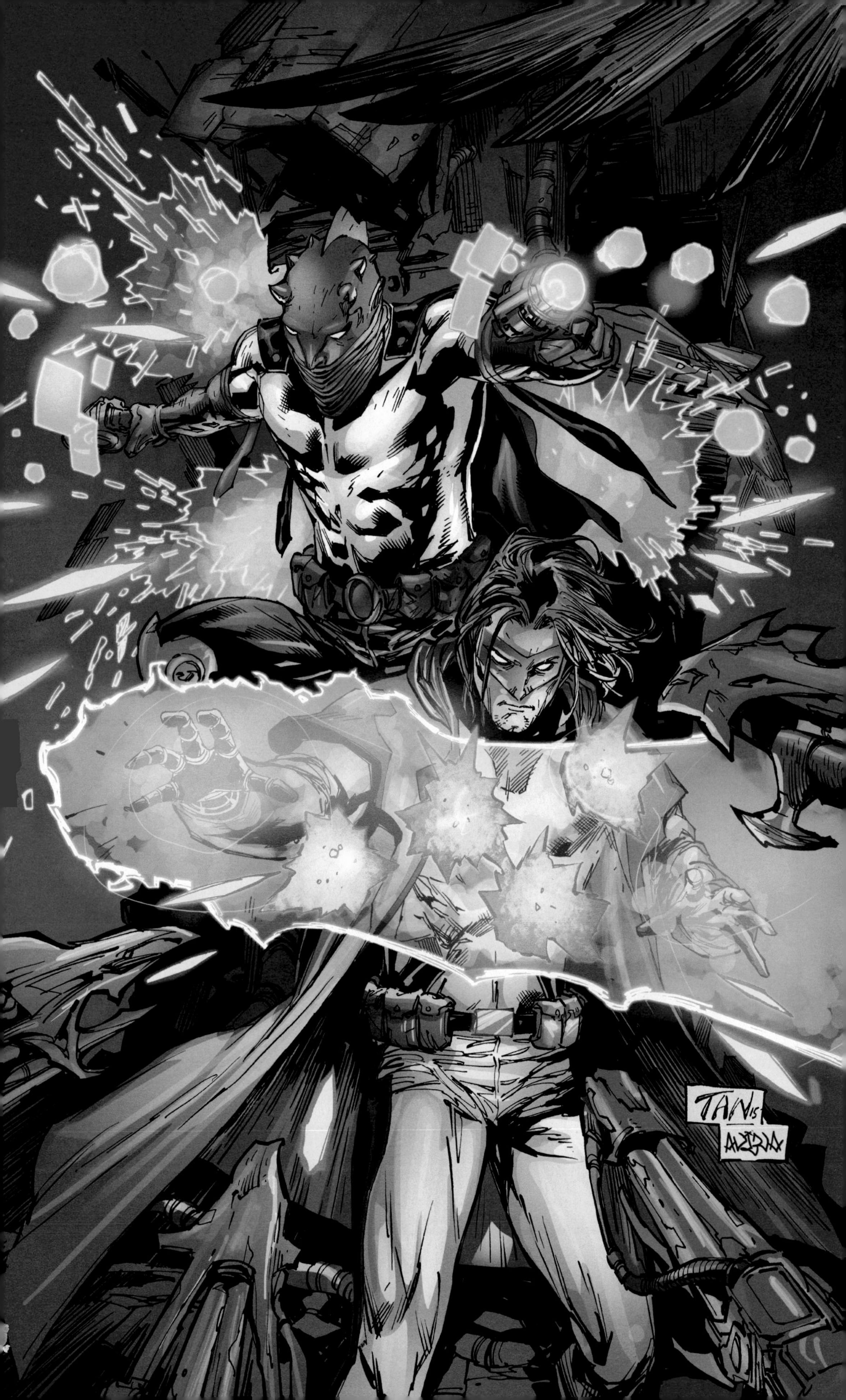

EMERGENCY STOP

ROBERT VENDITTI writer BILLY TAN & MARTIN COCCOLO pencillers MARK IRWIN & MARTIN COCCOLO inkers
TONY AVIÑA colorist DAVE SHARPE letterer BILLY TAN & TONY AVIÑA cover

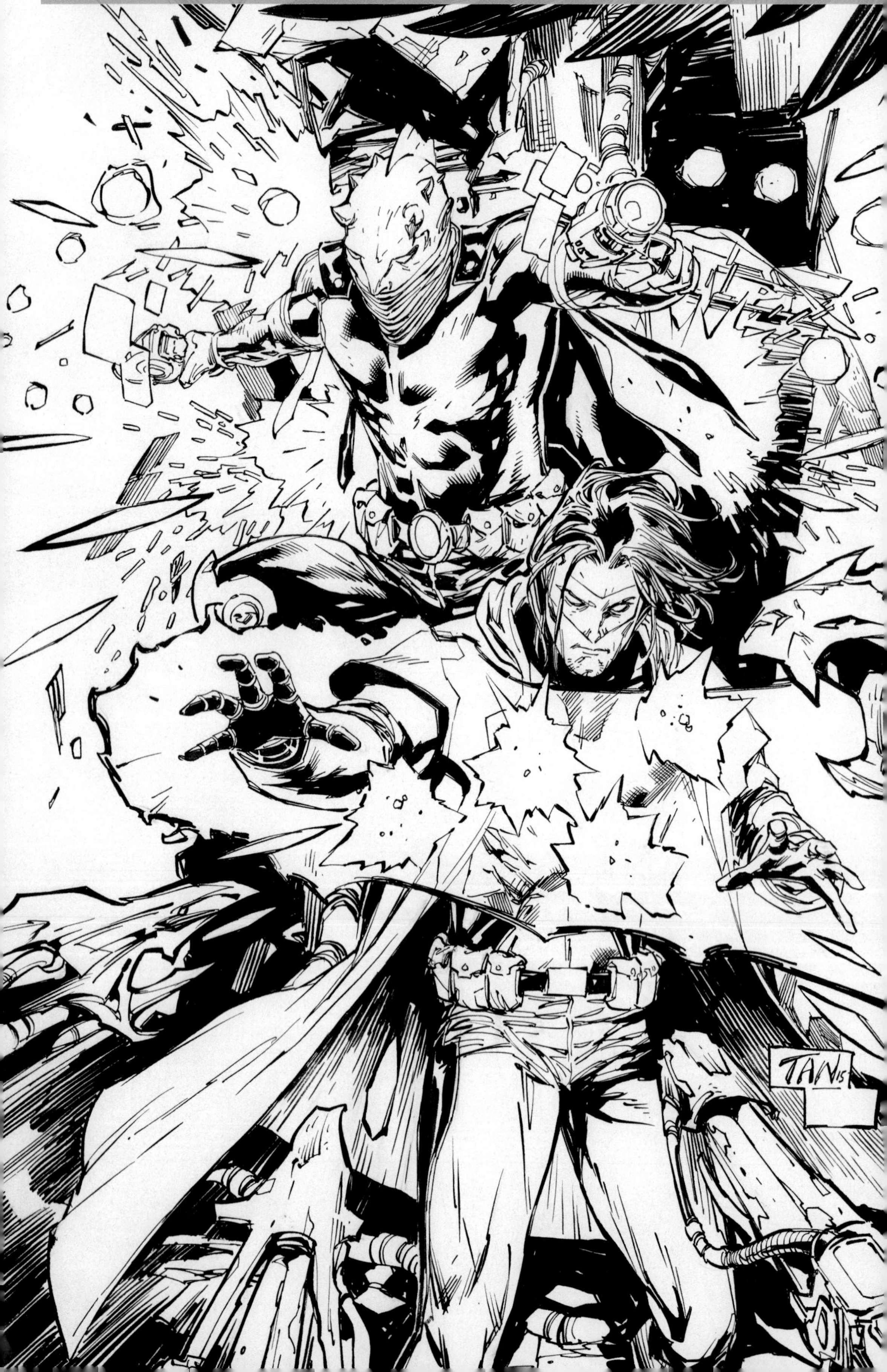

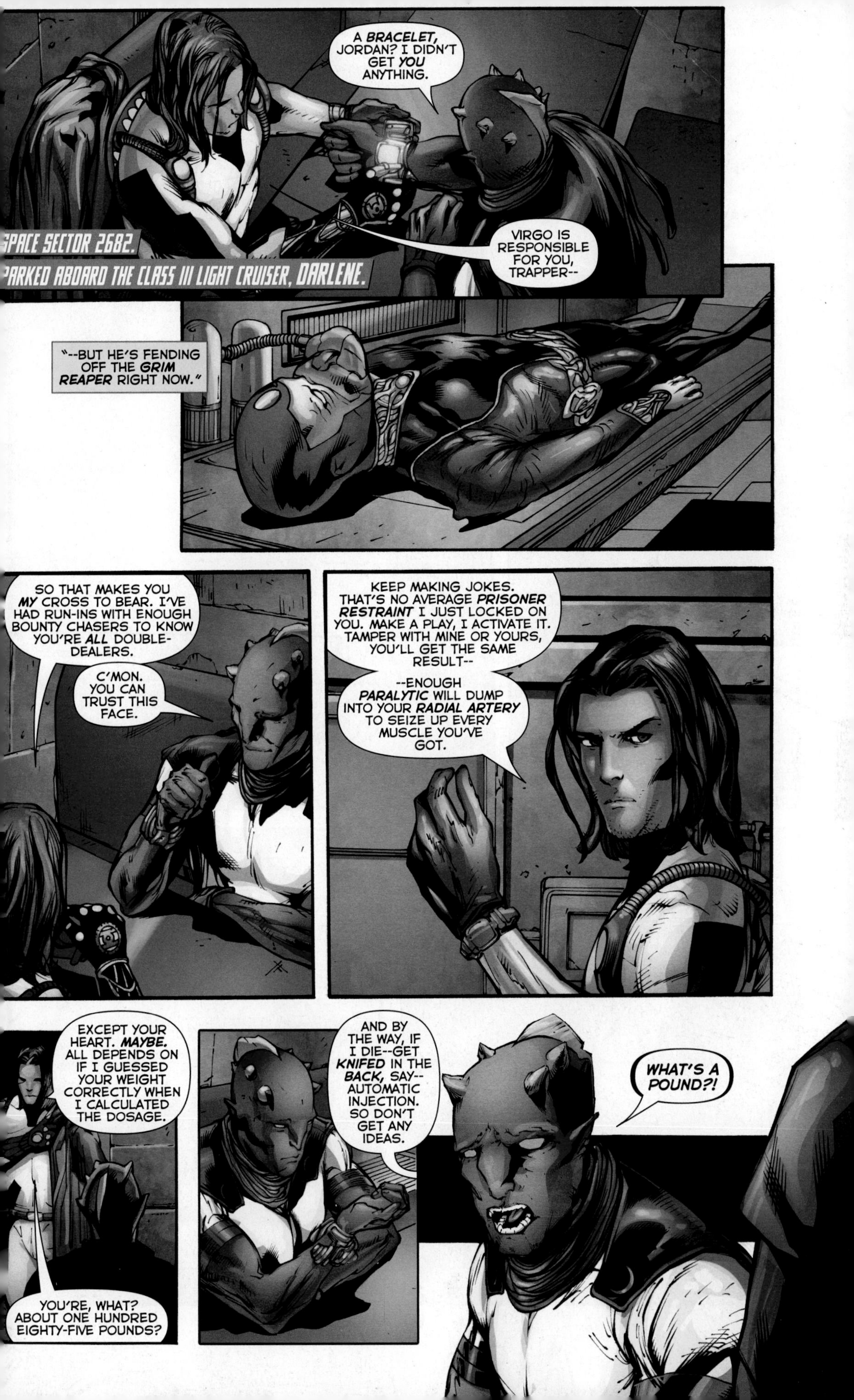
A BRACELET, JORDAN? I DIDN'T GET YOU ANYTHING.
SPACE SECTOR 2682.
PARKED ABOARD THE CLASS III LIGHT CRUISER, DARLENE.
VIRGO IS RESPONSIBLE FOR YOU, TRAPPER--
"--BUT HE'S FENDING OFF THE GRIM REAPER RIGHT NOW."
SO THAT MAKES YOU MY CROSS TO BEAR. I'VE HAD RUN-INS WITH ENOUGH BOUNTY CHASERS TO KNOW YOU'RE ALL DOUBLE-DEALERS.
C'MON. YOU CAN TRUST THIS FACE.
KEEP MAKING JOKES. THAT'S NO AVERAGE PRISONER RESTRAINT I JUST LOCKED ON YOU. MAKE A PLAY, I ACTIVATE IT. TAMPER WITH MINE OR YOURS, YOU'LL GET THE SAME RESULT--
--ENOUGH PARALYTIC WILL DUMP INTO YOUR RADIAL ARTERY TO SEIZE UP EVERY MUSCLE YOU'VE GOT.
EXCEPT YOUR HEART. MAYBE. ALL DEPENDS ON IF I GUESSED YOUR WEIGHT CORRECTLY WHEN I CALCULATED THE DOSAGE.
YOU'RE, WHAT? ABOUT ONE HUNDRED EIGHTY-FIVE POUNDS?
AND BY THE WAY, IF I DIE--GET KNIFED IN THE BACK, SAY--AUTOMATIC INJECTION. SO DON'T GET ANY IDEAS.
WHAT'S A POUND?!

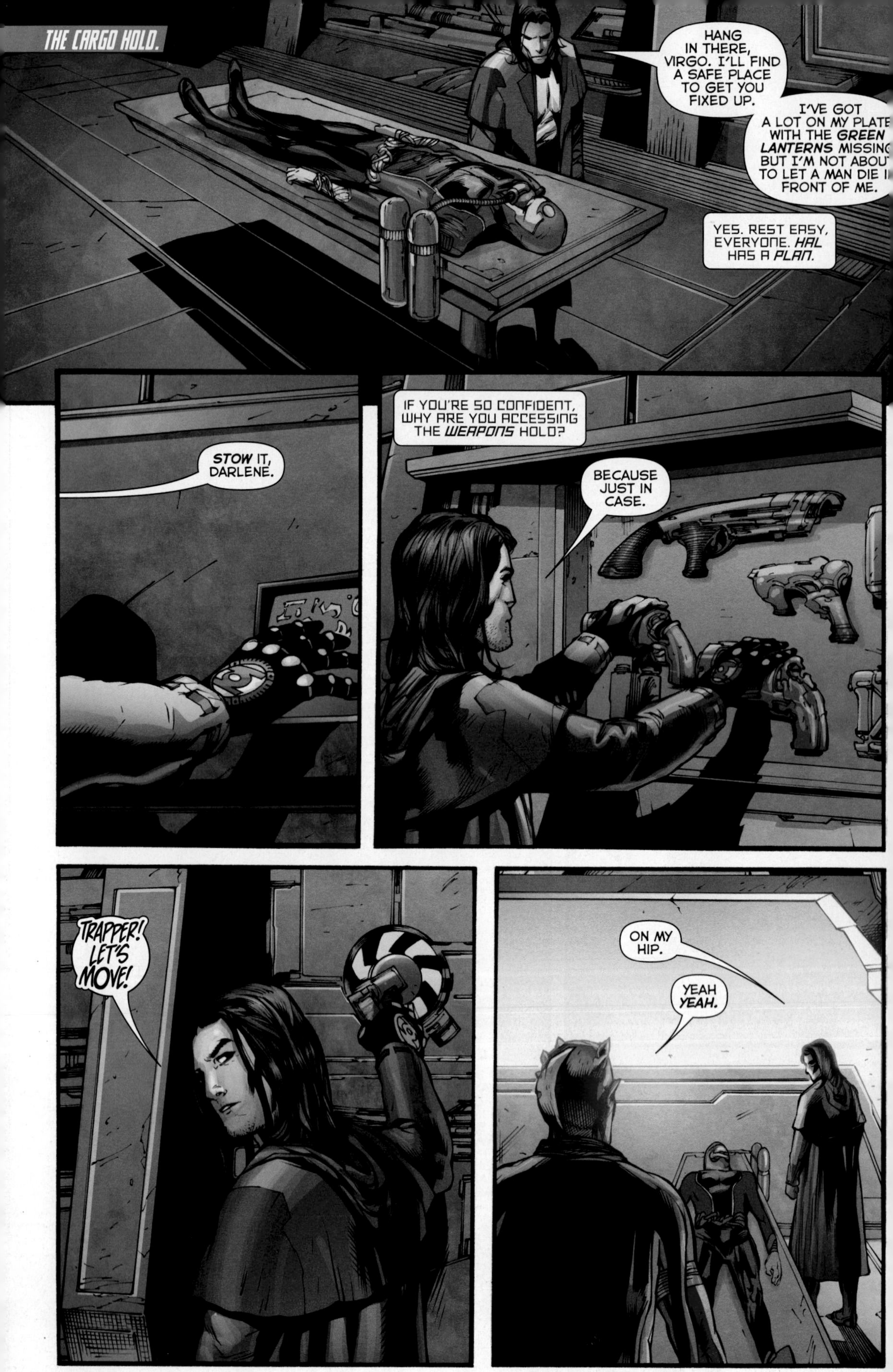
THE CARGO HOLD.
HANG IN THERE, VIRGO. I'LL FIND A SAFE PLACE TO GET YOU FIXED UP.
I'VE GOT A LOT ON MY PLATE WITH THE GREEN LANTERNS MISSING BUT I'M NOT ABOUT TO LET A MAN DIE IN FRONT OF ME.
YES. REST EASY, EVERYONE. HAL HAS A PLAN.
STOW IT, DARLENE.
IF YOU'RE SO CONFIDENT, WHY ARE YOU ACCESSING THE WEAPONS HOLD?
BECAUSE JUST IN CASE.
TRAPPER! LET'S MOVE!
ON MY HIP.
YEAH YEAH.

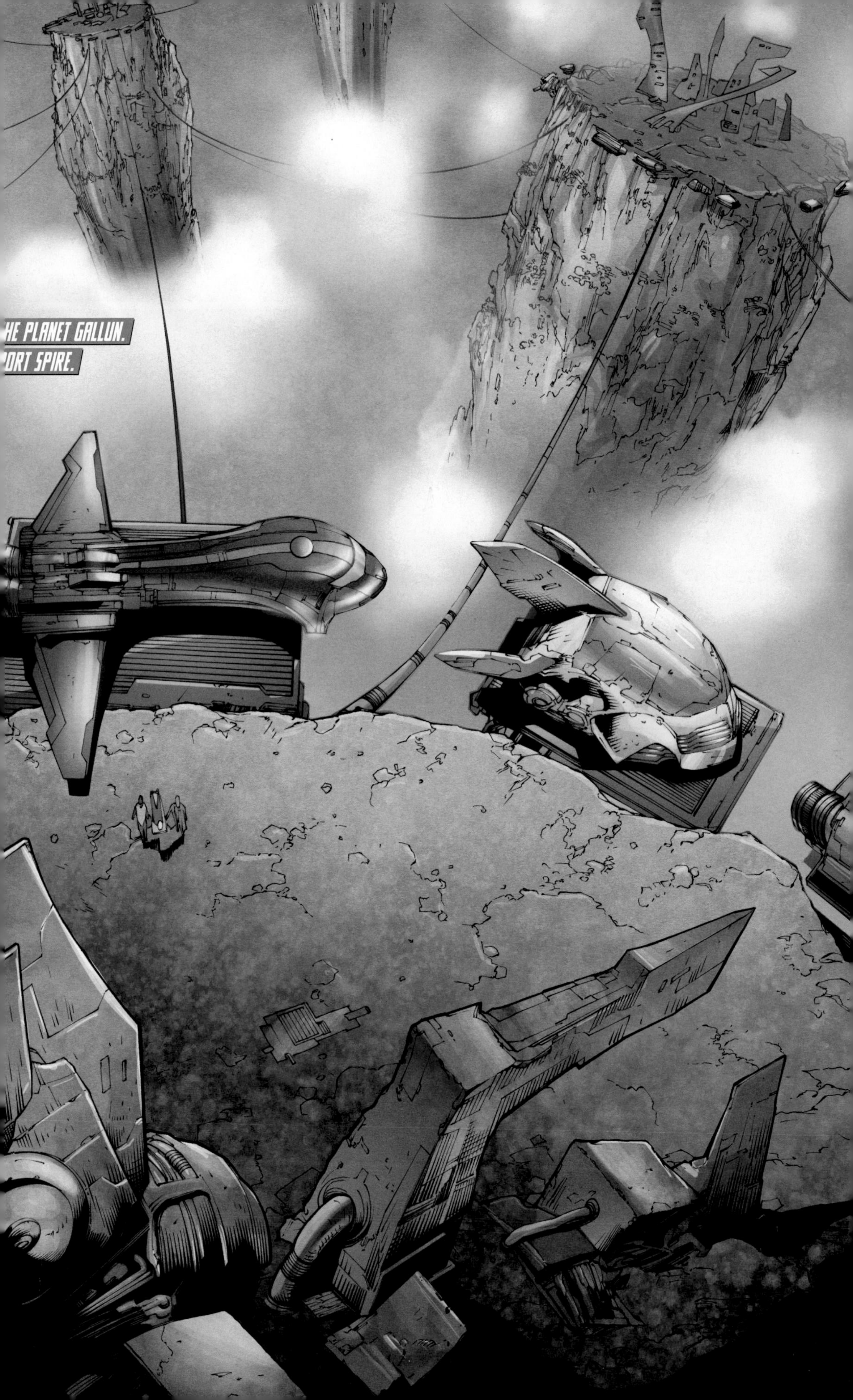
HE PLANET GALLUN.
ORT SPIRE.

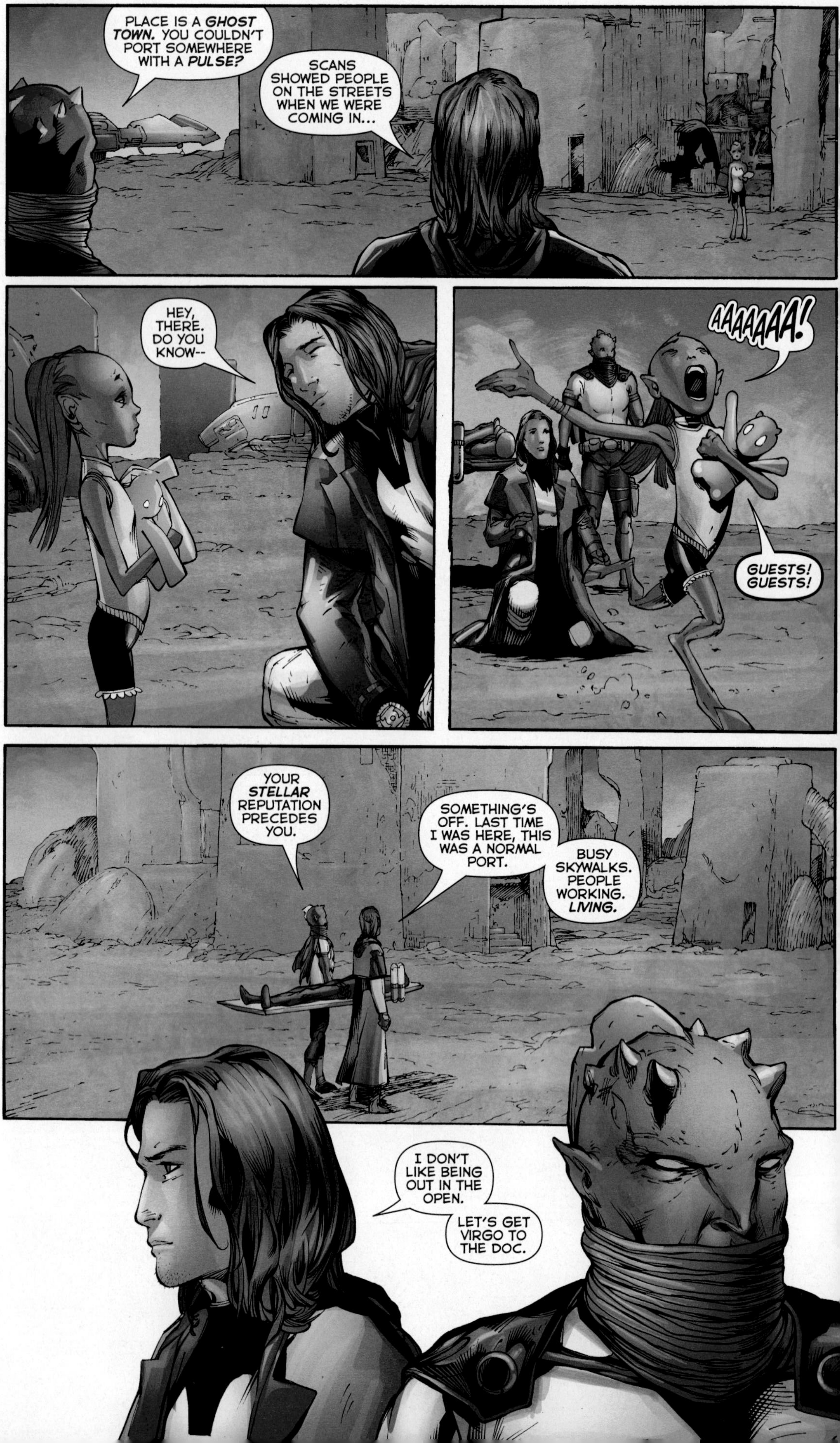
PLACE IS A *GHOST TOWN.* YOU COULDN'T PORT SOMEWHERE WITH A *PULSE?*
SCANS SHOWED PEOPLE ON THE STREETS WHEN WE WERE COMING IN...
HEY, THERE. DO YOU KNOW--
AAAAAAA!
GUESTS! GUESTS!
YOUR *STELLAR* REPUTATION PRECEDES YOU.
SOMETHING'S OFF. LAST TIME I WAS HERE, THIS WAS A NORMAL PORT.
BUSY SKYWALKS. PEOPLE WORKING. *LIVING.*
I DON'T LIKE BEING OUT IN THE OPEN.
LET'S GET VIRGO TO THE DOC.

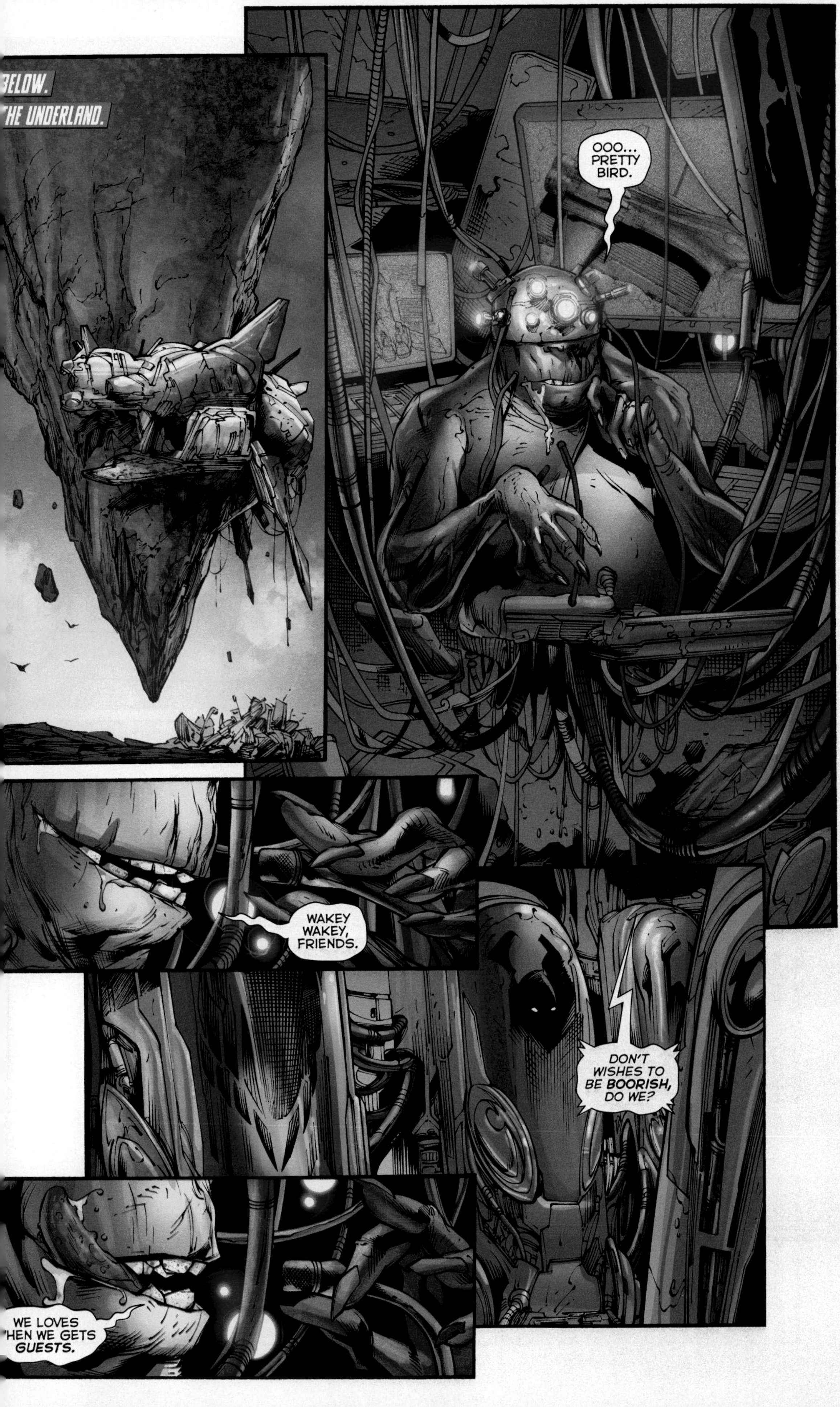
BELOW.
THE UNDERLAND.
OOO... PRETTY BIRD.
WAKEY WAKEY, FRIENDS.
DON'T WISHES TO BE BOORISH, DO WE?
WE LOVES HEN WE GETS GUESTS.

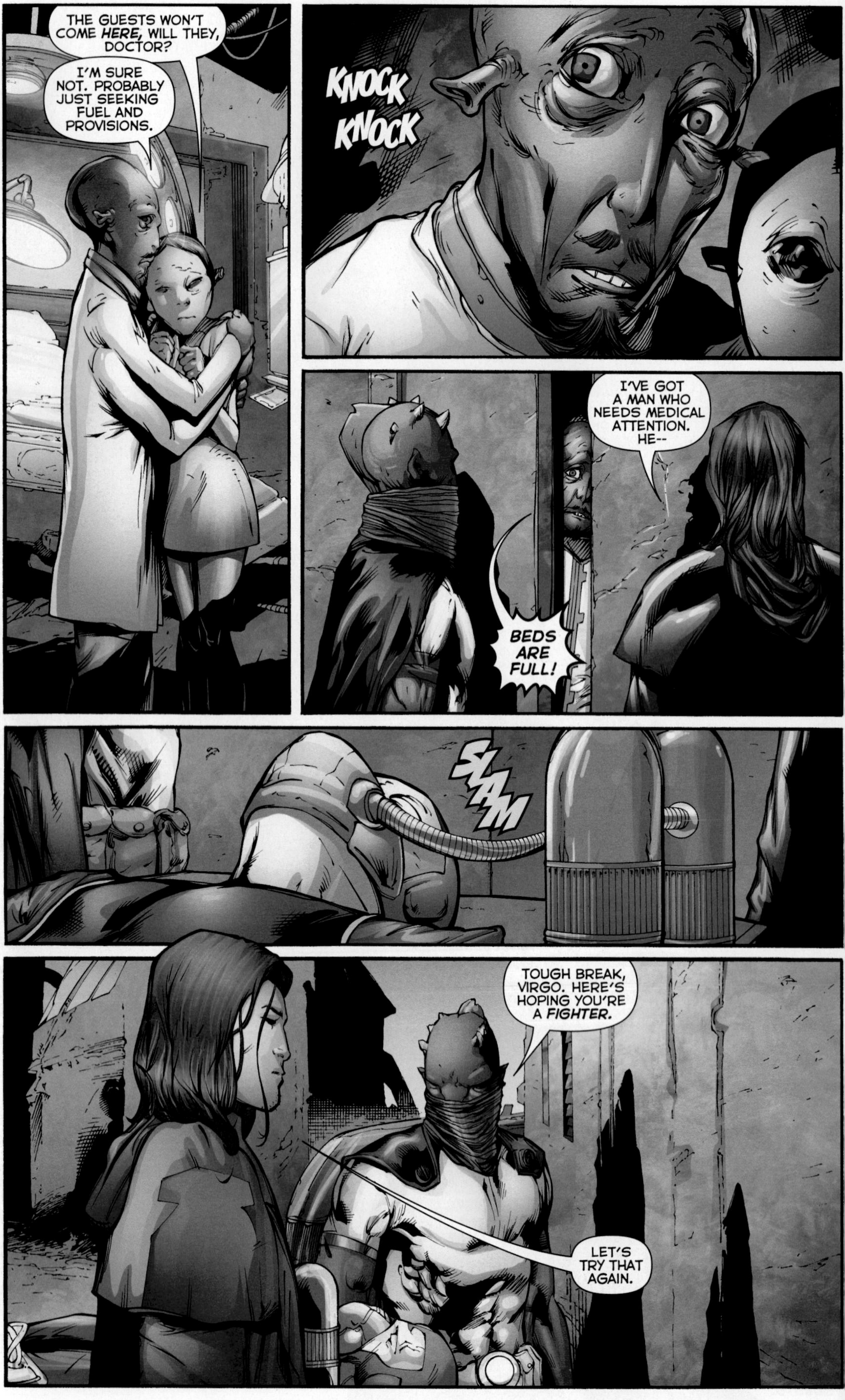

THE GUESTS WON'T COME *HERE*, WILL THEY, DOCTOR?
I'M SURE NOT. PROBABLY JUST SEEKING FUEL AND PROVISIONS.
KNOCK KNOCK
I'VE GOT A MAN WHO NEEDS MEDICAL ATTENTION. HE--
BEDS ARE FULL!
SLAM
TOUGH BREAK, VIRGO. HERE'S HOPING YOU'RE A *FIGHTER.*
LET'S TRY THAT AGAIN.

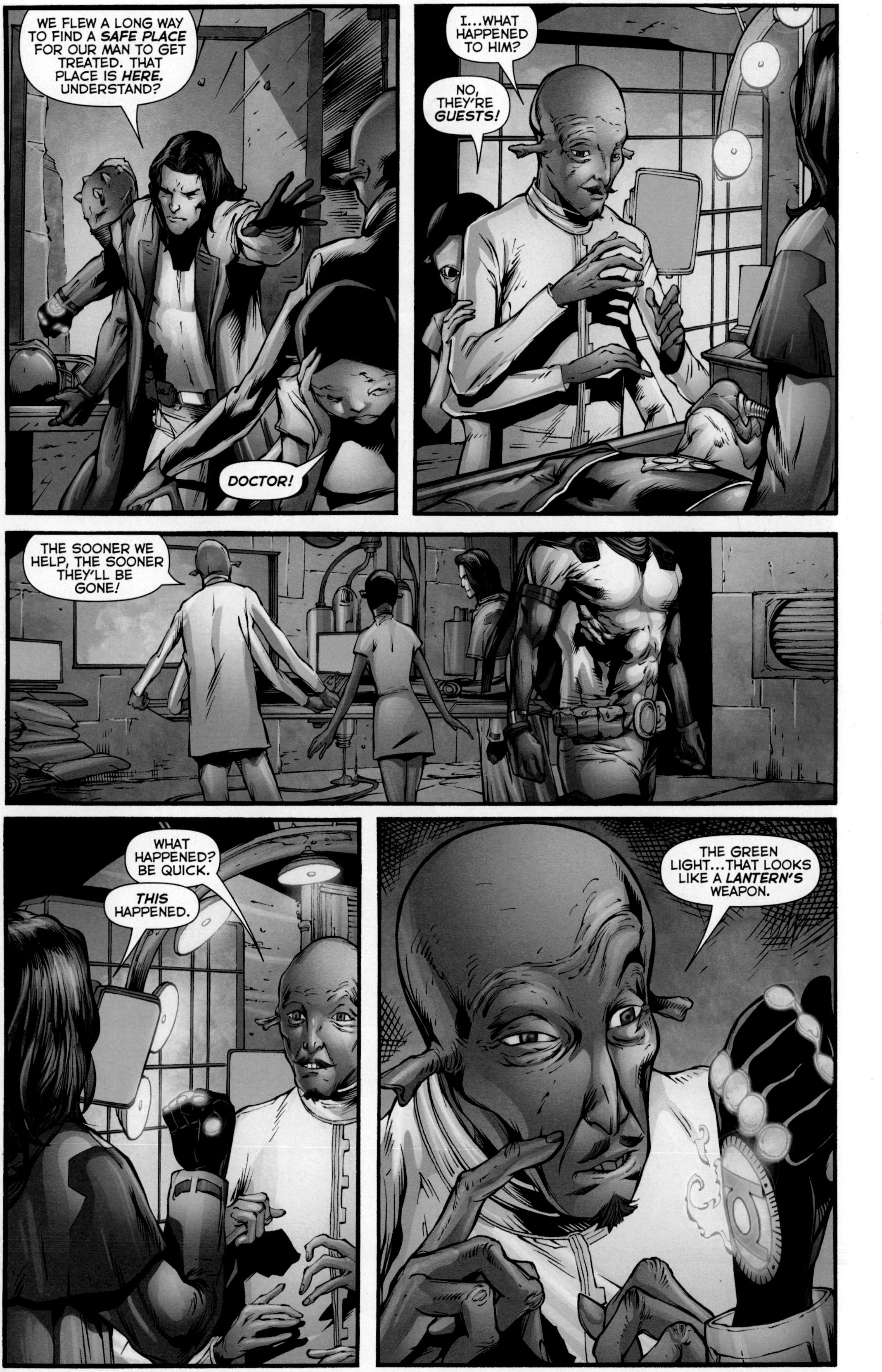
WE FLEW A LONG WAY TO FIND A SAFE PLACE FOR OUR MAN TO GET TREATED. THAT PLACE IS HERE. UNDERSTAND?
DOCTOR!
I...WHAT HAPPENED TO HIM?
NO, THEY'RE GUESTS!
THE SOONER WE HELP, THE SOONER THEY'LL BE GONE!
WHAT HAPPENED? BE QUICK.
THIS HAPPENED.
THE GREEN LIGHT...THAT LOOKS LIKE A LANTERN'S WEAPON.

BUT WAY MORE *POWERFUL* THAN A RING. AND WITH A *DODGIER* INTERFACE.

WHEN I SAY I'M FOCUSING EVERY OUNCE OF *WILLPOWER* I HAVE TO KEEP THIS THING FROM *ERUPTING*, I'M NOT KIDDING. IT'S EXHAUSTING.

AND THAT'S WITH *YEARS* OF BEING A LANTERN UNDER MY BELT. IMAGINE WHAT IT'D DO TO A FIRST-TIMER TRYING IT ON WITHOUT PERMISSION.

SPEAKING AS A MEDICAL PROFESSIONAL, I SUSPECT *SEVERE TRAUMA* TO THE BRAIN WOULD RESULT.

YOU SEE? THIS TYPE OF CONDITION IS MORE COMMONLY ASSOCIATED WITH A *BLUNT FORCE* HEAD INJURY.

YOUR FRIEND'S BRAIN HAS RETREATED. *SHUT DOWN* TO CONCENTRATE ALL ITS ENERGIES ON HEALING.

I CAN ACCELERATE THE PROCESS.

JAEVA, BRING ME THE SUBCRANIAL STIMULATOR.

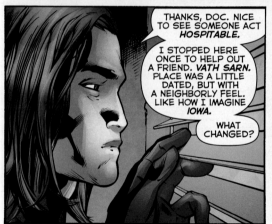

THANKS, DOC. NICE TO SEE SOMEONE ACT *HOSPITABLE.*

I STOPPED HERE ONCE TO HELP OUT A FRIEND. *VATH SARN.* PLACE WAS A LITTLE DATED, BUT WITH A NEIGHBORLY FEEL. LIKE HOW I IMAGINE *IOWA.*

WHAT CHANGED?

BE *QUICK,* JAEVA.

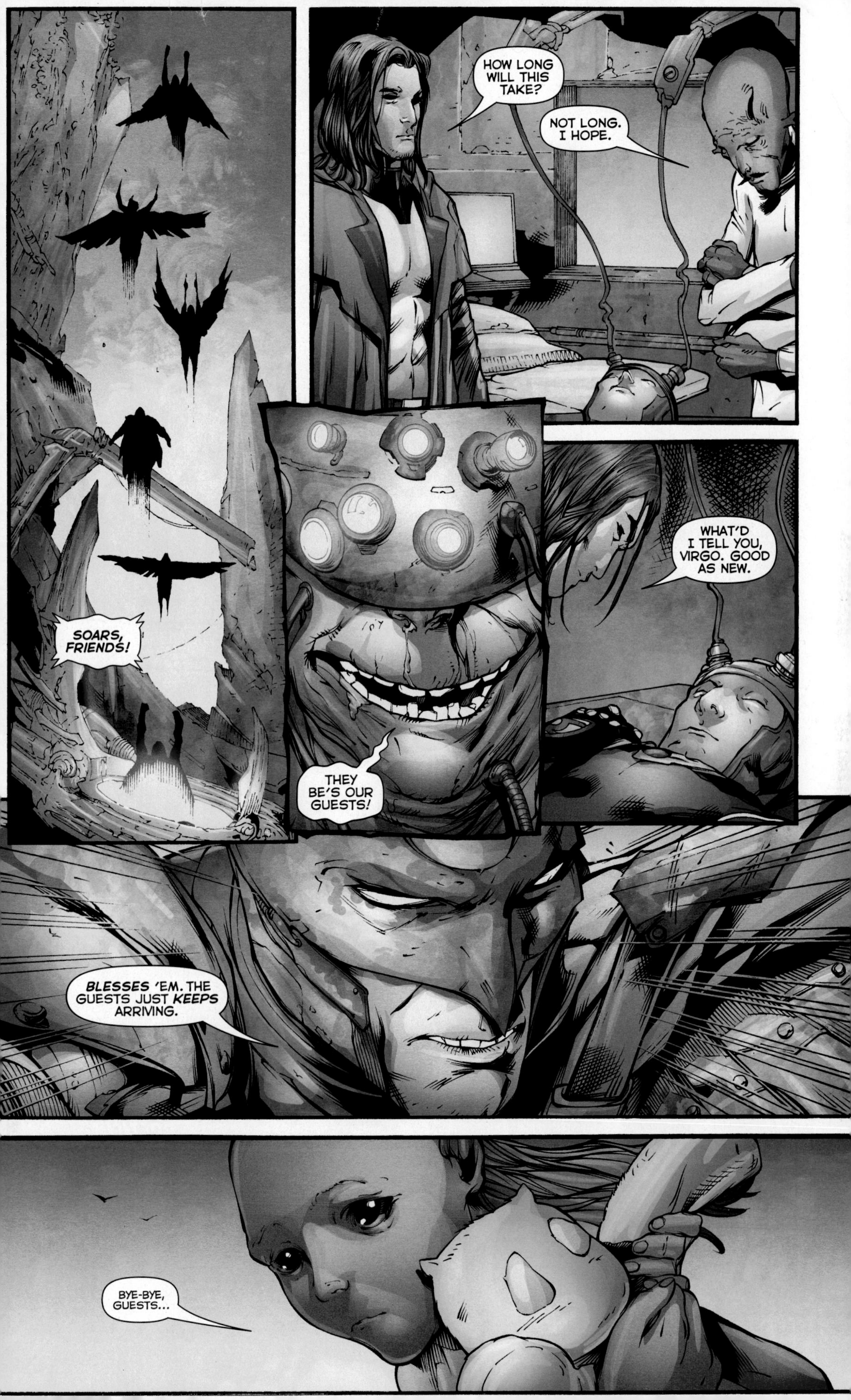
SOARS, FRIENDS!
HOW LONG WILL THIS TAKE?
NOT LONG. I HOPE.
THEY BE'S OUR GUESTS!
WHAT'D I TELL YOU, VIRGO. GOOD AS NEW.
BLESSES 'EM. THE GUESTS JUST KEEPS ARRIVING.
BYE-BYE, GUESTS...

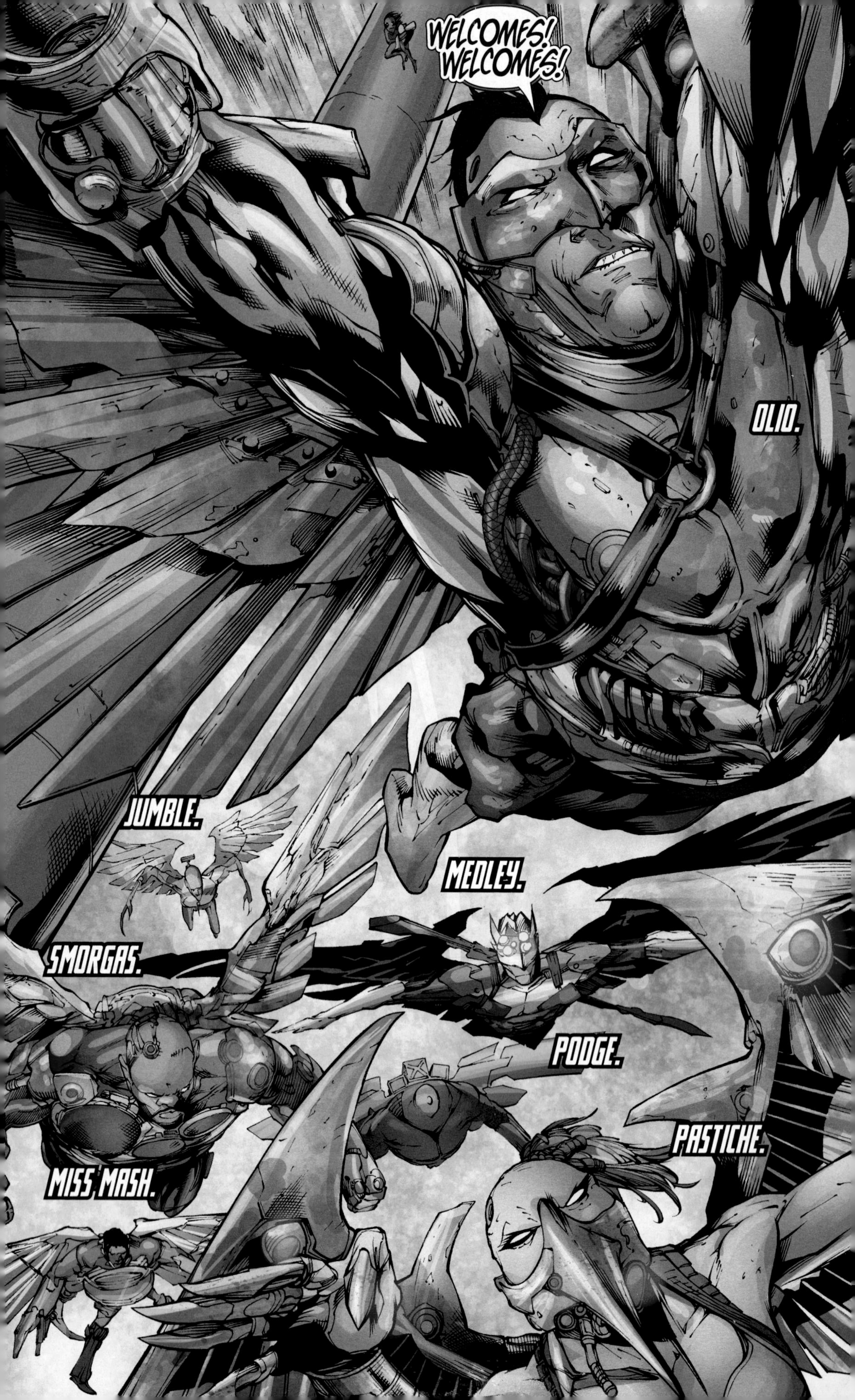
WELCOMES! WELCOMES!
OLIO.
JUMBLE.
MEDLEY.
SMORGAS.
PODGE.
PASTICHE.
MISS MASH.

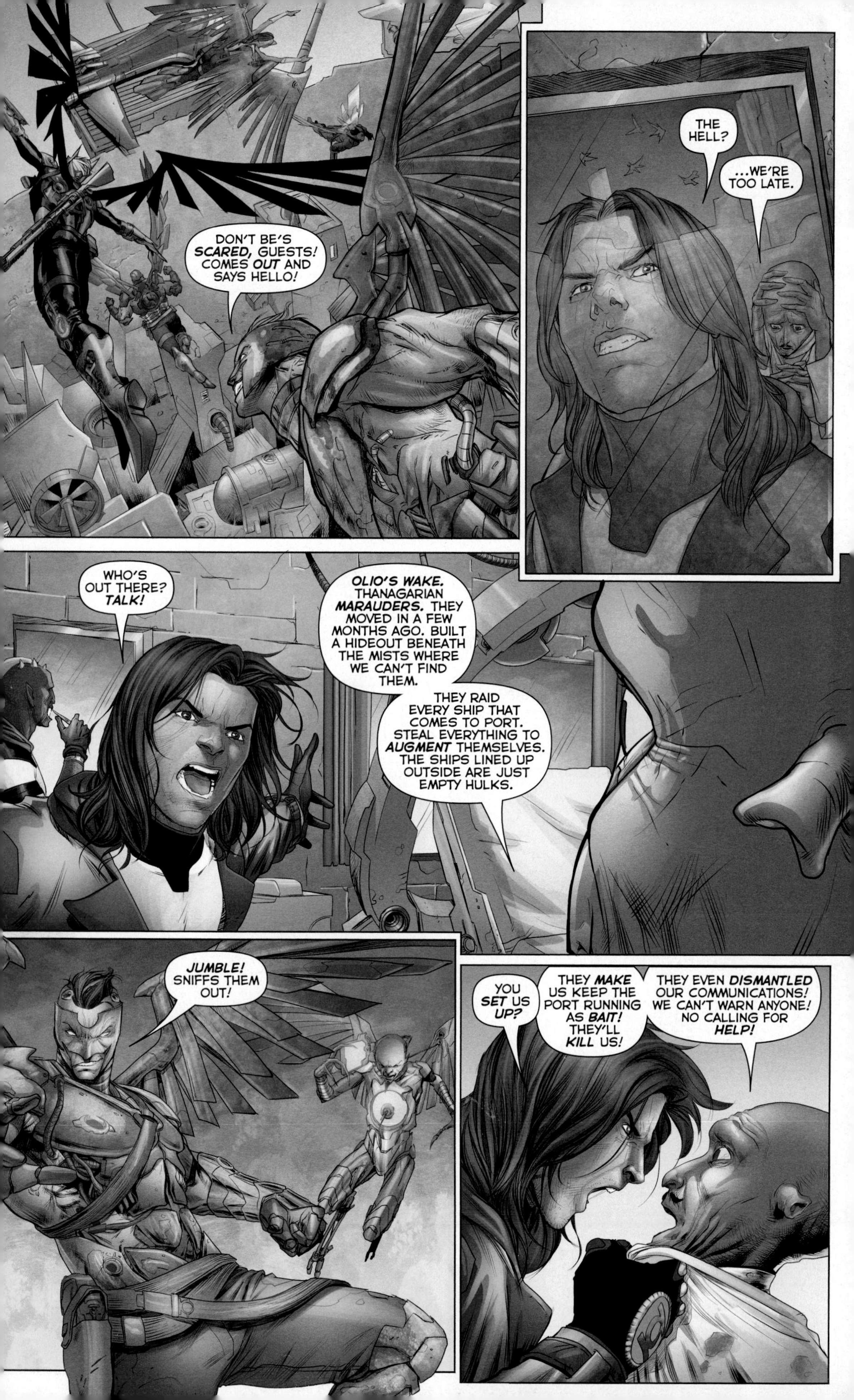

DON'T BE'S *SCARED,* GUESTS! COMES *OUT* AND SAYS HELLO!
THE HELL?
...WE'RE TOO LATE.
WHO'S OUT THERE? *TALK!*
OLIO'S WAKE. THANAGARIAN *MARAUDERS.* THEY MOVED IN A FEW MONTHS AGO. BUILT A HIDEOUT BENEATH THE MISTS WHERE WE CAN'T FIND THEM.
THEY RAID EVERY SHIP THAT COMES TO PORT. STEAL EVERYTHING TO *AUGMENT* THEMSELVES. THE SHIPS LINED UP OUTSIDE ARE JUST EMPTY HULKS.
JUMBLE! SNIFFS THEM OUT!
YOU *SET* US *UP?*
THEY *MAKE* US KEEP THE PORT RUNNING AS *BAIT!* THEY'LL *KILL* US!
THEY EVEN *DISMANTLED* OUR COMMUNICATIONS! WE CAN'T WARN ANYONE! NO CALLING FOR *HELP!*

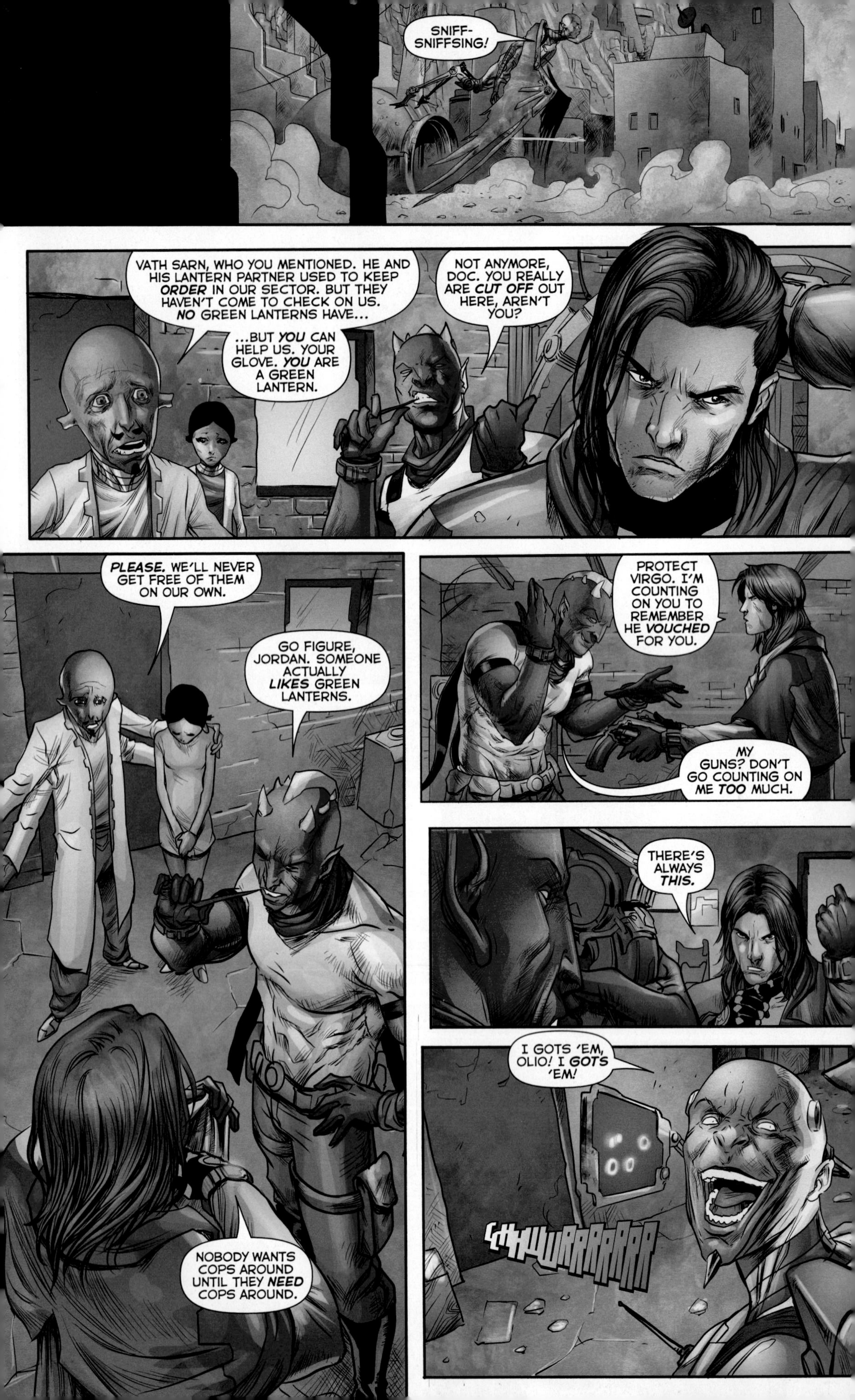
SNIFF-SNIFFSING!
VATH SARN, WHO YOU MENTIONED. HE AND HIS LANTERN PARTNER USED TO KEEP ORDER IN OUR SECTOR. BUT THEY HAVEN'T COME TO CHECK ON US. NO GREEN LANTERNS HAVE...
...BUT YOU CAN HELP US. YOUR GLOVE. YOU ARE A GREEN LANTERN.
NOT ANYMORE, DOC. YOU REALLY ARE CUT OFF OUT HERE, AREN'T YOU?
PLEASE. WE'LL NEVER GET FREE OF THEM ON OUR OWN.
GO FIGURE, JORDAN. SOMEONE ACTUALLY LIKES GREEN LANTERNS.
NOBODY WANTS COPS AROUND UNTIL THEY NEED COPS AROUND.
PROTECT VIRGO. I'M COUNTING ON YOU TO REMEMBER HE VOUCHED FOR YOU.
MY GUNS? DON'T GO COUNTING ON ME TOO MUCH.
THERE'S ALWAYS THIS.
I GOTS 'EM, OLIO! I GOTS 'EM!
CHHWURRRRRRR

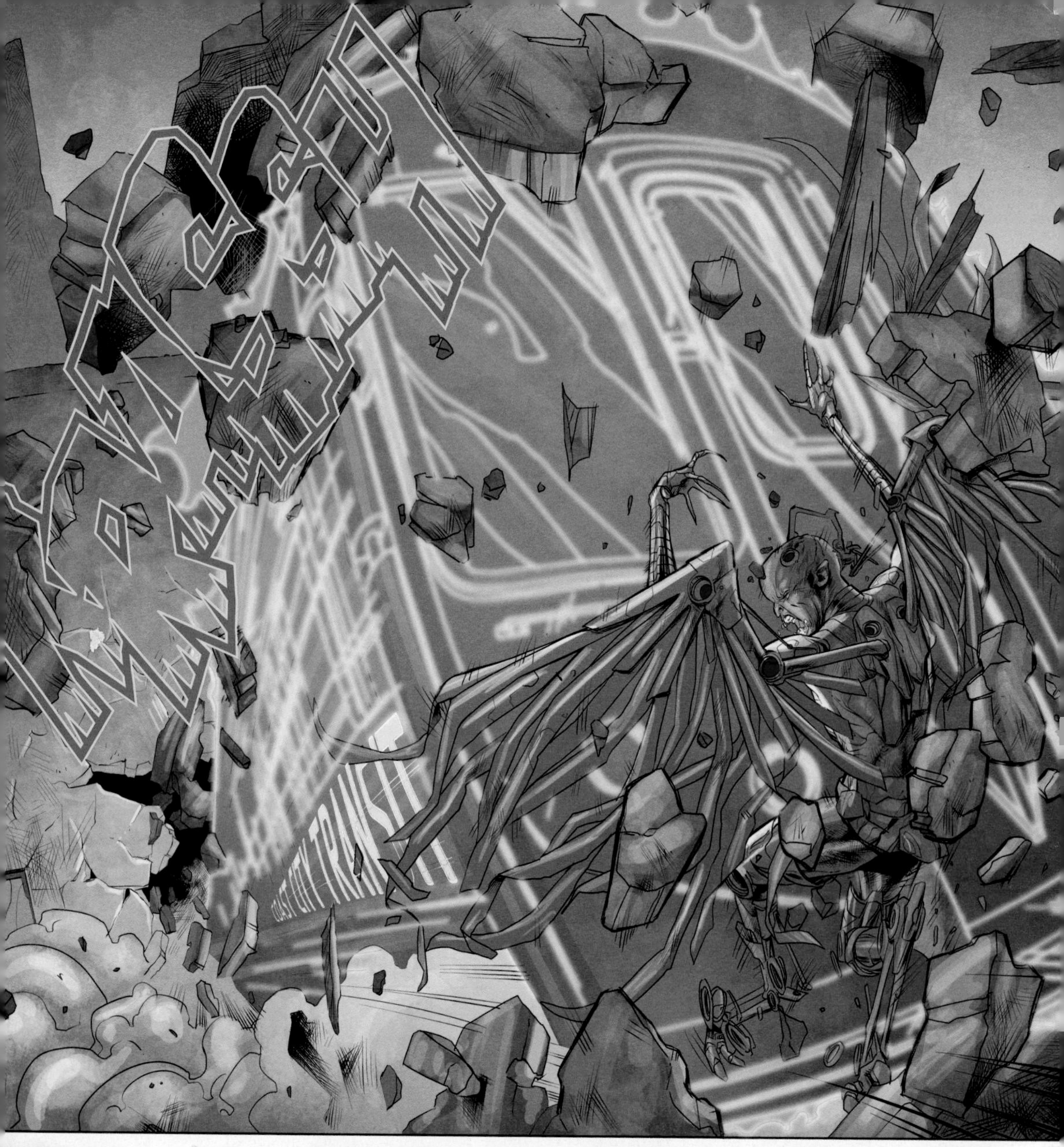
COAST CITY TRANSIT

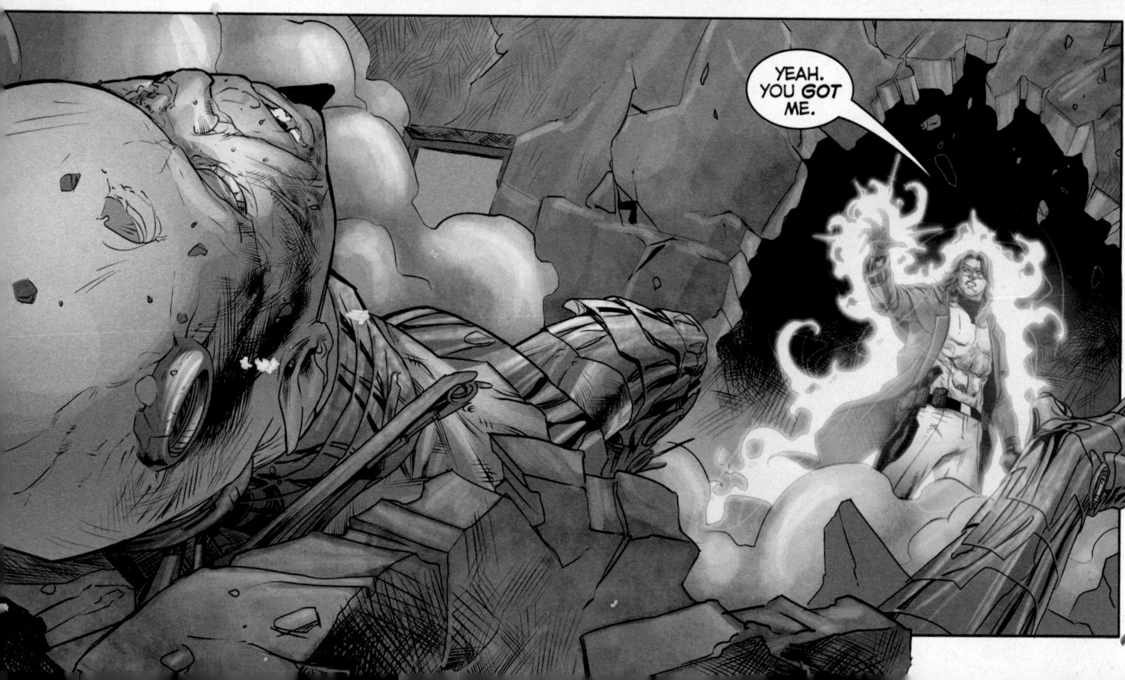
YEAH. YOU GOT ME.

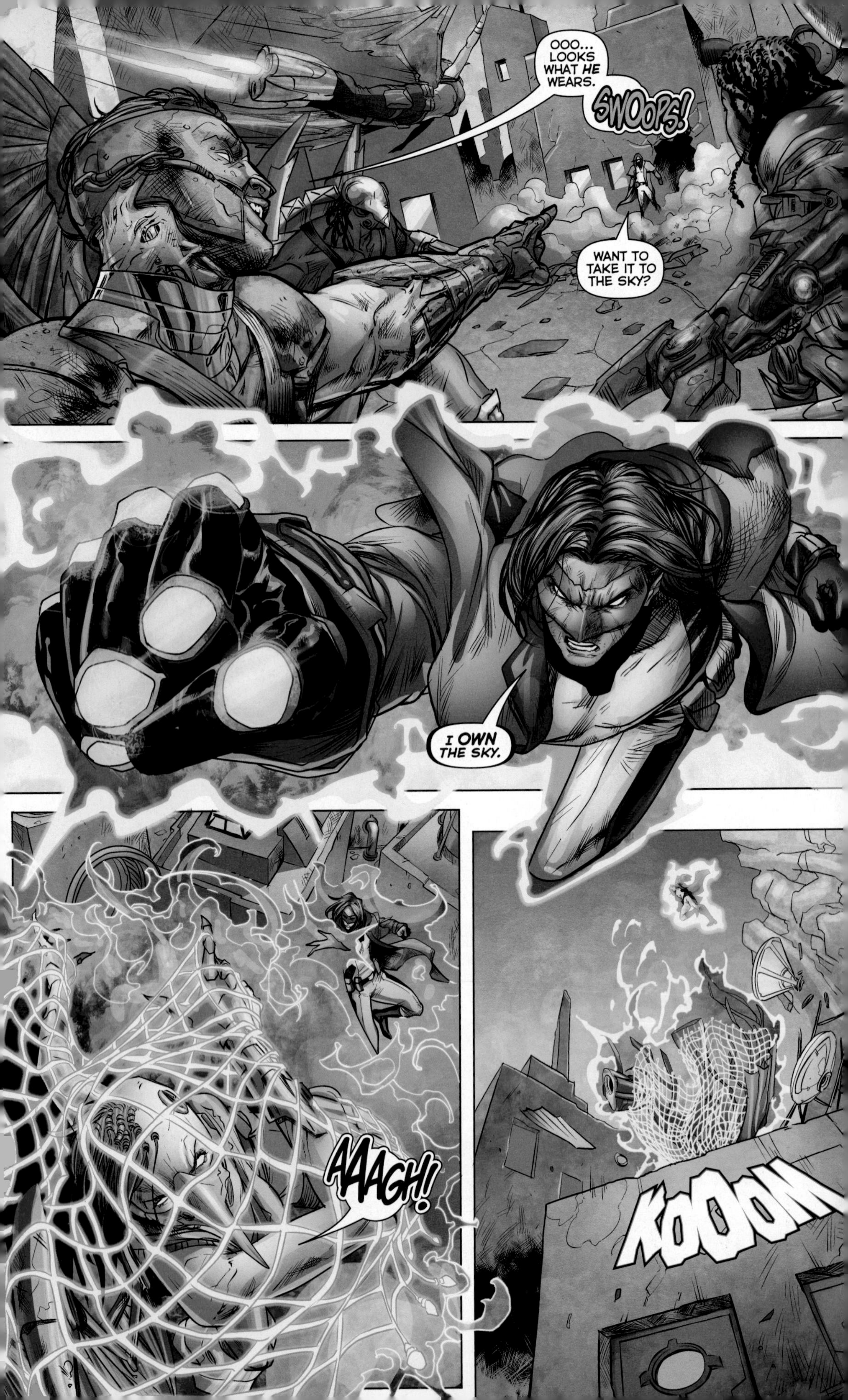
OOO... LOOKS WHAT HE WEARS.
SWOOPS!
WANT TO TAKE IT TO THE SKY?
I OWN THE SKY.
AAAGH!
KOOOM

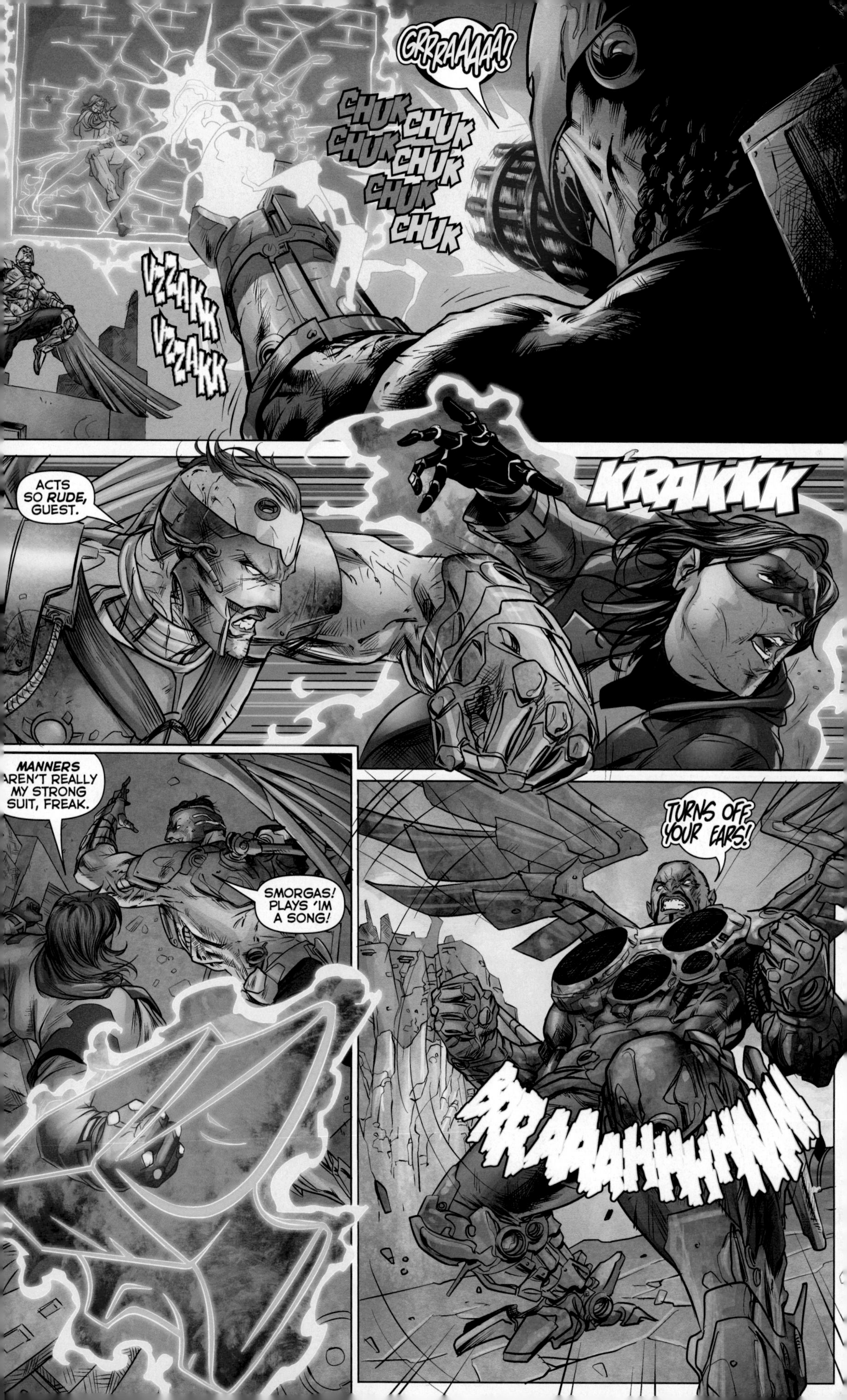
GRRRAAAAA!
CHUK CHUK
CHUK CHUK
CHUK
CHUK
VZZAKK
VZZAKK
ACTS SO RUDE, GUEST.
KRAKKK
MANNERS AREN'T REALLY MY STRONG SUIT, FREAK.
SMORGAS! PLAYS 'IM A SONG!
TURNS OFF YOUR EARS!
BRRAAAAHHHHMM

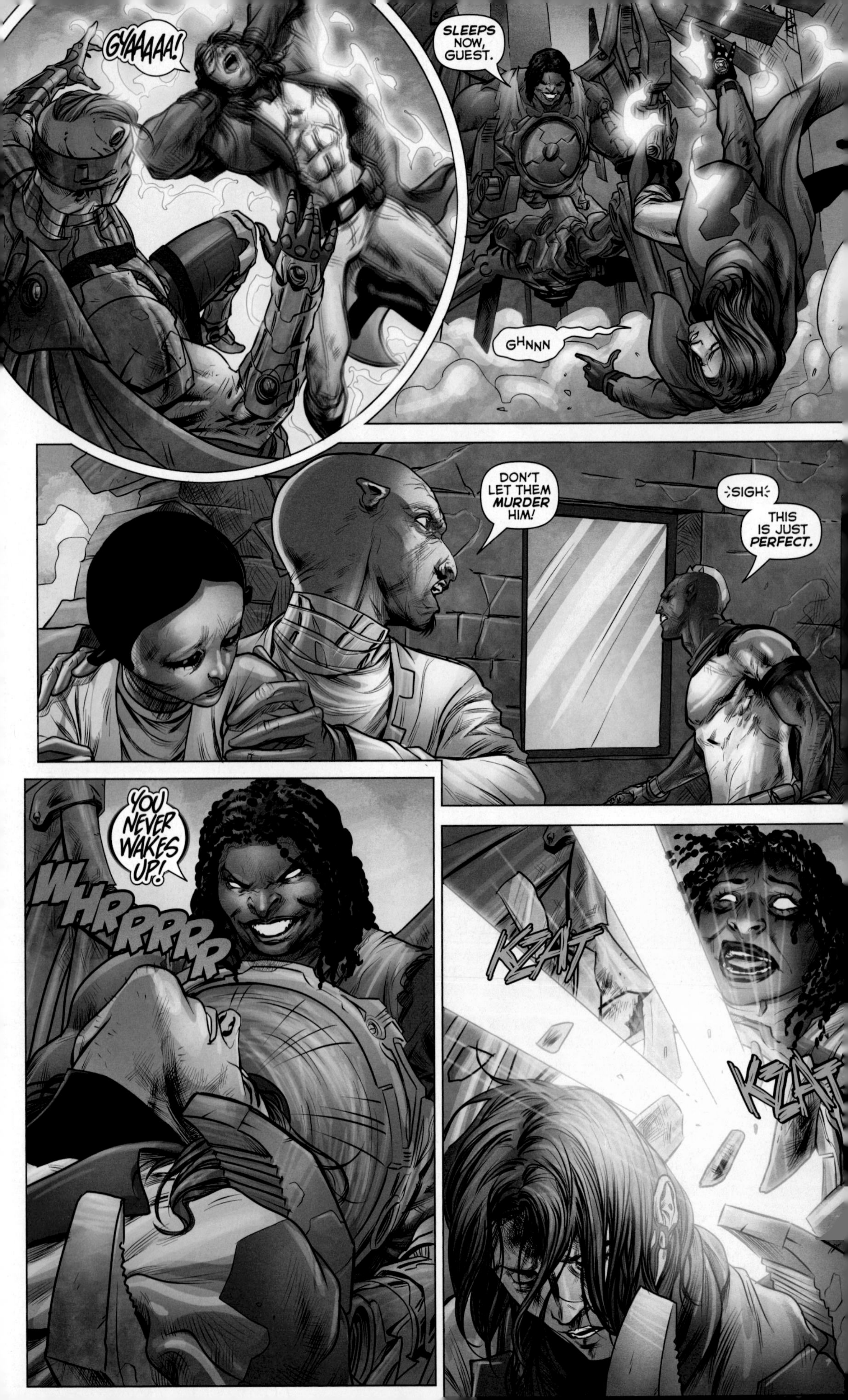
GYAAAAA!
SLEEPS NOW, GUEST.
GHNNN
DON'T LET THEM *MURDER* HIM!
SIGH
THIS IS JUST *PERFECT.*
YOU NEVER WAKES UP!
WHRRRRR
KZAT
KZAT

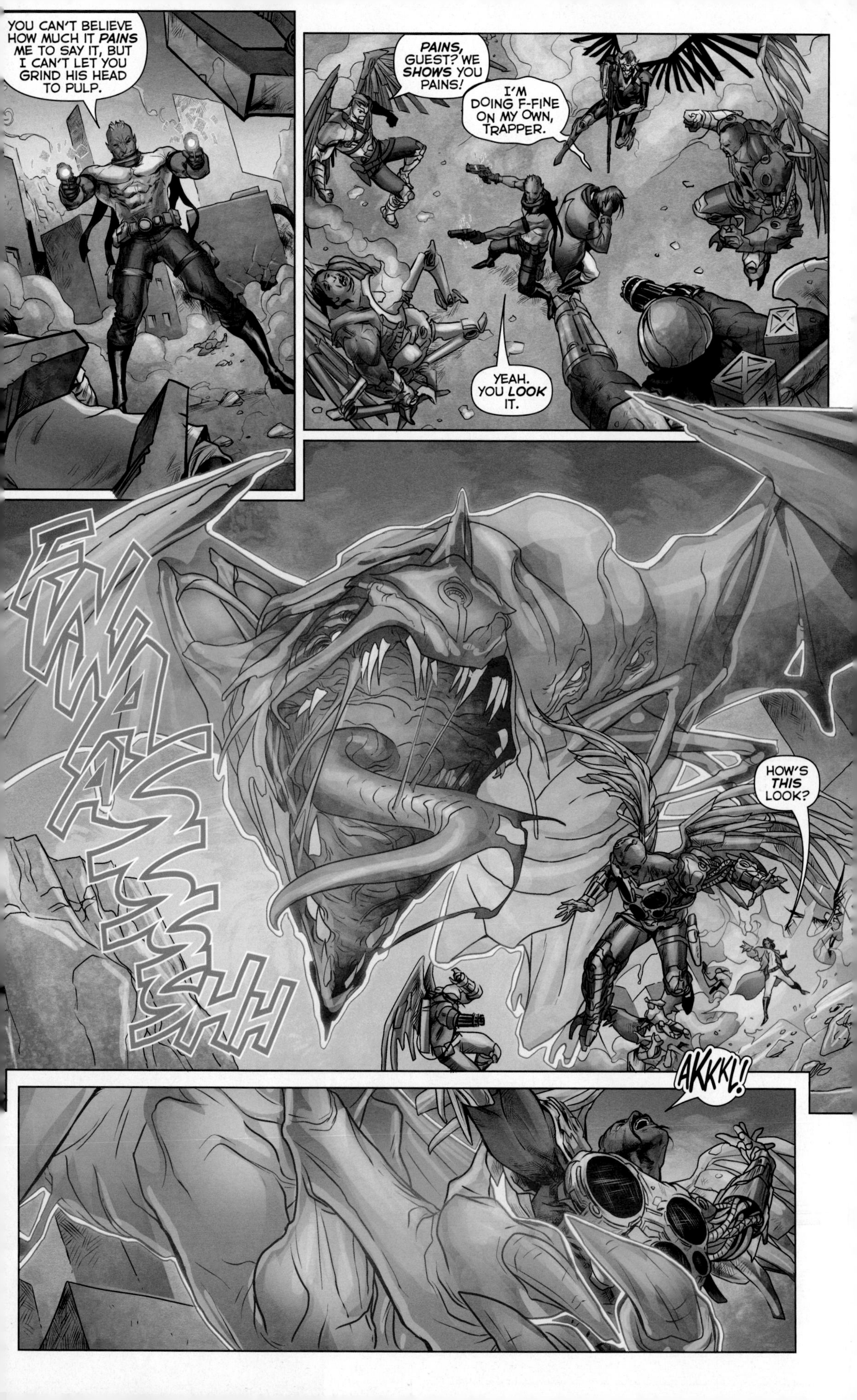
YOU CAN'T BELIEVE HOW MUCH IT PAINS ME TO SAY IT, BUT I CAN'T LET YOU GRIND HIS HEAD TO PULP.
PAINS, GUEST? WE SHOWS YOU PAINS!
I'M DOING F-FINE ON MY OWN, TRAPPER.
YEAH. YOU LOOK IT.
FWAASSHH
HOW'S THIS LOOK?
AKKKL!

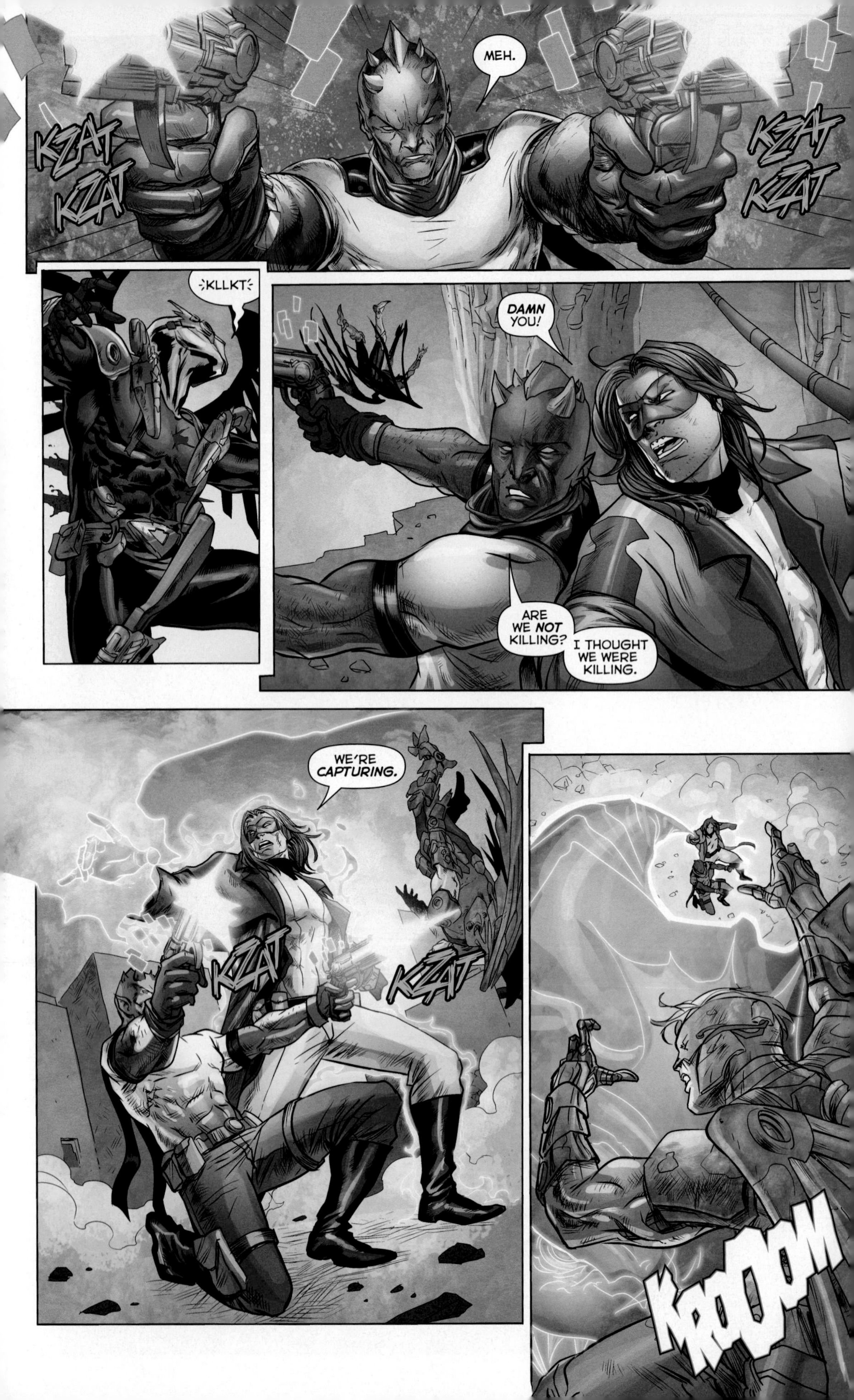

MEH.
KZAT KZAT
KZAT KZAT
KLLKT
DAMN YOU!
ARE WE NOT KILLING?
I THOUGHT WE WERE KILLING.
WE'RE CAPTURING.
KZAT
KZAT
KROOOM

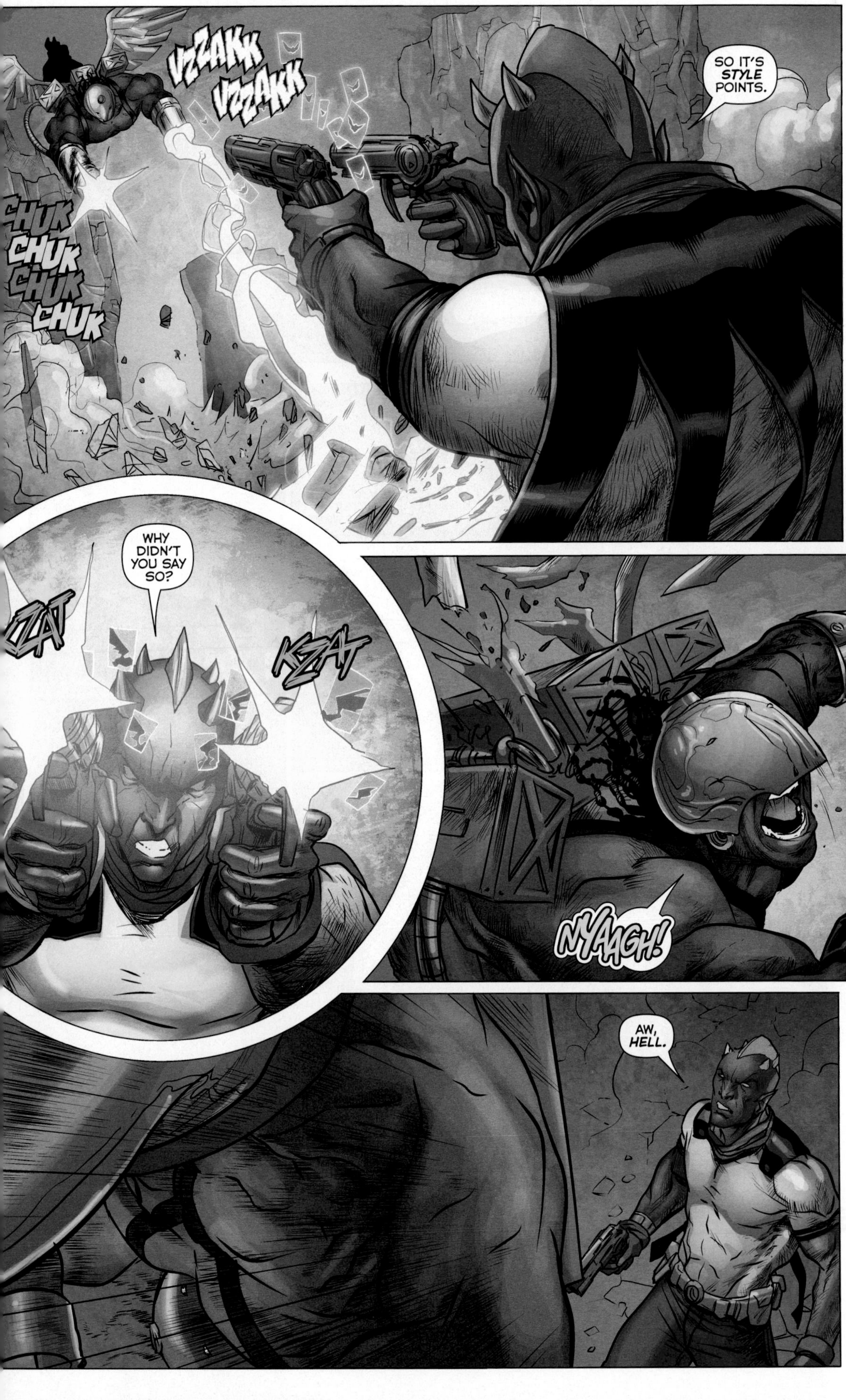
VZZAKK
VZZAKK
SO IT'S *STYLE* POINTS.
CHUK
CHUK
CHUK
CHUK
WHY DIDN'T YOU SAY SO?
KZAT
KZAT
NYAAGH!
AW, HELL.

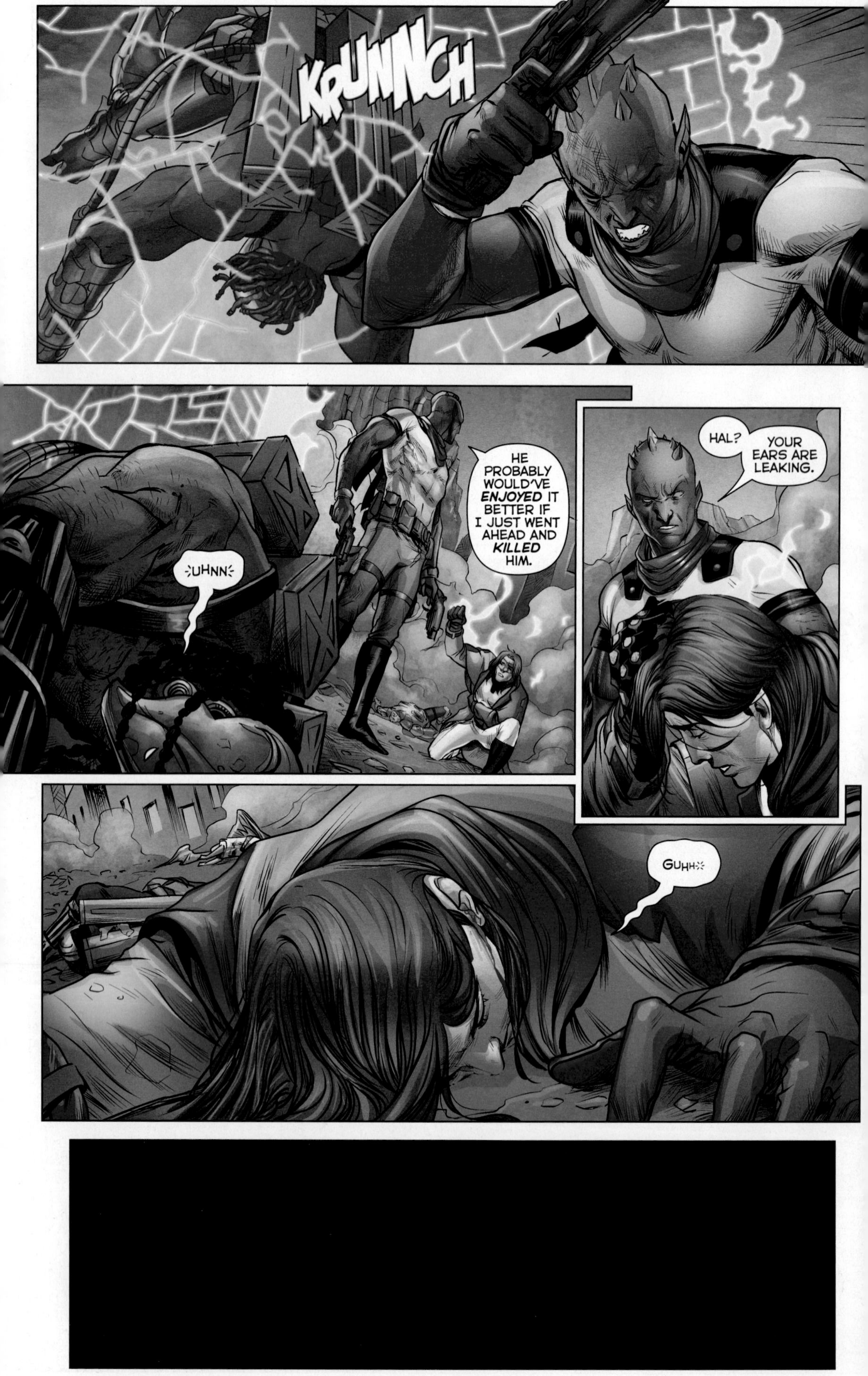
KRUNNCH
UHNN
HE PROBABLY WOULD'VE ENJOYED IT BETTER IF I JUST WENT AHEAD AND KILLED HIM.
HAL?
YOUR EARS ARE LEAKING.
GUHH

[redacted]

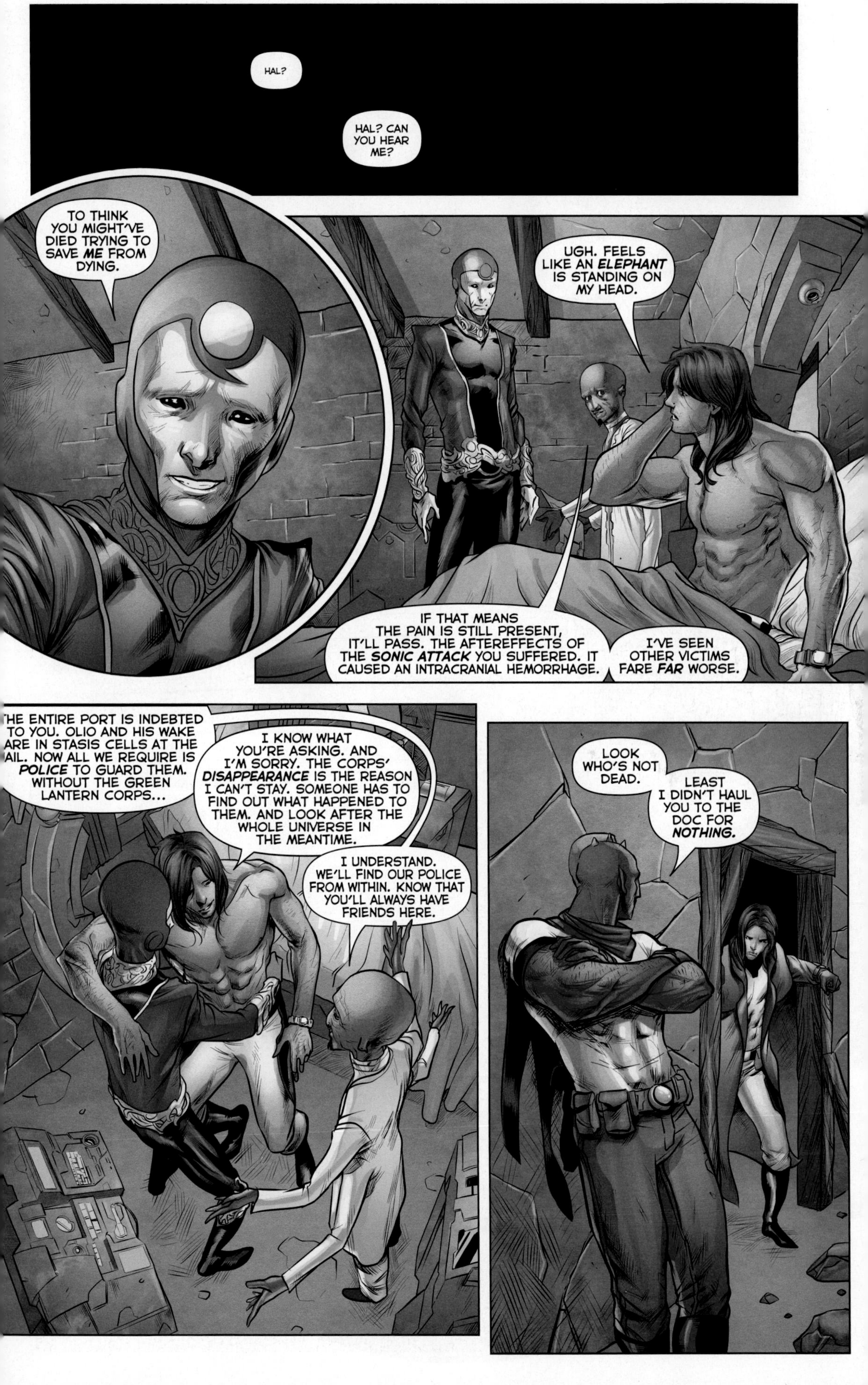
HAL?
HAL? CAN YOU HEAR ME?
TO THINK YOU MIGHT'VE DIED TRYING TO SAVE ME FROM DYING.
UGH. FEELS LIKE AN ELEPHANT IS STANDING ON MY HEAD.
IF THAT MEANS THE PAIN IS STILL PRESENT, IT'LL PASS. THE AFTEREFFECTS OF THE SONIC ATTACK YOU SUFFERED. IT CAUSED AN INTRACRANIAL HEMORRHAGE.
I'VE SEEN OTHER VICTIMS FARE FAR WORSE.
THE ENTIRE PORT IS INDEBTED TO YOU. OLIO AND HIS WAKE ARE IN STASIS CELLS AT THE AIL. NOW ALL WE REQUIRE IS POLICE TO GUARD THEM. WITHOUT THE GREEN LANTERN CORPS...
I KNOW WHAT YOU'RE ASKING. AND I'M SORRY. THE CORPS' DISAPPEARANCE IS THE REASON I CAN'T STAY. SOMEONE HAS TO FIND OUT WHAT HAPPENED TO THEM. AND LOOK AFTER THE WHOLE UNIVERSE IN THE MEANTIME.
I UNDERSTAND. WE'LL FIND OUR POLICE FROM WITHIN. KNOW THAT YOU'LL ALWAYS HAVE FRIENDS HERE.
LOOK WHO'S NOT DEAD.
LEAST I DIDN'T HAUL YOU TO THE DOC FOR NOTHING.

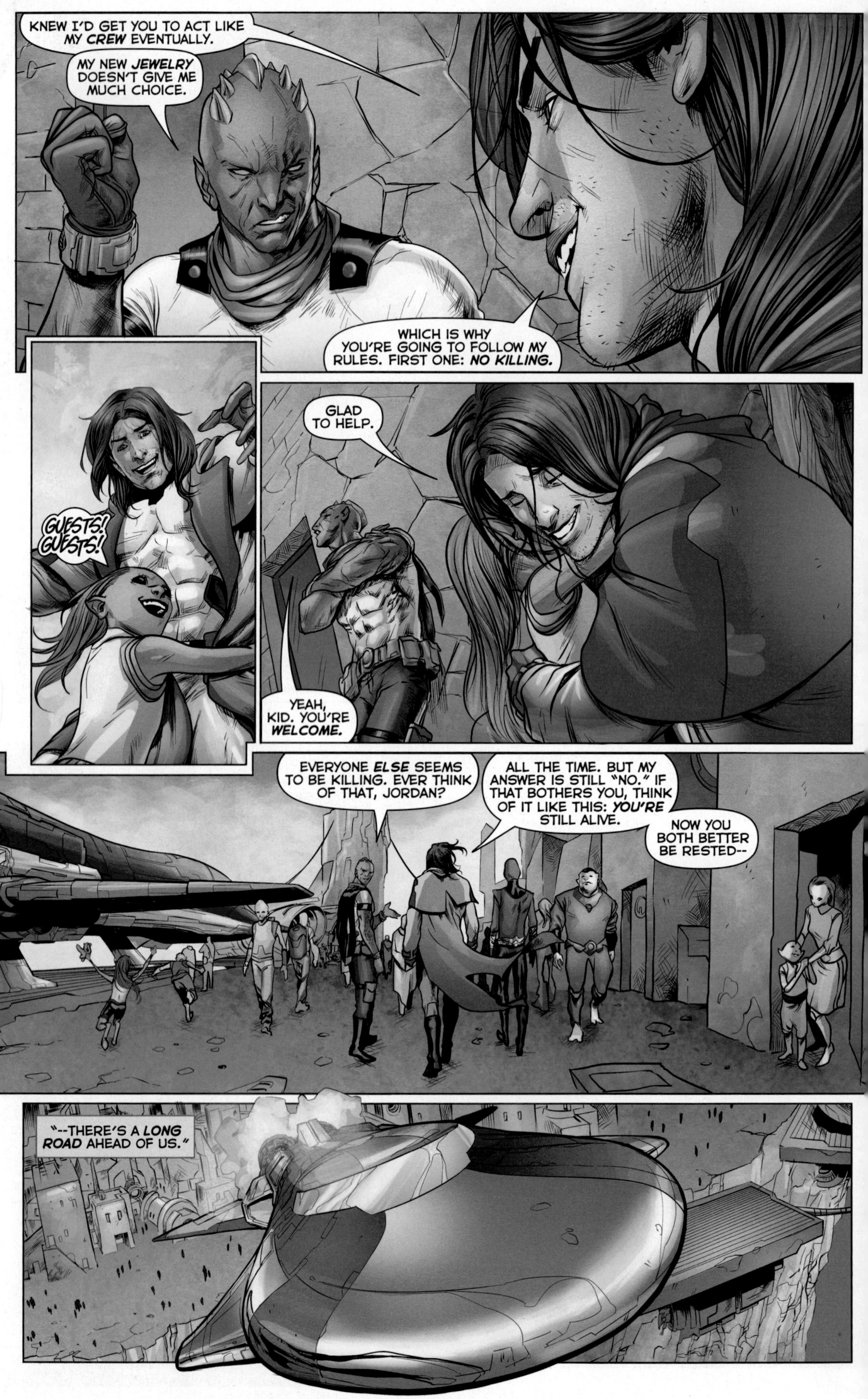
KNEW I'D GET YOU TO ACT LIKE MY CREW EVENTUALLY.
MY NEW JEWELRY DOESN'T GIVE ME MUCH CHOICE.
WHICH IS WHY YOU'RE GOING TO FOLLOW MY RULES. FIRST ONE: NO KILLING.
GUESTS! GUESTS!
GLAD TO HELP.
YEAH, KID. YOU'RE WELCOME.
EVERYONE ELSE SEEMS TO BE KILLING. EVER THINK OF THAT, JORDAN?
ALL THE TIME. BUT MY ANSWER IS STILL "NO." IF THAT BOTHERS YOU, THINK OF IT LIKE THIS: YOU'RE STILL ALIVE.
NOW YOU BOTH BETTER BE RESTED--
"--THERE'S A LONG ROAD AHEAD OF US."

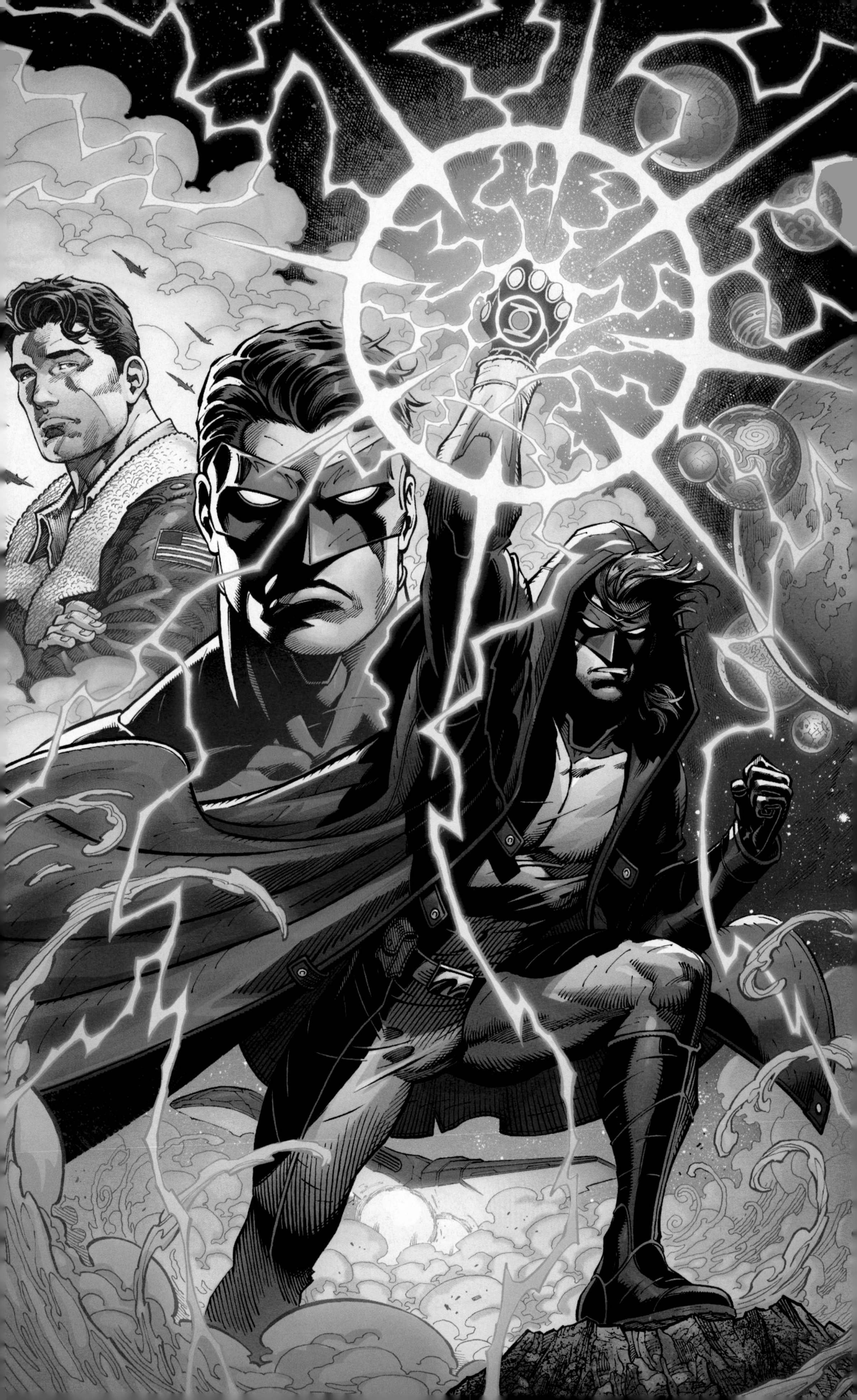

IN THE GRAY

ROBERT VENDITTI writer PASCAL ALIXE & MARTIN COCCOLO artists TONY AVIÑA, PETE PANTAZIS & HI-FI colorists DAVE SHARPE letterer IAN CHURCHILL & HI-FI cover

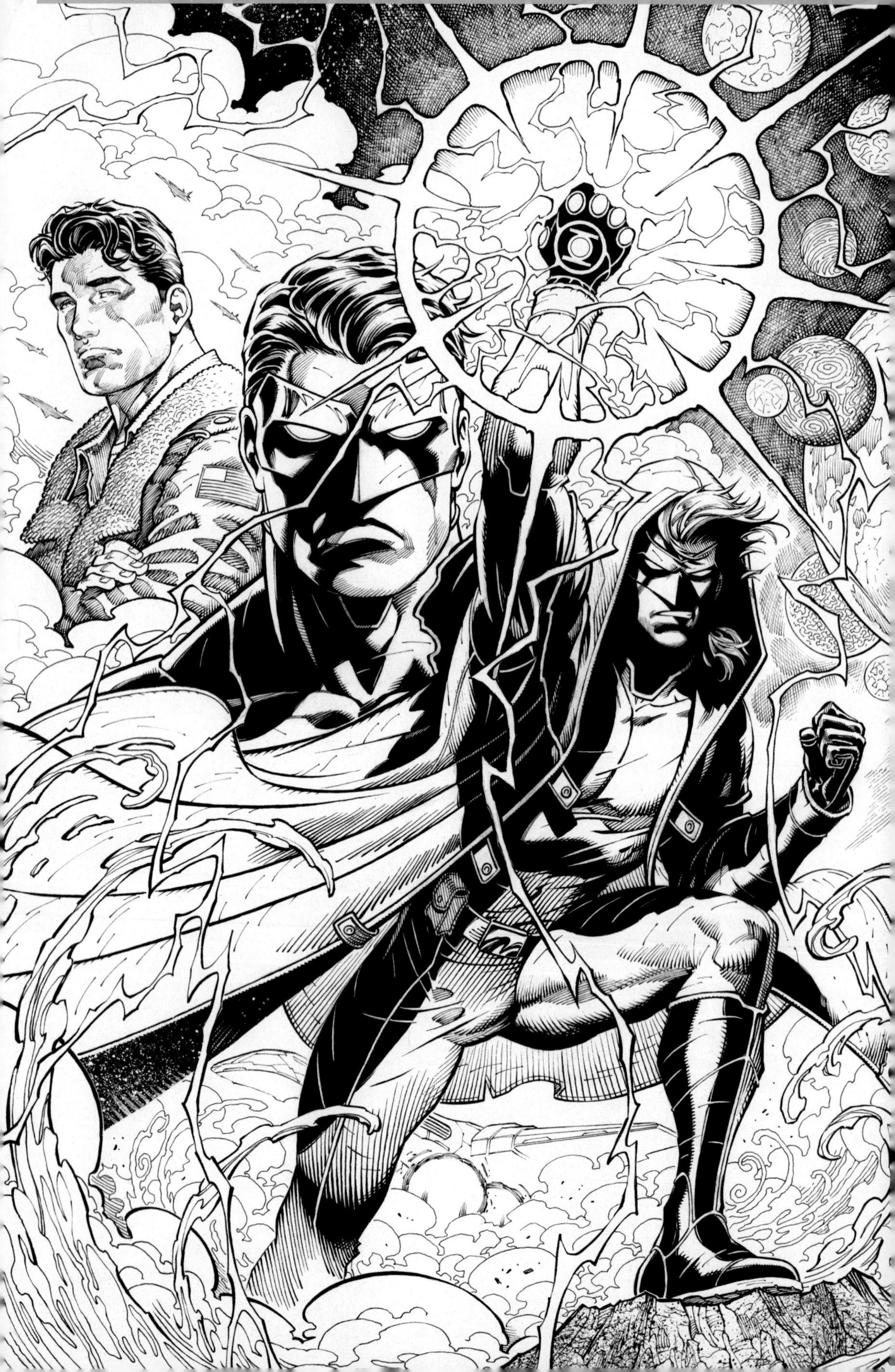

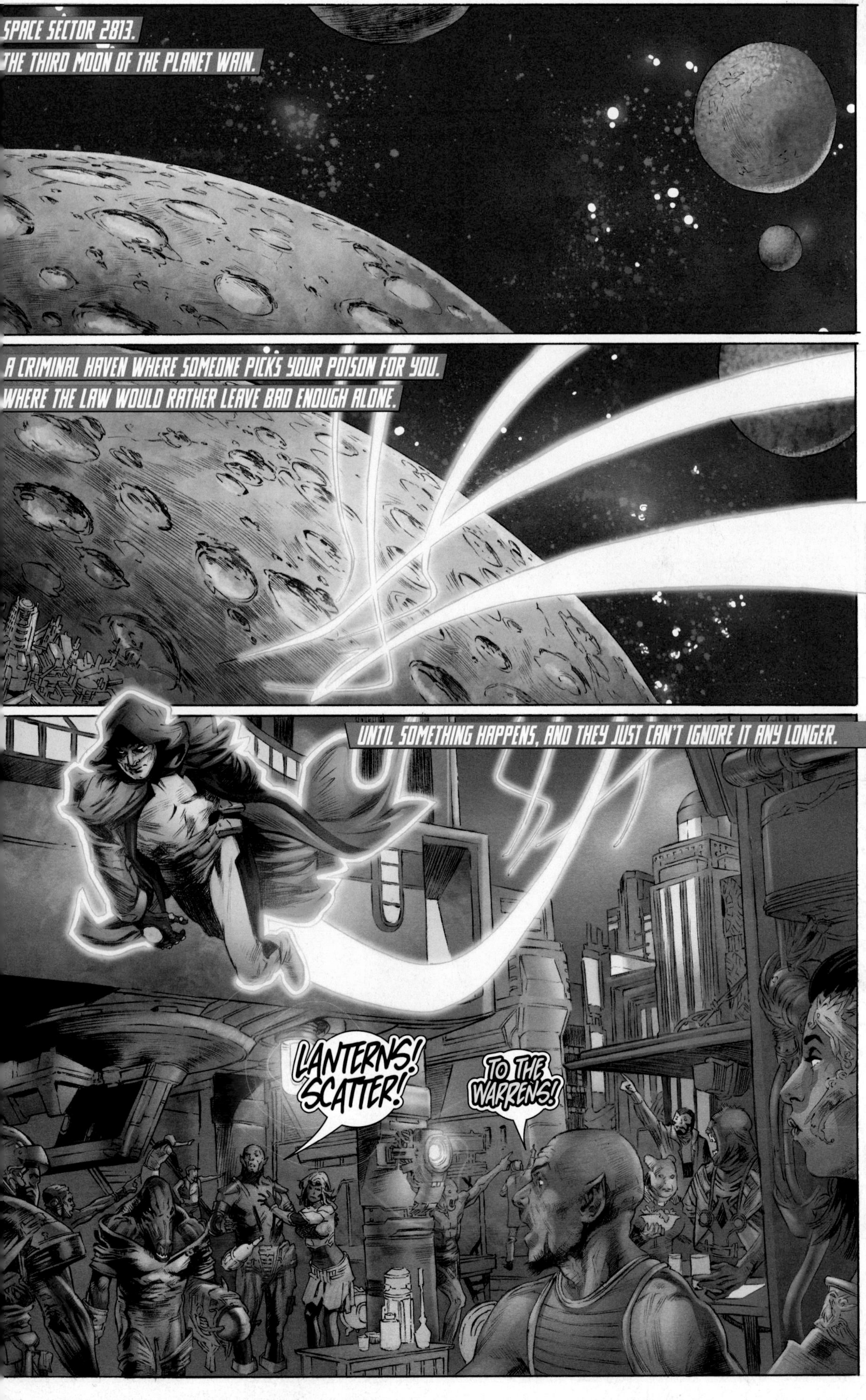
SPACE SECTOR 2813.
THE THIRD MOON OF THE PLANET WAIN.
A CRIMINAL HAVEN WHERE SOMEONE PICKS YOUR POISON FOR YOU.
WHERE THE LAW WOULD RATHER LEAVE BAD ENOUGH ALONE.
UNTIL SOMETHING HAPPENS, AND THEY JUST CAN'T IGNORE IT ANY LONGER.
LANTERNS! SCATTER!
TO THE WARRENS!

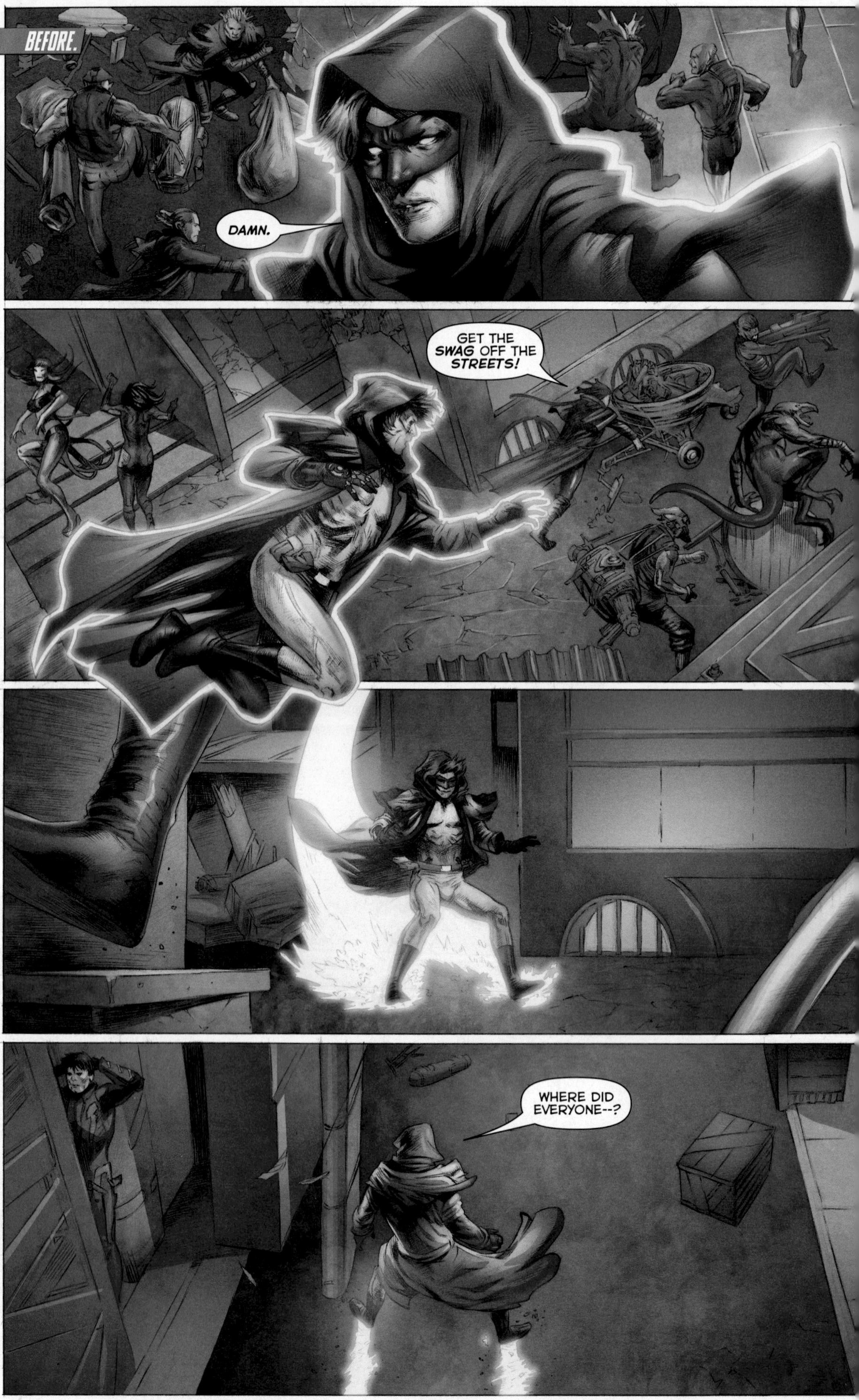
BEFORE.
DAMN.
GET THE SWAG OFF THE STREETS!
WHERE DID EVERYONE--?

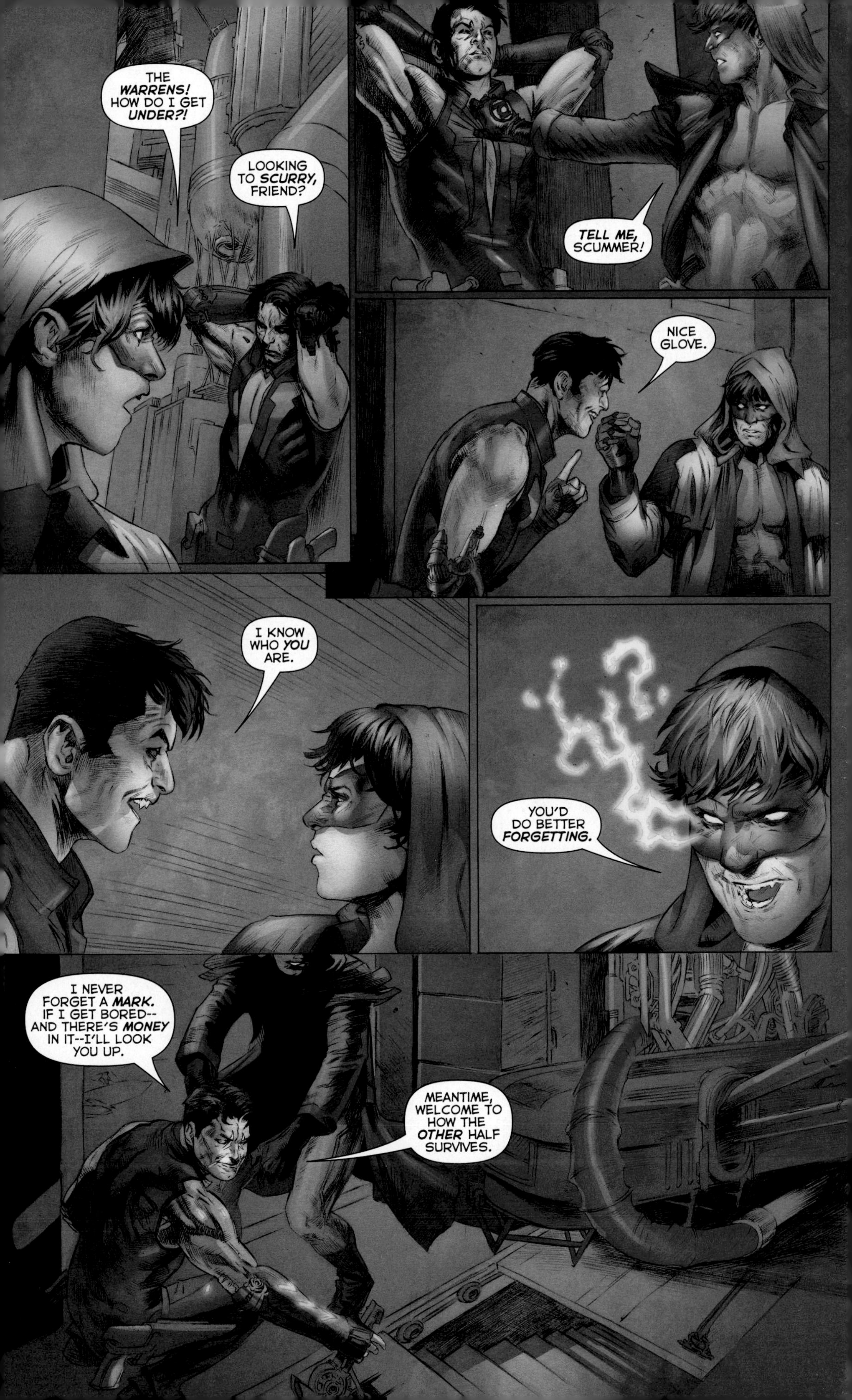
THE WARRENS! HOW DO I GET UNDER?!
LOOKING TO SCURRY, FRIEND?
TELL ME, SCUMMER!
NICE GLOVE.
I KNOW WHO YOU ARE.
YOU'D DO BETTER FORGETTING.
I NEVER FORGET A MARK. IF I GET BORED-- AND THERE'S MONEY IN IT--I'LL LOOK YOU UP.
MEANTIME, WELCOME TO HOW THE OTHER HALF SURVIVES.

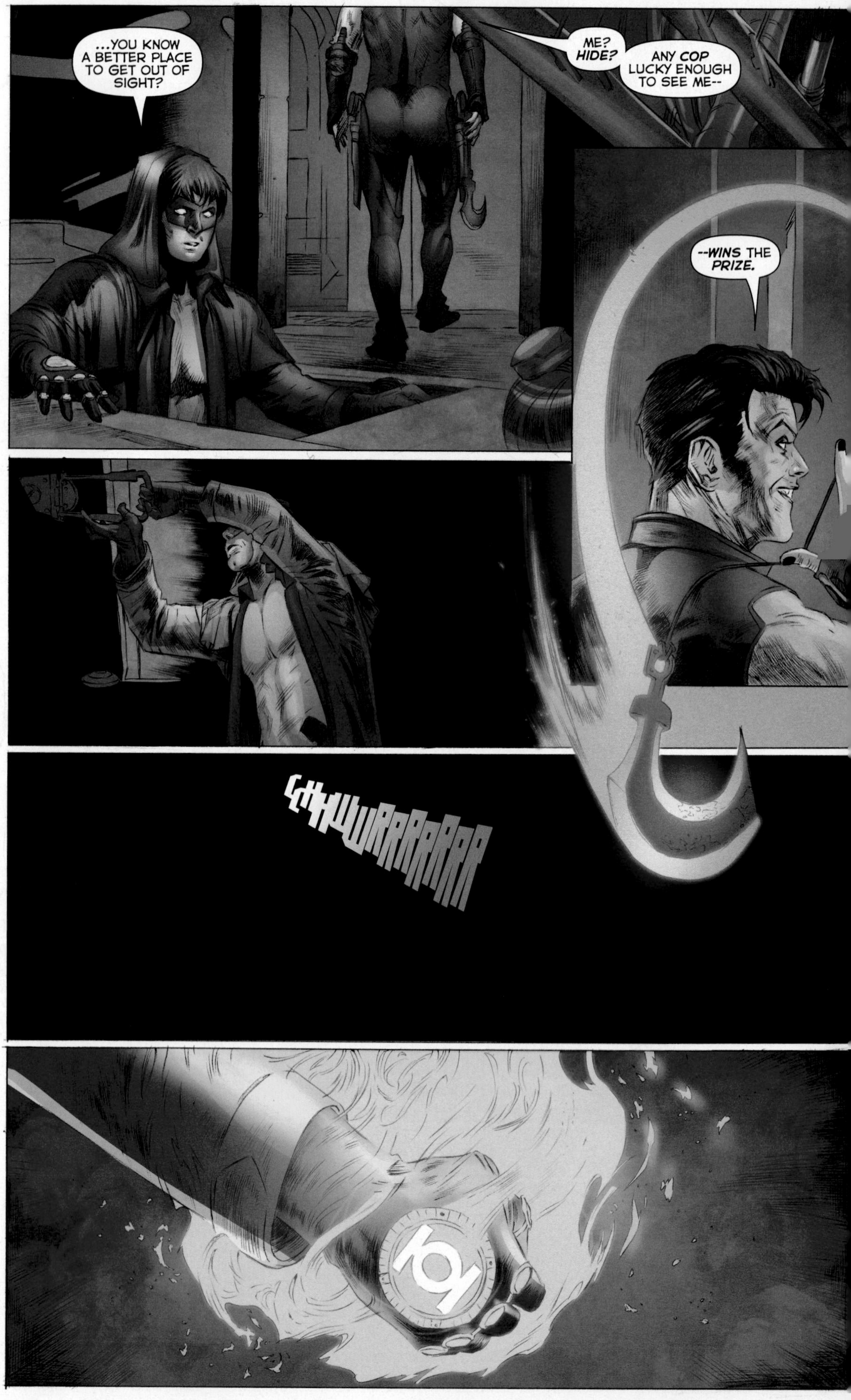
...YOU KNOW A BETTER PLACE TO GET OUT OF SIGHT?
ME? HIDE?
ANY COP LUCKY ENOUGH TO SEE ME--
--WINS THE PRIZE.
CHHWURRRRRRR

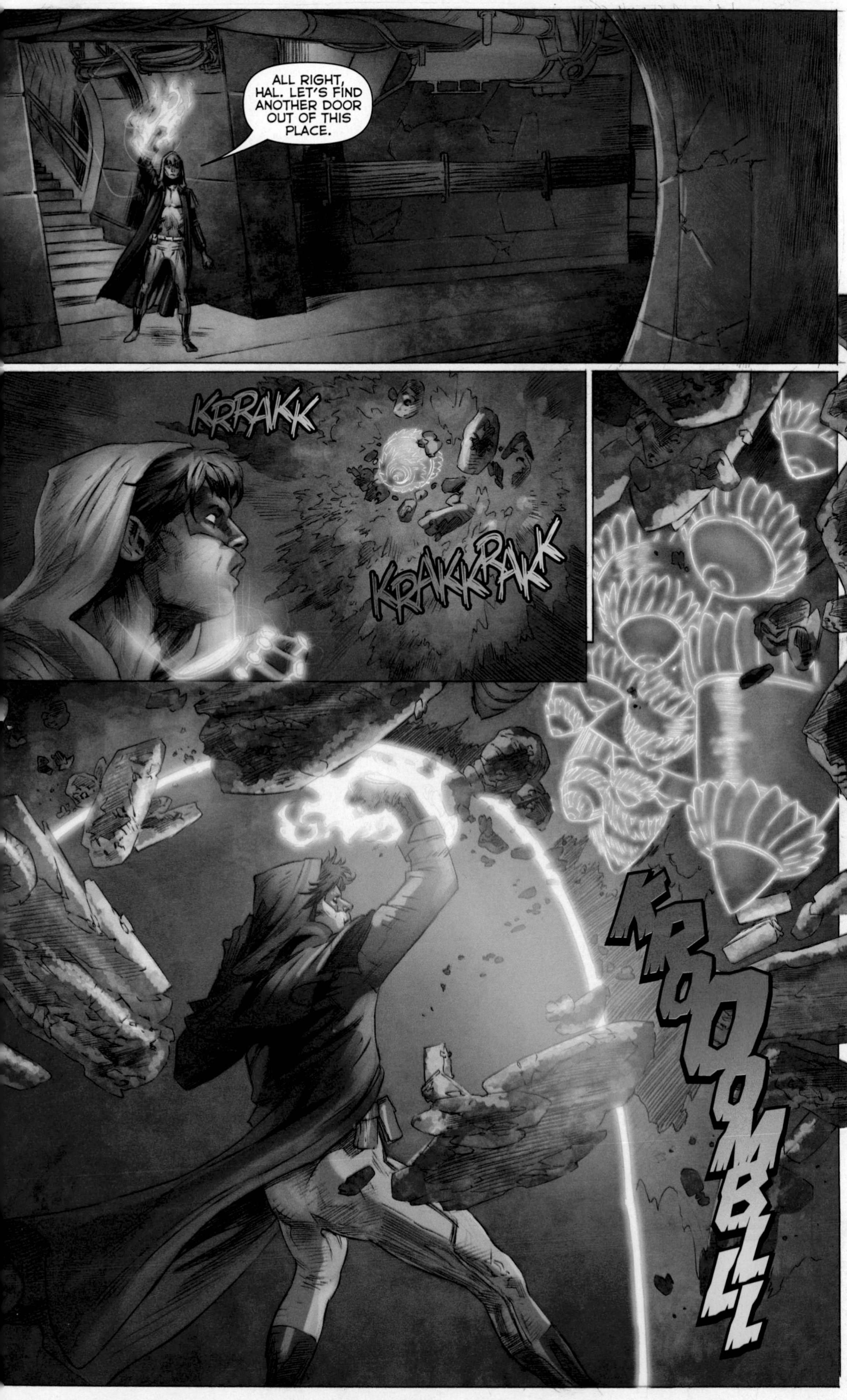
ALL RIGHT, HAL. LET'S FIND ANOTHER DOOR OUT OF THIS PLACE.
KRRAKK
KRAKKRAKK
KROOOMBLLL

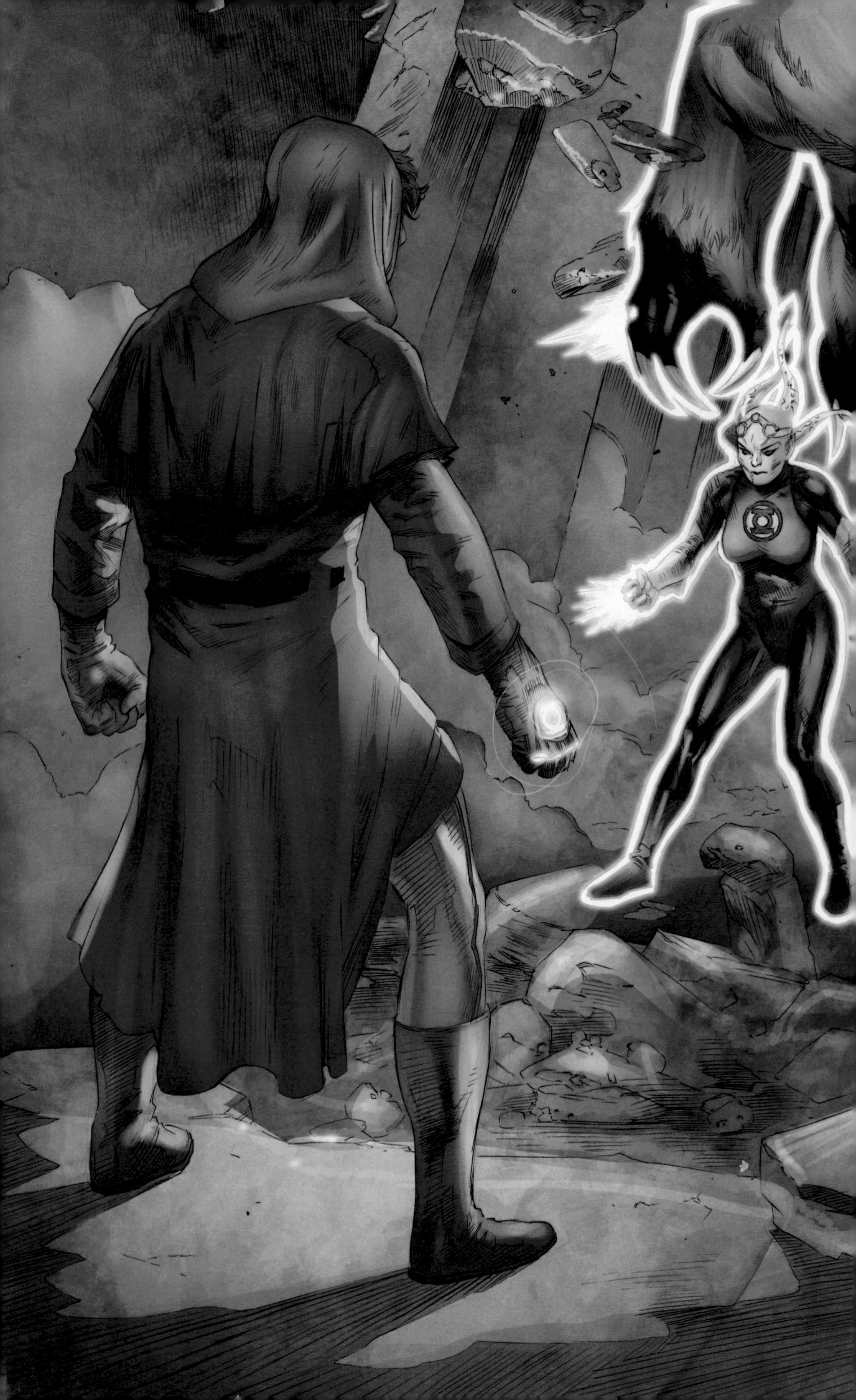

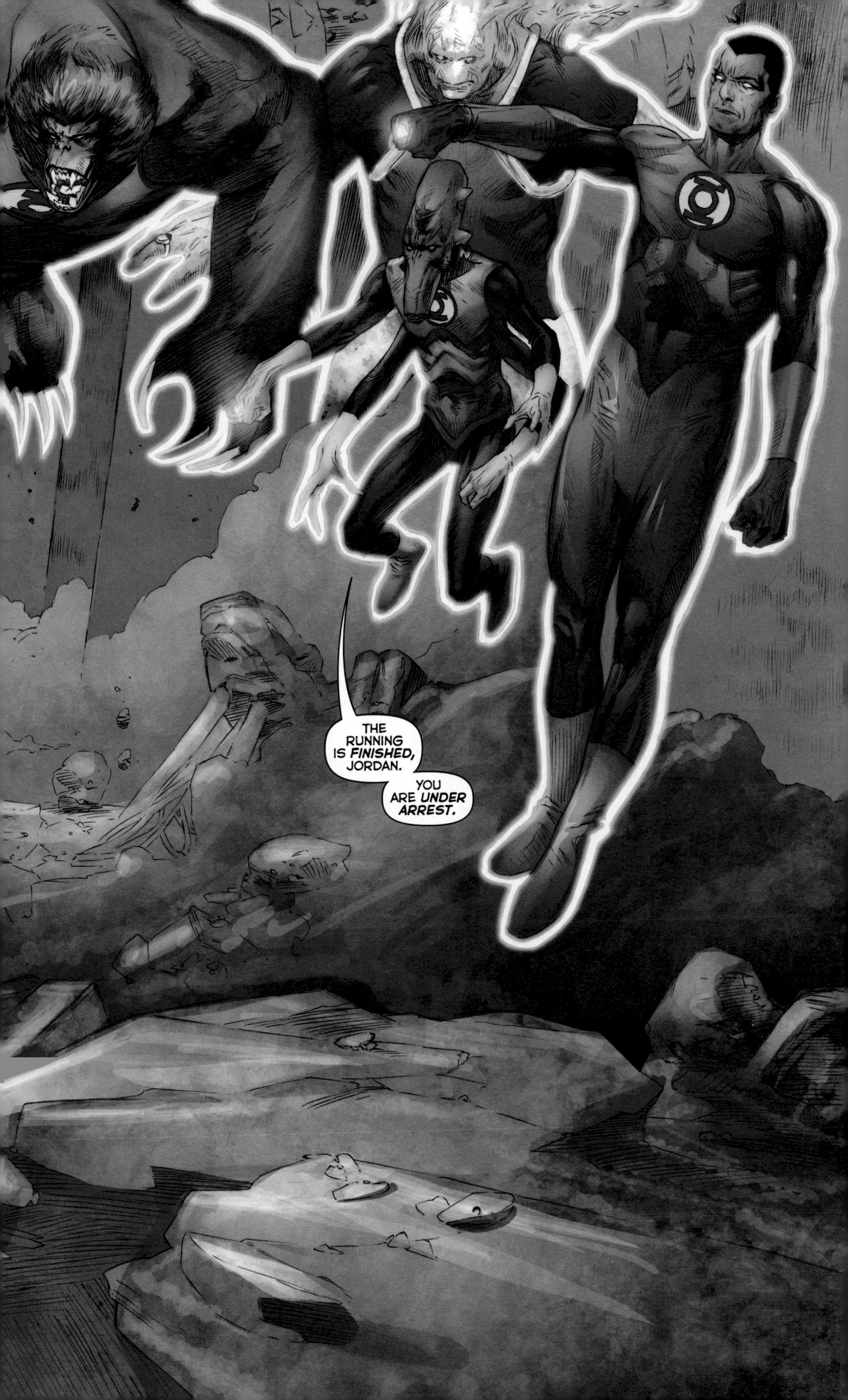
THE RUNNING IS *FINISHED*, JORDAN.
YOU ARE *UNDER ARREST.*

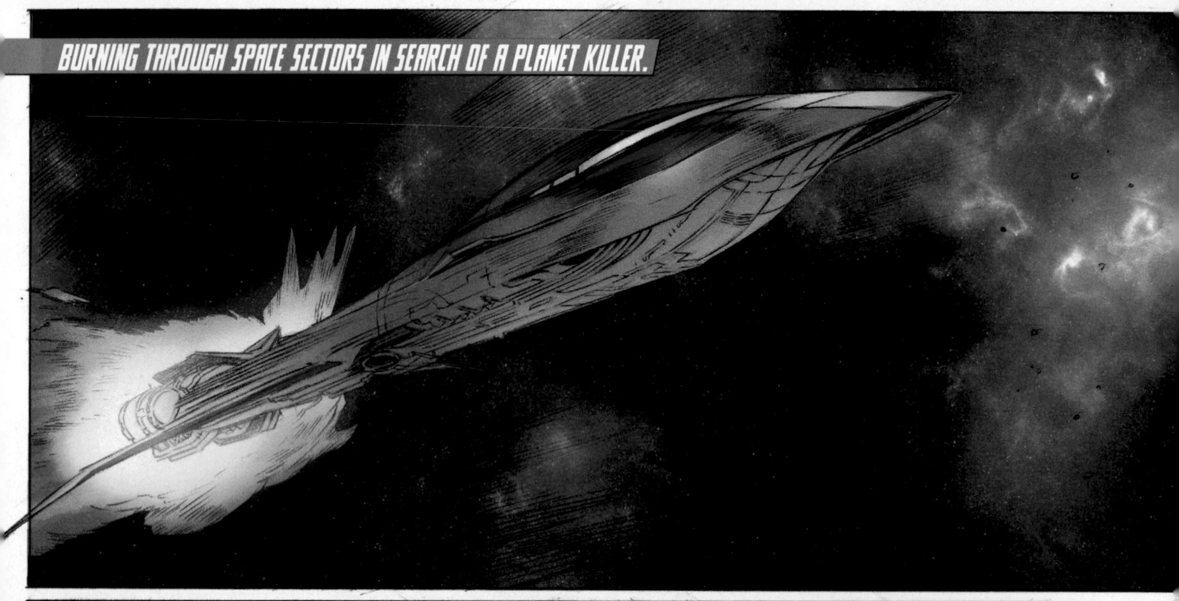
BURNING THROUGH SPACE SECTORS IN SEARCH OF A PLANET KILLER.

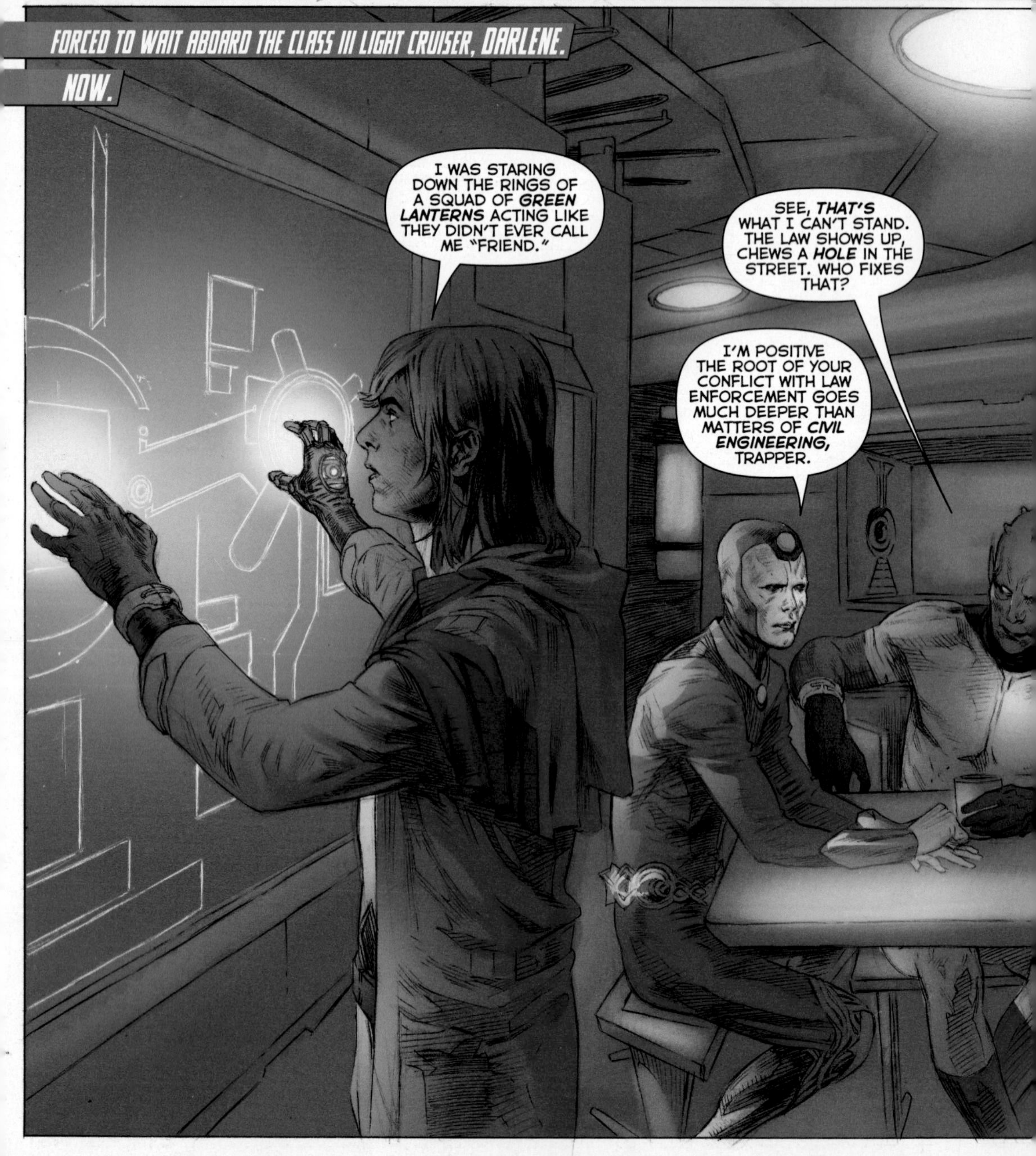
FORCED TO WAIT ABOARD THE CLASS III LIGHT CRUISER, DARLENE.
NOW.
I WAS STARING DOWN THE RINGS OF A SQUAD OF GREEN LANTERNS ACTING LIKE THEY DIDN'T EVER CALL ME "FRIEND."
SEE, THAT'S WHAT I CAN'T STAND. THE LAW SHOWS UP, CHEWS A HOLE IN THE STREET. WHO FIXES THAT?
I'M POSITIVE THE ROOT OF YOUR CONFLICT WITH LAW ENFORCEMENT GOES MUCH DEEPER THAN MATTERS OF CIVIL ENGINEERING, TRAPPER.

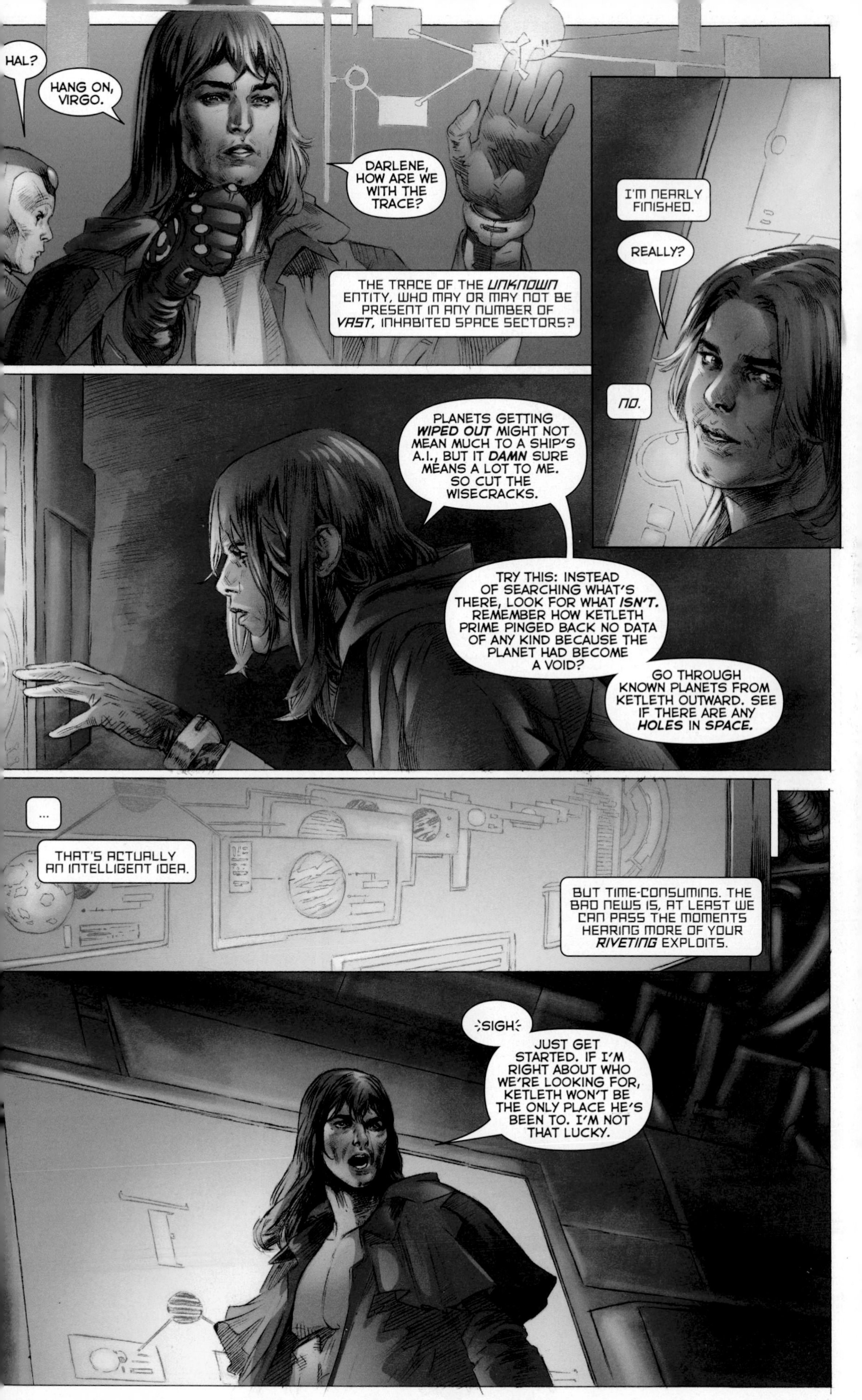
HAL?
HANG ON, VIRGO.
DARLENE, HOW ARE WE WITH THE TRACE?
THE TRACE OF THE UNKNOWN ENTITY, WHO MAY OR MAY NOT BE PRESENT IN ANY NUMBER OF VAST, INHABITED SPACE SECTORS?
I'M NEARLY FINISHED.
REALLY?
NO.
PLANETS GETTING WIPED OUT MIGHT NOT MEAN MUCH TO A SHIP'S A.I., BUT IT DAMN SURE MEANS A LOT TO ME. SO CUT THE WISECRACKS.
TRY THIS: INSTEAD OF SEARCHING WHAT'S THERE, LOOK FOR WHAT ISN'T. REMEMBER HOW KETLETH PRIME PINGED BACK NO DATA OF ANY KIND BECAUSE THE PLANET HAD BECOME A VOID?
GO THROUGH KNOWN PLANETS FROM KETLETH OUTWARD. SEE IF THERE ARE ANY HOLES IN SPACE.
...
THAT'S ACTUALLY AN INTELLIGENT IDEA.
BUT TIME-CONSUMING. THE BAD NEWS IS, AT LEAST WE CAN PASS THE MOMENTS HEARING MORE OF YOUR RIVETING EXPLOITS.
SIGH
JUST GET STARTED. IF I'M RIGHT ABOUT WHO WE'RE LOOKING FOR, KETLETH WON'T BE THE ONLY PLACE HE'S BEEN TO. I'M NOT THAT LUCKY.

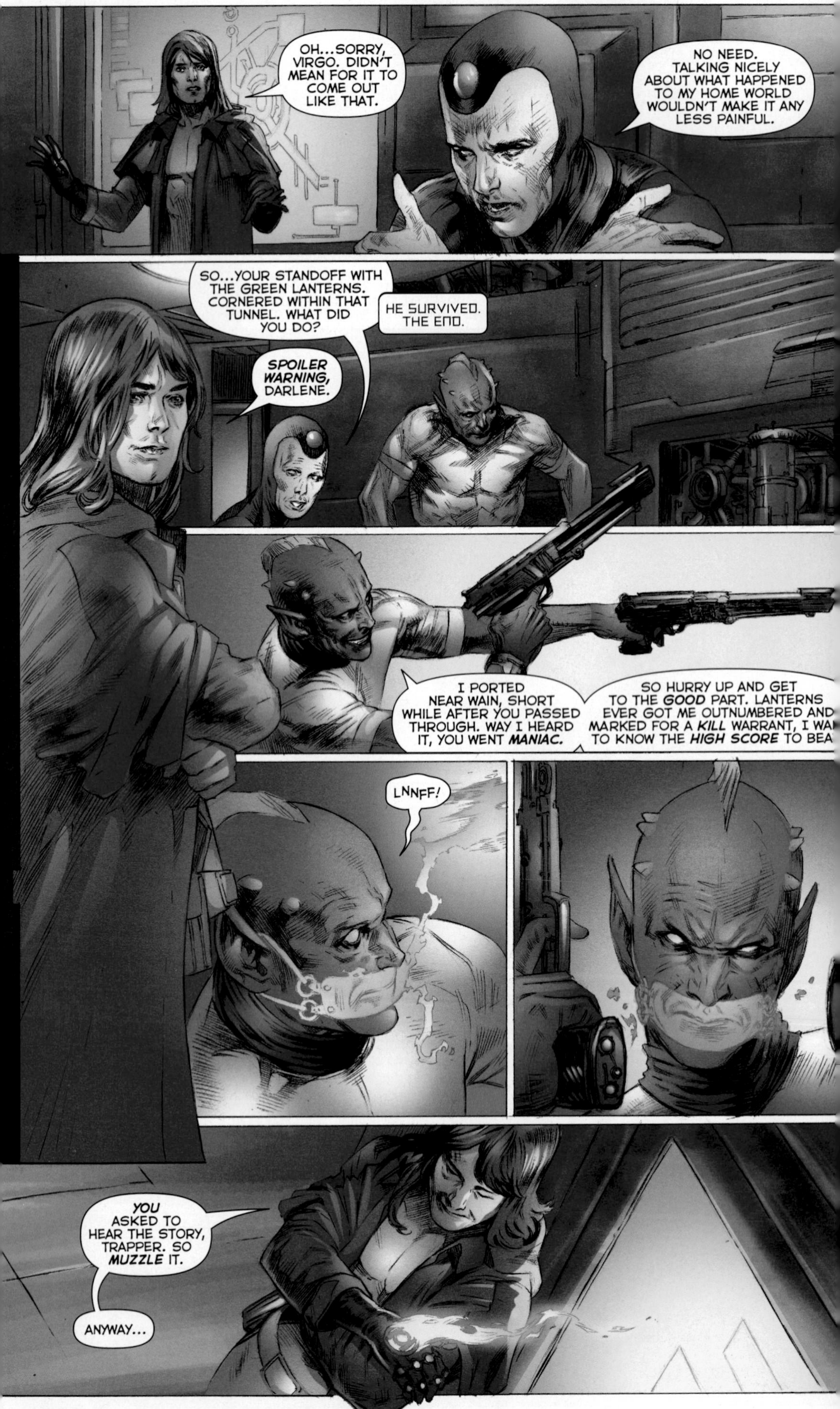
OH...SORRY, VIRGO. DIDN'T MEAN FOR IT TO COME OUT LIKE THAT.
NO NEED. TALKING NICELY ABOUT WHAT HAPPENED TO MY HOME WORLD WOULDN'T MAKE IT ANY LESS PAINFUL.
SO...YOUR STANDOFF WITH THE GREEN LANTERNS. CORNERED WITHIN THAT TUNNEL. WHAT DID YOU DO?
HE SURVIVED. THE END.
SPOILER WARNING, DARLENE.
I PORTED NEAR WAIN, SHORT WHILE AFTER YOU PASSED THROUGH. WAY I HEARD IT, YOU WENT MANIAC.
SO HURRY UP AND GET TO THE GOOD PART. LANTERNS EVER GOT ME OUTNUMBERED AND MARKED FOR A KILL WARRANT, I WA
TO KNOW THE HIGH SCORE TO BEA
LNNFF!
YOU ASKED TO HEAR THE STORY, TRAPPER. SO MUZZLE IT.
ANYWAY...

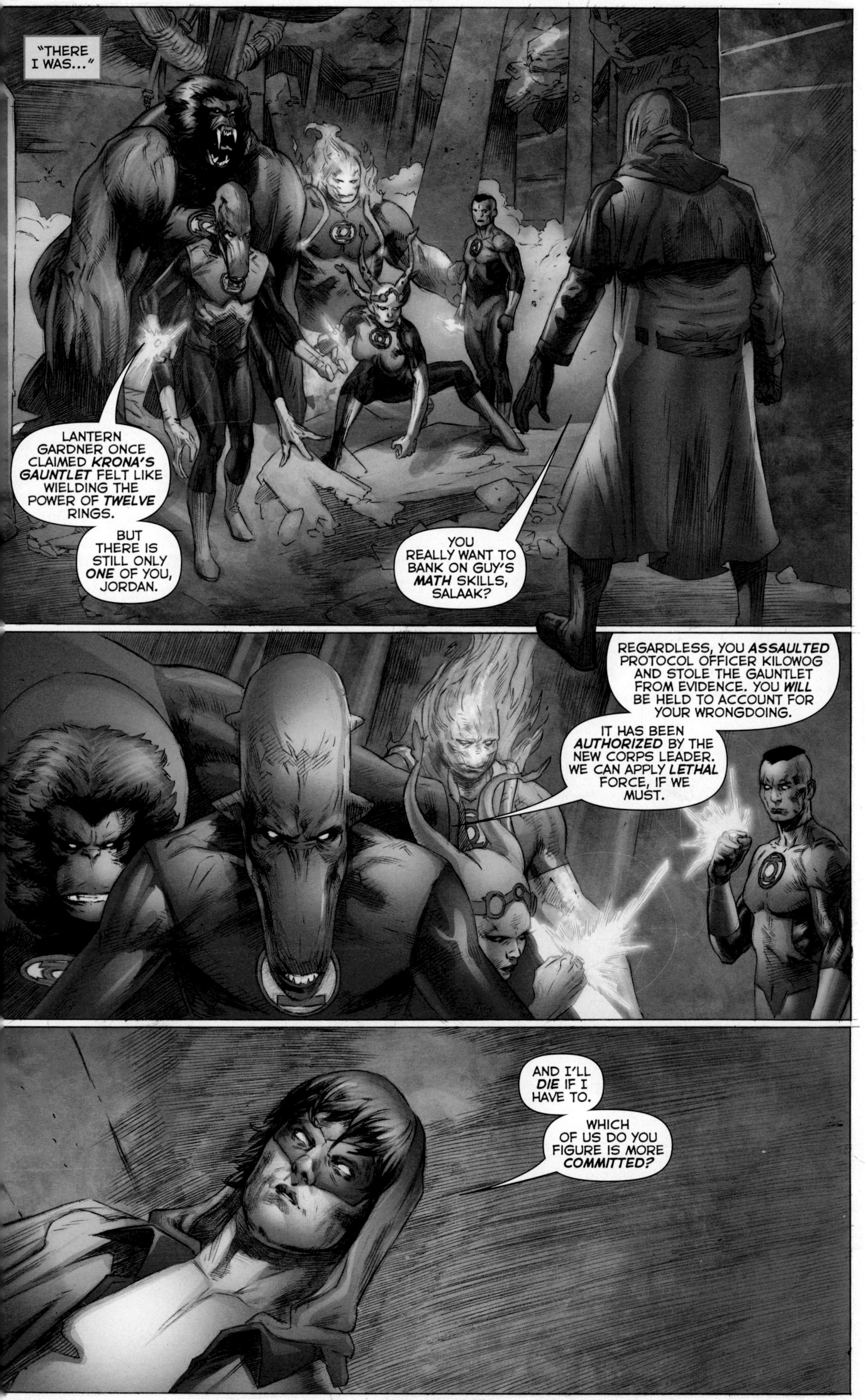
"THERE I WAS..."
LANTERN GARDNER ONCE CLAIMED KRONA'S GAUNTLET FELT LIKE WIELDING THE POWER OF TWELVE RINGS.
BUT THERE IS STILL ONLY ONE OF YOU, JORDAN.
YOU REALLY WANT TO BANK ON GUY'S MATH SKILLS, SALAAK?
REGARDLESS, YOU ASSAULTED PROTOCOL OFFICER KILOWOG AND STOLE THE GAUNTLET FROM EVIDENCE. YOU WILL BE HELD TO ACCOUNT FOR YOUR WRONGDOING.
IT HAS BEEN AUTHORIZED BY THE NEW CORPS LEADER. WE CAN APPLY LETHAL FORCE, IF WE MUST.
AND I'LL DIE IF I HAVE TO.
WHICH OF US DO YOU FIGURE IS MORE COMMITTED?

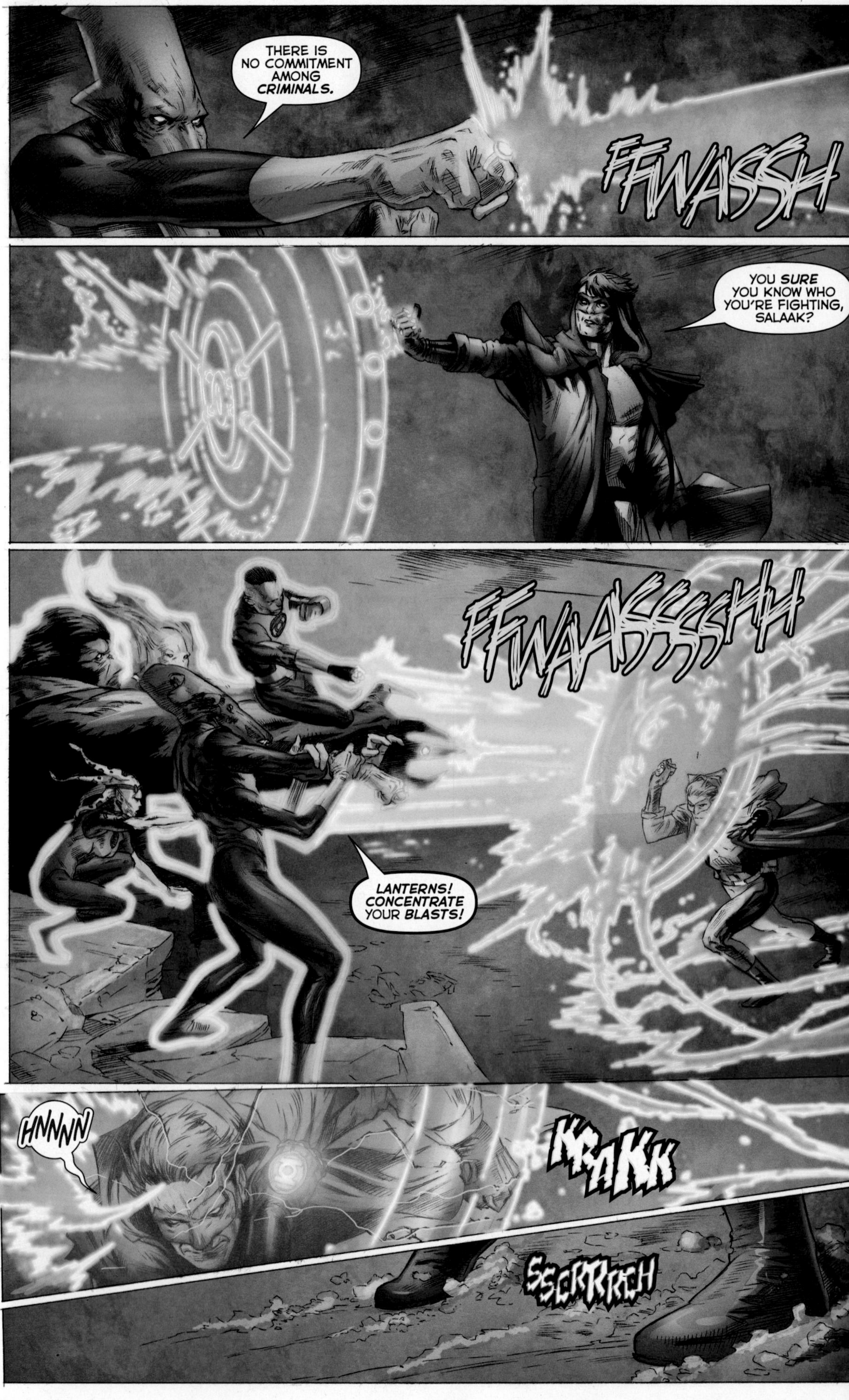
THERE IS NO COMMITMENT AMONG CRIMINALS.
FFWASSH
YOU SURE YOU KNOW WHO YOU'RE FIGHTING, SALAAK?
FFWAASSSSHH
LANTERNS! CONCENTRATE YOUR BLASTS!
HNNNN
KRAKK
SSCRRRCH

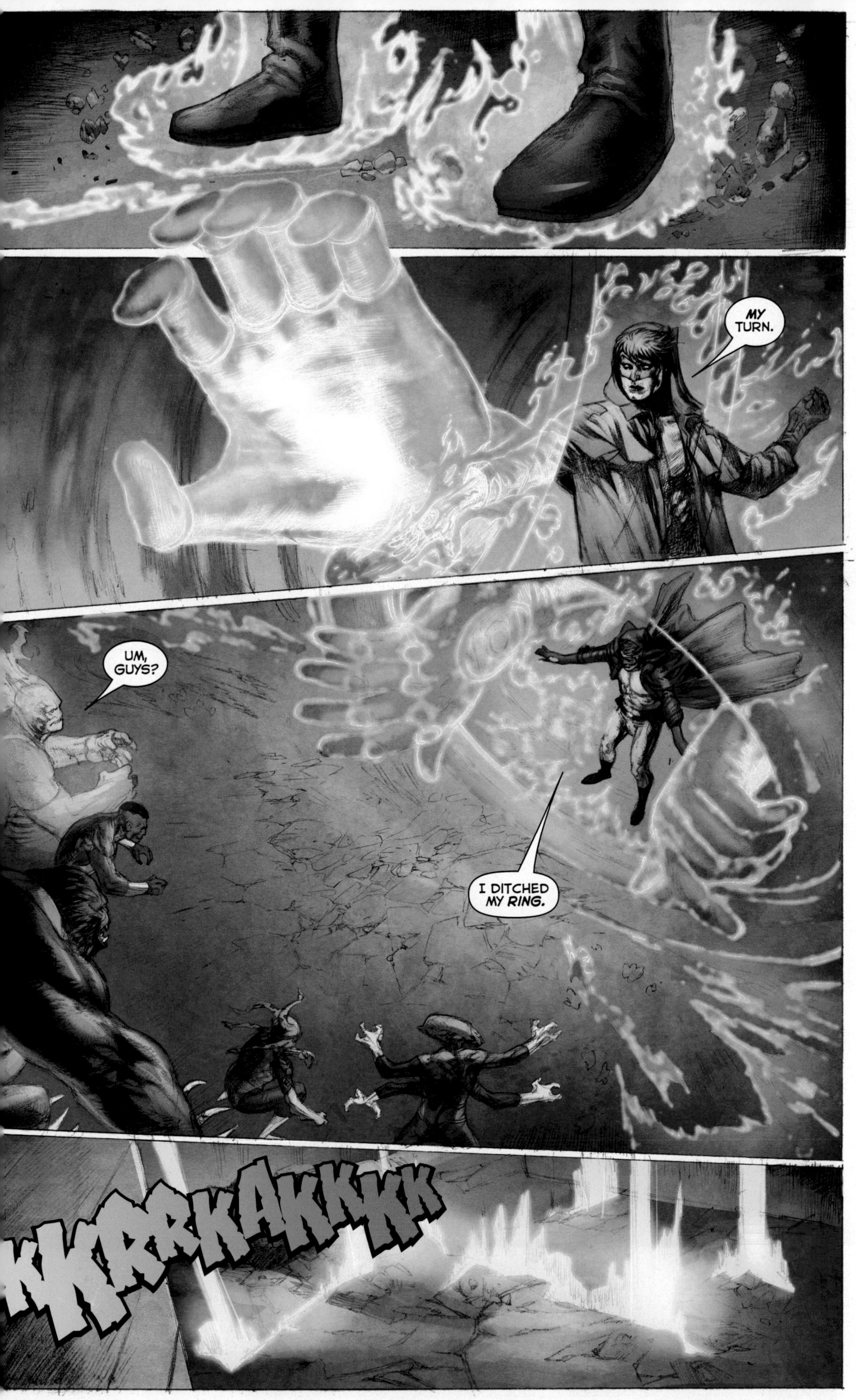
MY TURN.
UM, GUYS?
I DITCHED MY RING.
KKRRKAKKKK

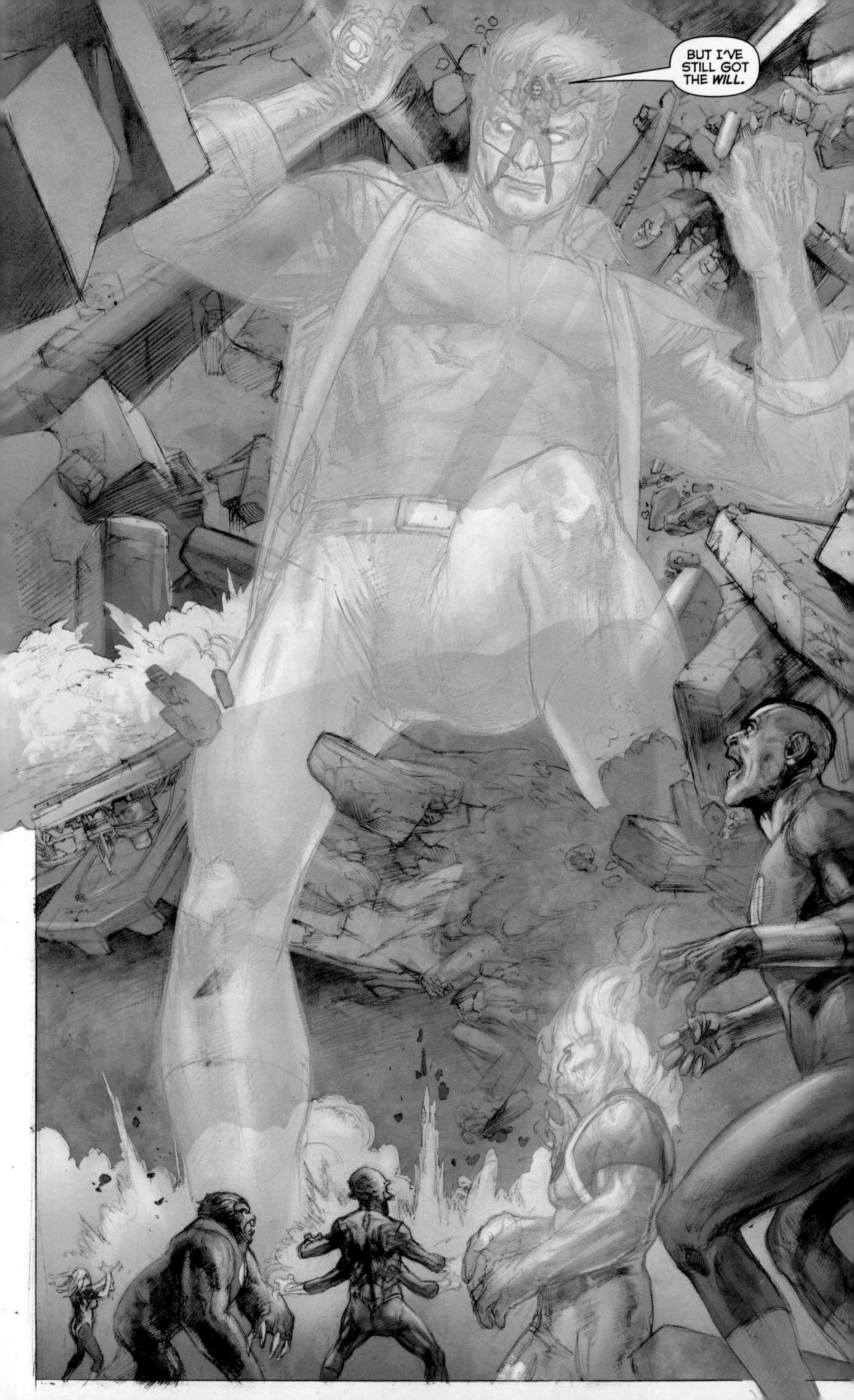
BUT I'VE STILL GOT THE *WILL.*

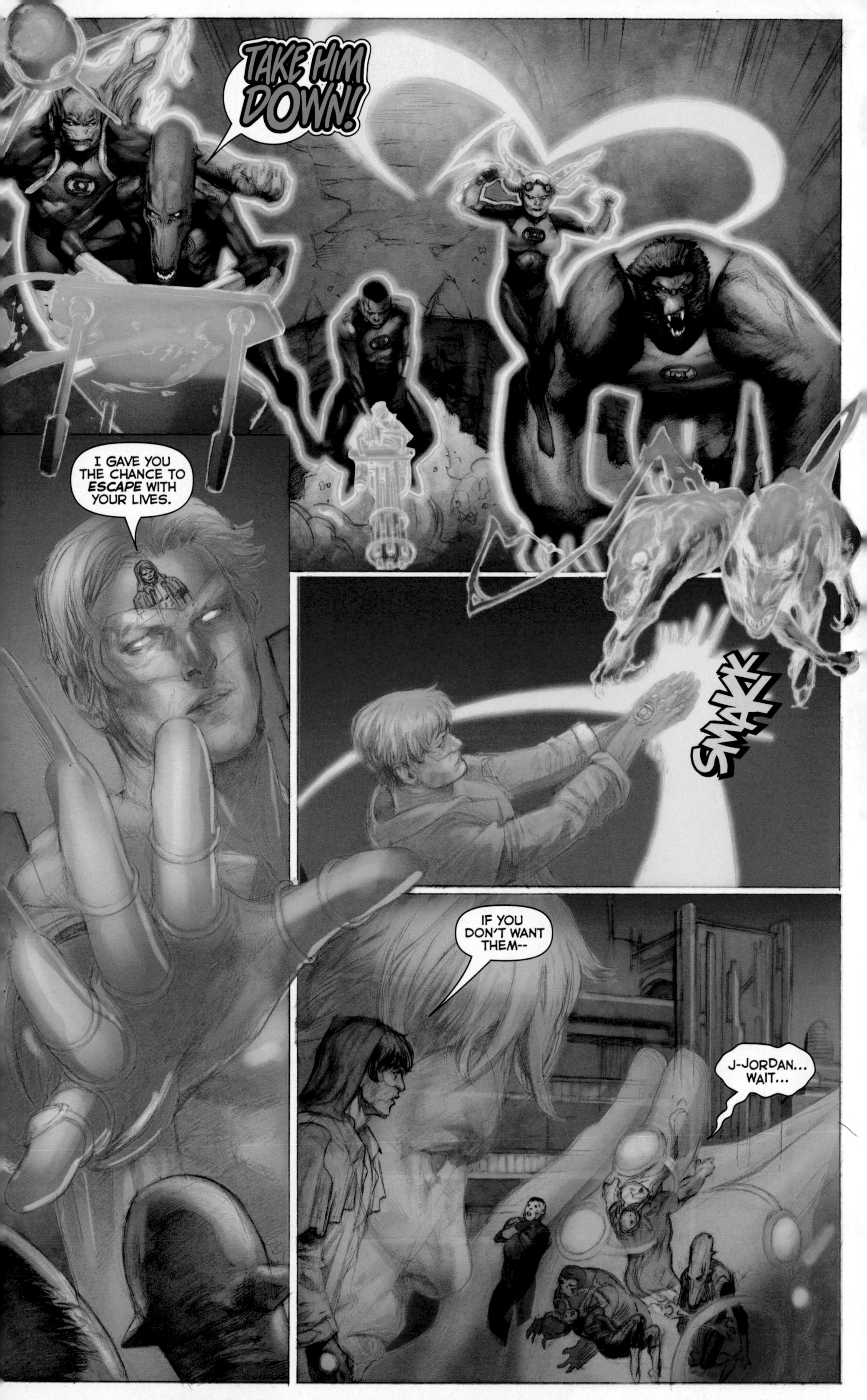
TAKE HIM DOWN!
I GAVE YOU THE CHANCE TO ESCAPE WITH YOUR LIVES.
SMAKK
IF YOU DON'T WANT THEM--
J-JORDAN... WAIT...

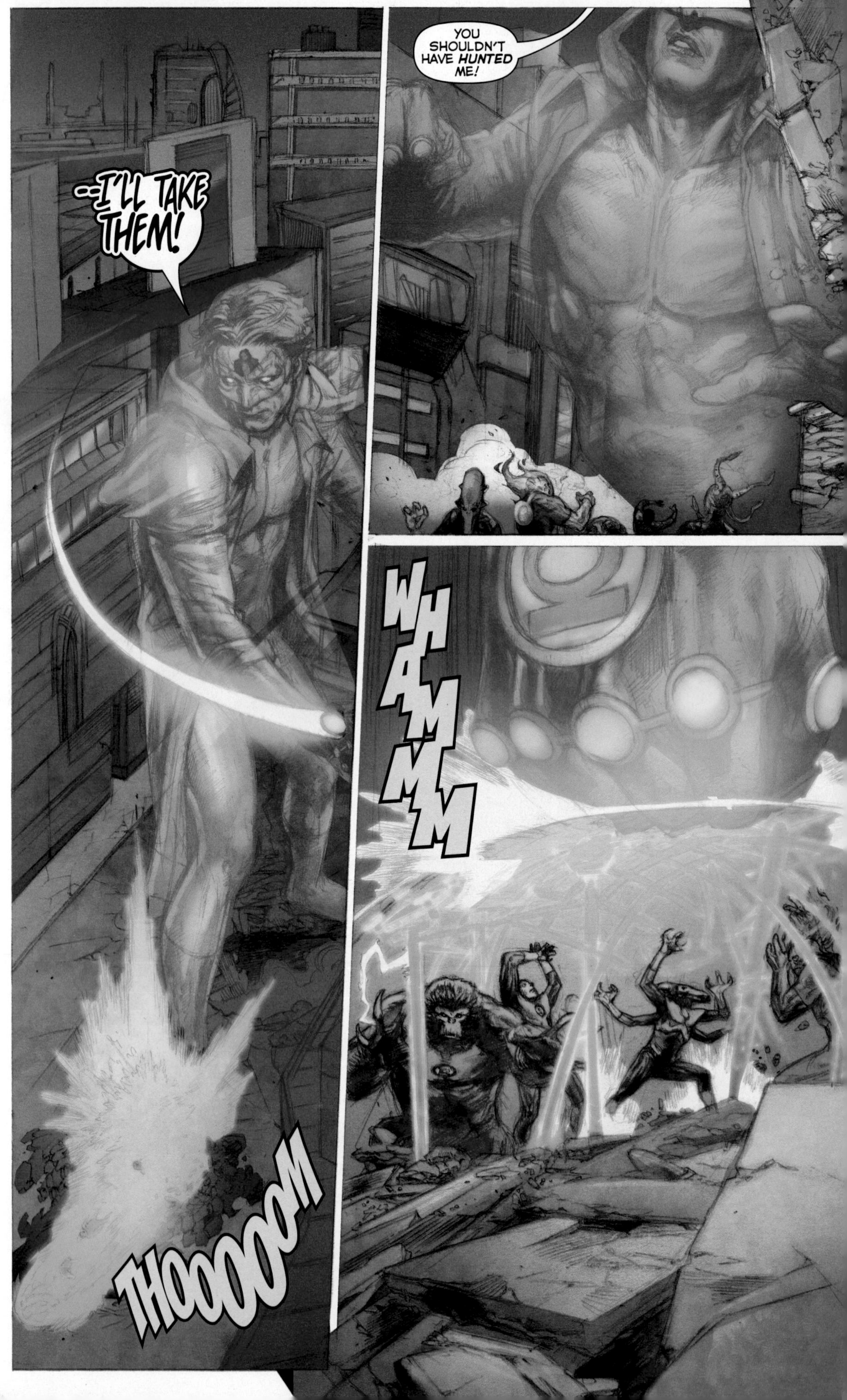
--I'LL TAKE THEM!
YOU SHOULDN'T HAVE HUNTED ME!
THOOOOOM
WHAMMMM

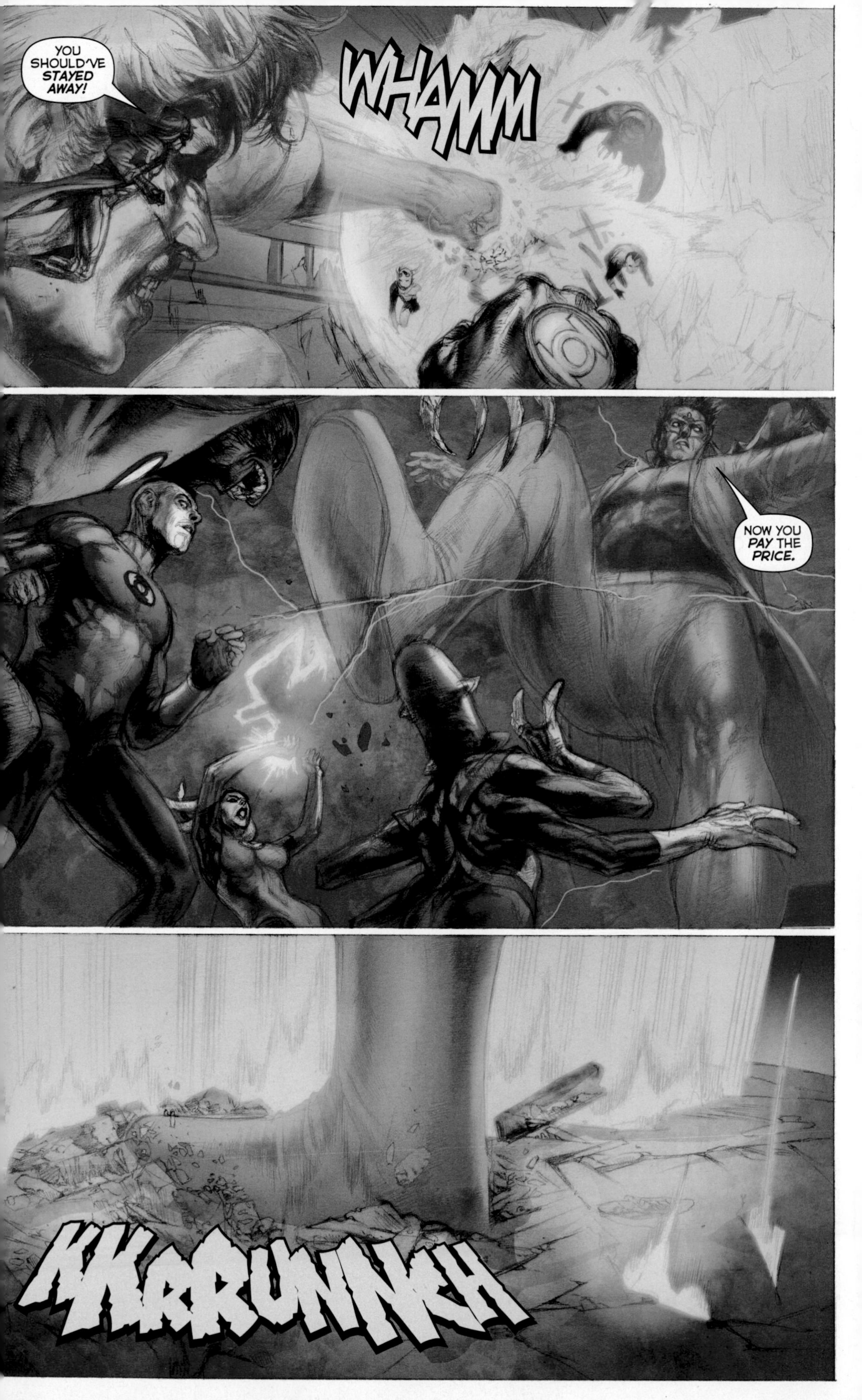
YOU SHOULD'VE STAYED AWAY!
WHAMM
NOW YOU PAY THE PRICE.
KKRRUNNKH

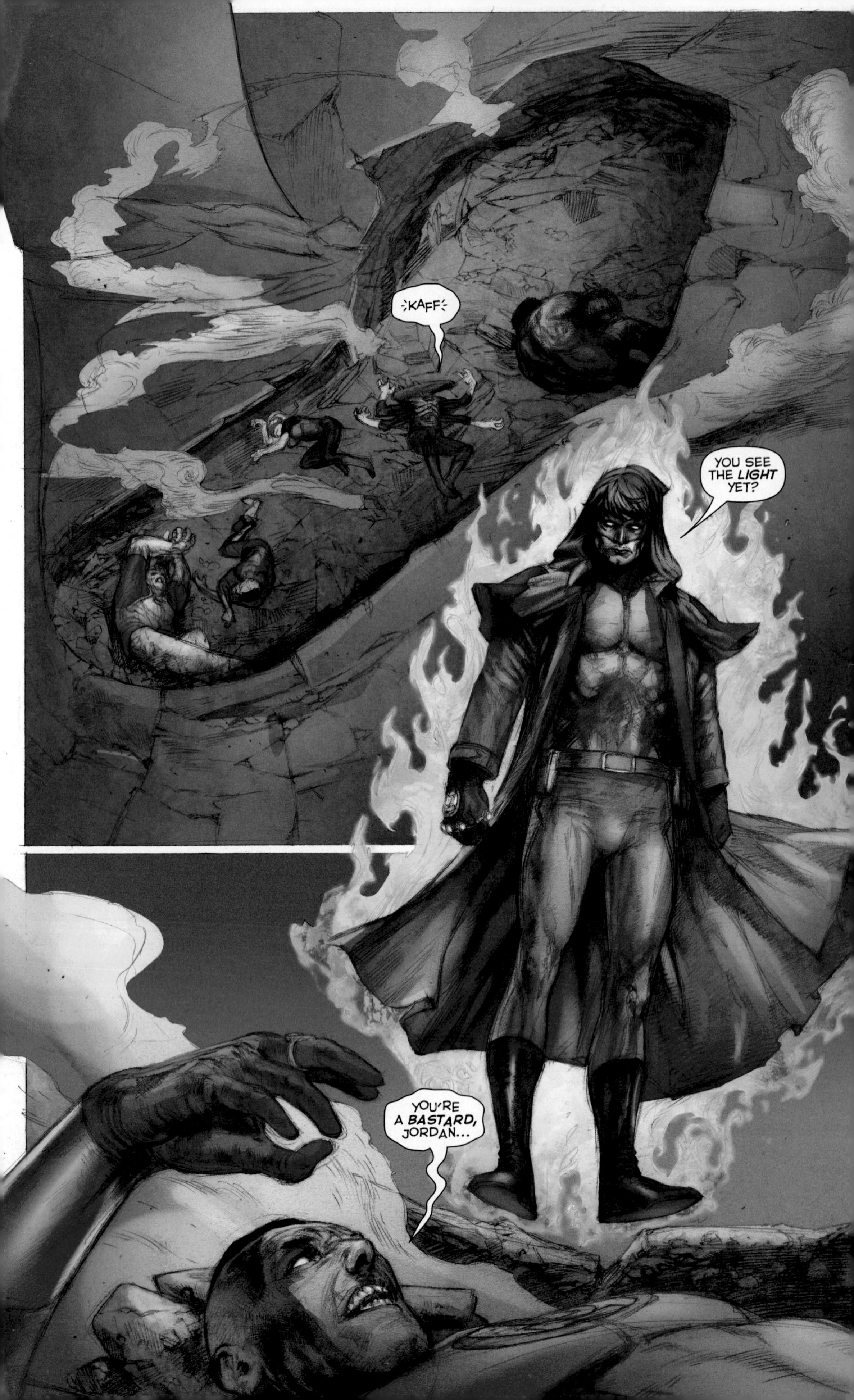
KAFF
YOU SEE THE LIGHT YET?
YOU'RE A BASTARD, JORDAN...

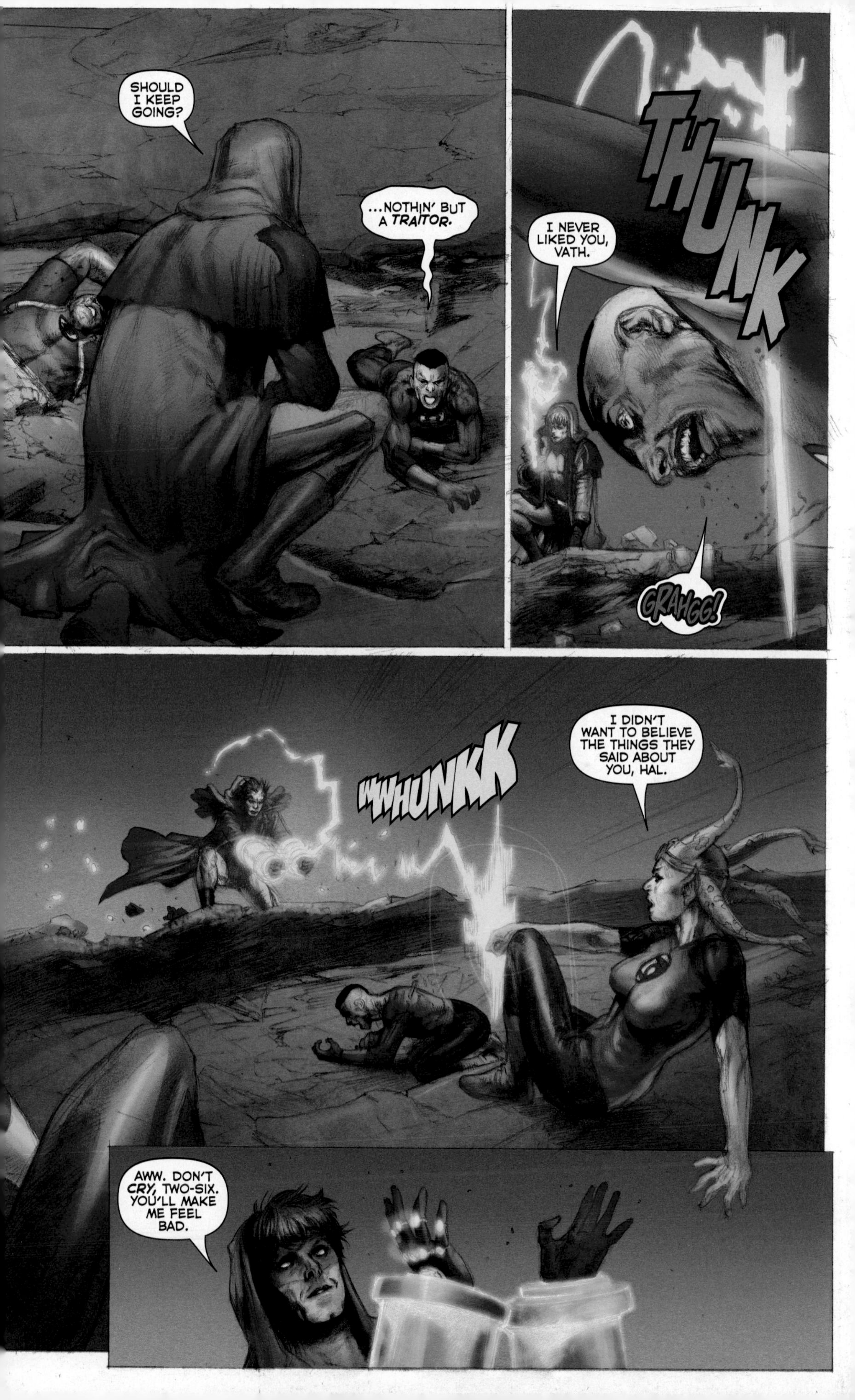

SHOULD I KEEP GOING?
...NOTHIN' BUT A TRAITOR.
THUNK
I NEVER LIKED YOU, VATH.
GRAHGG!
WWHUNKK
I DIDN'T WANT TO BELIEVE THE THINGS THEY SAID ABOUT YOU, HAL.
AWW. DON'T CRY, TWO-SIX. YOU'LL MAKE ME FEEL BAD.

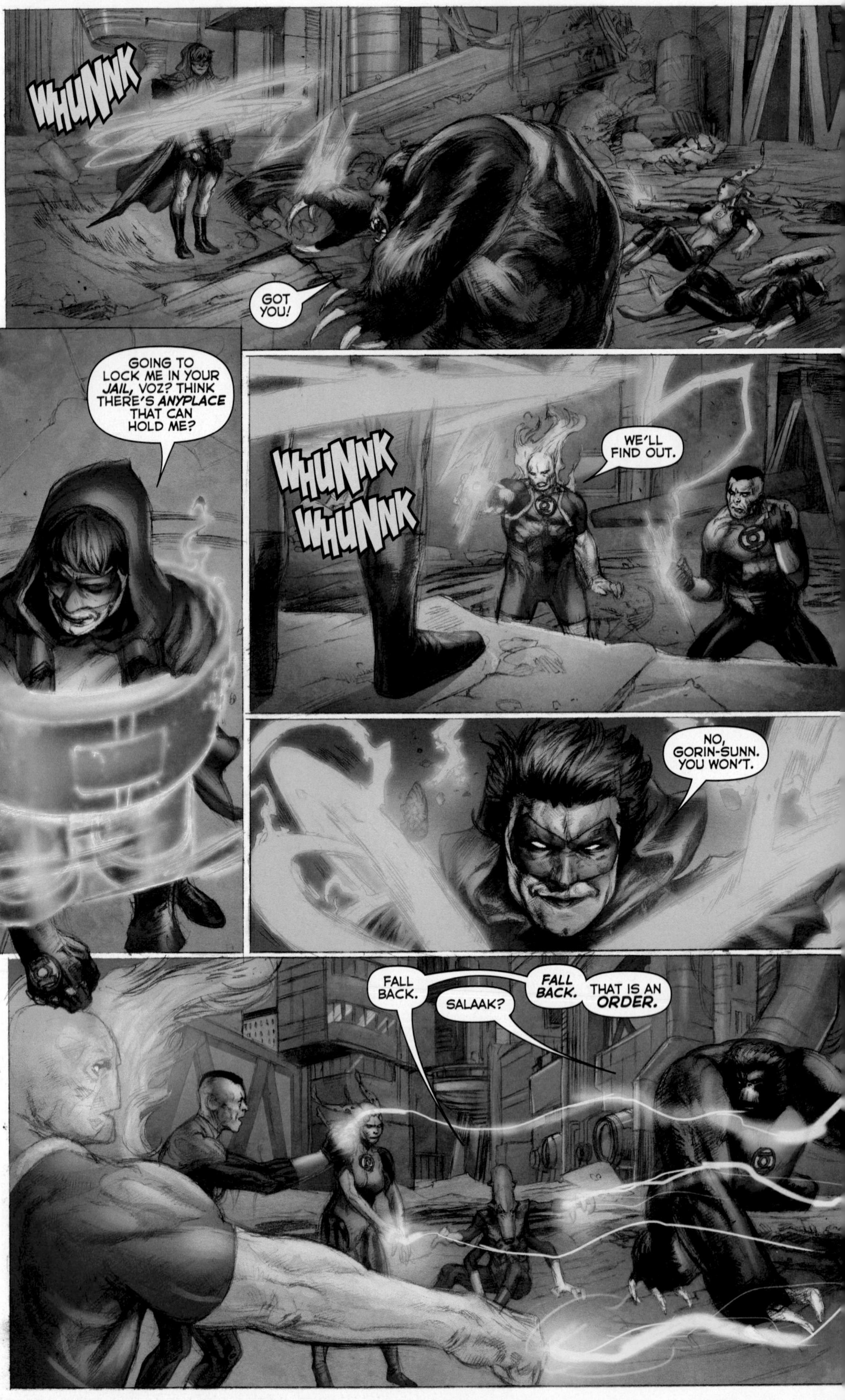
WHUNNK
GOT YOU!
GOING TO LOCK ME IN YOUR JAIL, VOZ? THINK THERE'S ANYPLACE THAT CAN HOLD ME?
WHUNNK
WHUNNK
WE'LL FIND OUT.
NO, GORIN-SUNN. YOU WON'T.
FALL BACK.
FALL BACK.
THAT IS AN ORDER.
SALAAK?

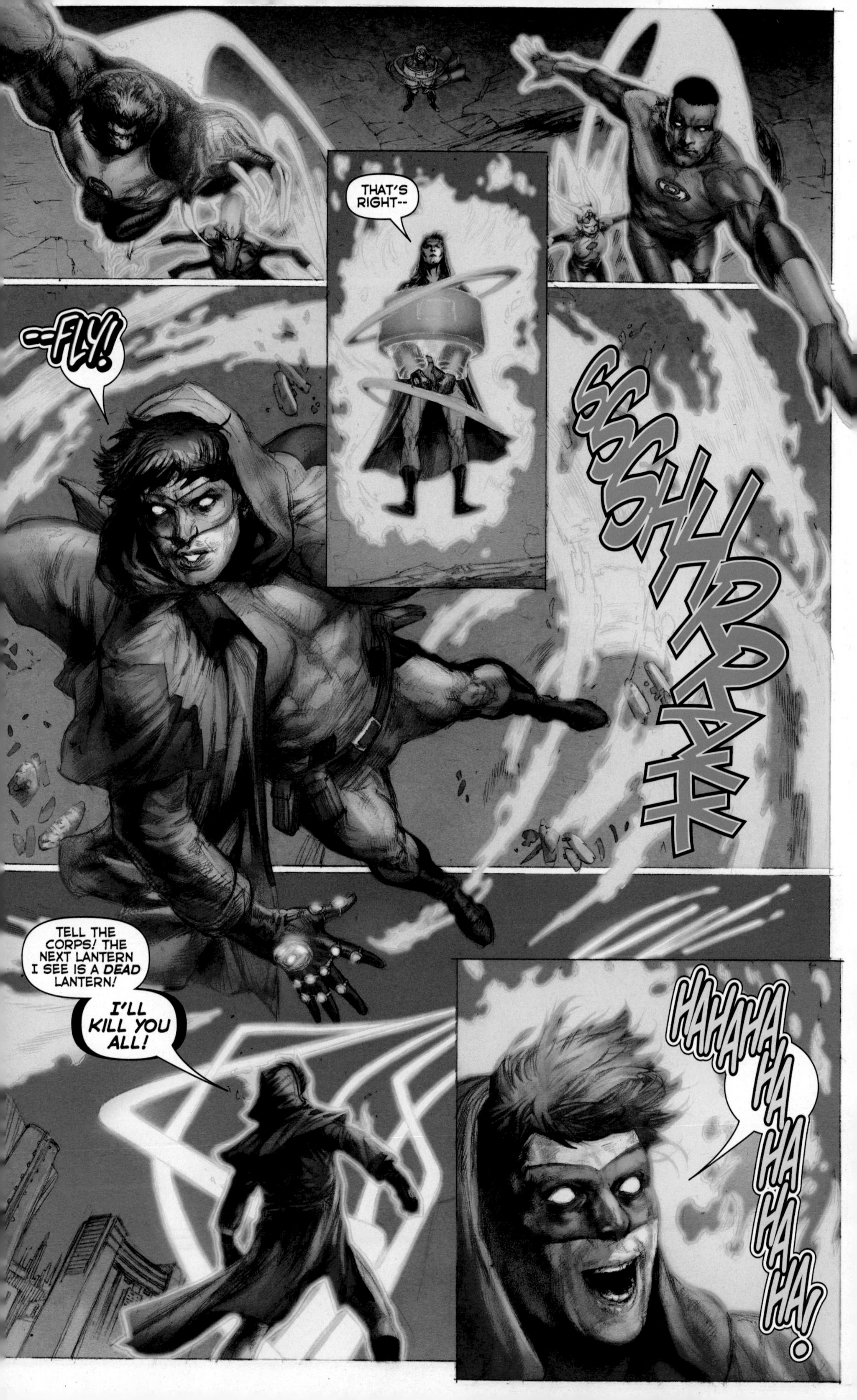
THAT'S RIGHT--
--FLY!
SSSHHRRAAKK
TELL THE CORPS! THE NEXT LANTERN I SEE IS A *DEAD* LANTERN!
I'LL KILL YOU ALL!
HAHAHAHAHAHAHAHAHA!

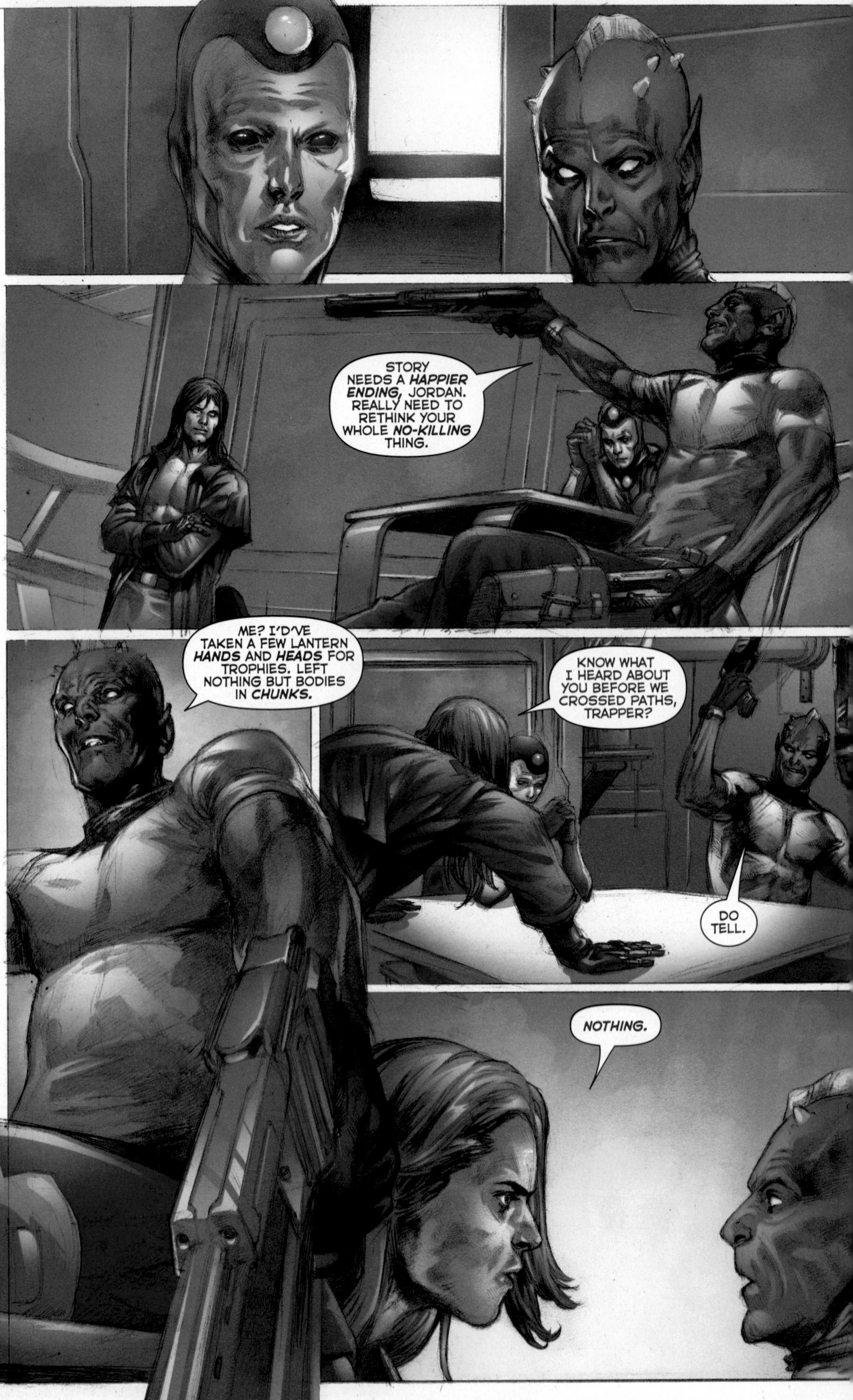
STORY NEEDS A HAPPIER ENDING, JORDAN. REALLY NEED TO RETHINK YOUR WHOLE NO-KILLING THING.
ME? I'D'VE TAKEN A FEW LANTERN HANDS AND HEADS FOR TROPHIES. LEFT NOTHING BUT BODIES IN CHUNKS.
KNOW WHAT I HEARD ABOUT YOU BEFORE WE CROSSED PATHS, TRAPPER?
DO TELL.
NOTHING.

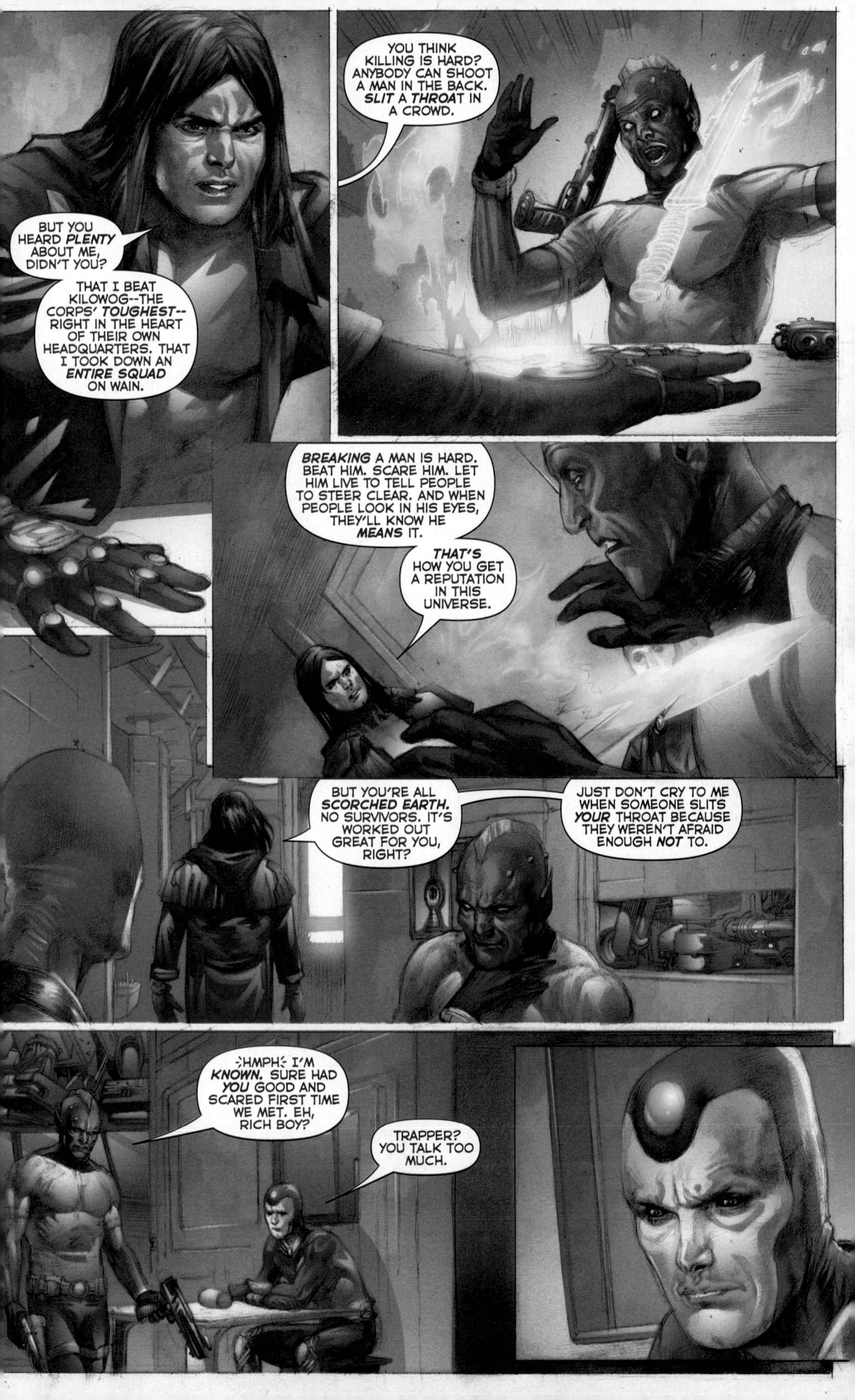
BUT YOU HEARD *PLENTY* ABOUT ME, DIDN'T YOU?
THAT I BEAT KILOWOG--THE CORPS' *TOUGHEST*--RIGHT IN THE HEART OF THEIR OWN HEADQUARTERS. THAT I TOOK DOWN AN *ENTIRE SQUAD* ON WAIN.
YOU THINK KILLING IS HARD? ANYBODY CAN SHOOT A MAN IN THE BACK. *SLIT A THROAT* IN A CROWD.
BREAKING A MAN IS HARD. BEAT HIM. SCARE HIM. LET HIM LIVE TO TELL PEOPLE TO STEER CLEAR. AND WHEN PEOPLE LOOK IN HIS EYES, THEY'LL KNOW HE *MEANS* IT.
THAT'S HOW YOU GET A REPUTATION IN THIS UNIVERSE.
BUT YOU'RE ALL *SCORCHED EARTH.* NO SURVIVORS. IT'S WORKED OUT GREAT FOR YOU, RIGHT?
JUST DON'T CRY TO ME WHEN SOMEONE SLITS *YOUR* THROAT BECAUSE THEY WEREN'T AFRAID ENOUGH *NOT* TO.
-HMPH- I'M *KNOWN.* SURE HAD *YOU* GOOD AND SCARED FIRST TIME WE MET. EH, RICH BOY?
TRAPPER? YOU TALK TOO MUCH.

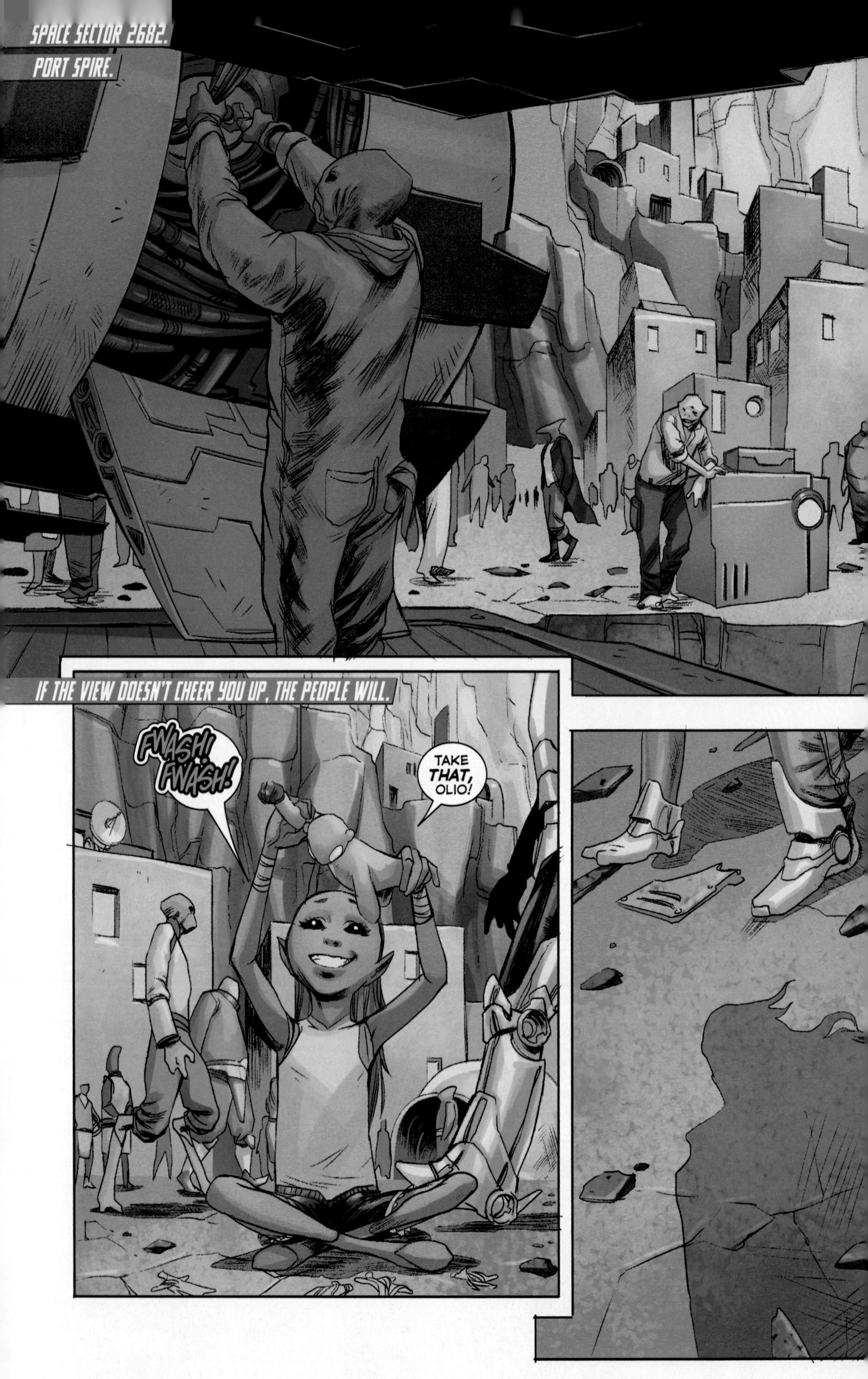
SPACE SECTOR 2682.
PORT SPIRE.
IF THE VIEW DOESN'T CHEER YOU UP, THE PEOPLE WILL.
FWASH! FWASH!
TAKE THAT, OLIO!

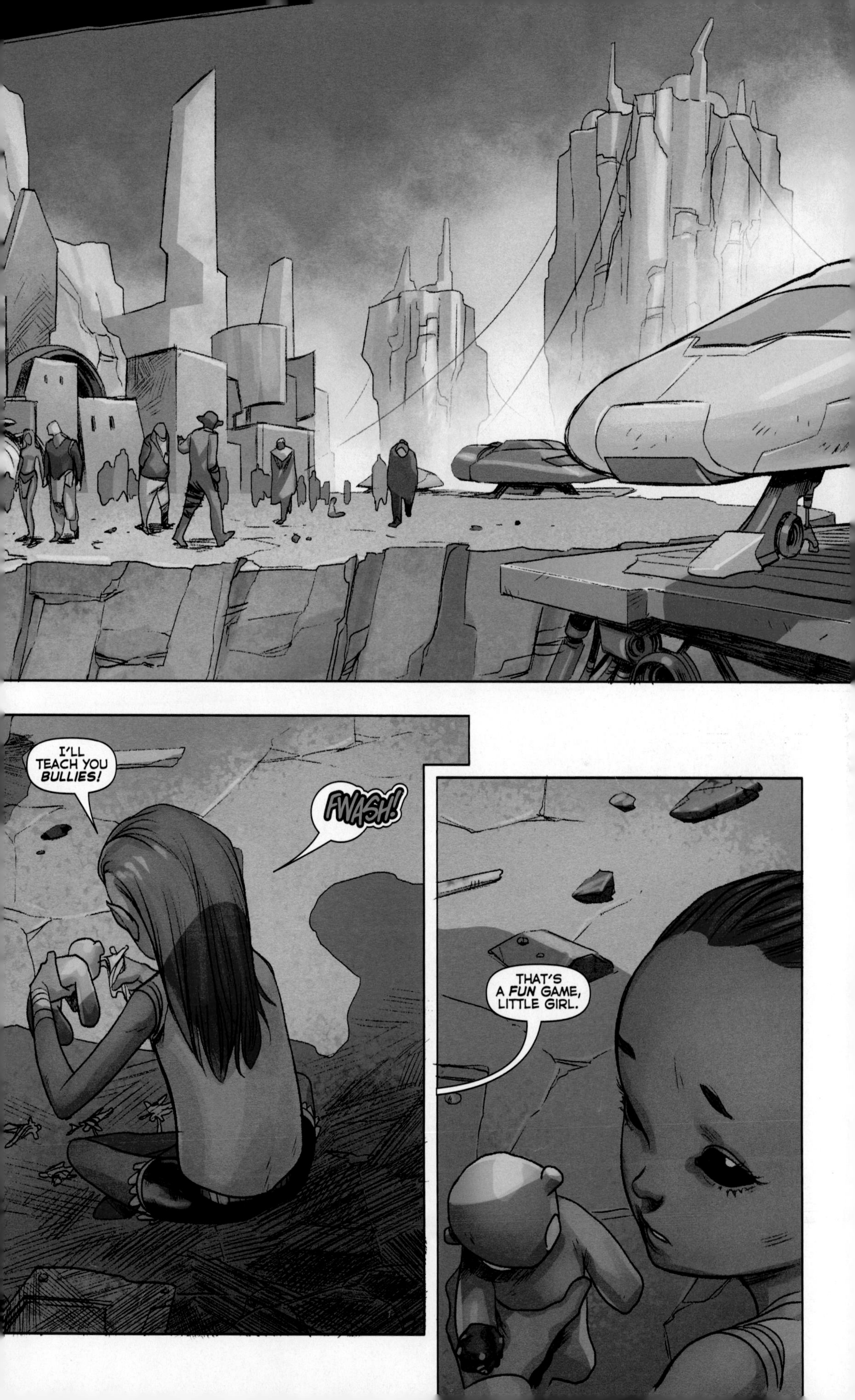
I'LL TEACH YOU BULLIES!
FWASH!
THAT'S A FUN GAME, LITTLE GIRL.

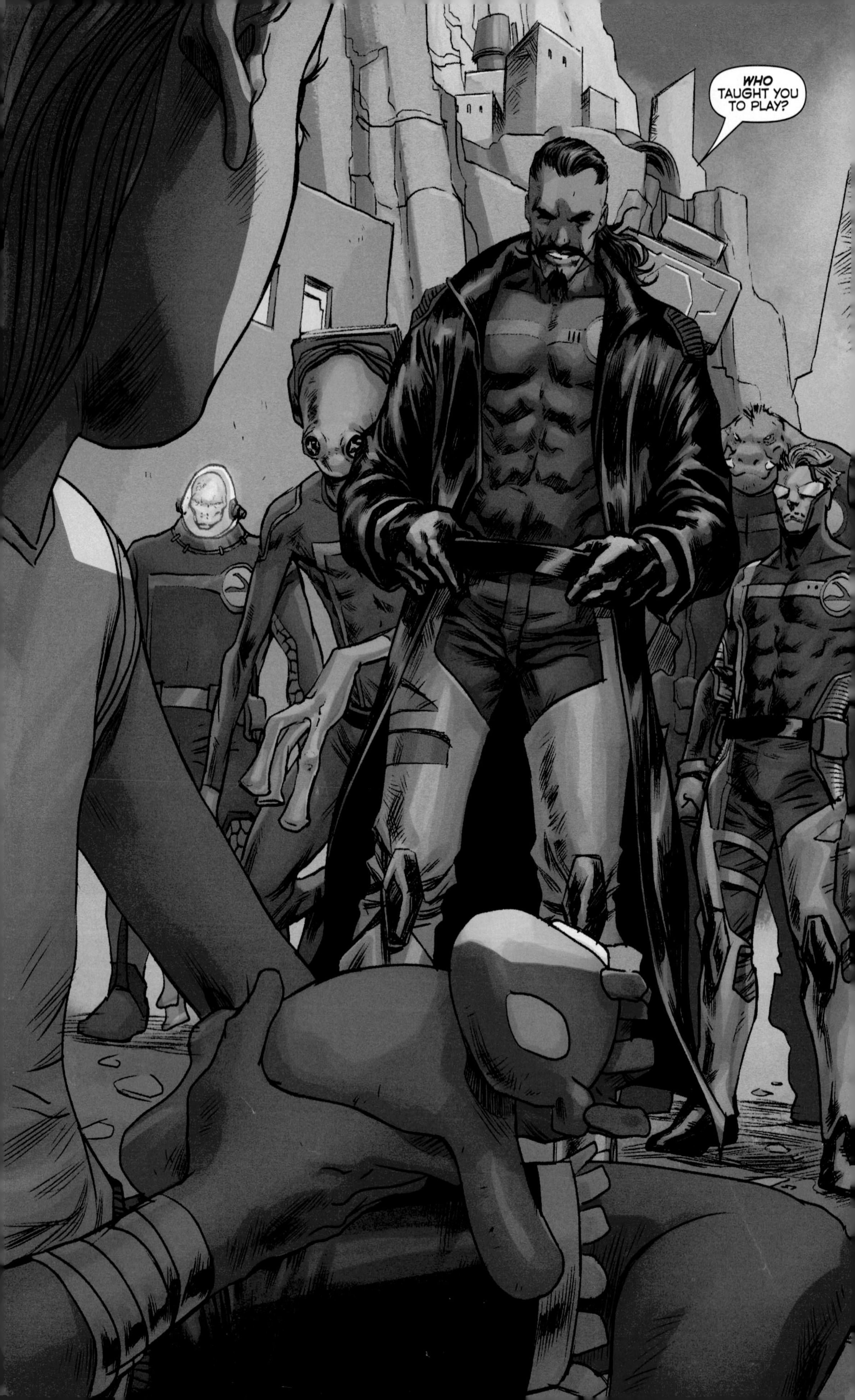
WHO TAUGHT YOU TO PLAY?

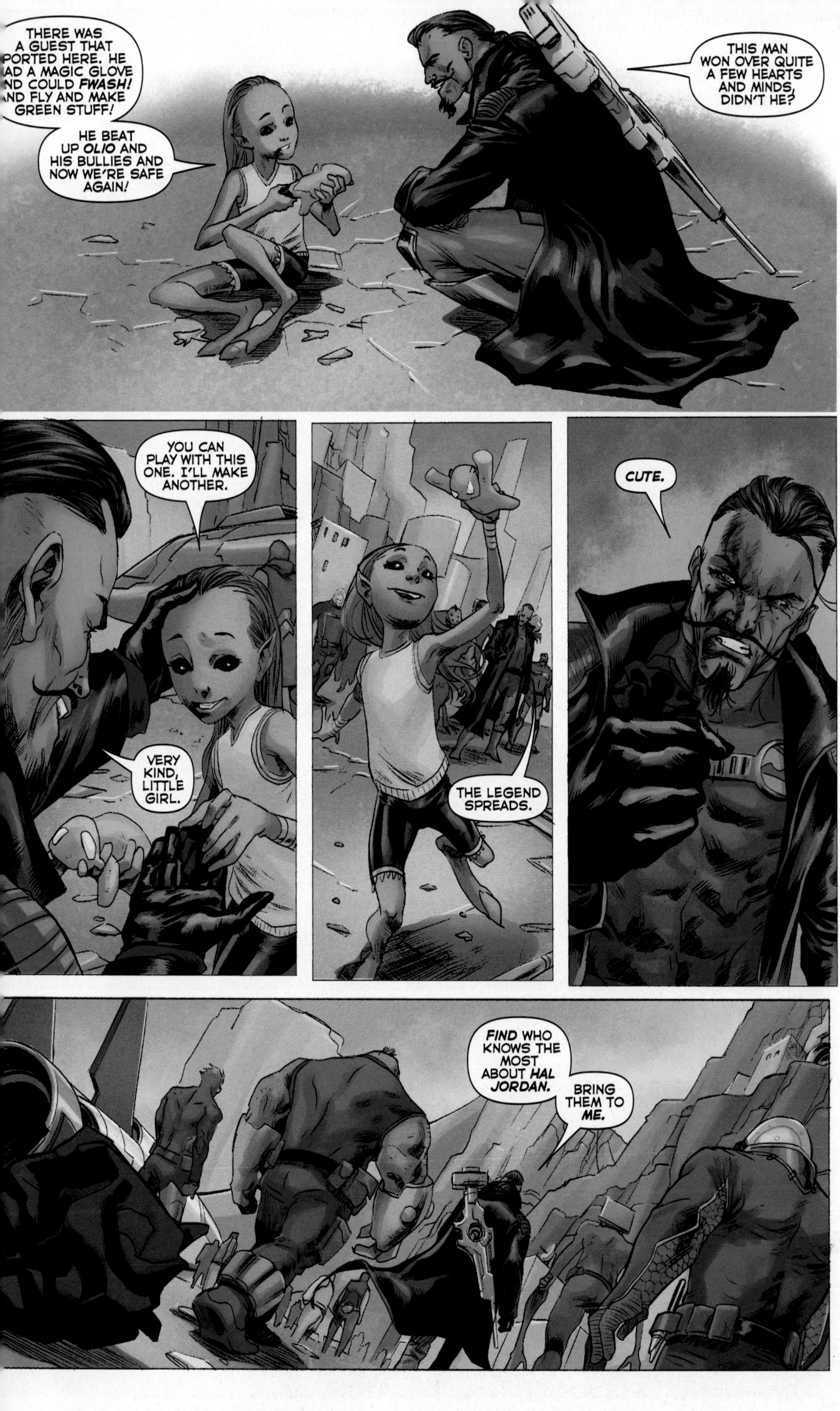
THERE WAS A GUEST THAT PORTED HERE. HE HAD A MAGIC GLOVE AND COULD FWASH! AND FLY AND MAKE GREEN STUFF!
HE BEAT UP OLIO AND HIS BULLIES AND NOW WE'RE SAFE AGAIN!
THIS MAN WON OVER QUITE A FEW HEARTS AND MINDS, DIDN'T HE?
YOU CAN PLAY WITH THIS ONE. I'LL MAKE ANOTHER.
VERY KIND, LITTLE GIRL.
THE LEGEND SPREADS.
CUTE.
FIND WHO KNOWS THE MOST ABOUT HAL JORDAN.
BRING THEM TO ME.

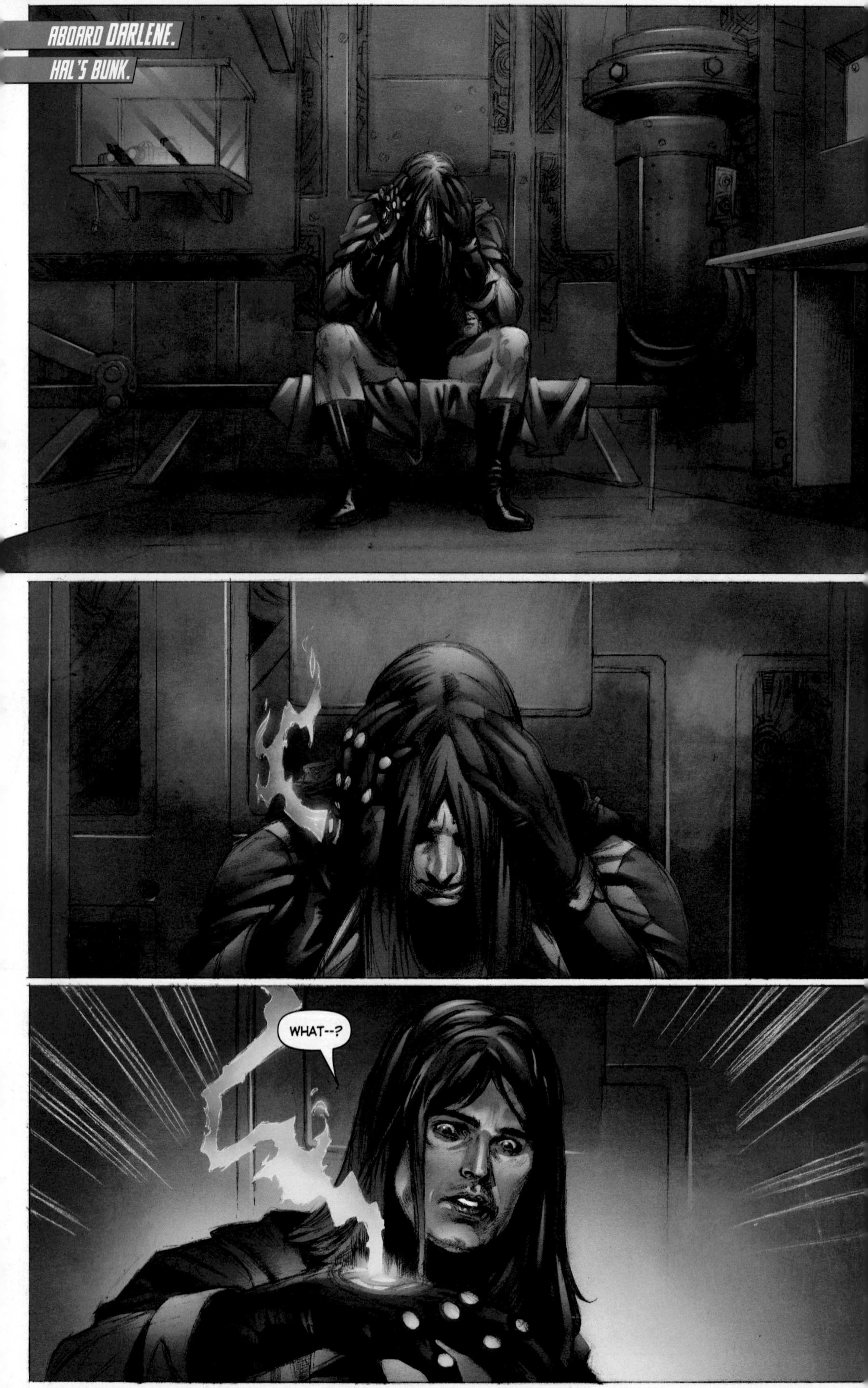
ABOARD DARLENE.
HAL'S BUNK.
WHAT--?

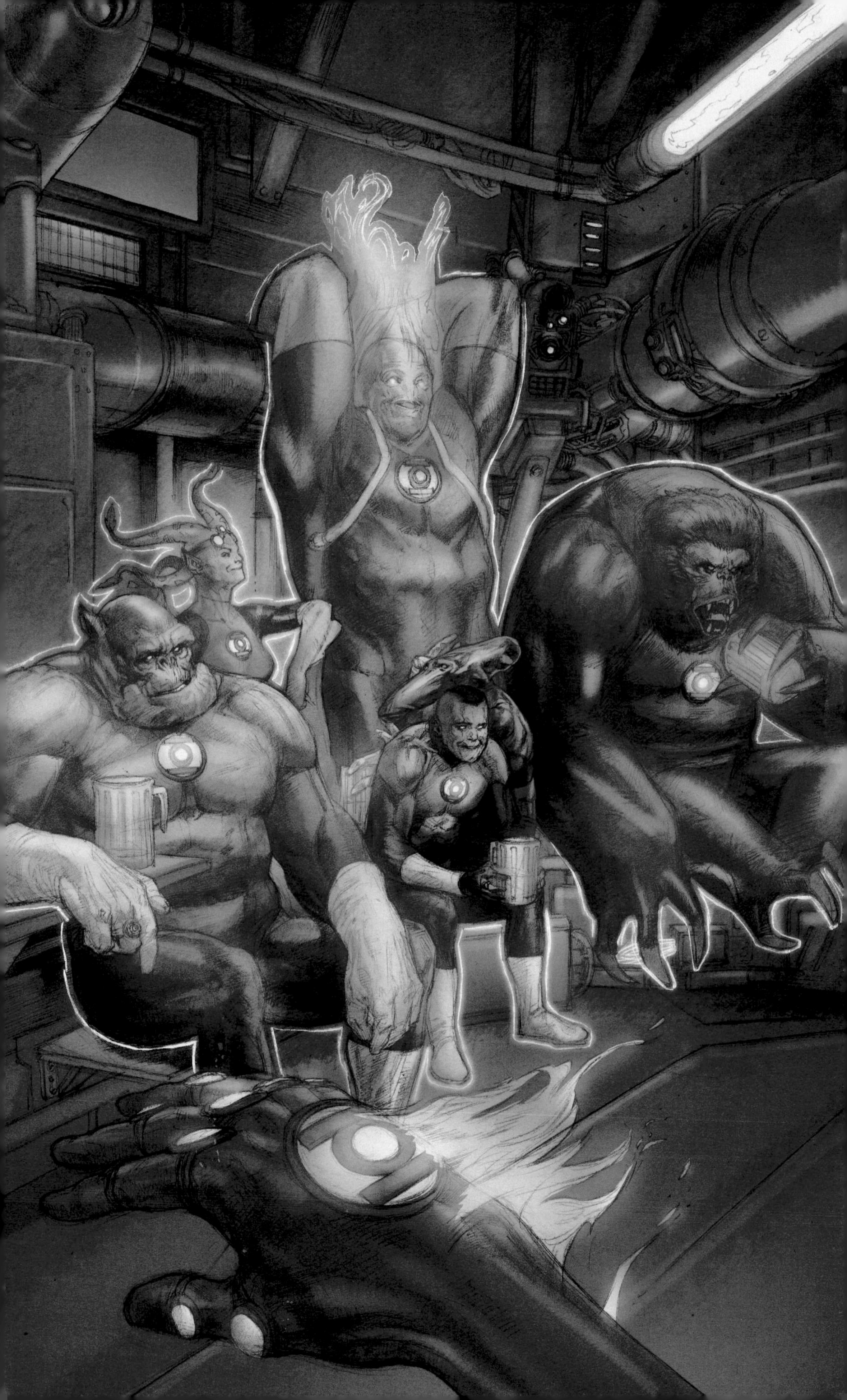

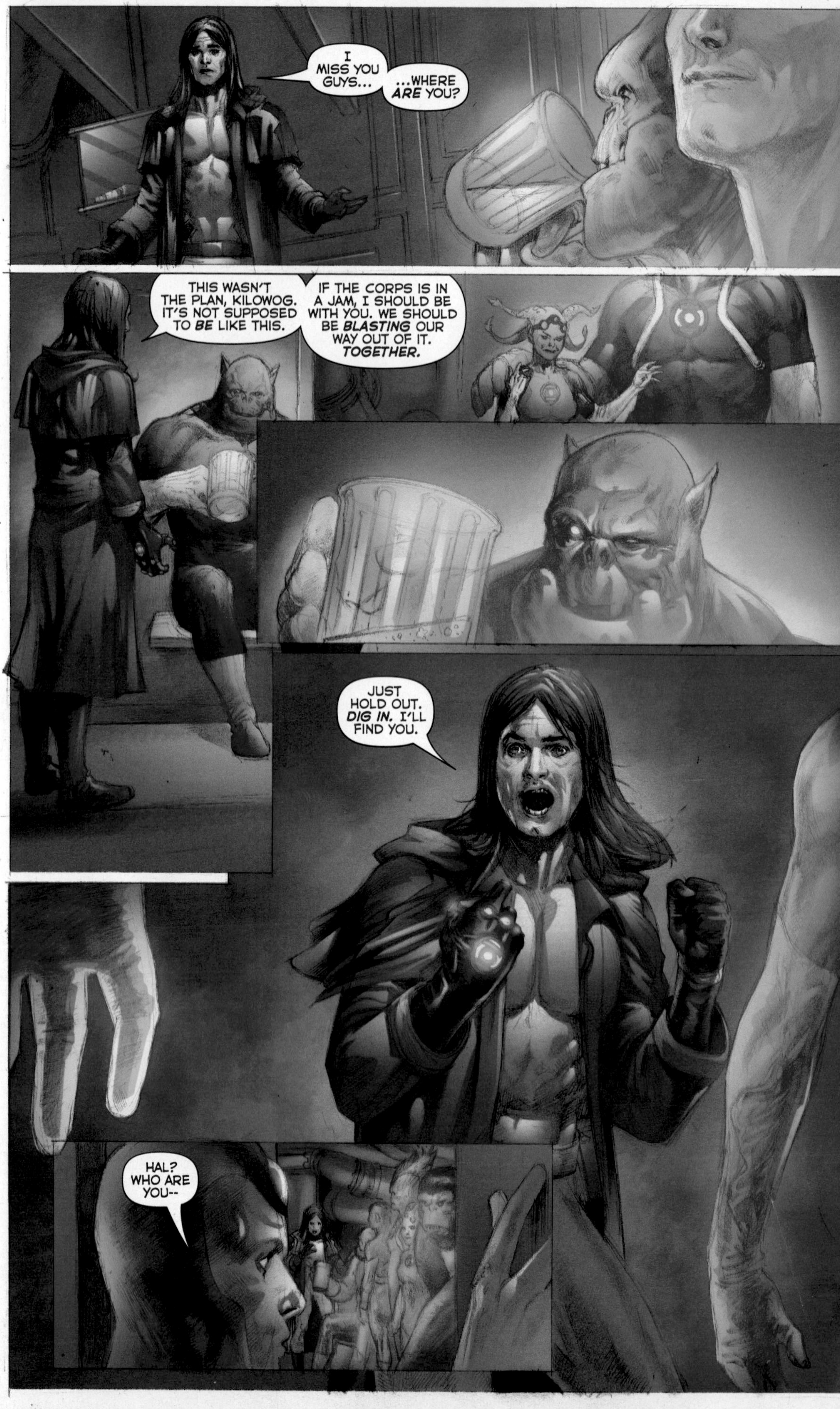
I MISS YOU GUYS...
...WHERE *ARE* YOU?
THIS WASN'T THE PLAN, KILOWOG. IT'S NOT SUPPOSED TO *BE* LIKE THIS.
IF THE CORPS IS IN A JAM, I SHOULD BE WITH YOU. WE SHOULD BE *BLASTING* OUR WAY OUT OF IT. *TOGETHER.*
JUST HOLD OUT. *DIG IN.* I'LL FIND YOU.
HAL? WHO ARE YOU--

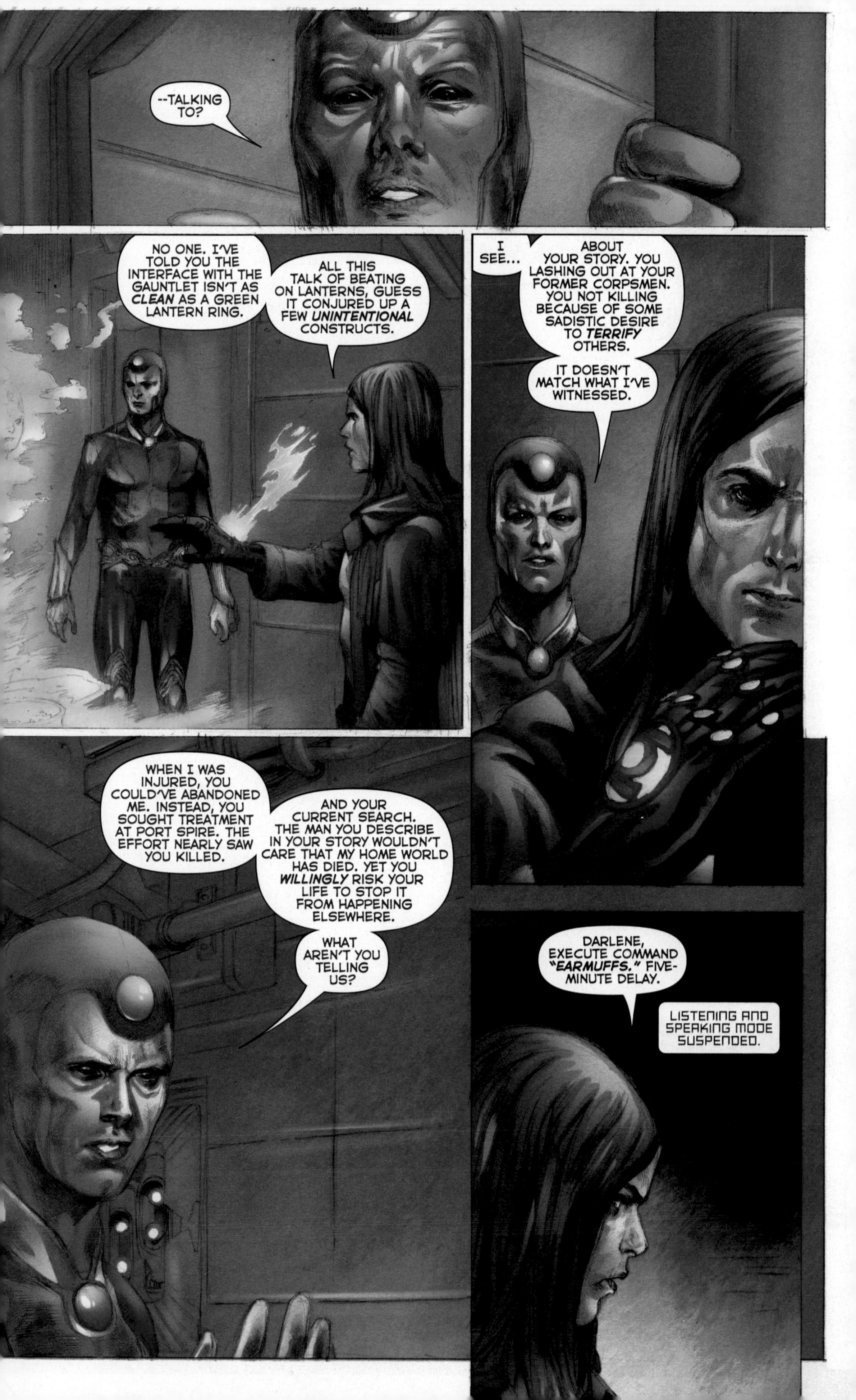
--TALKING TO?
NO ONE. I'VE TOLD YOU THE INTERFACE WITH THE GAUNTLET ISN'T AS CLEAN AS A GREEN LANTERN RING.
ALL THIS TALK OF BEATING ON LANTERNS, GUESS IT CONJURED UP A FEW UNINTENTIONAL CONSTRUCTS.
I SEE...
ABOUT YOUR STORY. YOU LASHING OUT AT YOUR FORMER CORPSMEN. YOU NOT KILLING BECAUSE OF SOME SADISTIC DESIRE TO TERRIFY OTHERS.
IT DOESN'T MATCH WHAT I'VE WITNESSED.
WHEN I WAS INJURED, YOU COULD'VE ABANDONED ME. INSTEAD, YOU SOUGHT TREATMENT AT PORT SPIRE. THE EFFORT NEARLY SAW YOU KILLED.
AND YOUR CURRENT SEARCH. THE MAN YOU DESCRIBE IN YOUR STORY WOULDN'T CARE THAT MY HOME WORLD HAS DIED. YET YOU WILLINGLY RISK YOUR LIFE TO STOP IT FROM HAPPENING ELSEWHERE.
WHAT AREN'T YOU TELLING US?
DARLENE, EXECUTE COMMAND "EARMUFFS." FIVE-MINUTE DELAY.
LISTENING AND SPEAKING MODE SUSPENDED.

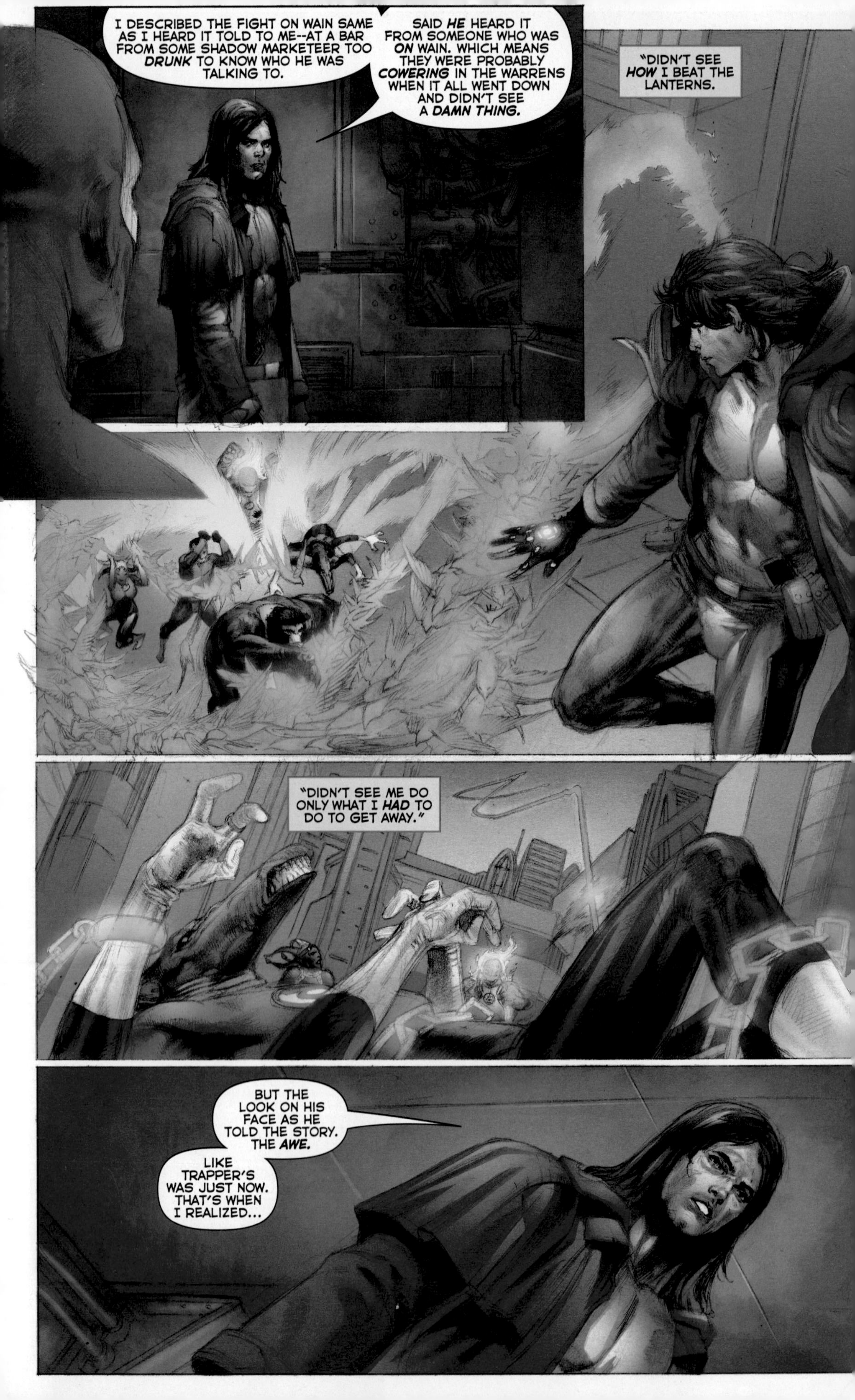
I DESCRIBED THE FIGHT ON WAIN SAME AS I HEARD IT TOLD TO ME--AT A BAR FROM SOME SHADOW MARKETEER TOO DRUNK TO KNOW WHO HE WAS TALKING TO.
SAID HE HEARD IT FROM SOMEONE WHO WAS ON WAIN. WHICH MEANS THEY WERE PROBABLY COWERING IN THE WARRENS WHEN IT ALL WENT DOWN AND DIDN'T SEE A DAMN THING.
"DIDN'T SEE HOW I BEAT THE LANTERNS.
"DIDN'T SEE ME DO ONLY WHAT I HAD TO DO TO GET AWAY."
BUT THE LOOK ON HIS FACE AS HE TOLD THE STORY. THE AWE.
LIKE TRAPPER'S WAS JUST NOW. THAT'S WHEN I REALIZED...

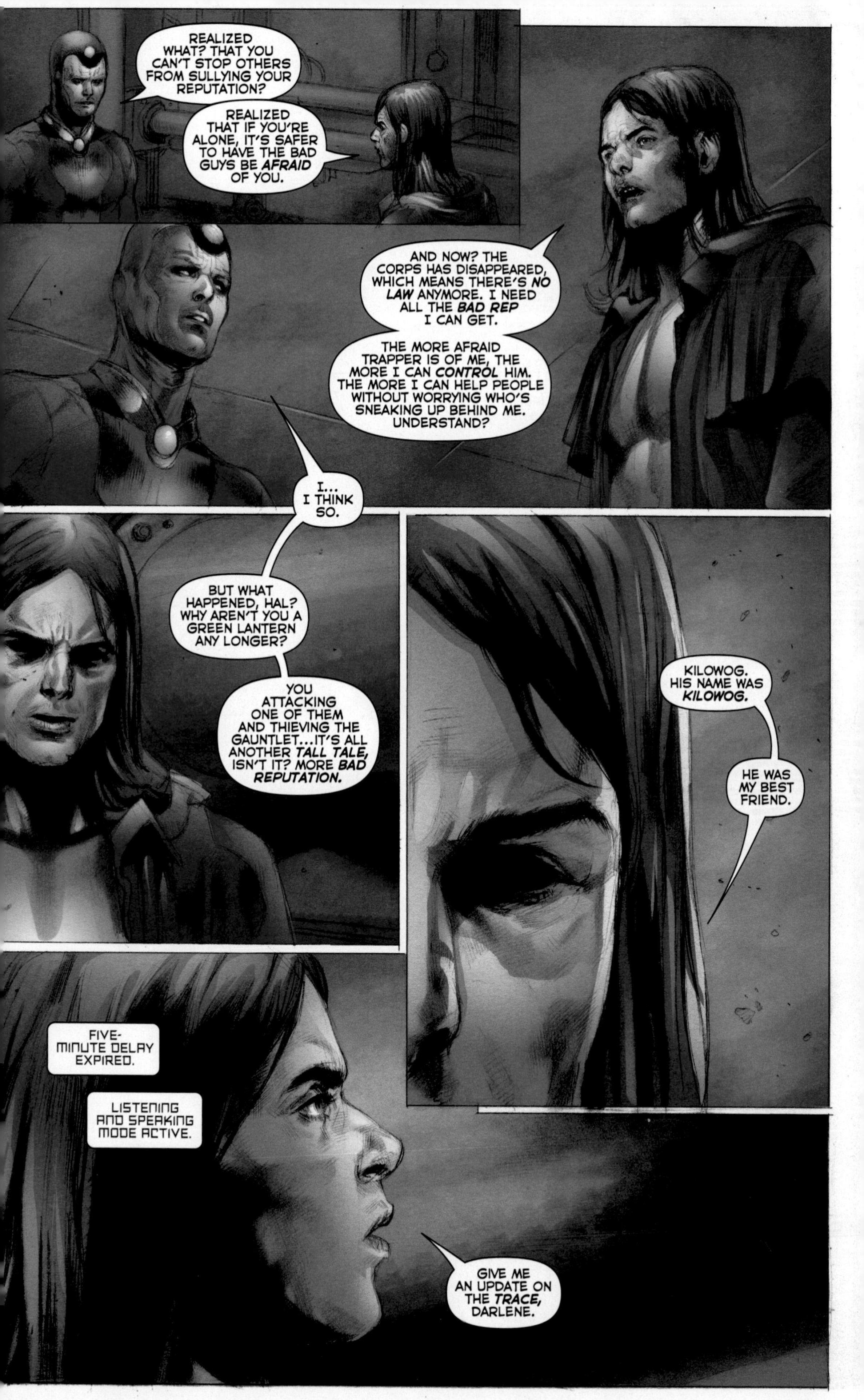
REALIZED WHAT? THAT YOU CAN'T STOP OTHERS FROM SULLYING YOUR REPUTATION?
REALIZED THAT IF YOU'RE ALONE, IT'S SAFER TO HAVE THE BAD GUYS BE *AFRAID* OF YOU.
AND NOW? THE CORPS HAS DISAPPEARED, WHICH MEANS THERE'S *NO LAW* ANYMORE. I NEED ALL THE *BAD REP* I CAN GET.
THE MORE AFRAID TRAPPER IS OF ME, THE MORE I CAN *CONTROL* HIM. THE MORE I CAN HELP PEOPLE WITHOUT WORRYING WHO'S SNEAKING UP BEHIND ME. UNDERSTAND?
I... I THINK SO.
BUT WHAT HAPPENED, HAL? WHY AREN'T YOU A GREEN LANTERN ANY LONGER?
YOU ATTACKING ONE OF THEM AND THIEVING THE GAUNTLET...IT'S ALL ANOTHER *TALL TALE,* ISN'T IT? MORE *BAD REPUTATION.*
KILOWOG. HIS NAME WAS *KILOWOG.*
HE WAS MY BEST FRIEND.
FIVE-MINUTE DELAY EXPIRED.
LISTENING AND SPEAKING MODE ACTIVE.
GIVE ME AN UPDATE ON THE *TRACE,* DARLENE.

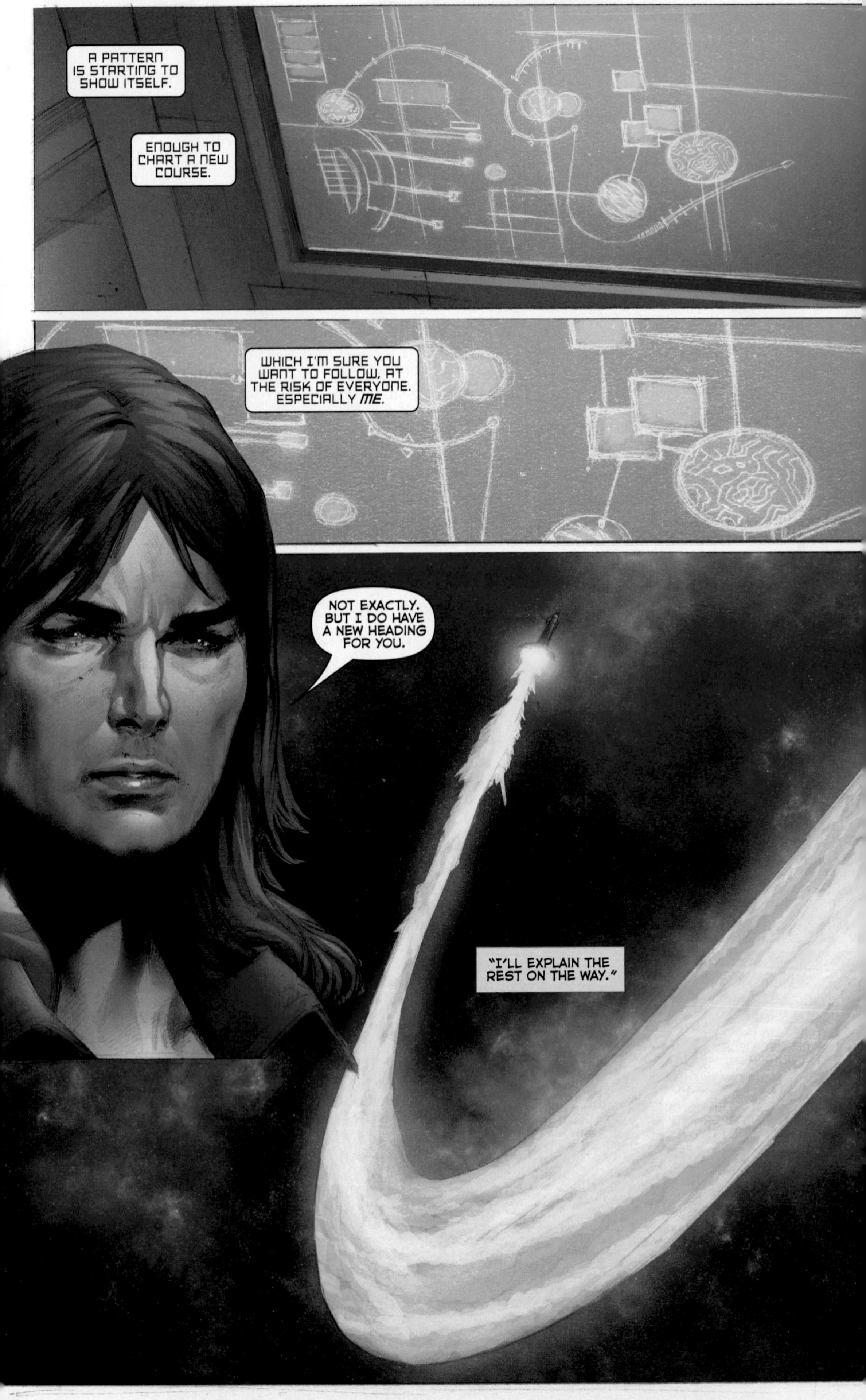
A PATTERN IS STARTING TO SHOW ITSELF.
ENOUGH TO CHART A NEW COURSE.
WHICH I'M SURE YOU WANT TO FOLLOW, AT THE RISK OF EVERYONE. ESPECIALLY *ME*.
NOT EXACTLY. BUT I DO HAVE A NEW HEADING FOR YOU.
"I'LL EXPLAIN THE REST ON THE WAY."

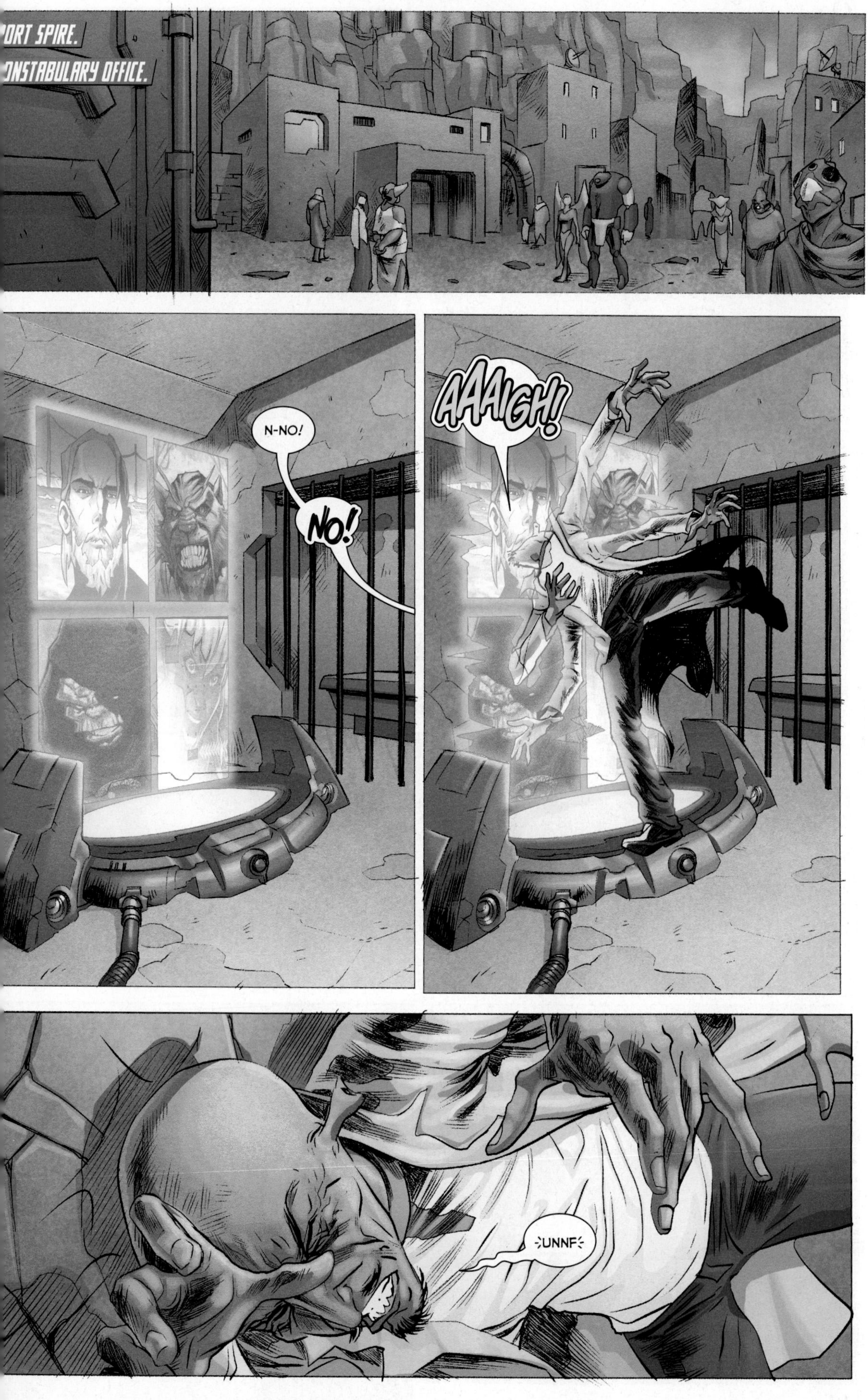
ORT SPIRE.
ONSTABULARY OFFICE.
N-NO!
NO!
AAAIGH!
UNNF

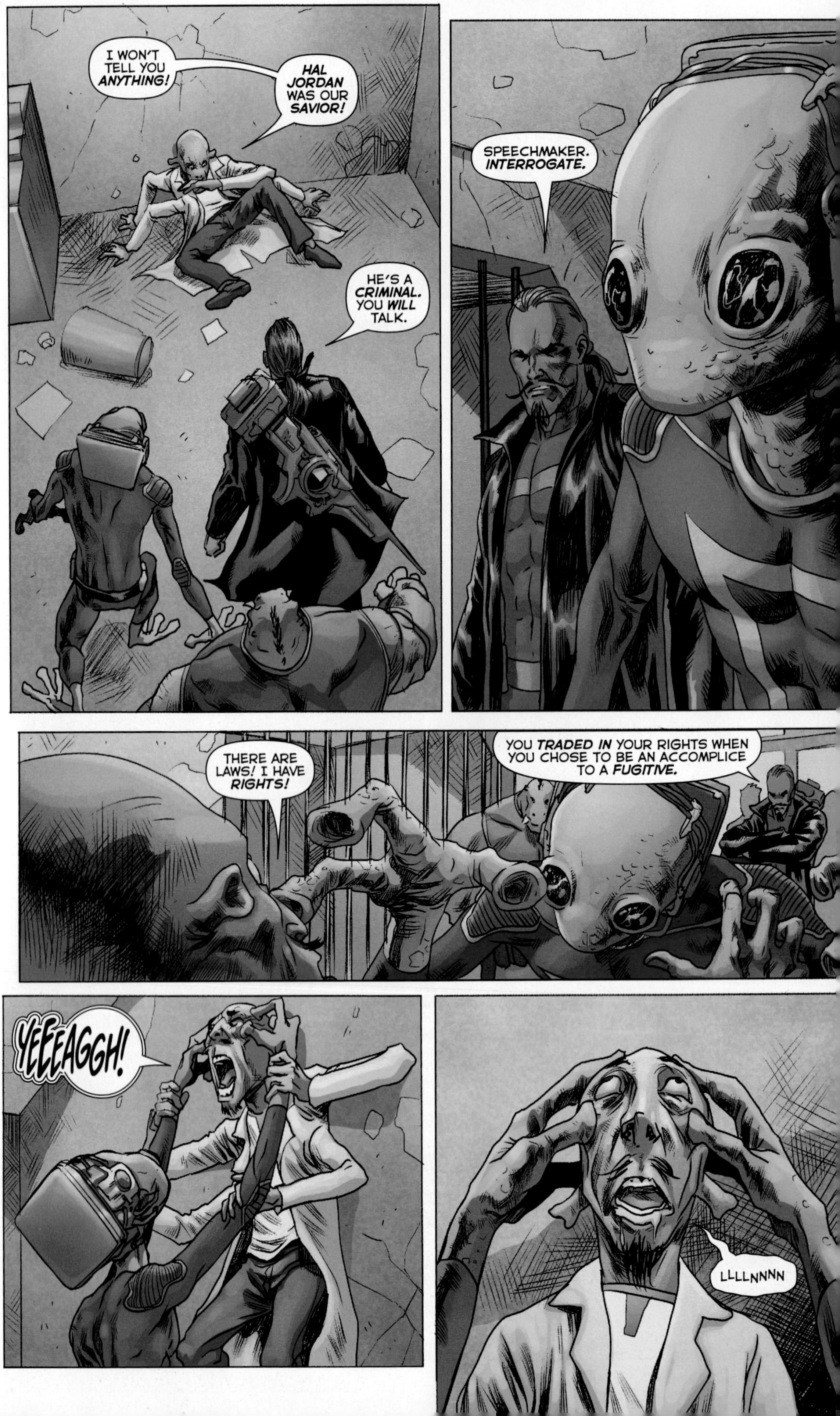

I WON'T TELL YOU *ANYTHING!*
HAL JORDAN WAS OUR *SAVIOR!*
HE'S A *CRIMINAL.* YOU *WILL* TALK.
SPEECHMAKER. *INTERROGATE.*
THERE ARE LAWS! I HAVE *RIGHTS!*
YOU *TRADED IN* YOUR RIGHTS WHEN YOU CHOSE TO BE AN ACCOMPLICE TO A *FUGITIVE.*
YEEEAGGH!
LLLLNNNN

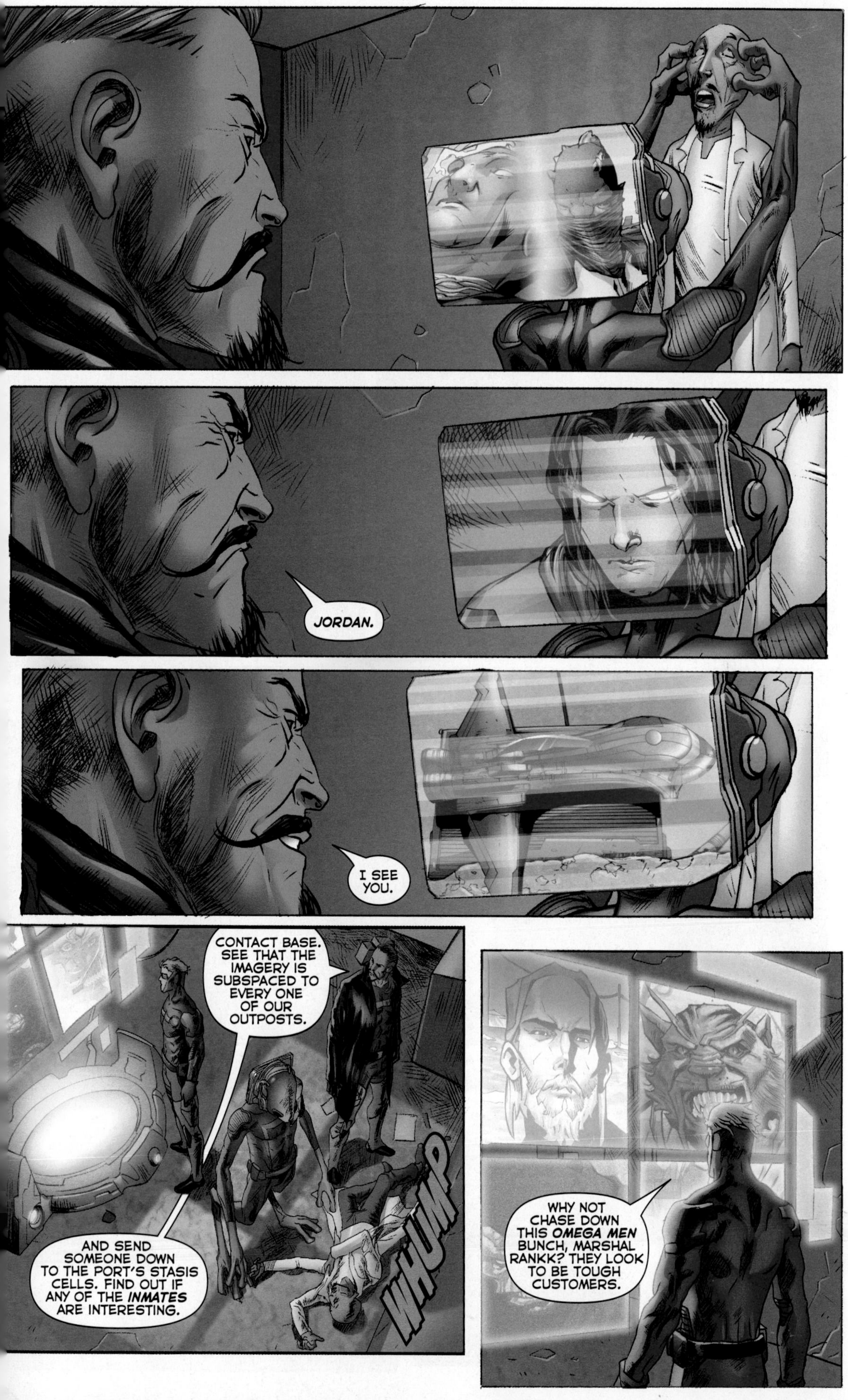
JORDAN.
I SEE YOU.
CONTACT BASE. SEE THAT THE IMAGERY IS SUBSPACED TO EVERY ONE OF OUR OUTPOSTS.
AND SEND SOMEONE DOWN TO THE PORT'S STASIS CELLS. FIND OUT IF ANY OF THE *INMATES* ARE INTERESTING.
WHUMP
WHY NOT CHASE DOWN THIS *OMEGA MEN* BUNCH, MARSHAL RANKK? THEY LOOK TO BE TOUGH CUSTOMERS.

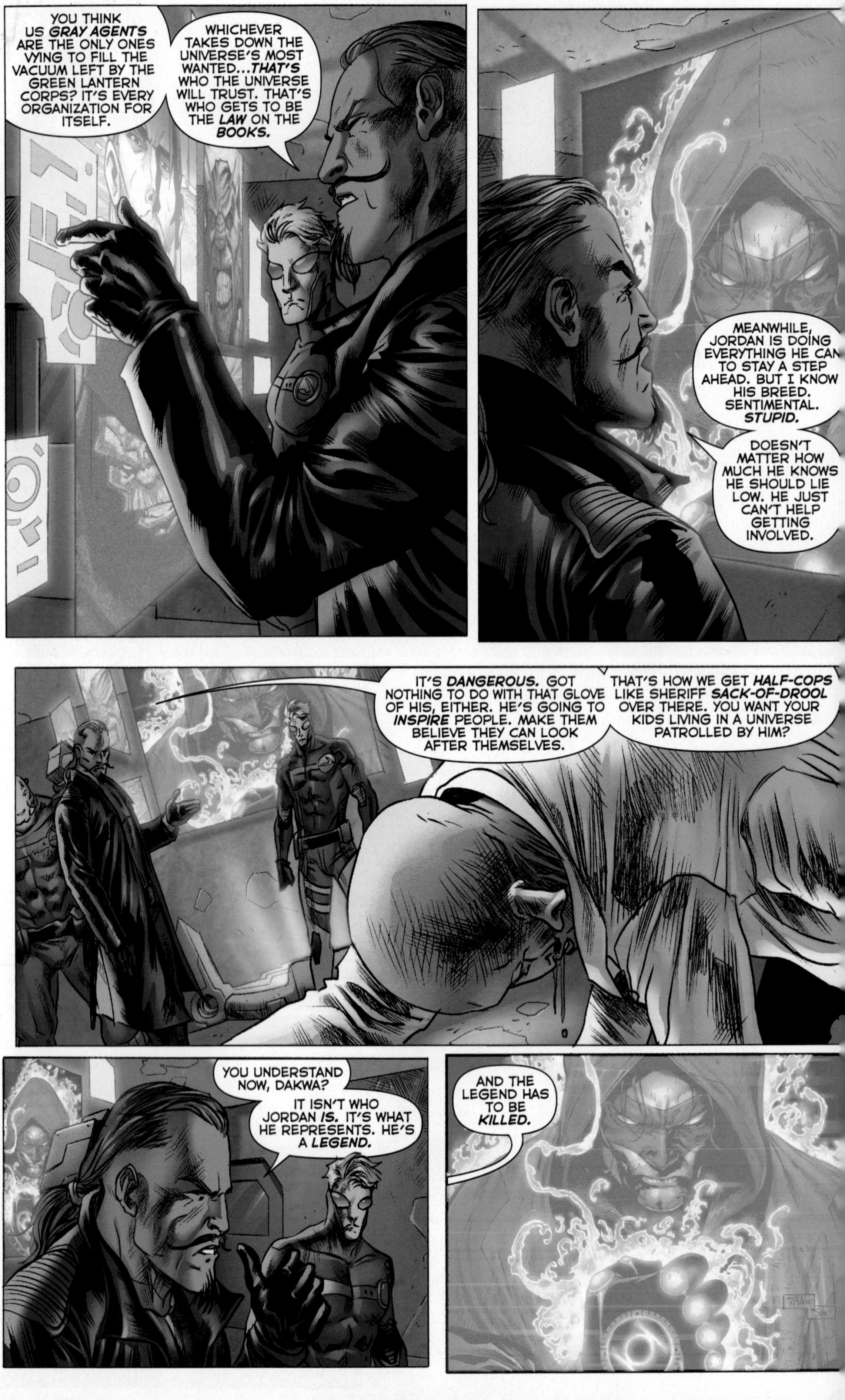
YOU THINK US GRAY AGENTS ARE THE ONLY ONES VYING TO FILL THE VACUUM LEFT BY THE GREEN LANTERN CORPS? IT'S EVERY ORGANIZATION FOR ITSELF.
WHICHEVER TAKES DOWN THE UNIVERSE'S MOST WANTED...THAT'S WHO THE UNIVERSE WILL TRUST. THAT'S WHO GETS TO BE THE LAW ON THE BOOKS.
MEANWHILE, JORDAN IS DOING EVERYTHING HE CAN TO STAY A STEP AHEAD. BUT I KNOW HIS BREED. SENTIMENTAL. STUPID.
DOESN'T MATTER HOW MUCH HE KNOWS HE SHOULD LIE LOW. HE JUST CAN'T HELP GETTING INVOLVED.
IT'S DANGEROUS. GOT NOTHING TO DO WITH THAT GLOVE OF HIS, EITHER. HE'S GOING TO INSPIRE PEOPLE. MAKE THEM BELIEVE THEY CAN LOOK AFTER THEMSELVES.
THAT'S HOW WE GET HALF-COPS LIKE SHERIFF SACK-OF-DROOL OVER THERE. YOU WANT YOUR KIDS LIVING IN A UNIVERSE PATROLLED BY HIM?
YOU UNDERSTAND NOW, DAKWA?
IT ISN'T WHO JORDAN IS. IT'S WHAT HE REPRESENTS. HE'S A LEGEND.
AND THE LEGEND HAS TO BE KILLED.

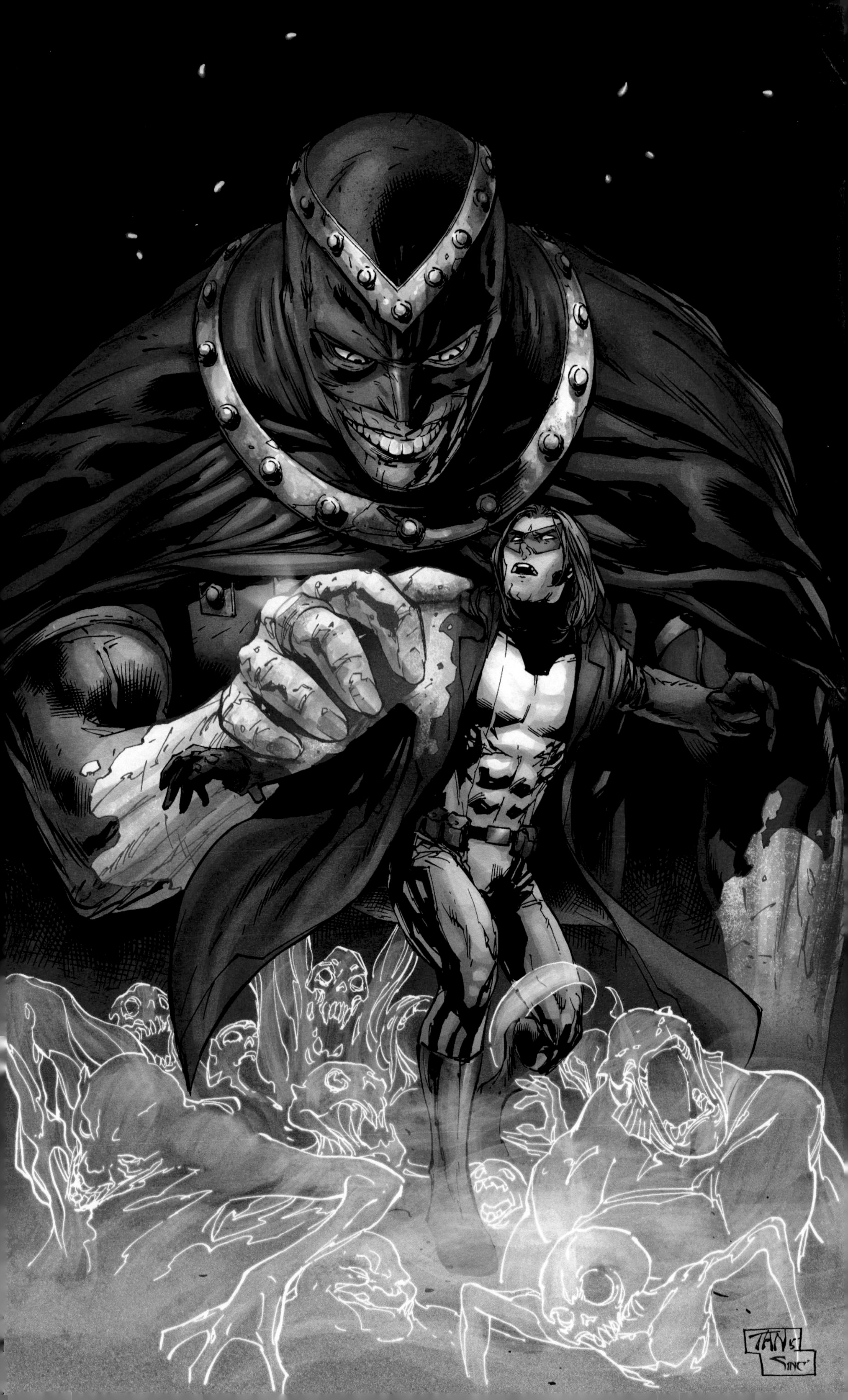

IDLE HAND

ROBERT VENDITTI writer **BILLY TAN** penciller **MARK IRWIN** inker **ALEX SINCLAIR** colorist **DAVE SHARPE** letterer **BILLY TAN & ALEX SINCLAIR** cover

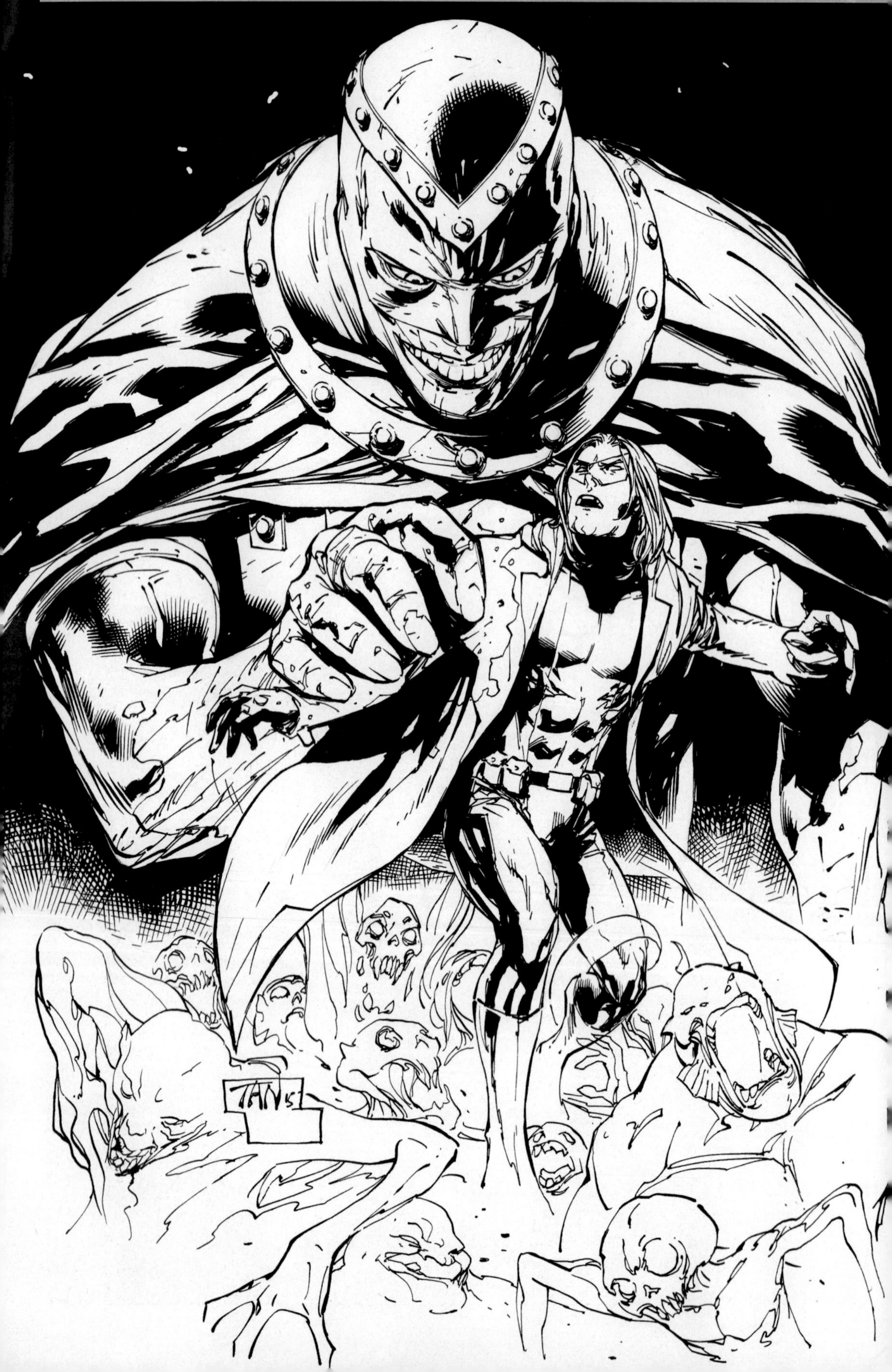

TAN 15

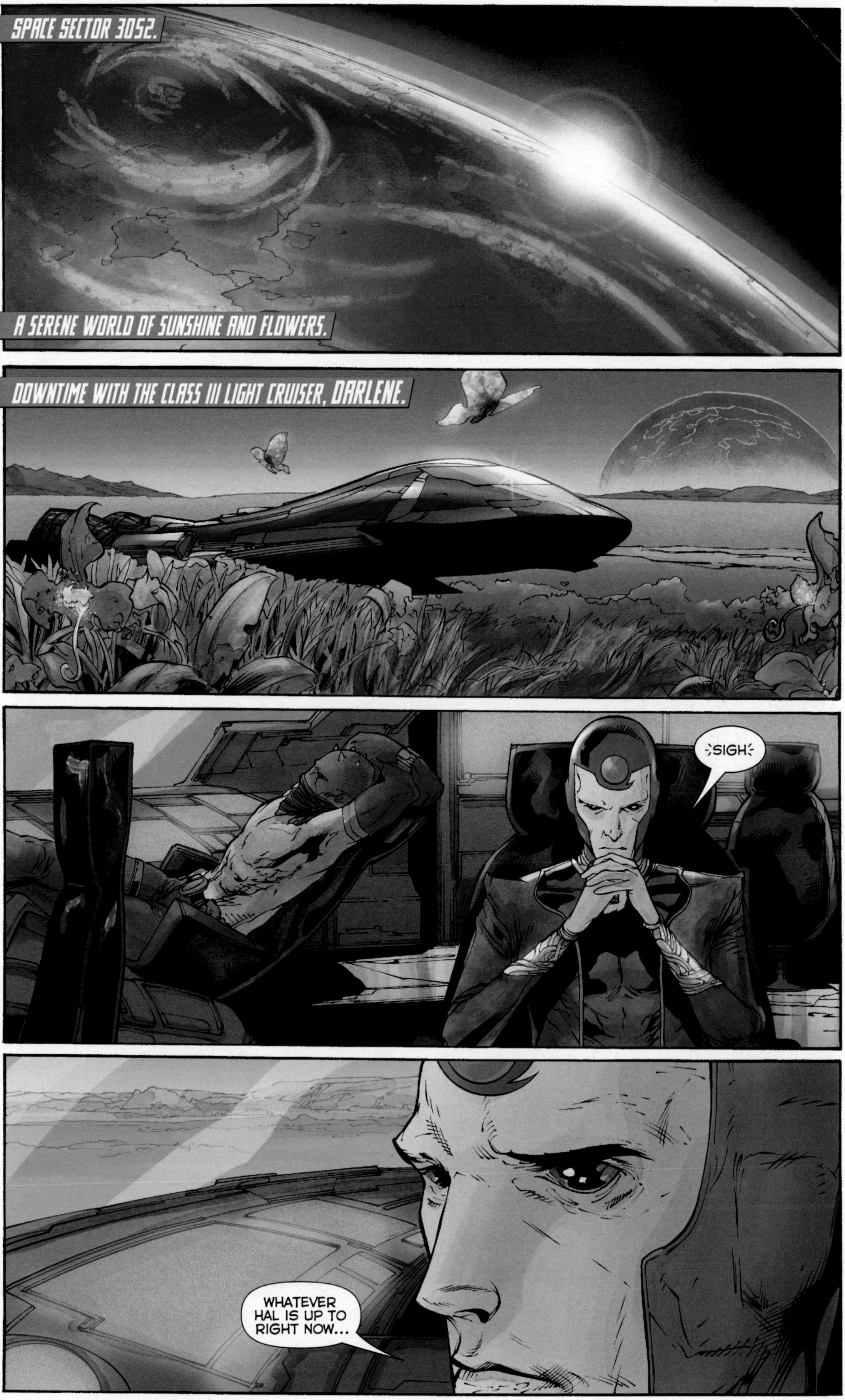

SPACE SECTOR 3052.
A SERENE WORLD OF SUNSHINE AND FLOWERS.
DOWNTIME WITH THE CLASS III LIGHT CRUISER, DARLENE.
SIGH
WHATEVER HAL IS UP TO RIGHT NOW...

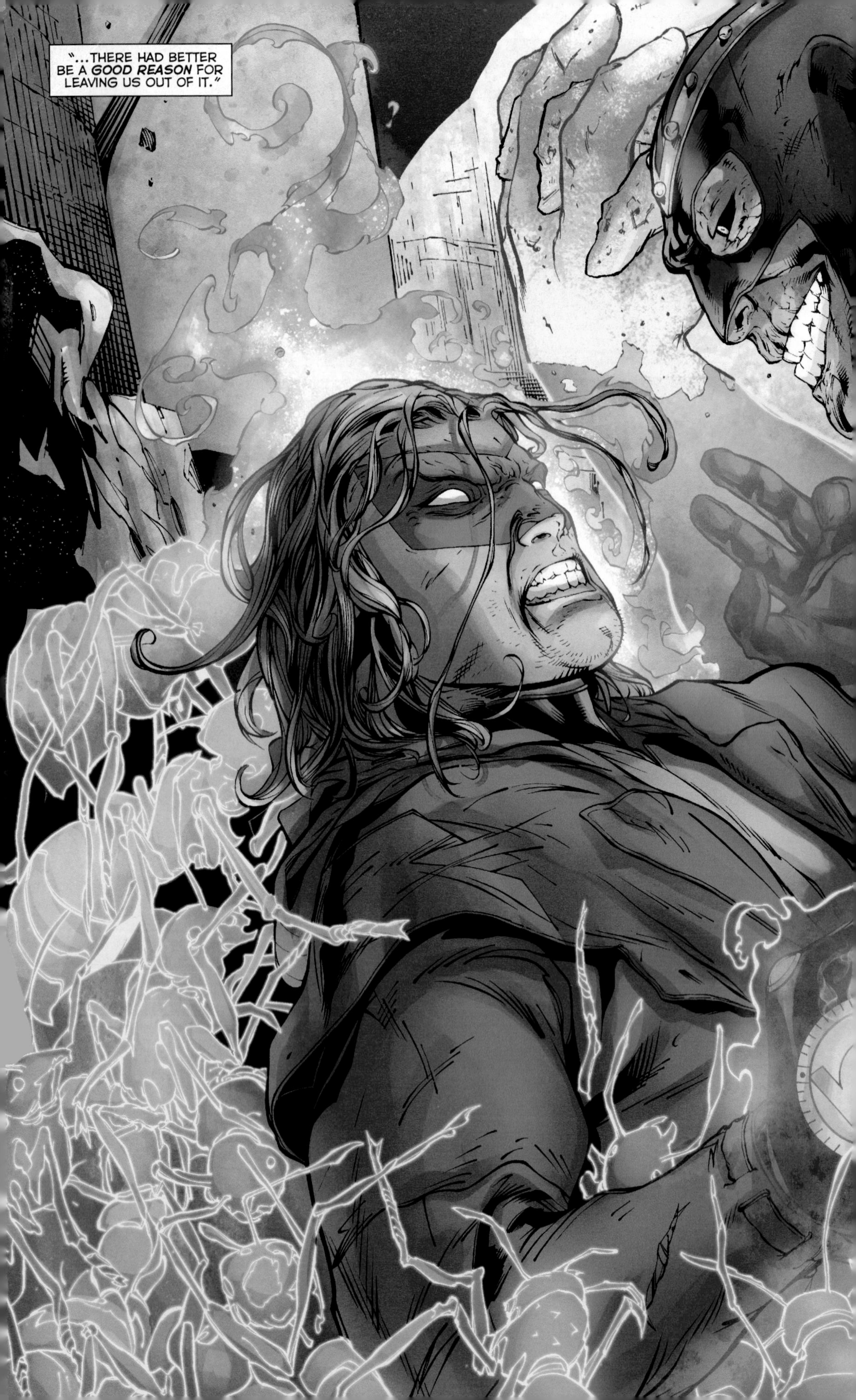
"...THERE HAD BETTER BE A GOOD REASON FOR LEAVING US OUT OF IT."

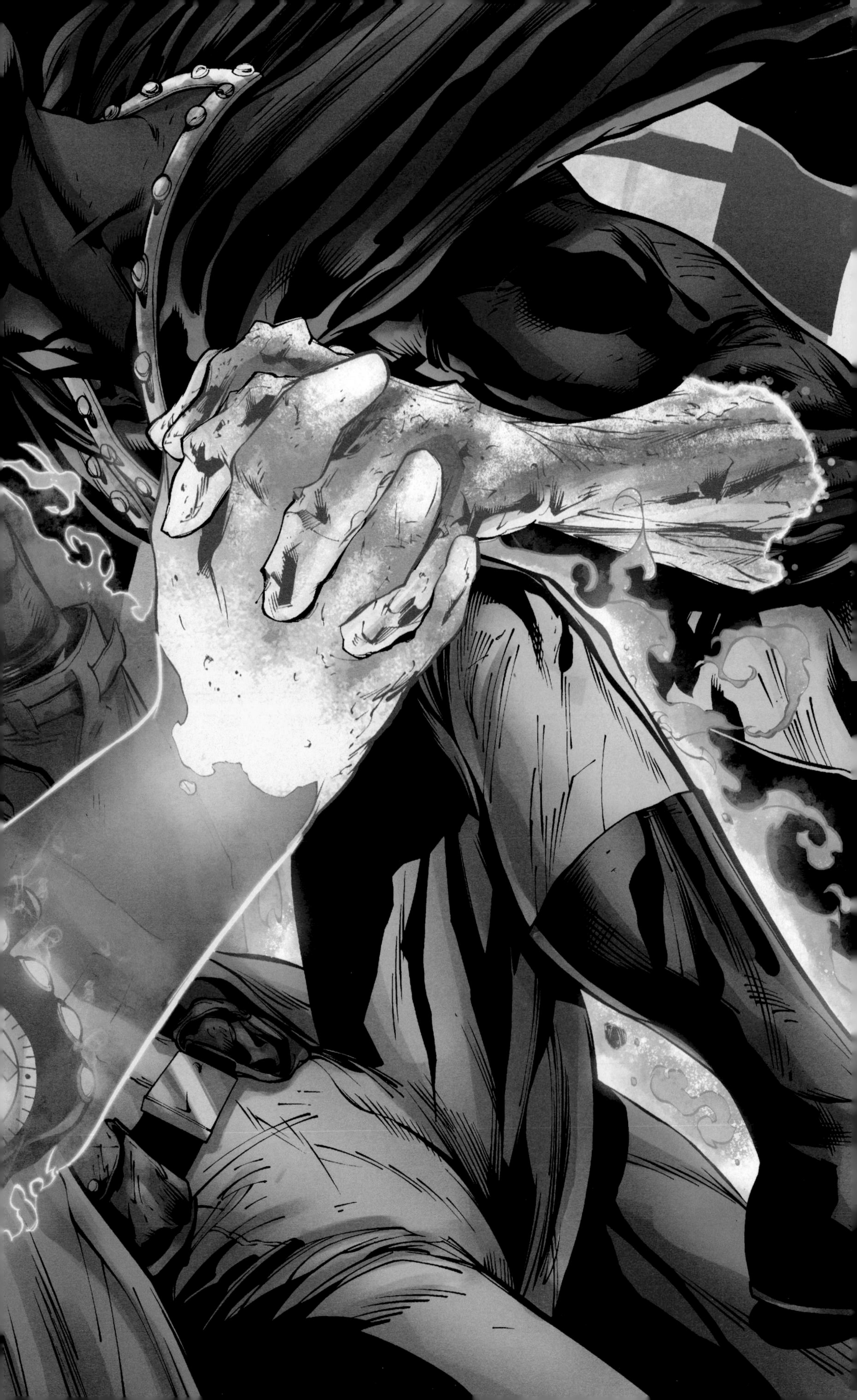

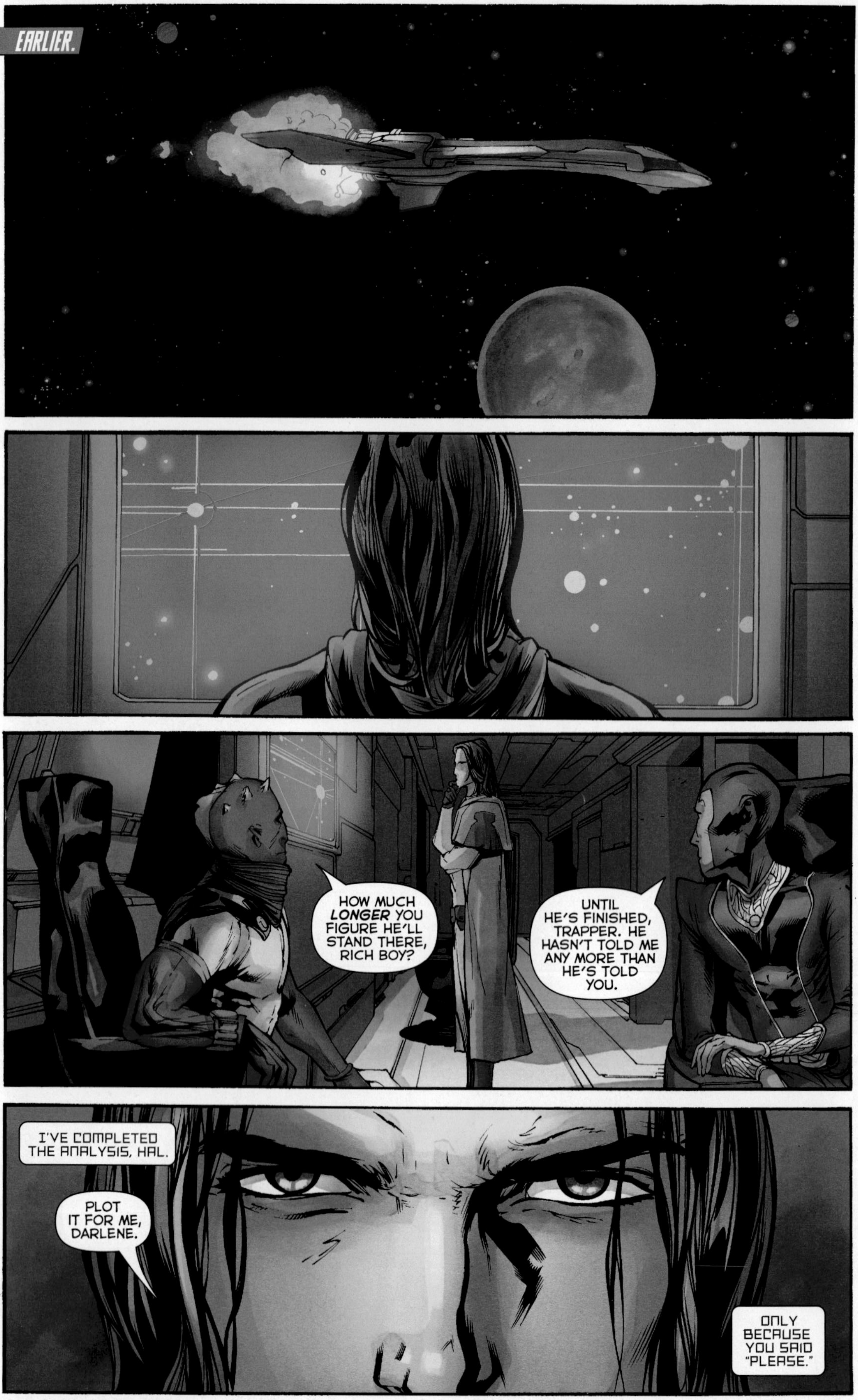
EARLIER.
HOW MUCH LONGER YOU FIGURE HE'LL STAND THERE, RICH BOY?
UNTIL HE'S FINISHED, TRAPPER. HE HASN'T TOLD ME ANY MORE THAN HE'S TOLD YOU.
I'VE COMPLETED THE ANALYSIS, HAL.
PLOT IT FOR ME, DARLENE.
ONLY BECAUSE YOU SAID "PLEASE."

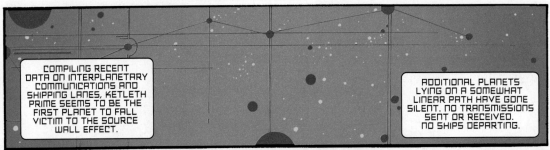

COMPILING RECENT DATA ON INTERPLANETARY COMMUNICATIONS AND SHIPPING LANES, KETLETH PRIME SEEMS TO BE THE FIRST PLANET TO FALL VICTIM TO THE SOURCE WALL EFFECT.

ADDITIONAL PLANETS LYING ON A SOMEWHAT LINEAR PATH HAVE GONE SILENT. NO TRANSMISSIONS SENT OR RECEIVED. NO SHIPS DEPARTING.

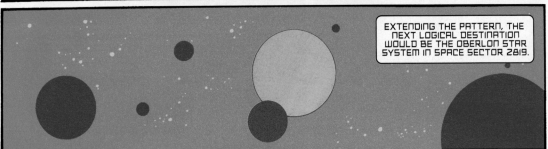

EXTENDING THE PATTERN, THE NEXT LOGICAL DESTINATION WOULD BE THE OBERLON STAR SYSTEM IN SPACE SECTOR 2819.

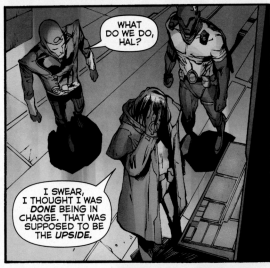

WHAT DO WE DO, HAL?

I SWEAR, I THOUGHT I WAS *DONE* BEING IN CHARGE. THAT WAS SUPPOSED TO BE THE *UPSIDE*.

WAIT.

DARLENE, SHOW ME THAT PATTERN AGAIN. ZOOM OUT.

OKAY...

SECTORS 3068, 2983, 2902, 2819. THAT FLIGHT PATH HAS HIM HEADING STRAIGHT TO...

OH NO...

WHAT IS IT? WHAT'S WRONG?

EVERYTHING IS WRONG, VIRGO. I HAVE TO GO. *NOW.*

YOU GUYS CAN'T GO WITH ME. EVEN IF YOU DID, YOU'D BE USELESS. STAY WITH DARLENE. SHE'LL KEEP YOU SAFE.

PTOO

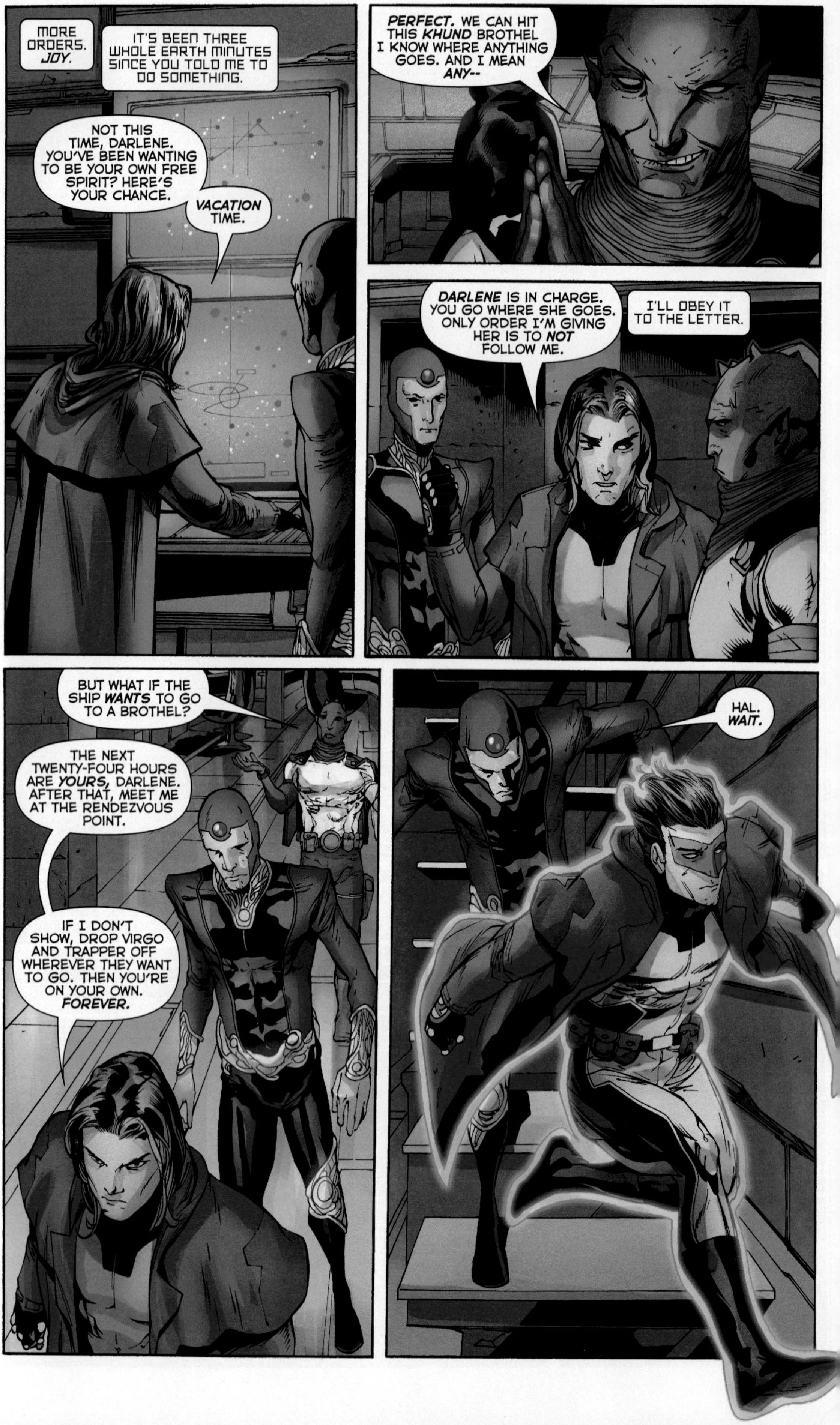
MORE ORDERS. JOY.
IT'S BEEN THREE WHOLE EARTH MINUTES SINCE YOU TOLD ME TO DO SOMETHING.
NOT THIS TIME, DARLENE. YOU'VE BEEN WANTING TO BE YOUR OWN FREE SPIRIT? HERE'S YOUR CHANCE.
VACATION TIME.
PERFECT. WE CAN HIT THIS KHUND BROTHEL I KNOW WHERE ANYTHING GOES. AND I MEAN ANY--
DARLENE IS IN CHARGE. YOU GO WHERE SHE GOES. ONLY ORDER I'M GIVING HER IS TO NOT FOLLOW ME.
I'LL OBEY IT TO THE LETTER.
BUT WHAT IF THE SHIP WANTS TO GO TO A BROTHEL?
THE NEXT TWENTY-FOUR HOURS ARE YOURS, DARLENE. AFTER THAT, MEET ME AT THE RENDEZVOUS POINT.
IF I DON'T SHOW, DROP VIRGO AND TRAPPER OFF WHEREVER THEY WANT TO GO. THEN YOU'RE ON YOUR OWN. FOREVER.
HAL. WAIT.

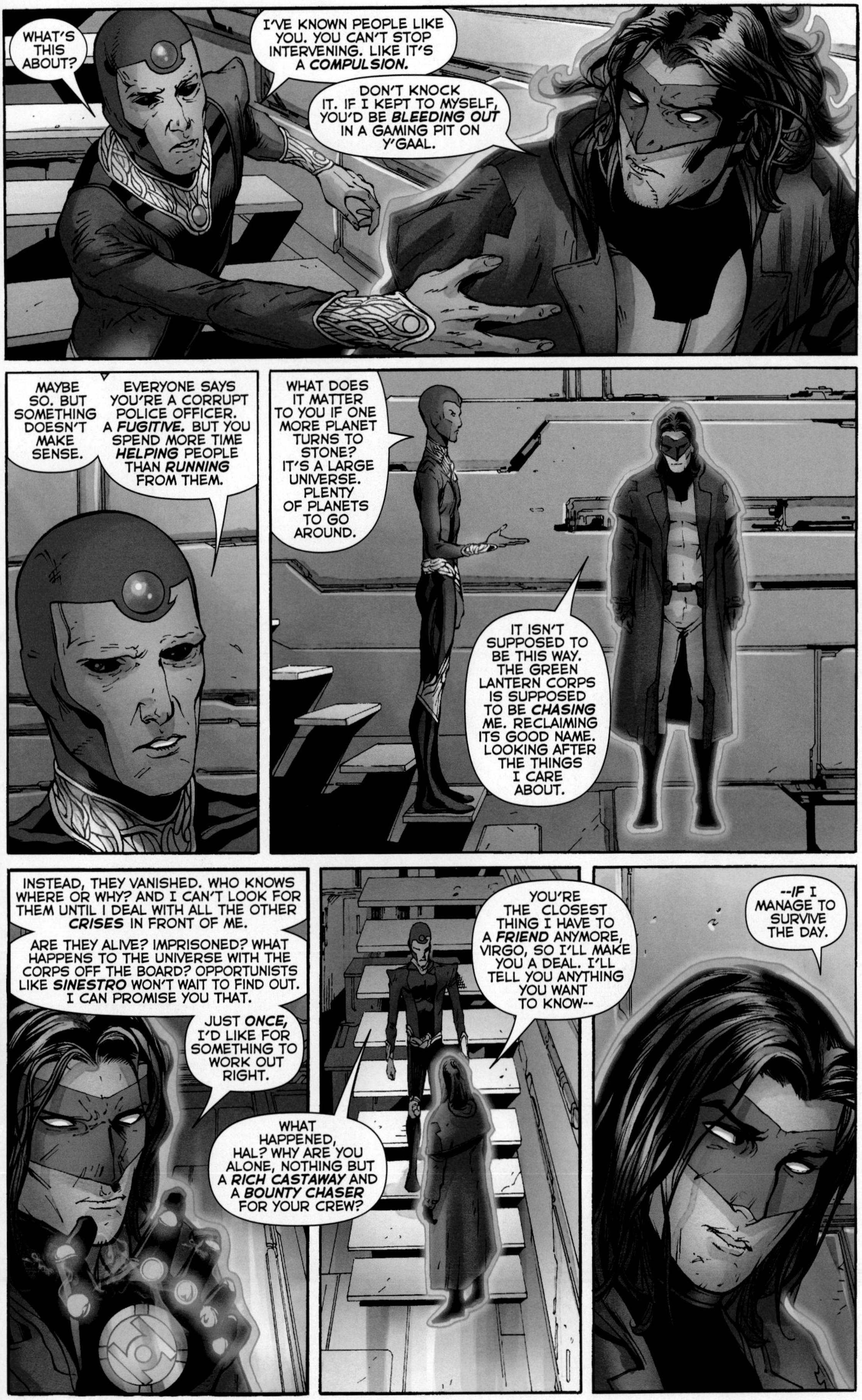
WHAT'S THIS ABOUT?
I'VE KNOWN PEOPLE LIKE YOU. YOU CAN'T STOP INTERVENING. LIKE IT'S A COMPULSION.
DON'T KNOCK IT. IF I KEPT TO MYSELF, YOU'D BE BLEEDING OUT IN A GAMING PIT ON Y'GAAL.
MAYBE SO. BUT SOMETHING DOESN'T MAKE SENSE.
EVERYONE SAYS YOU'RE A CORRUPT POLICE OFFICER. A FUGITIVE. BUT YOU SPEND MORE TIME HELPING PEOPLE THAN RUNNING FROM THEM.
WHAT DOES IT MATTER TO YOU IF ONE MORE PLANET TURNS TO STONE? IT'S A LARGE UNIVERSE. PLENTY OF PLANETS TO GO AROUND.
IT ISN'T SUPPOSED TO BE THIS WAY. THE GREEN LANTERN CORPS IS SUPPOSED TO BE CHASING ME. RECLAIMING ITS GOOD NAME. LOOKING AFTER THE THINGS I CARE ABOUT.
INSTEAD, THEY VANISHED. WHO KNOWS WHERE OR WHY? AND I CAN'T LOOK FOR THEM UNTIL I DEAL WITH ALL THE OTHER CRISES IN FRONT OF ME.
ARE THEY ALIVE? IMPRISONED? WHAT HAPPENS TO THE UNIVERSE WITH THE CORPS OFF THE BOARD? OPPORTUNISTS LIKE SINESTRO WON'T WAIT TO FIND OUT. I CAN PROMISE YOU THAT.
JUST ONCE, I'D LIKE FOR SOMETHING TO WORK OUT RIGHT.
WHAT HAPPENED, HAL? WHY ARE YOU ALONE, NOTHING BUT A RICH CASTAWAY AND A BOUNTY CHASER FOR YOUR CREW?
YOU'RE THE CLOSEST THING I HAVE TO A FRIEND ANYMORE, VIRGO, SO I'LL MAKE YOU A DEAL. I'LL TELL YOU ANYTHING YOU WANT TO KNOW--
--IF I MANAGE TO SURVIVE THE DAY.

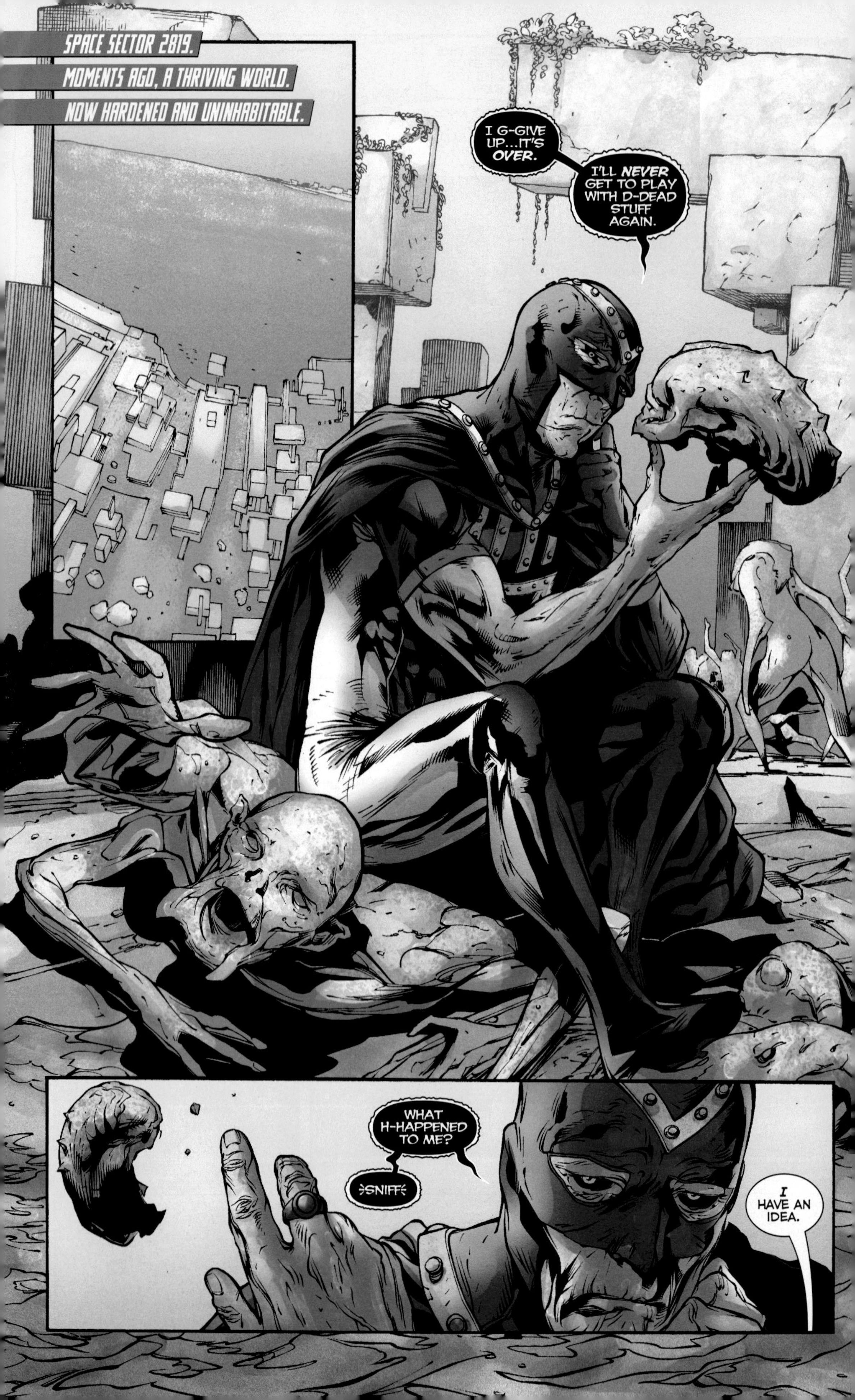
SPACE SECTOR 2819.
MOMENTS AGO, A THRIVING WORLD.
NOW HARDENED AND UNINHABITABLE.
I G-GIVE UP...IT'S OVER.
I'LL NEVER GET TO PLAY WITH D-DEAD STUFF AGAIN.
WHAT H-HAPPENED TO ME?
SNIFF
I HAVE AN IDEA.

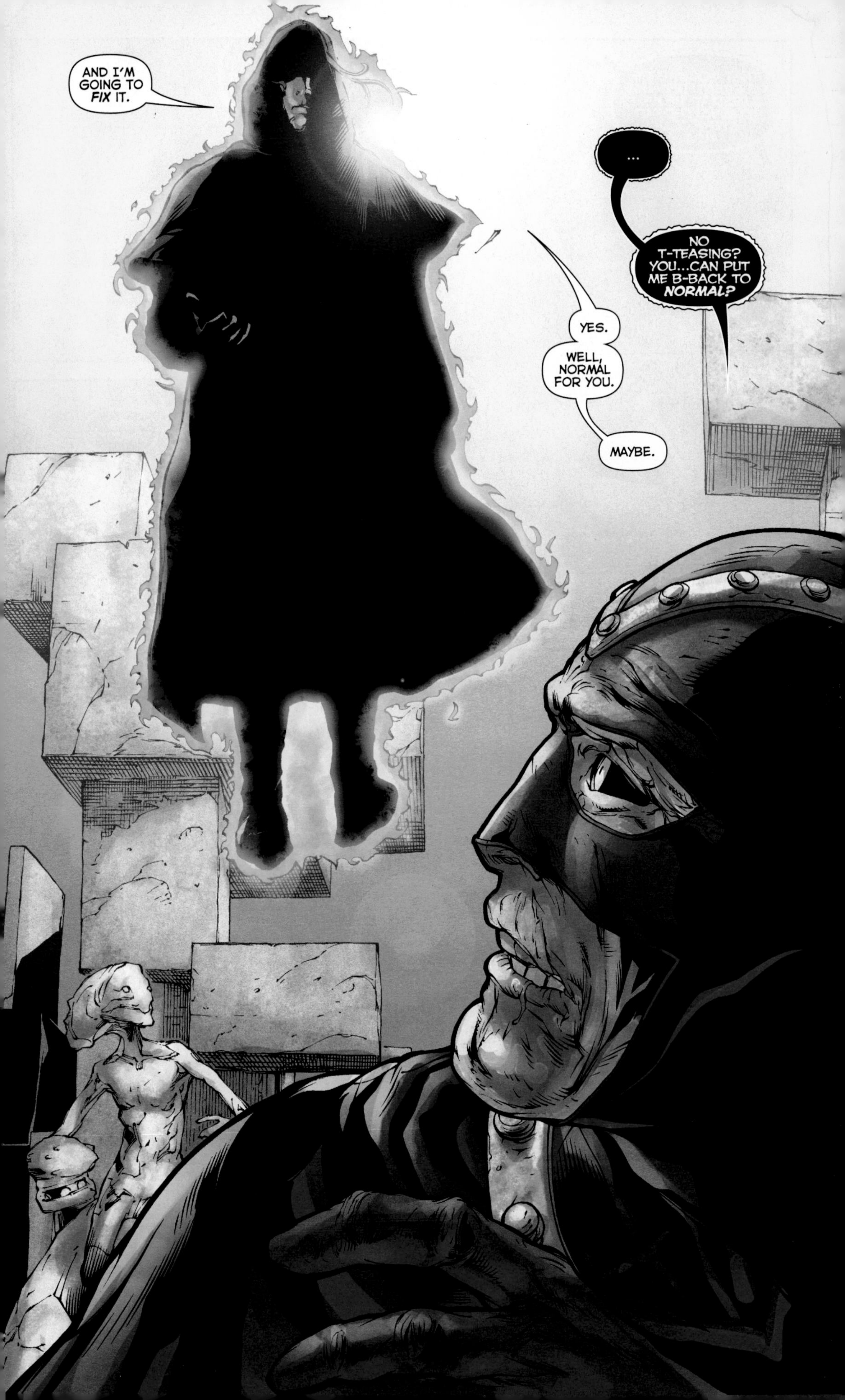
AND I'M GOING TO *FIX* IT.
...
NO T-TEASING? YOU...CAN PUT ME B-BACK TO ***NORMAL?***
YES.
WELL, NORMAL FOR YOU.
MAYBE.

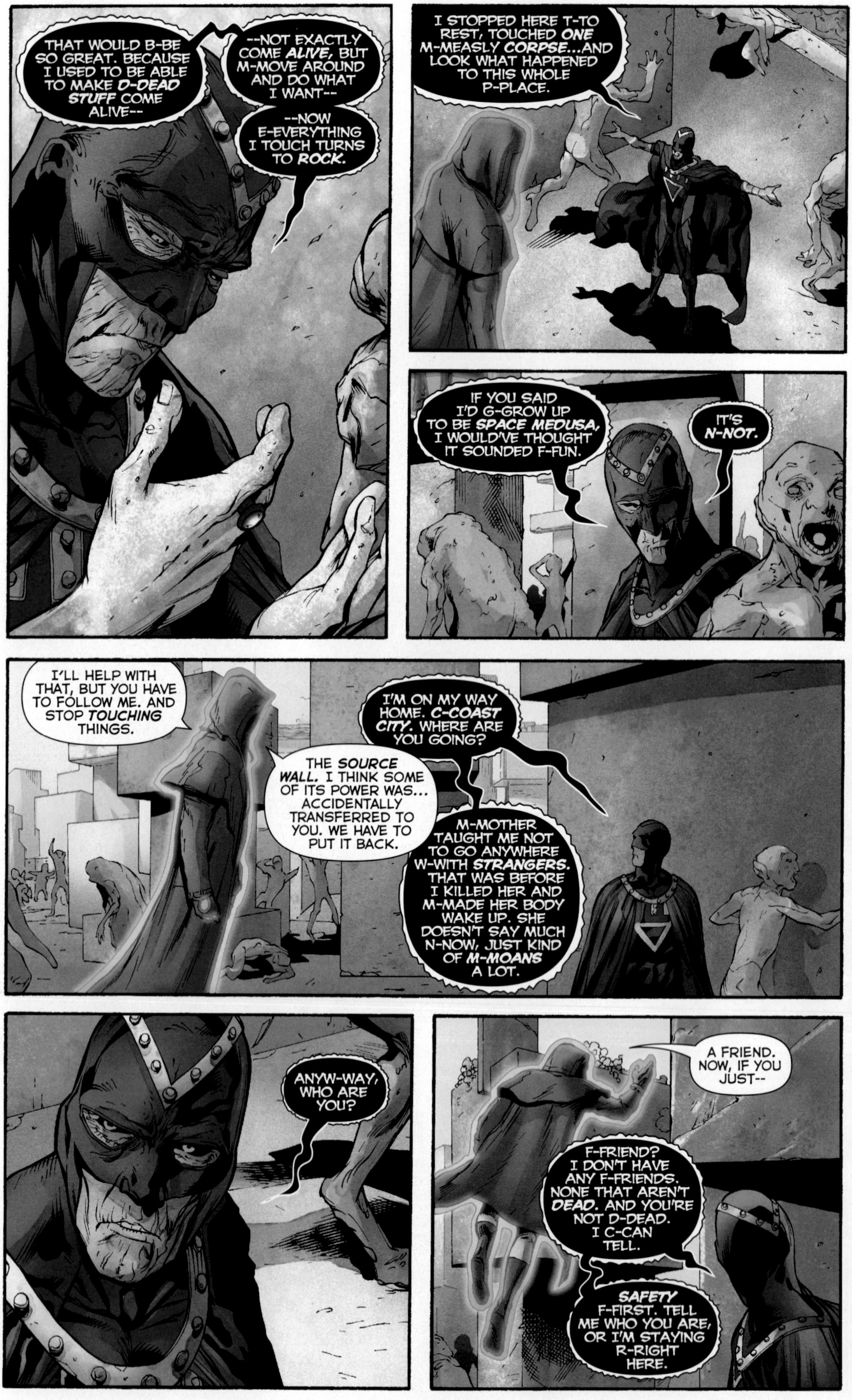
THAT WOULD B-BE SO GREAT. BECAUSE I USED TO BE ABLE TO MAKE D-DEAD STUFF COME ALIVE--
--NOT EXACTLY COME ALIVE, BUT M-MOVE AROUND AND DO WHAT I WANT--
--NOW E-EVERYTHING I TOUCH TURNS TO ROCK.
I STOPPED HERE T-TO REST, TOUCHED ONE M-MEASLY CORPSE...AND LOOK WHAT HAPPENED TO THIS WHOLE P-PLACE.
IF YOU SAID I'D G-GROW UP TO BE SPACE MEDUSA, I WOULD'VE THOUGHT IT SOUNDED F-FUN.
IT'S N-NOT.
I'LL HELP WITH THAT, BUT YOU HAVE TO FOLLOW ME. AND STOP TOUCHING THINGS.
I'M ON MY WAY HOME. C-COAST CITY. WHERE ARE YOU GOING?
THE SOURCE WALL. I THINK SOME OF ITS POWER WAS... ACCIDENTALLY TRANSFERRED TO YOU. WE HAVE TO PUT IT BACK.
M-MOTHER TAUGHT ME NOT TO GO ANYWHERE W-WITH STRANGERS. THAT WAS BEFORE I KILLED HER AND M-MADE HER BODY WAKE UP. SHE DOESN'T SAY MUCH N-NOW, JUST KIND OF M-MOANS A LOT.
ANYW-WAY, WHO ARE YOU?
A FRIEND. NOW, IF YOU JUST--
F-FRIEND? I DON'T HAVE ANY F-FRIENDS. NONE THAT AREN'T DEAD. AND YOU'RE NOT D-DEAD. I C-CAN TELL.
SAFETY F-FIRST. TELL ME WHO YOU ARE, OR I'M STAYING R-RIGHT HERE.

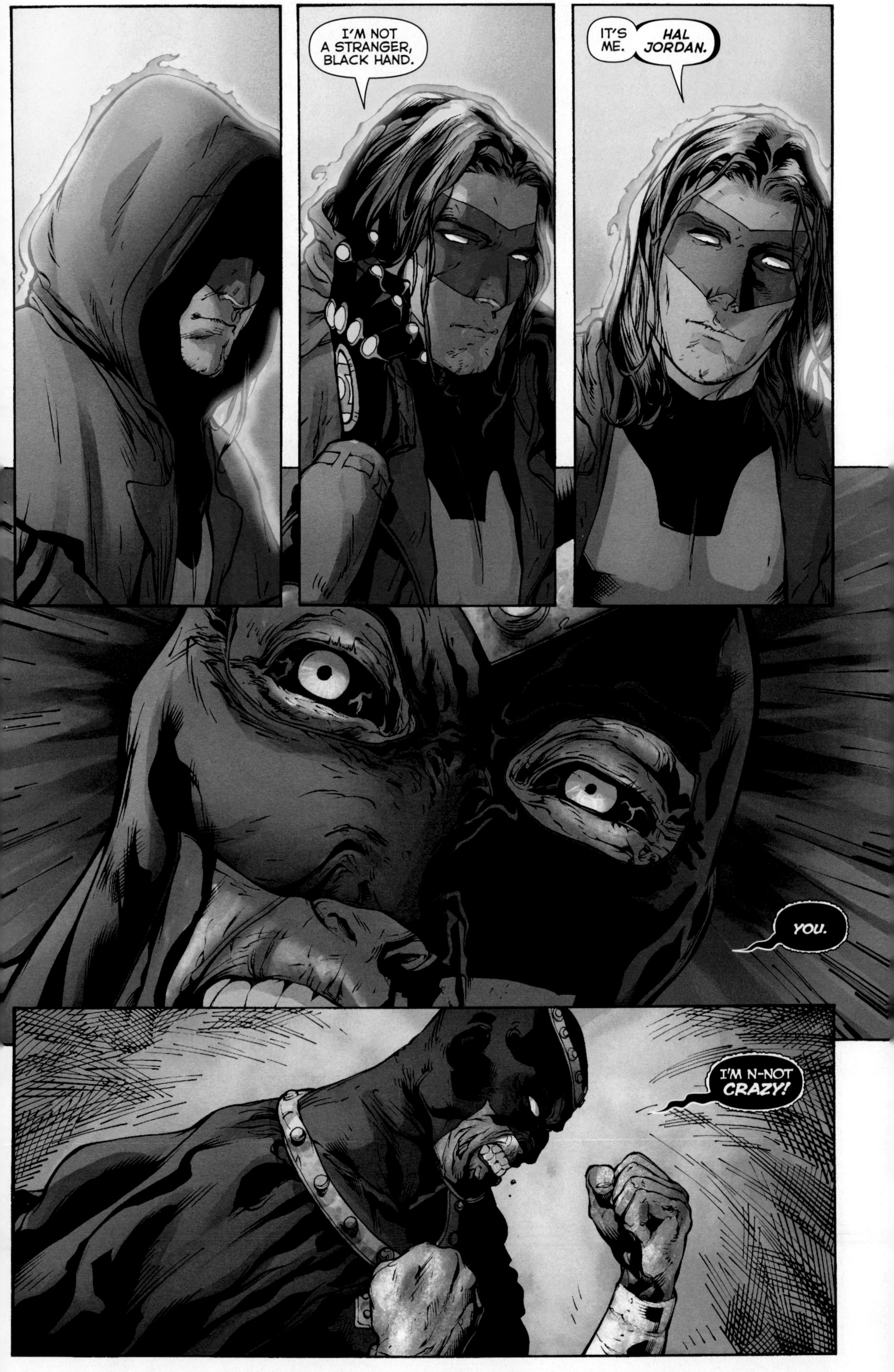
I'M NOT A STRANGER, BLACK HAND.
IT'S ME.
HAL JORDAN.
YOU.
I'M N-NOT CRAZY!

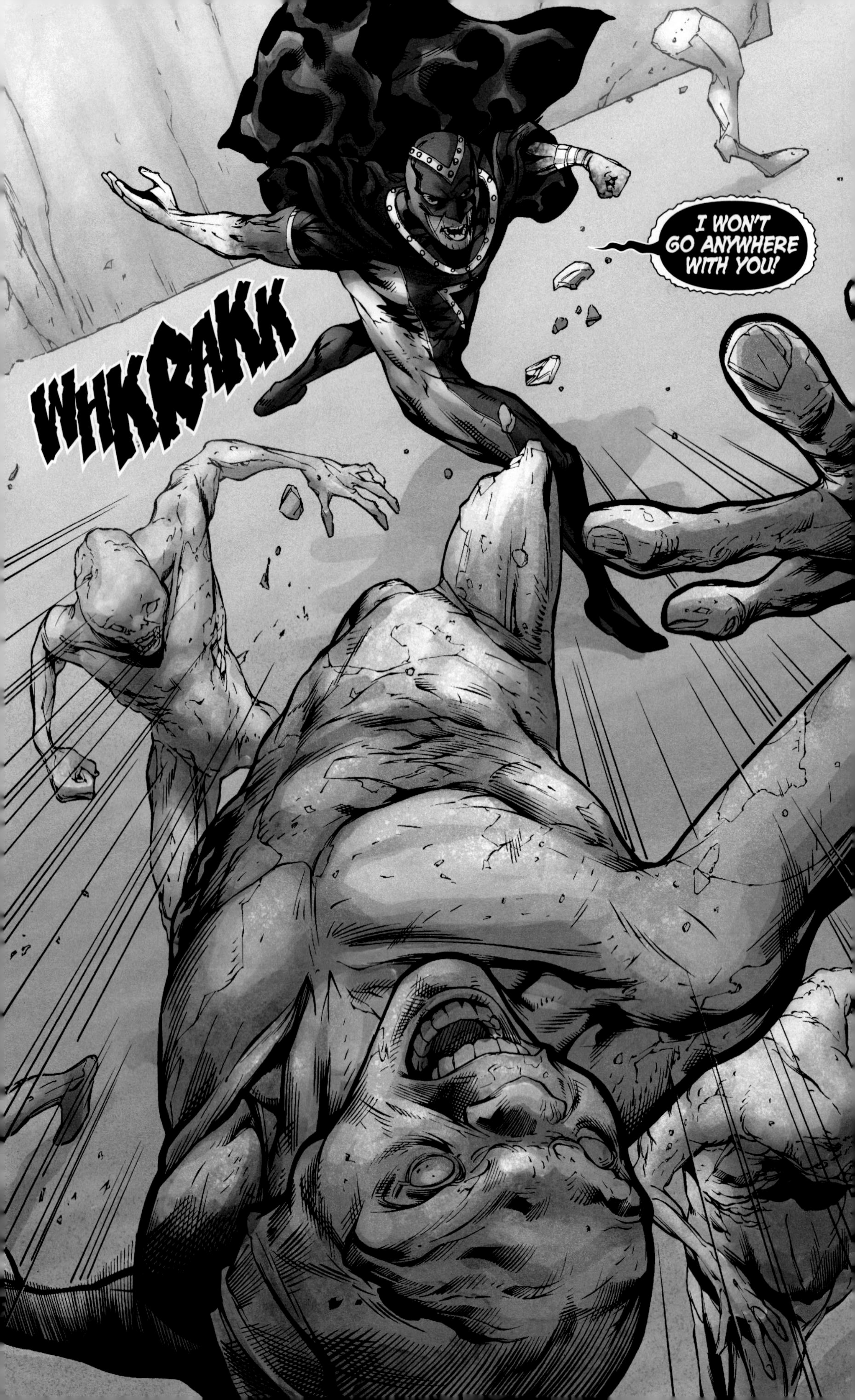
WHKRAKK
I WON'T GO ANYWHERE WITH YOU!

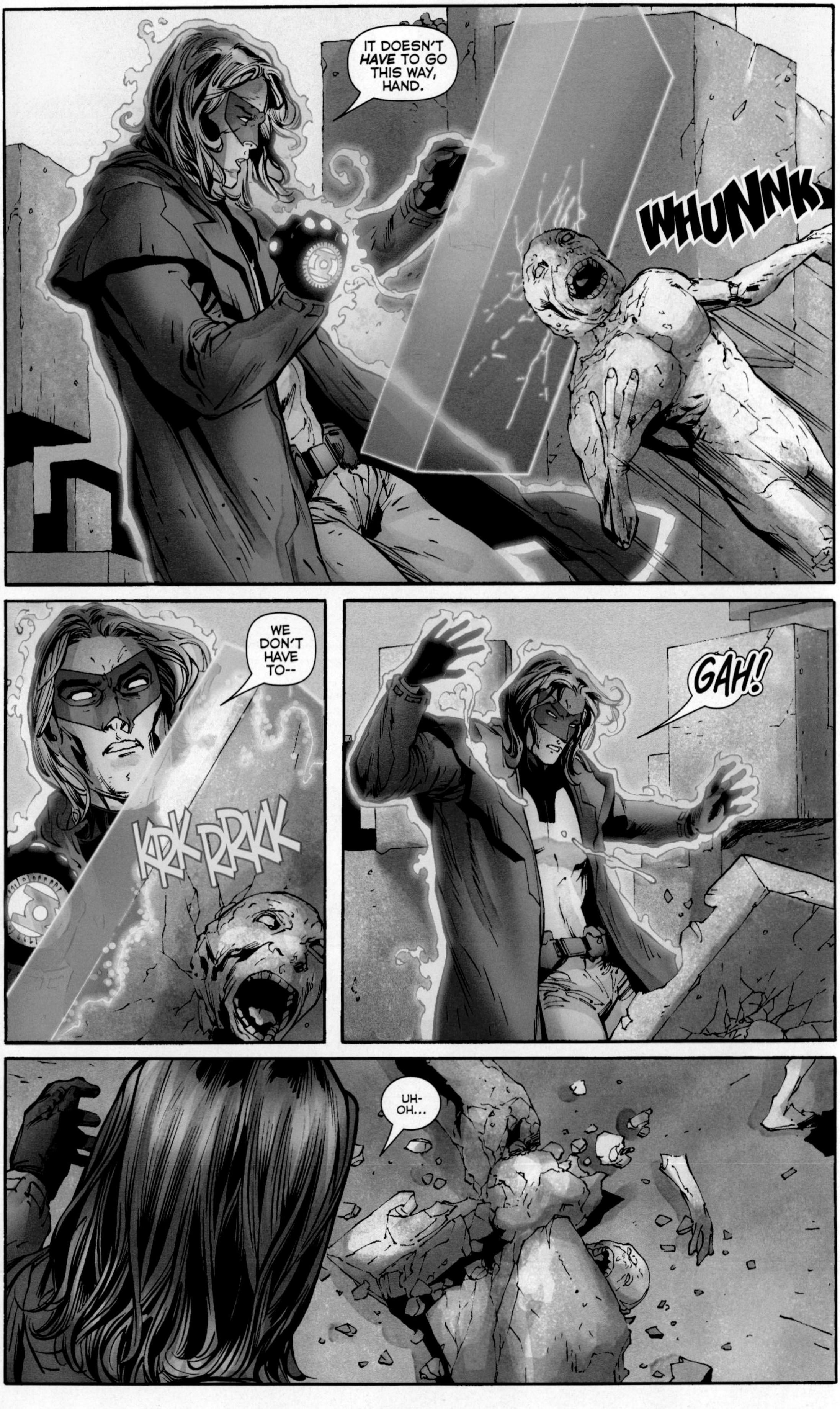
IT DOESN'T *HAVE* TO GO THIS WAY, HAND.
WHUNNK!
WE DON'T HAVE TO--
KRRK RRKK
GAH!
UH-OH...

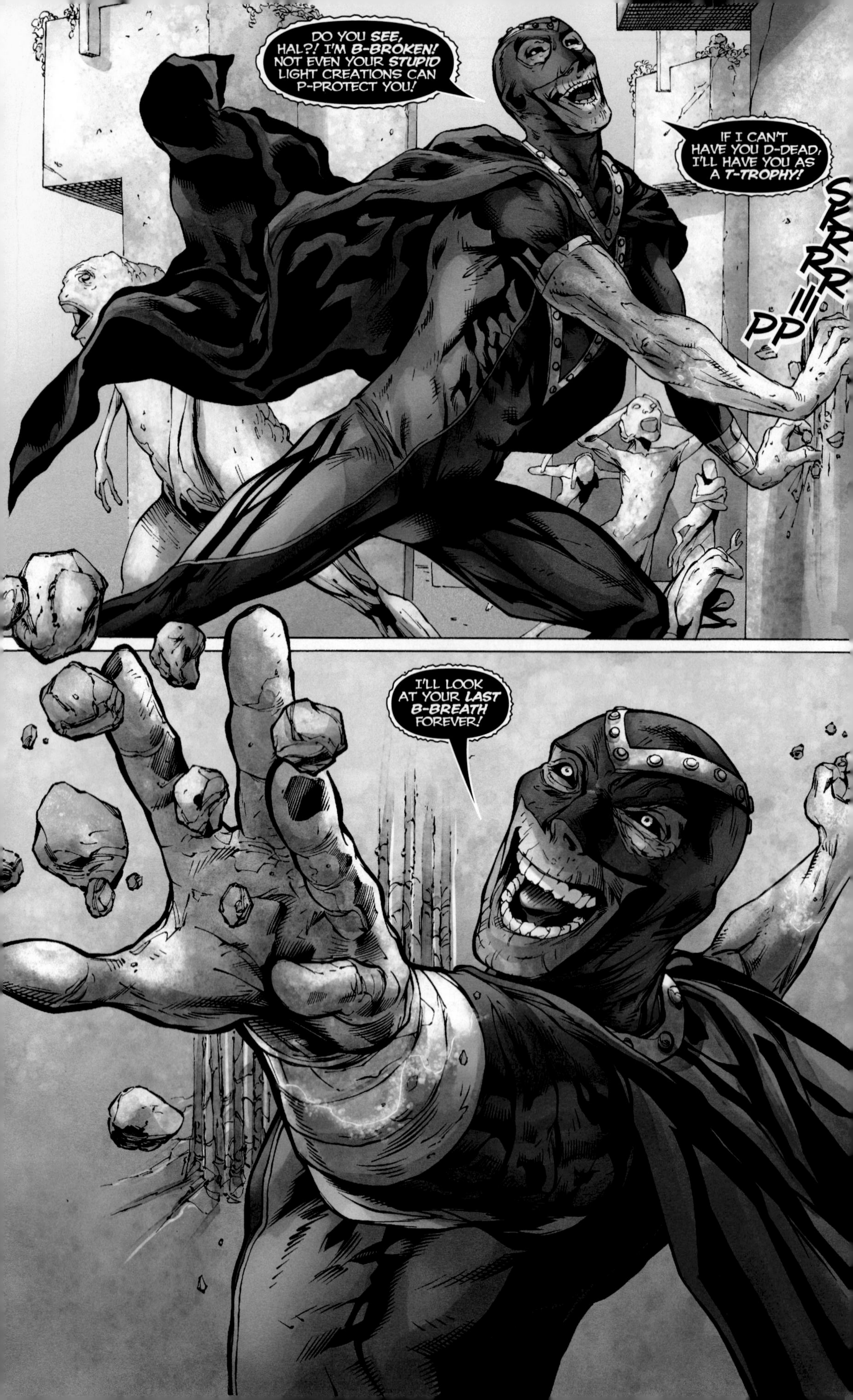
DO YOU SEE, HAL?! I'M B-BROKEN! NOT EVEN YOUR STUPID LIGHT CREATIONS CAN P-PROTECT YOU!
IF I CAN'T HAVE YOU D-DEAD, I'LL HAVE YOU AS A T-TROPHY!
SKRRRIIPP
I'LL LOOK AT YOUR LAST B-BREATH FOREVER!

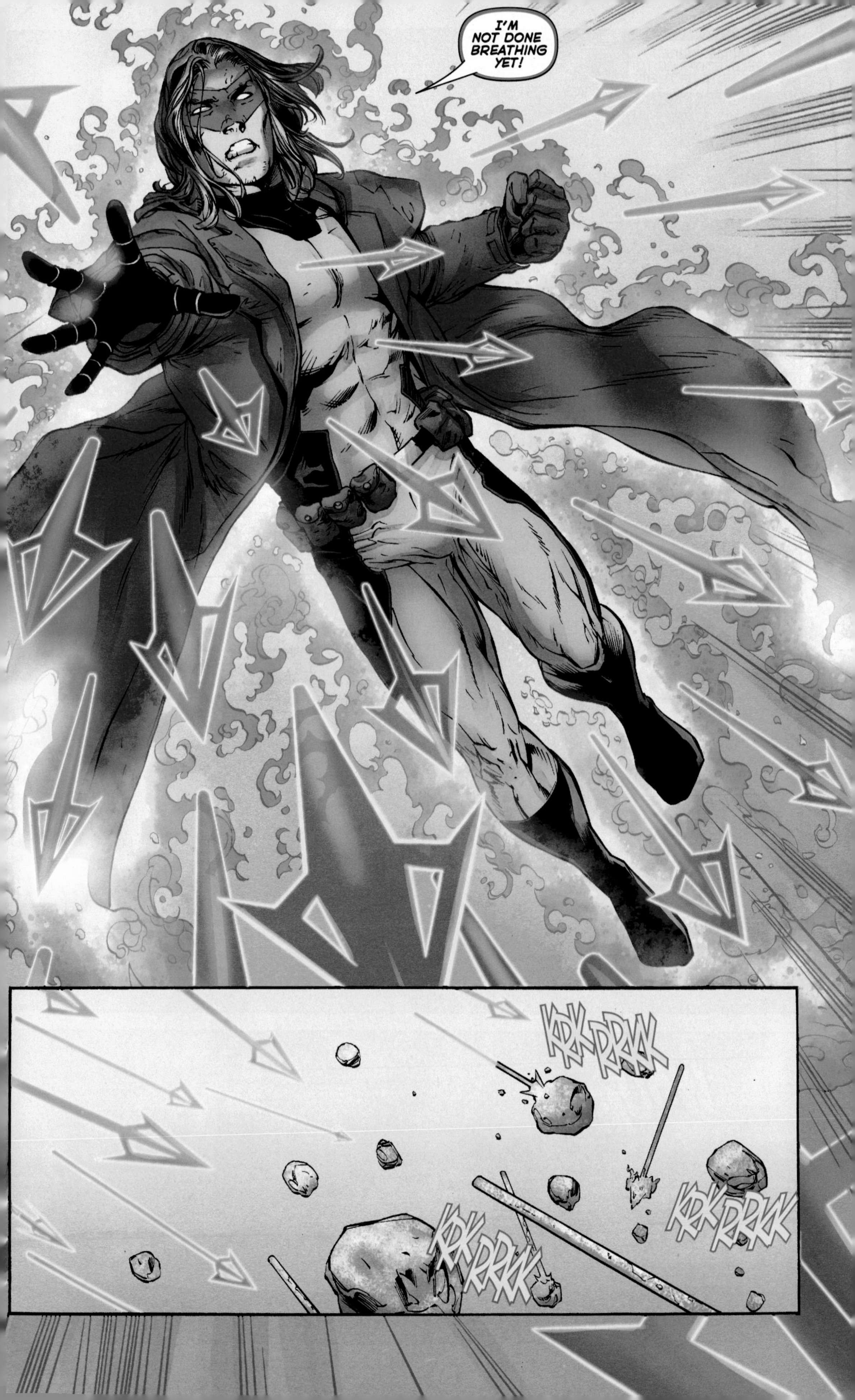
I'M NOT DONE BREATHING YET!
KRK-RRAK
KRK-RRRK
KRK-RRRK

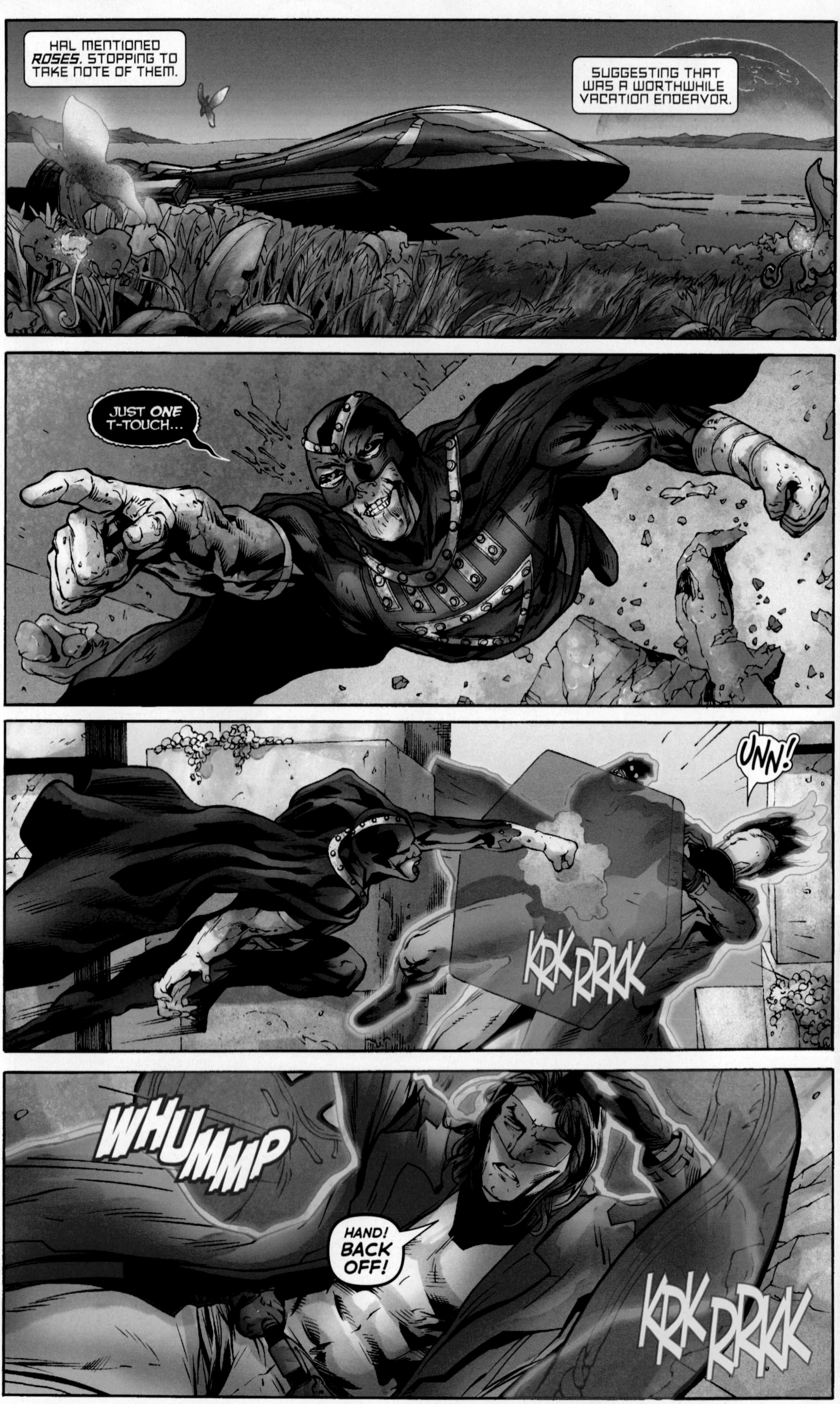
HAL MENTIONED ROSES, STOPPING TO TAKE NOTE OF THEM.
SUGGESTING THAT WAS A WORTHWHILE VACATION ENDEAVOR.
JUST ONE T-TOUCH...
UNN!
KRK RRKK
WHUMMP
HAND! BACK OFF!
KRK RRKK

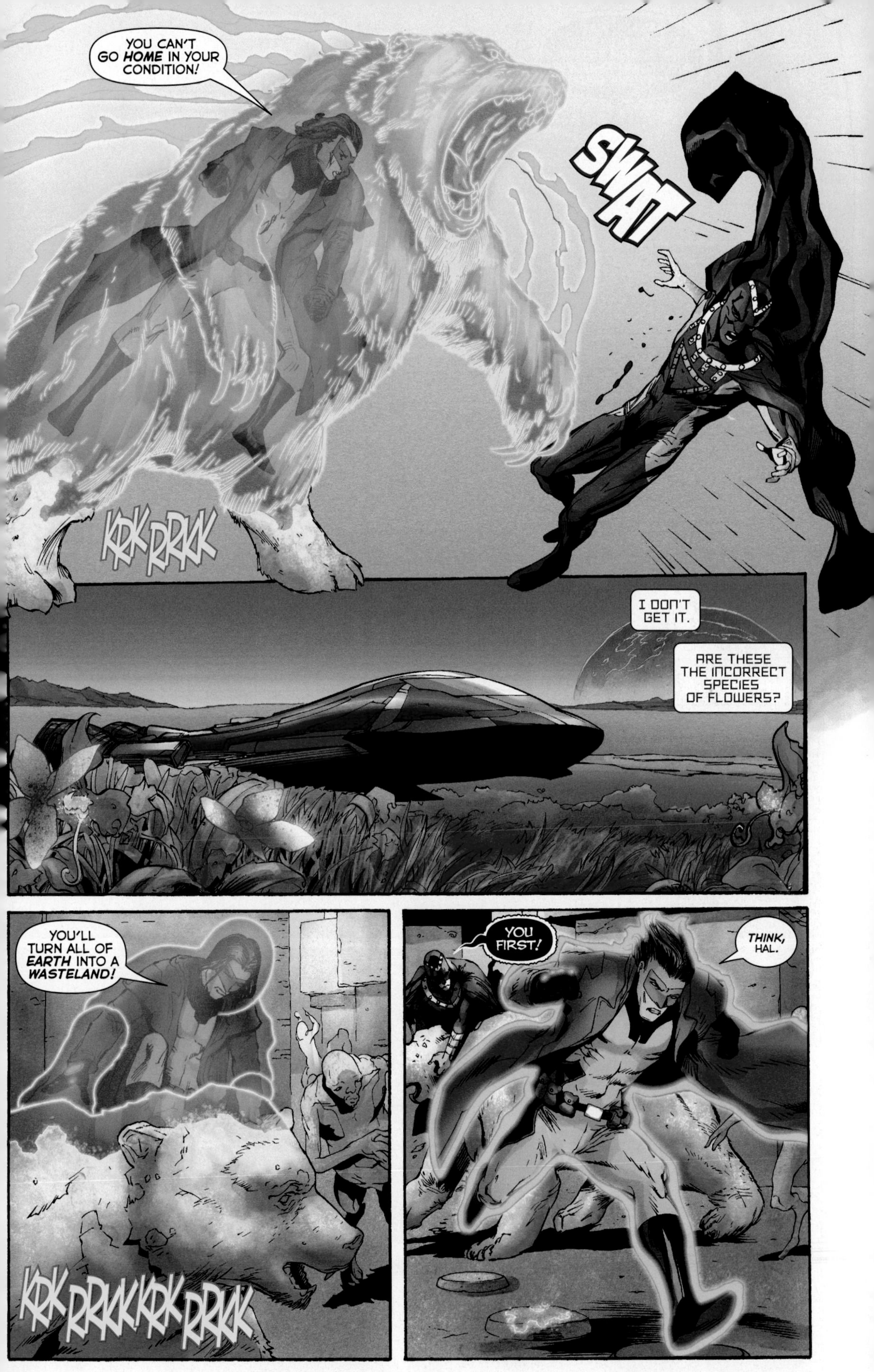
YOU CAN'T GO HOME IN YOUR CONDITION!
SWAT
KRK RRKK
I DON'T GET IT.
ARE THESE THE INCORRECT SPECIES OF FLOWERS?
YOU'LL TURN ALL OF EARTH INTO A WASTELAND!
KRK RRKK KRK RRKK
YOU FIRST!
THINK, HAL.

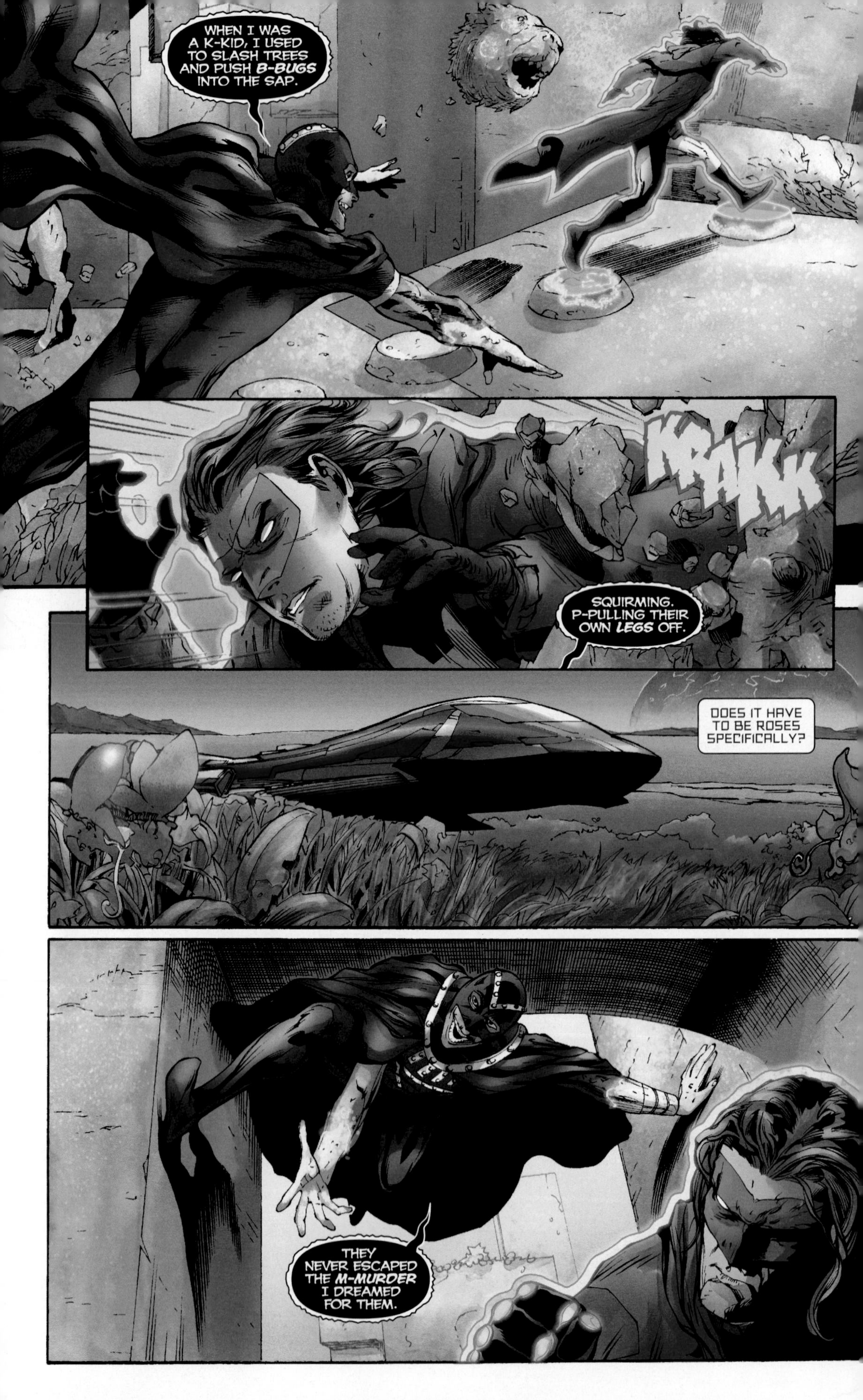
WHEN I WAS A K-KID, I USED TO SLASH TREES AND PUSH B-BUGS INTO THE SAP.
KRAKK
SQUIRMING. P-PULLING THEIR OWN LEGS OFF.
DOES IT HAVE TO BE ROSES SPECIFICALLY?
THEY NEVER ESCAPED THE M-MURDER I DREAMED FOR THEM.

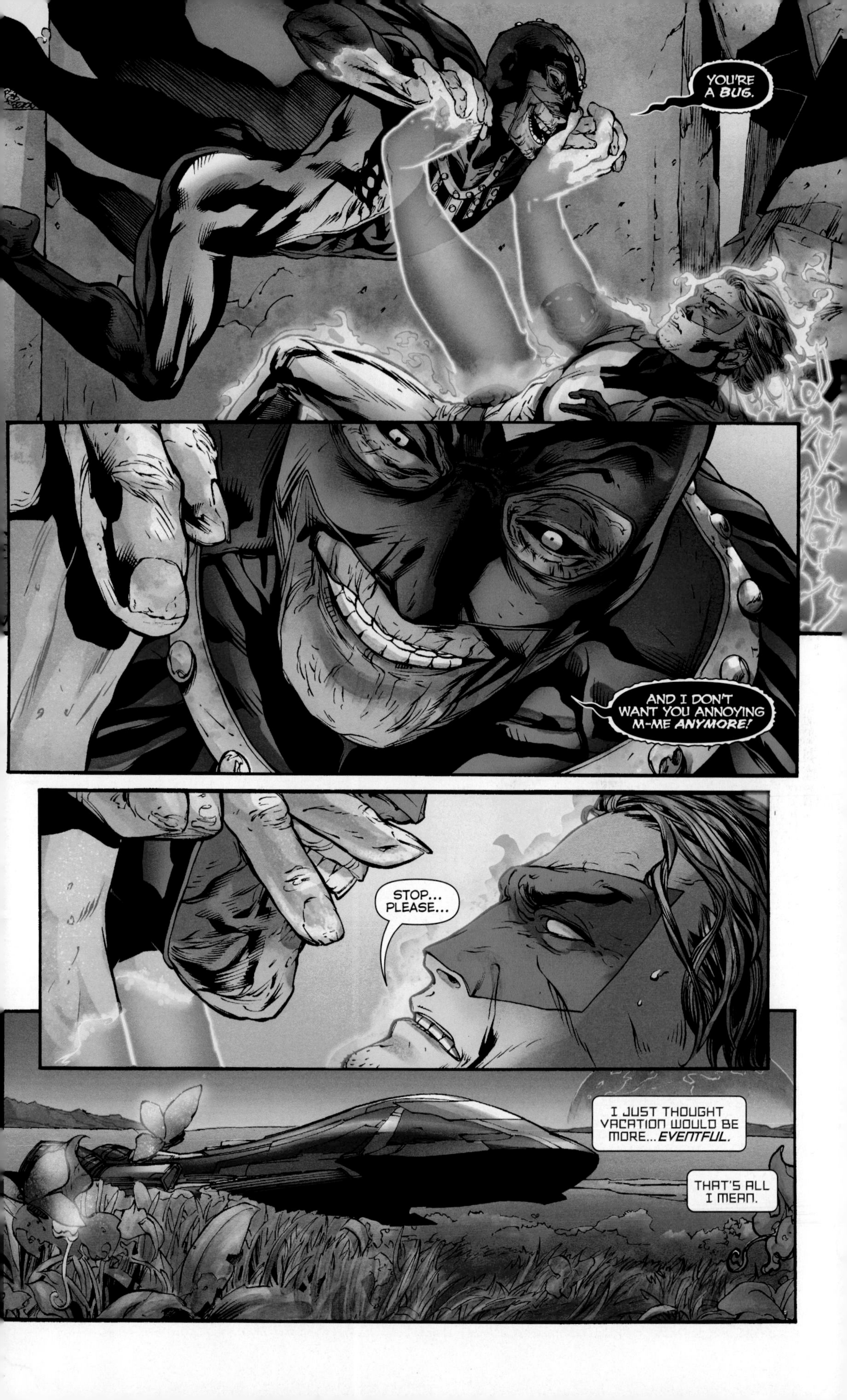
YOU'RE A *BUG.*
AND I DON'T WANT YOU ANNOYING M-ME *ANYMORE!*
STOP... PLEASE...
I JUST THOUGHT VACATION WOULD BE MORE... *EVENTFUL.*
THAT'S ALL I MEAN.

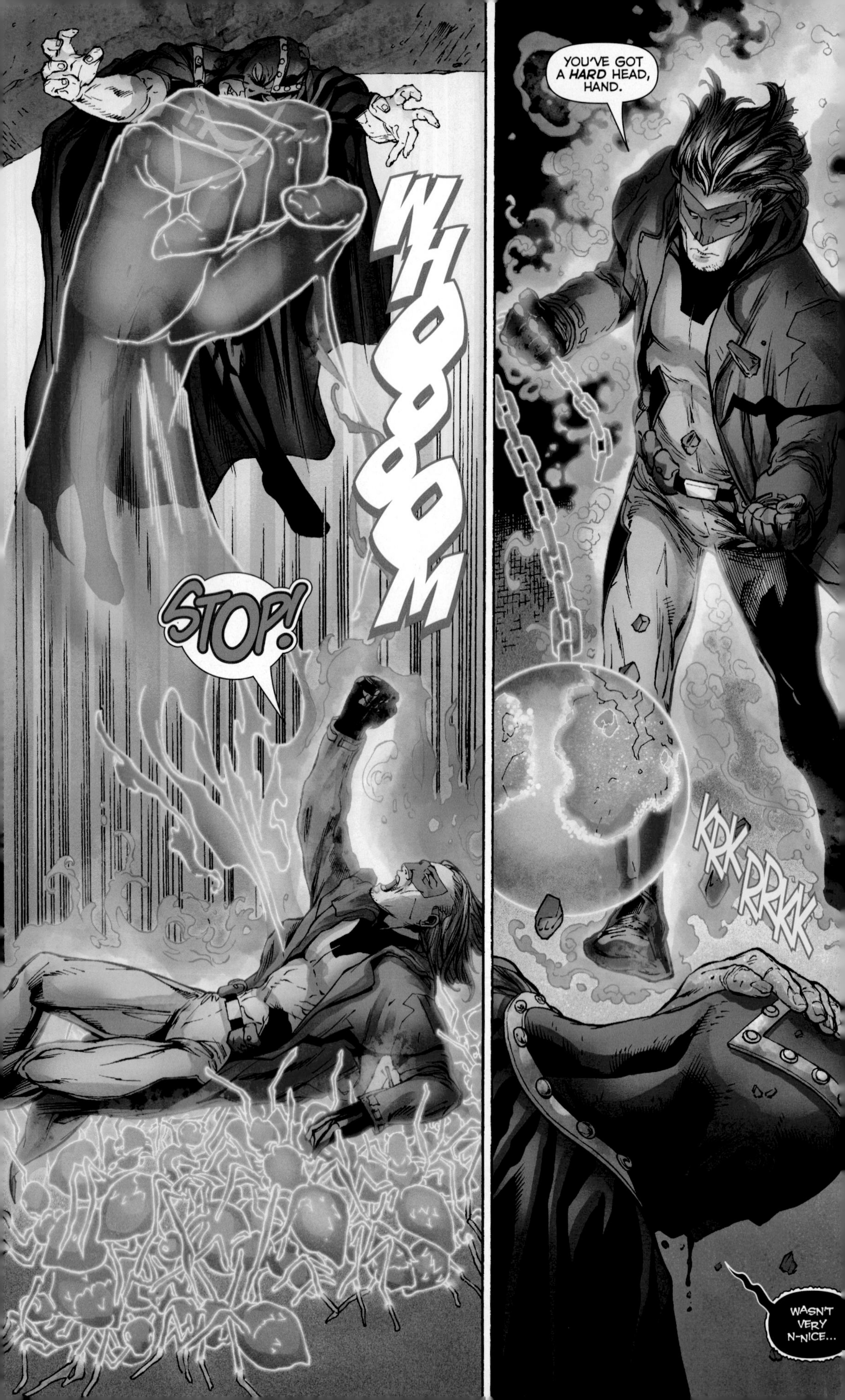
WHOOOOM
STOP!
YOU'VE GOT A HARD HEAD, HAND.
KRK RRKK
WASN'T VERY N-NICE...

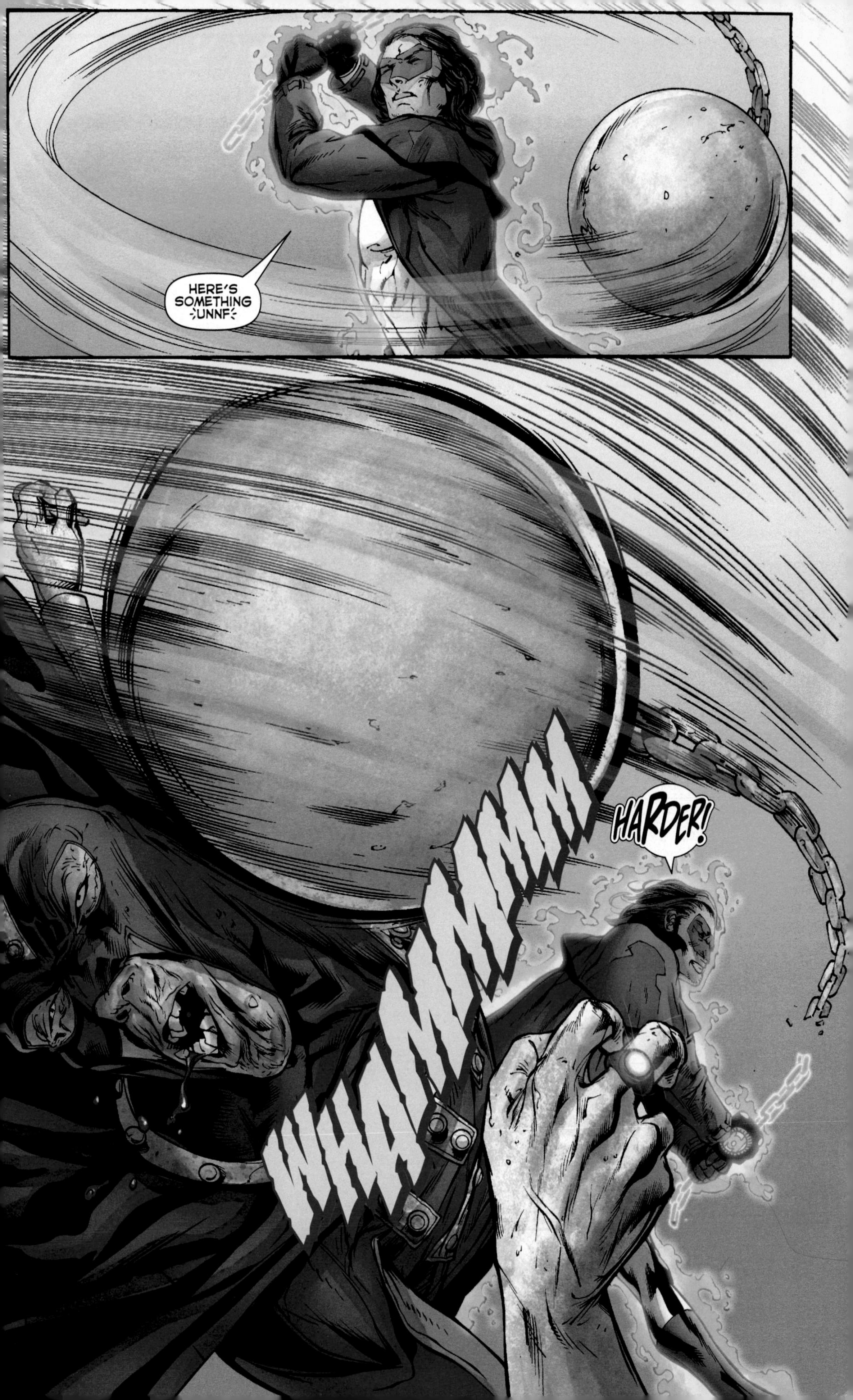
HERE'S SOMETHING -UNNF-
WHAMMMM
HARDER!

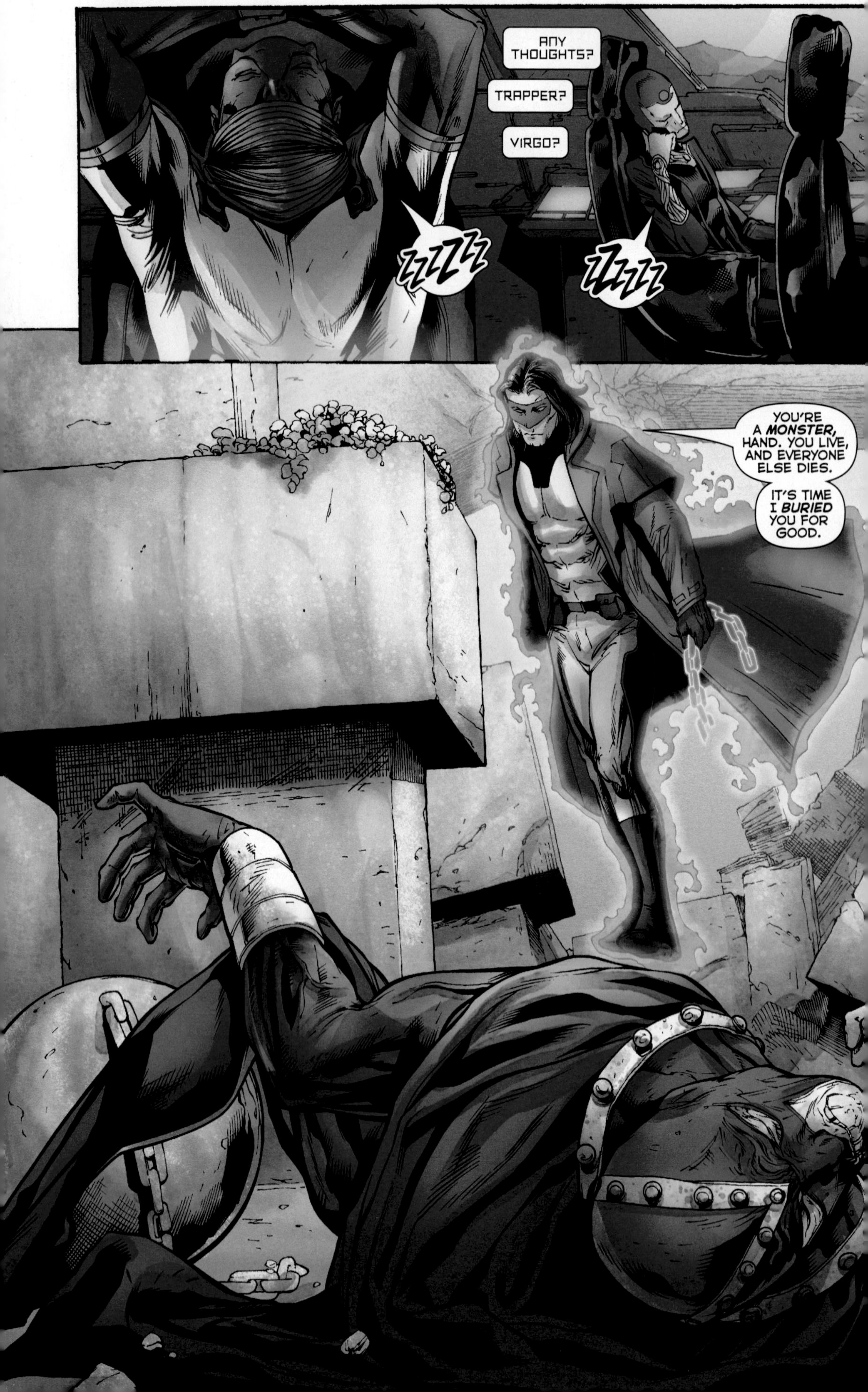
ANY THOUGHTS?
TRAPPER?
VIRGO?
ZZZZZZ
ZZZZZZ
YOU'RE A *MONSTER,* HAND. YOU LIVE, AND EVERYONE ELSE DIES.
IT'S TIME I *BURIED* YOU FOR GOOD.

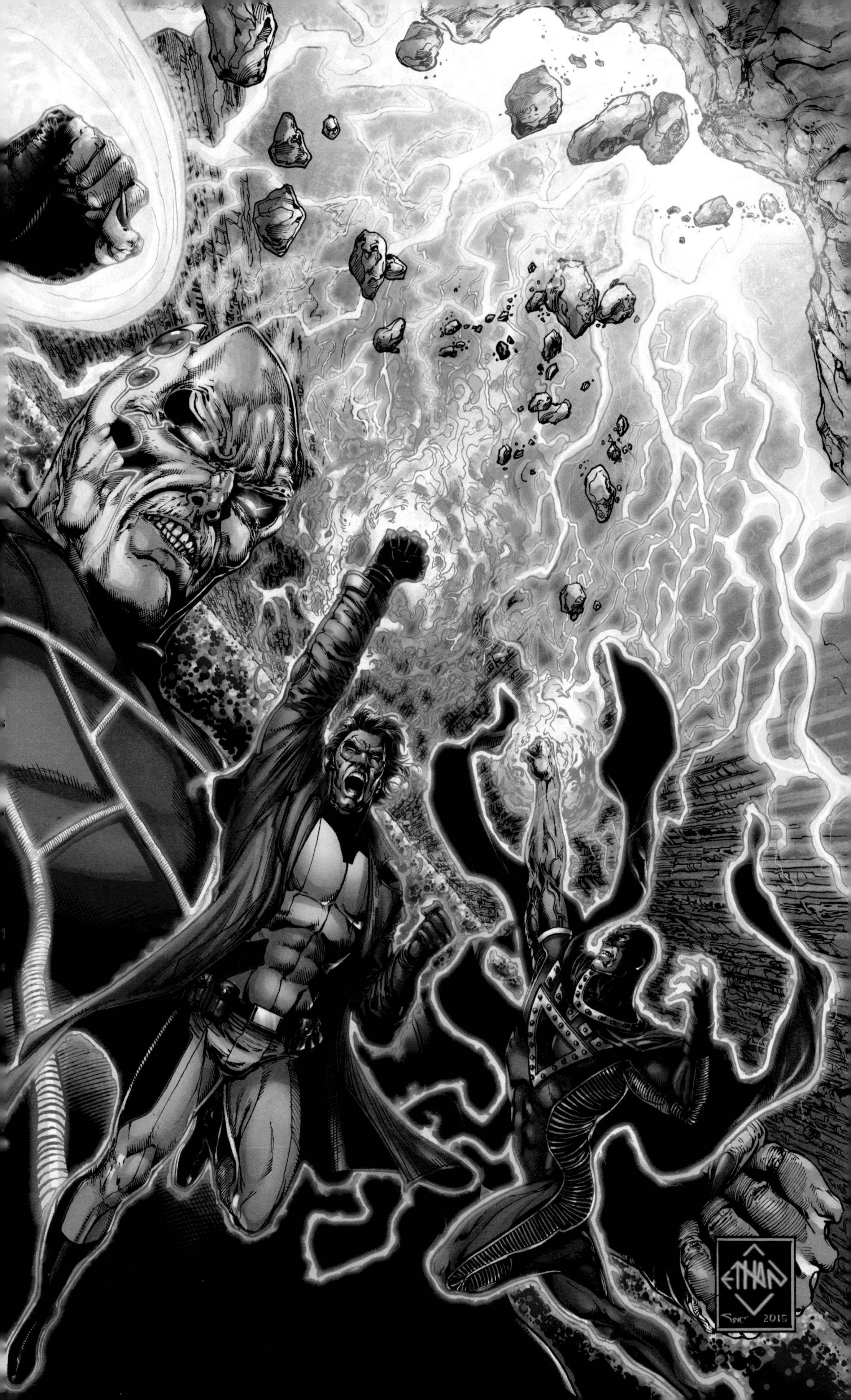

LAID TO REST

ROBERT VENDITTI writer **BILLY TAN** penciller **MARK IRWIN** inker **ALEX SINCLAIR** colorist **DAVE SHARPE** letterer **ETHAN VAN SCIVER & ALEX SINCLAIR** cover

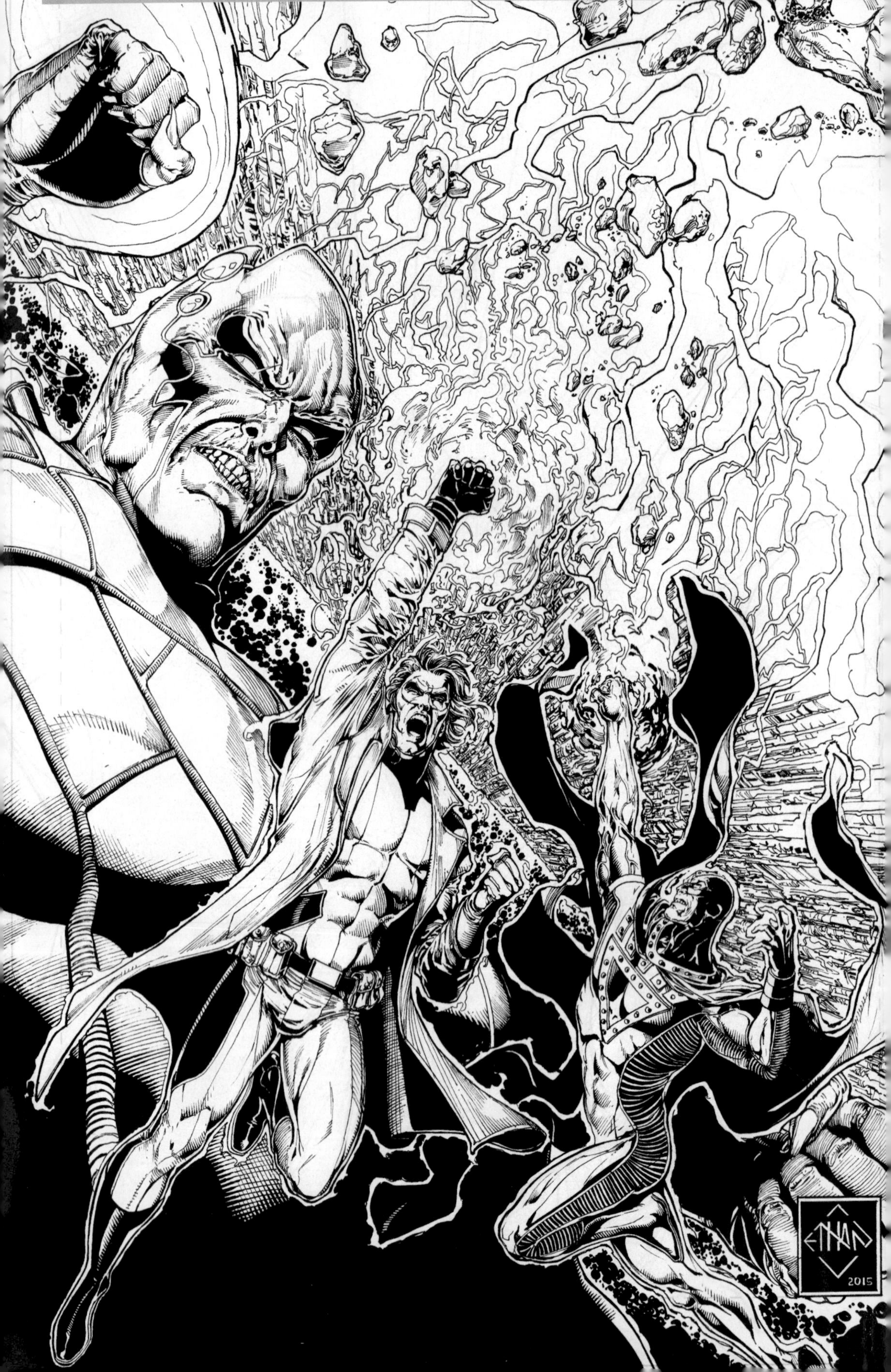
ETHAN
2015

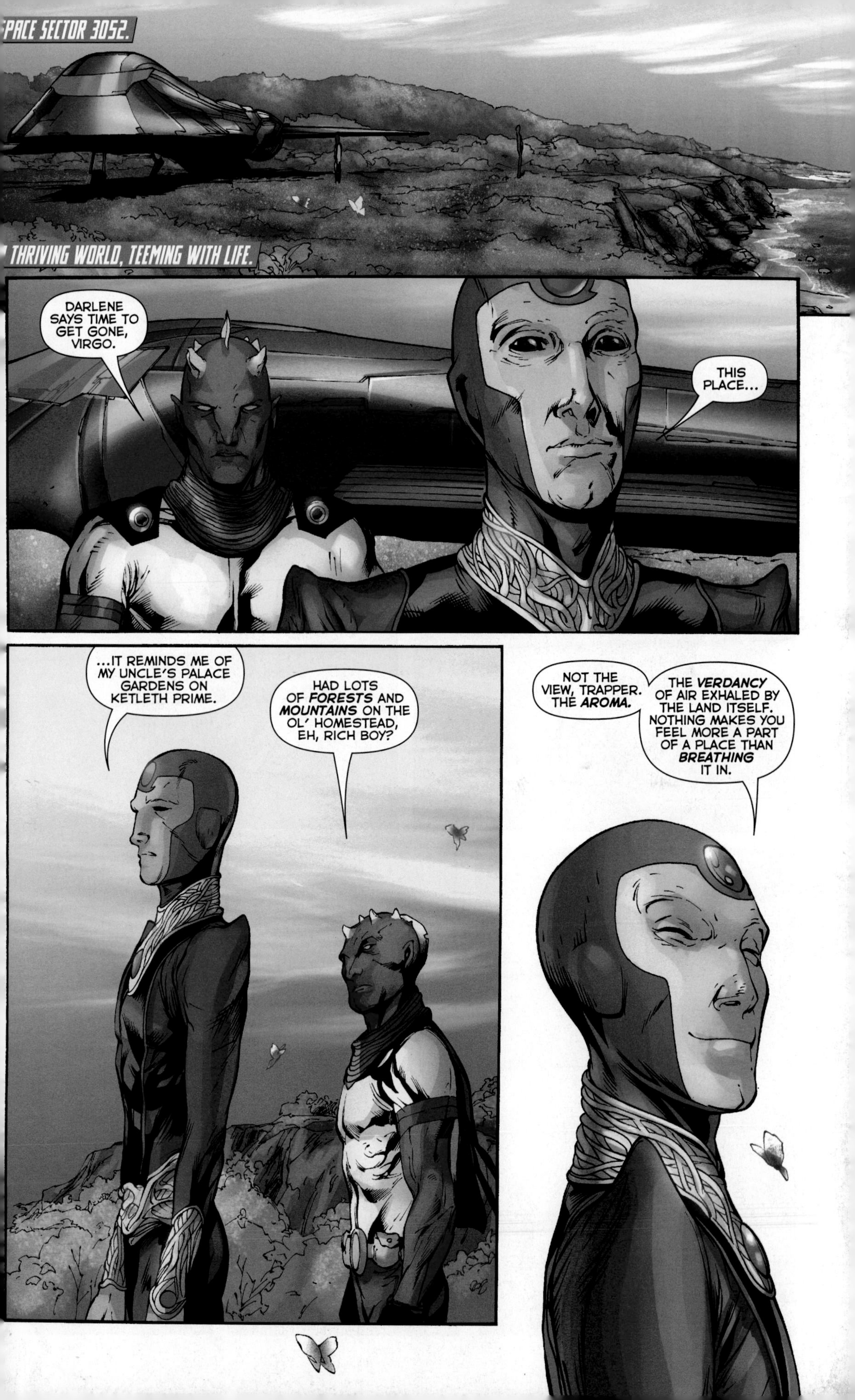
PACE SECTOR 3052.
THRIVING WORLD, TEEMING WITH LIFE.
DARLENE SAYS TIME TO GET GONE, VIRGO.
THIS PLACE...
...IT REMINDS ME OF MY UNCLE'S PALACE GARDENS ON KETLETH PRIME.
HAD LOTS OF FORESTS AND MOUNTAINS ON THE OL' HOMESTEAD, EH, RICH BOY?
NOT THE VIEW, TRAPPER. THE AROMA.
THE VERDANCY OF AIR EXHALED BY THE LAND ITSELF. NOTHING MAKES YOU FEEL MORE A PART OF A PLACE THAN BREATHING IT IN.

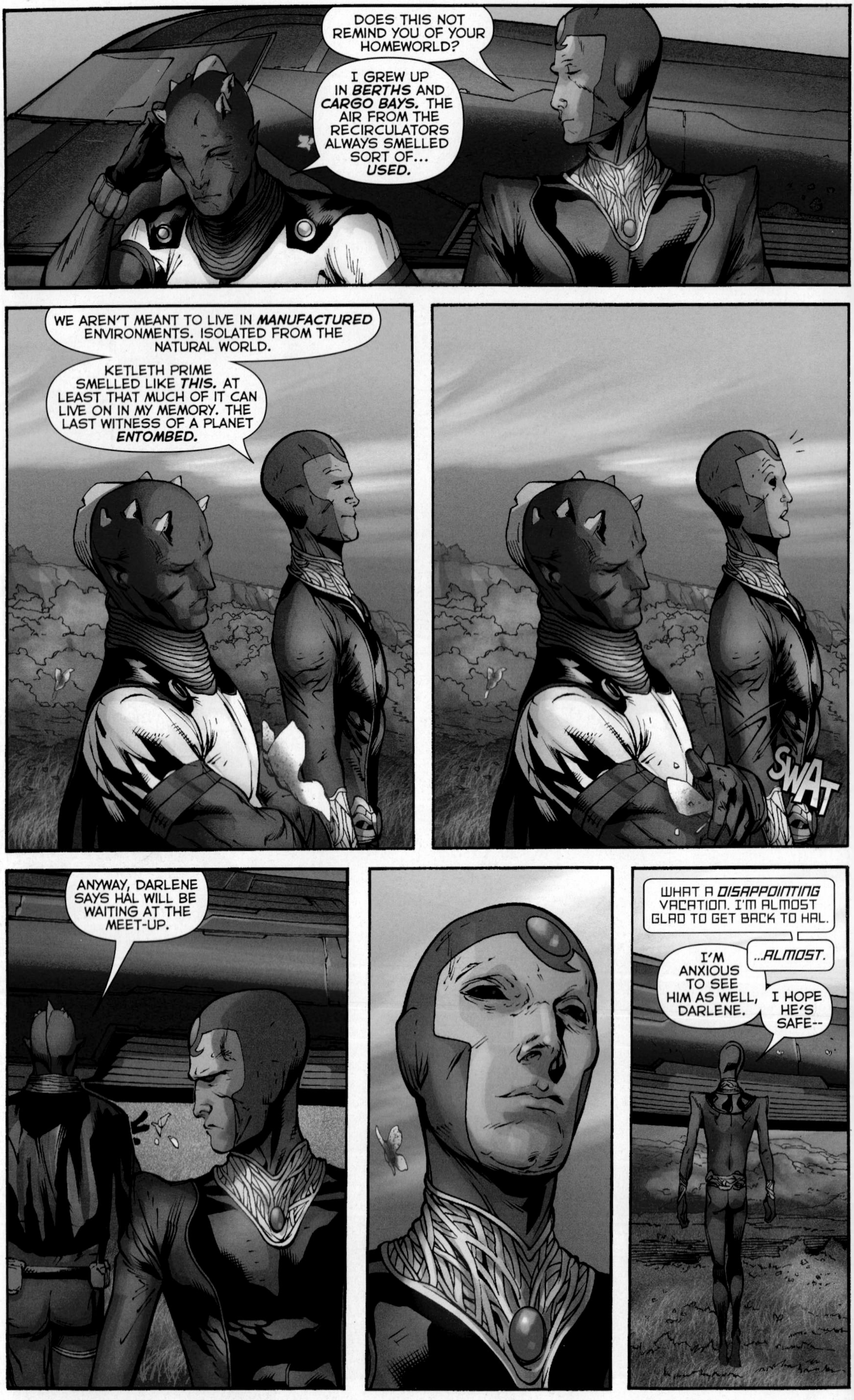
DOES THIS NOT REMIND YOU OF YOUR HOMEWORLD?
I GREW UP IN BERTHS AND CARGO BAYS. THE AIR FROM THE RECIRCULATORS ALWAYS SMELLED SORT OF... USED.
WE AREN'T MEANT TO LIVE IN MANUFACTURED ENVIRONMENTS. ISOLATED FROM THE NATURAL WORLD.
KETLETH PRIME SMELLED LIKE THIS. AT LEAST THAT MUCH OF IT CAN LIVE ON IN MY MEMORY. THE LAST WITNESS OF A PLANET ENTOMBED.
SWAT
ANYWAY, DARLENE SAYS HAL WILL BE WAITING AT THE MEET-UP.
WHAT A DISAPPOINTING VACATION. I'M ALMOST GLAD TO GET BACK TO HAL.
...ALMOST.
I'M ANXIOUS TO SEE HIM AS WELL, DARLENE.
I HOPE HE'S SAFE--

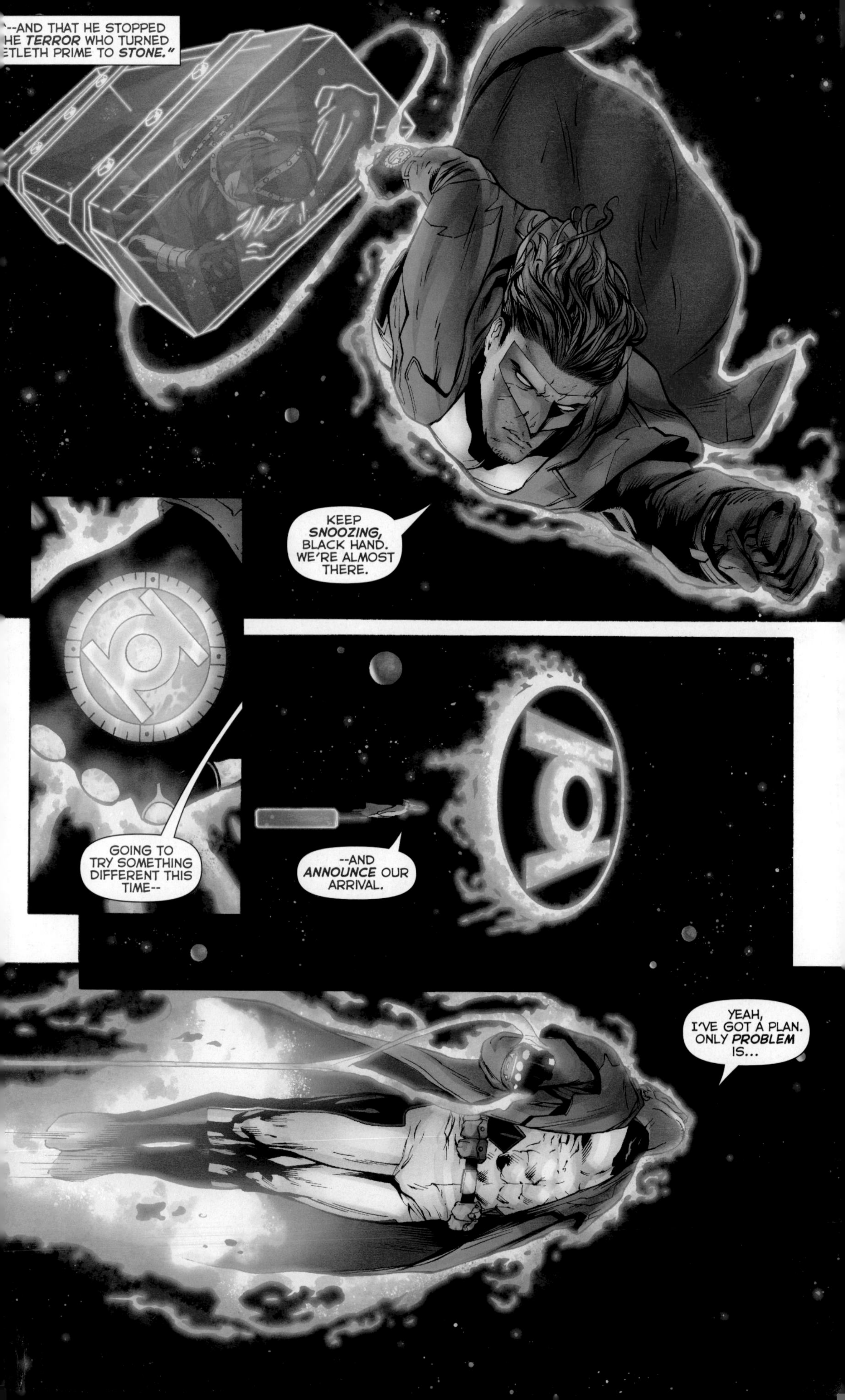
"--AND THAT HE STOPPED HE TERROR WHO TURNED ETLETH PRIME TO STONE."
KEEP SNOOZING, BLACK HAND. WE'RE ALMOST THERE.
GOING TO TRY SOMETHING DIFFERENT THIS TIME--
--AND ANNOUNCE OUR ARRIVAL.
YEAH, I'VE GOT A PLAN. ONLY PROBLEM IS...

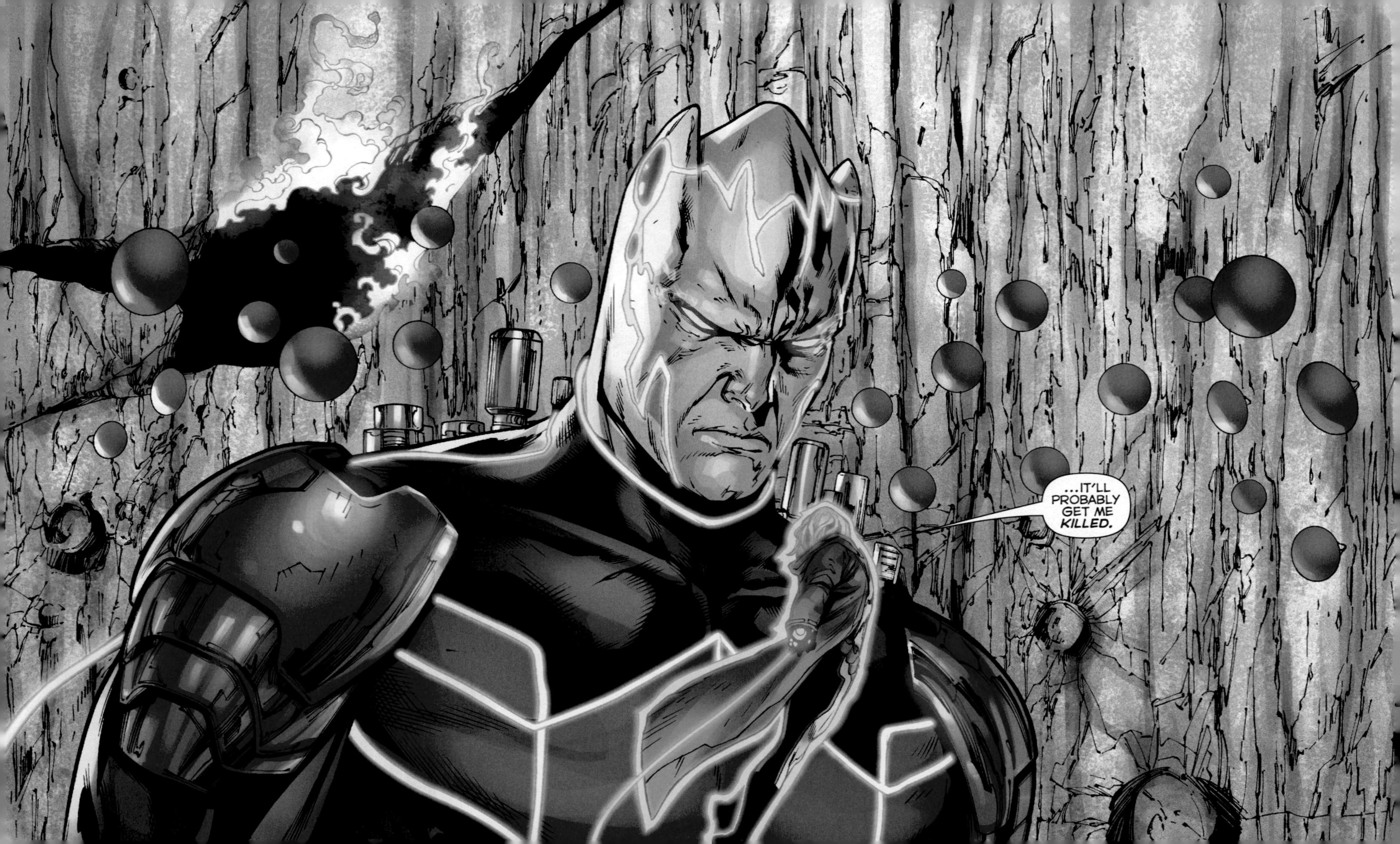
...IT'LL PROBABLY GET ME KILLED.

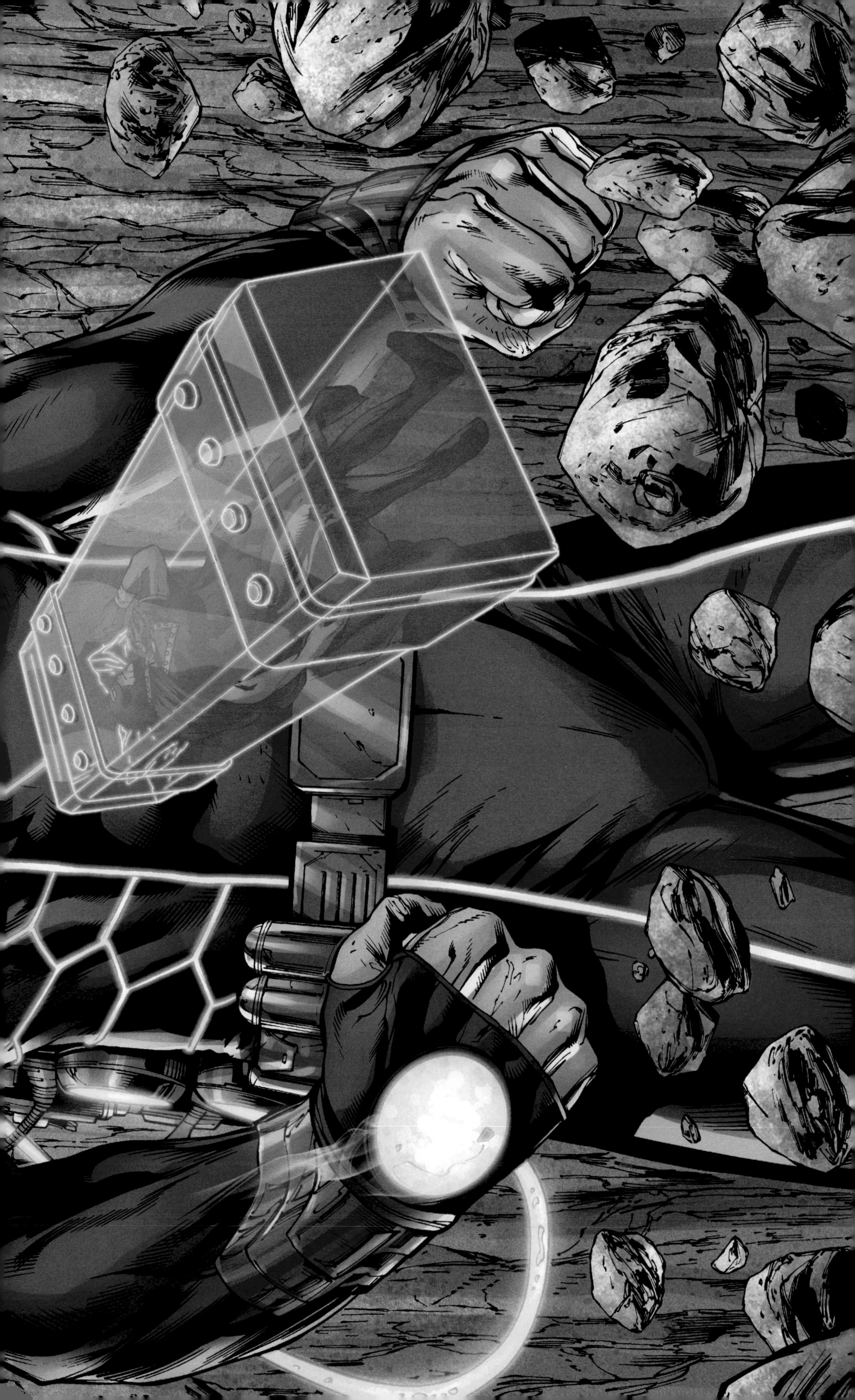

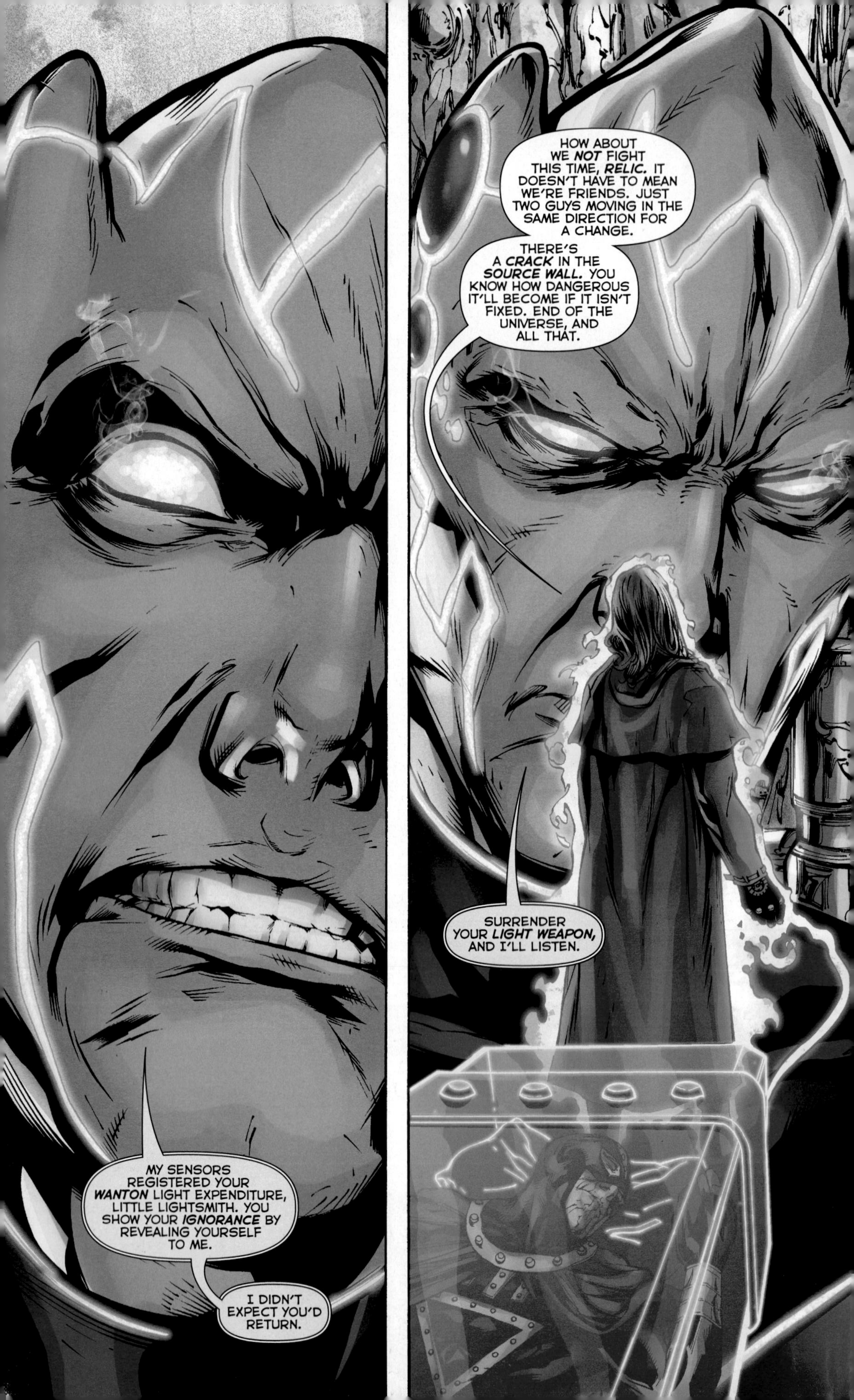
MY SENSORS REGISTERED YOUR *WANTON* LIGHT EXPENDITURE, LITTLE LIGHTSMITH. YOU SHOW YOUR *IGNORANCE* BY REVEALING YOURSELF TO ME.
I DIDN'T EXPECT YOU'D RETURN.
HOW ABOUT WE *NOT* FIGHT THIS TIME, *RELIC.* IT DOESN'T HAVE TO MEAN WE'RE FRIENDS. JUST TWO GUYS MOVING IN THE SAME DIRECTION FOR A CHANGE.
THERE'S A *CRACK* IN THE *SOURCE WALL.* YOU KNOW HOW DANGEROUS IT'LL BECOME IF IT ISN'T FIXED. END OF THE UNIVERSE, AND ALL THAT.
SURRENDER YOUR *LIGHT WEAPON,* AND I'LL LISTEN.

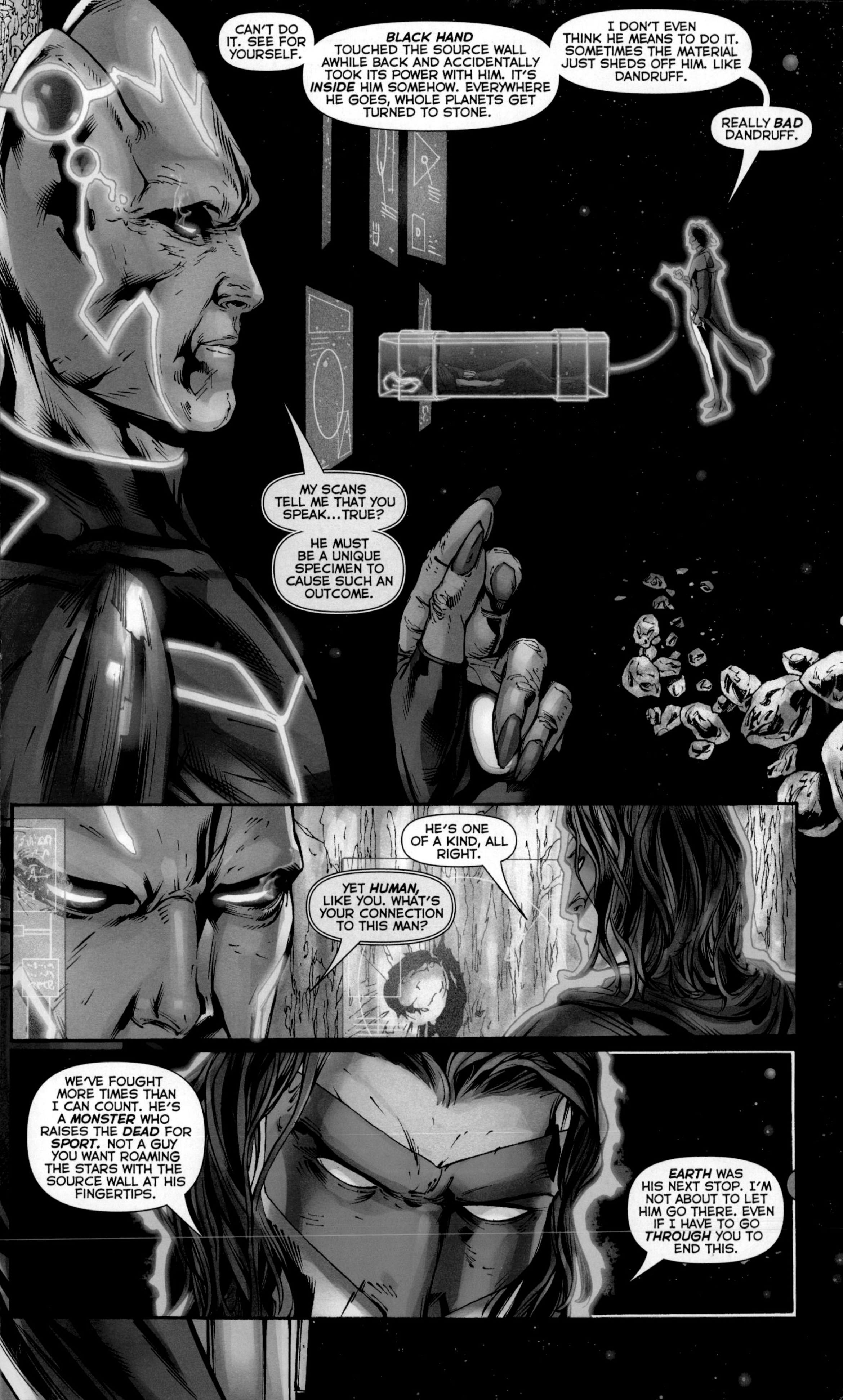
CAN'T DO IT. SEE FOR YOURSELF.
BLACK HAND TOUCHED THE SOURCE WALL AWHILE BACK AND ACCIDENTALLY TOOK ITS POWER WITH HIM. IT'S INSIDE HIM SOMEHOW. EVERYWHERE HE GOES, WHOLE PLANETS GET TURNED TO STONE.
I DON'T EVEN THINK HE MEANS TO DO IT. SOMETIMES THE MATERIAL JUST SHEDS OFF HIM. LIKE DANDRUFF.
REALLY BAD DANDRUFF.
MY SCANS TELL ME THAT YOU SPEAK...TRUE?
HE MUST BE A UNIQUE SPECIMEN TO CAUSE SUCH AN OUTCOME.
HE'S ONE OF A KIND, ALL RIGHT.
YET HUMAN, LIKE YOU. WHAT'S YOUR CONNECTION TO THIS MAN?
WE'VE FOUGHT MORE TIMES THAN I CAN COUNT. HE'S A MONSTER WHO RAISES THE DEAD FOR SPORT. NOT A GUY YOU WANT ROAMING THE STARS WITH THE SOURCE WALL AT HIS FINGERTIPS.
EARTH WAS HIS NEXT STOP. I'M NOT ABOUT TO LET HIM GO THERE. EVEN IF I HAVE TO GO THROUGH YOU TO END THIS.

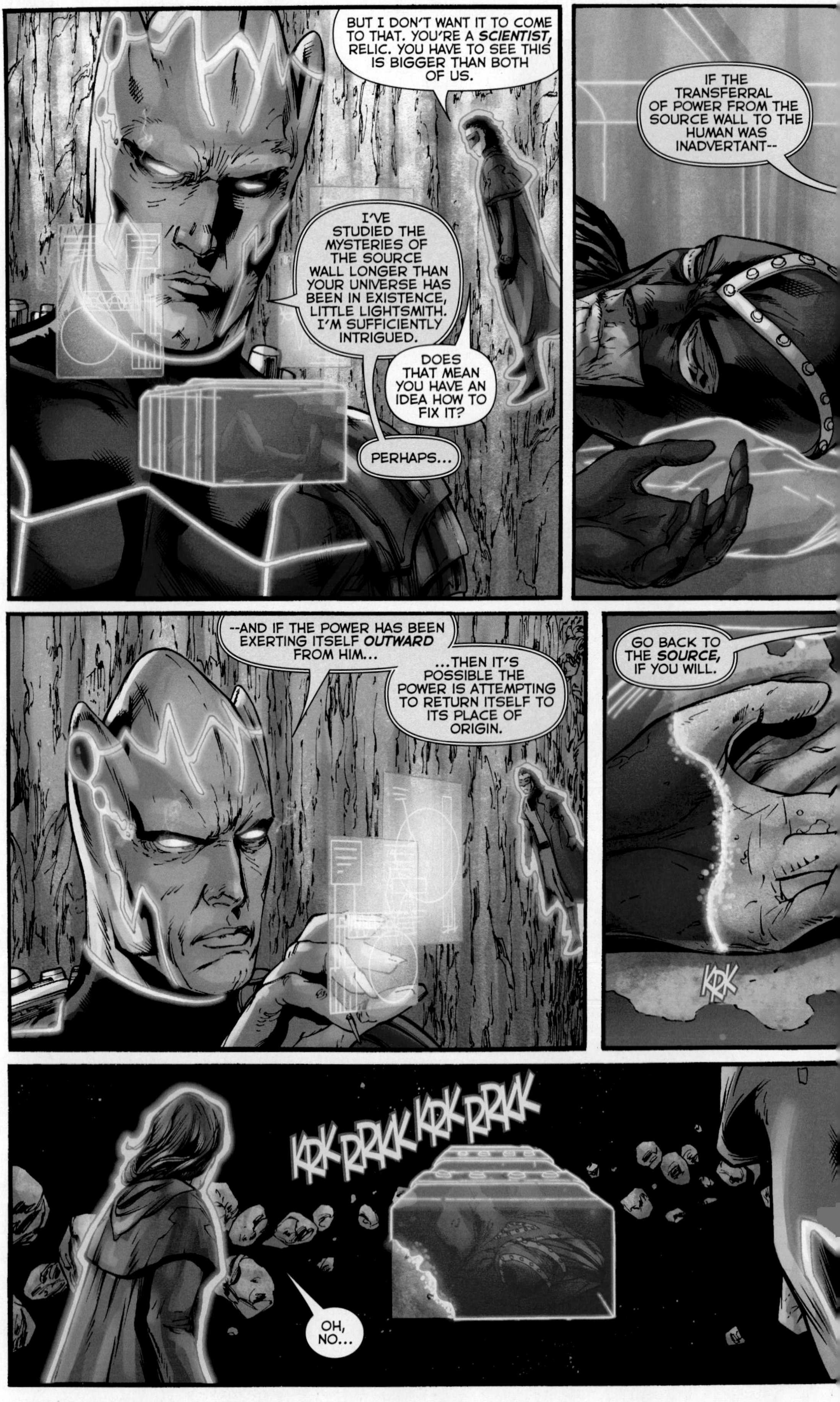
BUT I DON'T WANT IT TO COME TO THAT. YOU'RE A *SCIENTIST,* RELIC. YOU HAVE TO SEE THIS IS BIGGER THAN BOTH OF US.
I'VE STUDIED THE MYSTERIES OF THE SOURCE WALL LONGER THAN YOUR UNIVERSE HAS BEEN IN EXISTENCE, LITTLE LIGHTSMITH. I'M SUFFICIENTLY INTRIGUED.
DOES THAT MEAN YOU HAVE AN IDEA HOW TO FIX IT?
PERHAPS...
IF THE TRANSFERRAL OF POWER FROM THE SOURCE WALL TO THE HUMAN WAS INADVERTANT--
--AND IF THE POWER HAS BEEN EXERTING ITSELF *OUTWARD* FROM HIM...
...THEN IT'S POSSIBLE THE POWER IS ATTEMPTING TO RETURN ITSELF TO ITS PLACE OF ORIGIN.
GO BACK TO THE *SOURCE,* IF YOU WILL.
KRK
KRK RRKK KRK RRKK
OH, NO...

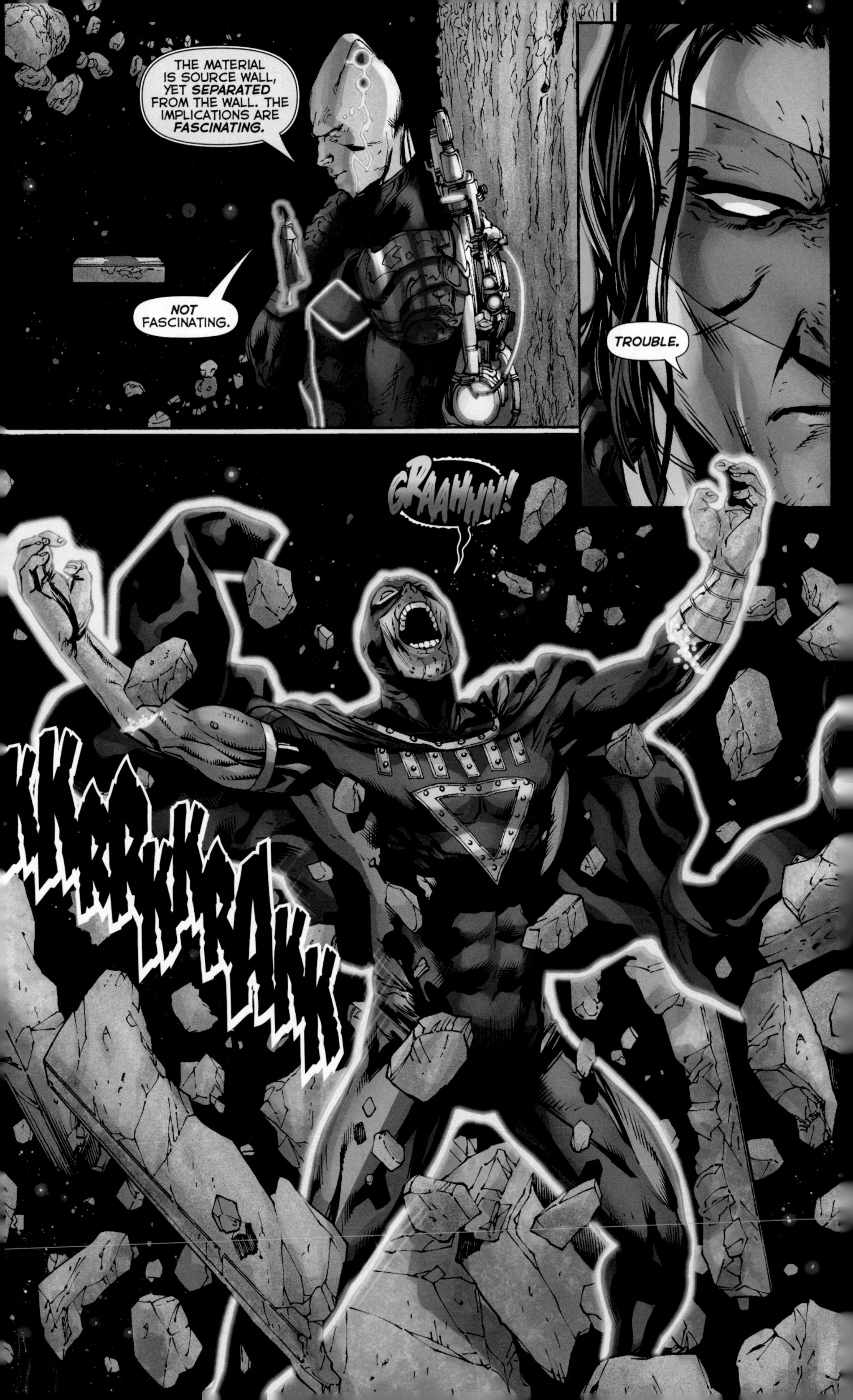
THE MATERIAL IS SOURCE WALL, YET SEPARATED FROM THE WALL. THE IMPLICATIONS ARE FASCINATING.
NOT FASCINATING.
TROUBLE.
GRAAHHH!
KKRRKKRAKK

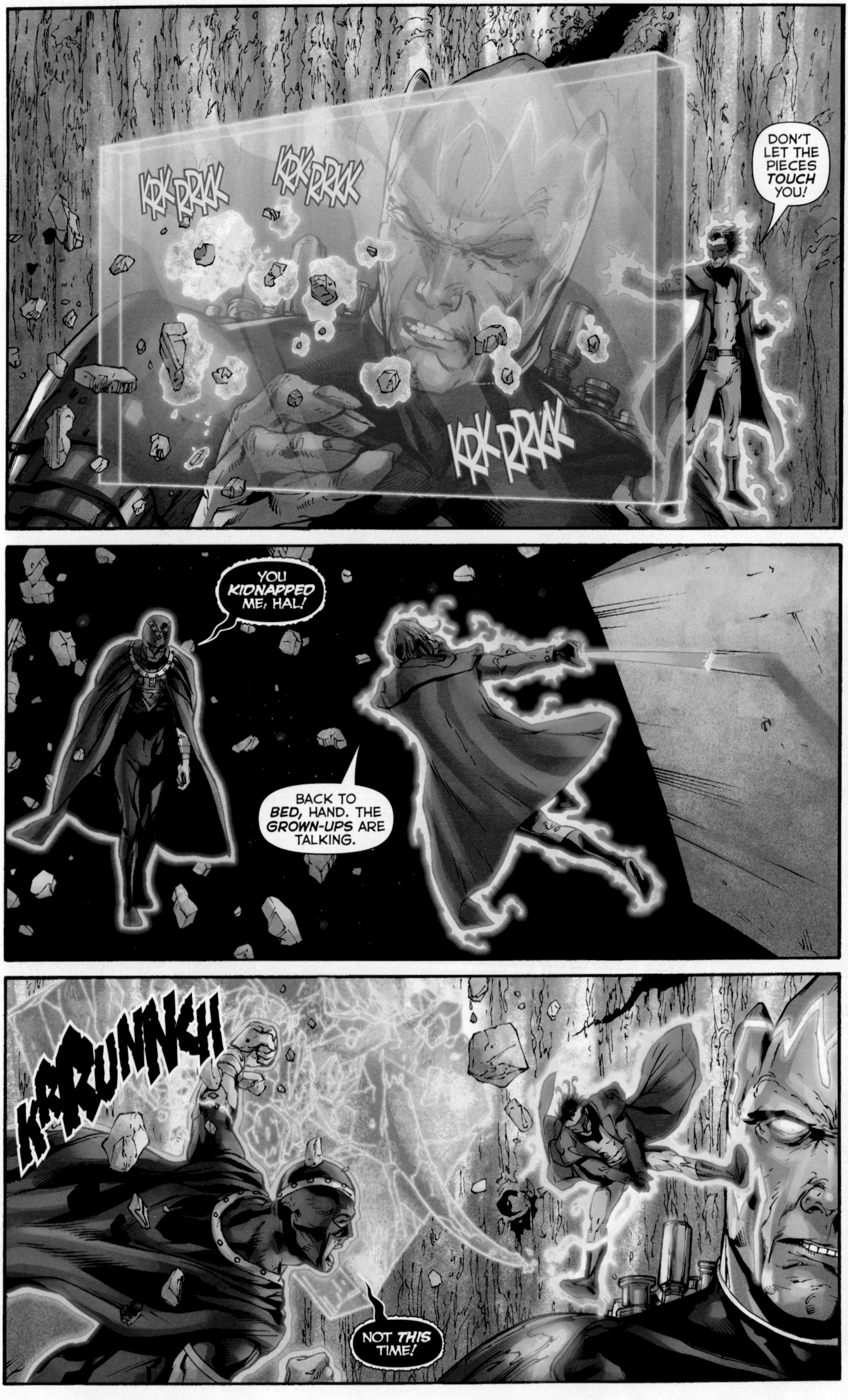
KRK RRKK
KRK RRKK
KRK RRKK
DON'T LET THE PIECES TOUCH YOU!
YOU KIDNAPPED ME, HAL!
BACK TO BED, HAND. THE GROWN-UPS ARE TALKING.
KARUNNCH
NOT THIS TIME!

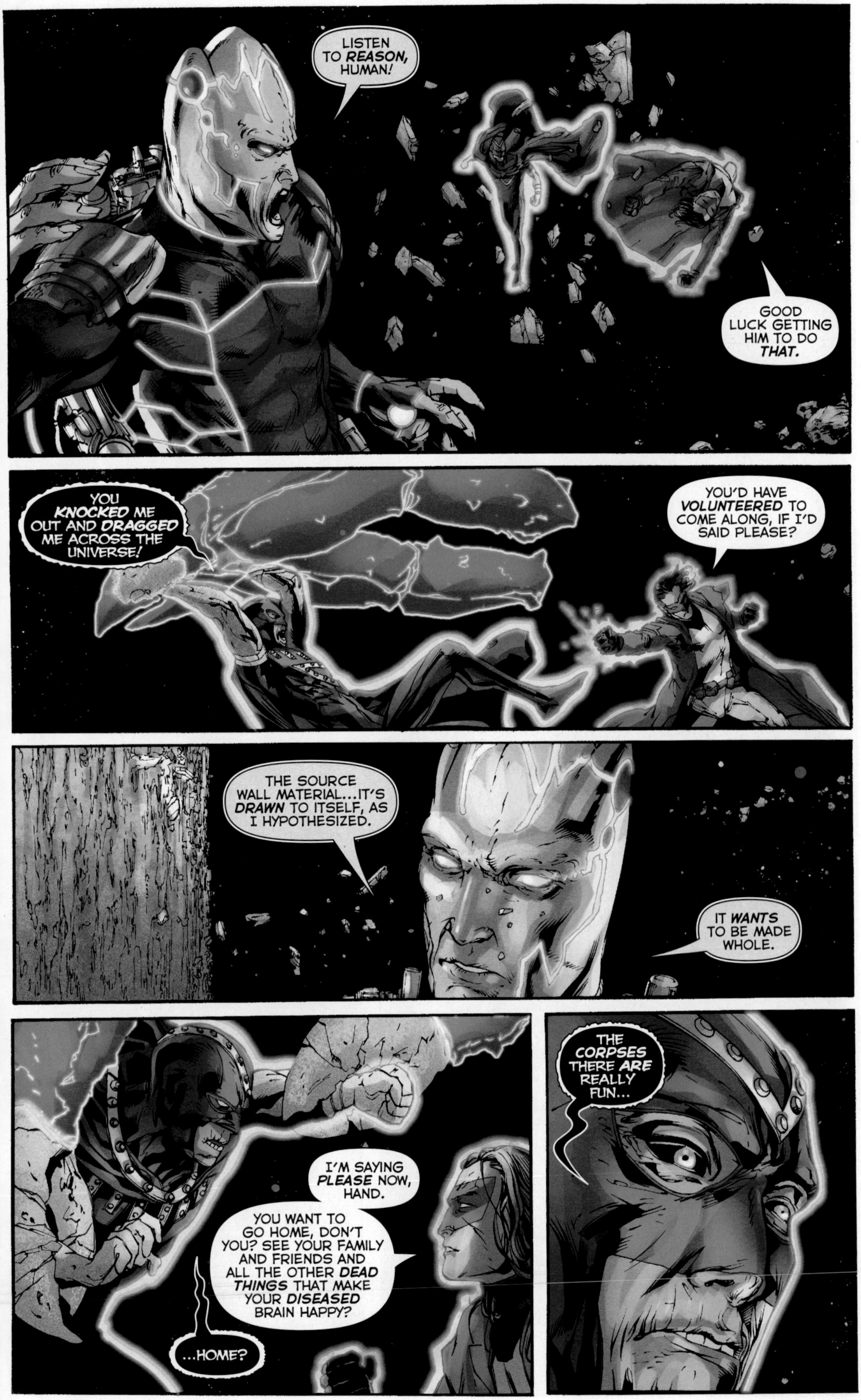
LISTEN TO REASON, HUMAN!
GOOD LUCK GETTING HIM TO DO THAT.
YOU KNOCKED ME OUT AND DRAGGED ME ACROSS THE UNIVERSE!
YOU'D HAVE VOLUNTEERED TO COME ALONG, IF I'D SAID PLEASE?
THE SOURCE WALL MATERIAL...IT'S DRAWN TO ITSELF, AS I HYPOTHESIZED.
IT WANTS TO BE MADE WHOLE.
I'M SAYING PLEASE NOW, HAND.
YOU WANT TO GO HOME, DON'T YOU? SEE YOUR FAMILY AND FRIENDS AND ALL THE OTHER DEAD THINGS THAT MAKE YOUR DISEASED BRAIN HAPPY?
...HOME?
THE CORPSES THERE ARE REALLY FUN...

AGH!

L'ET GO!

CARRY HIM TO THE *WALL*, COLLECTORS. PUT HIM BACK WHERE HE BELONGS.

KRK·RRKK

NO!

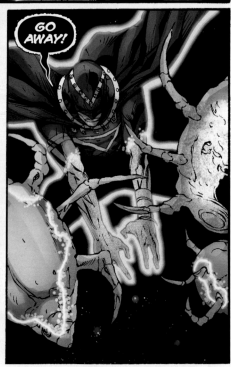

GO AWAY!

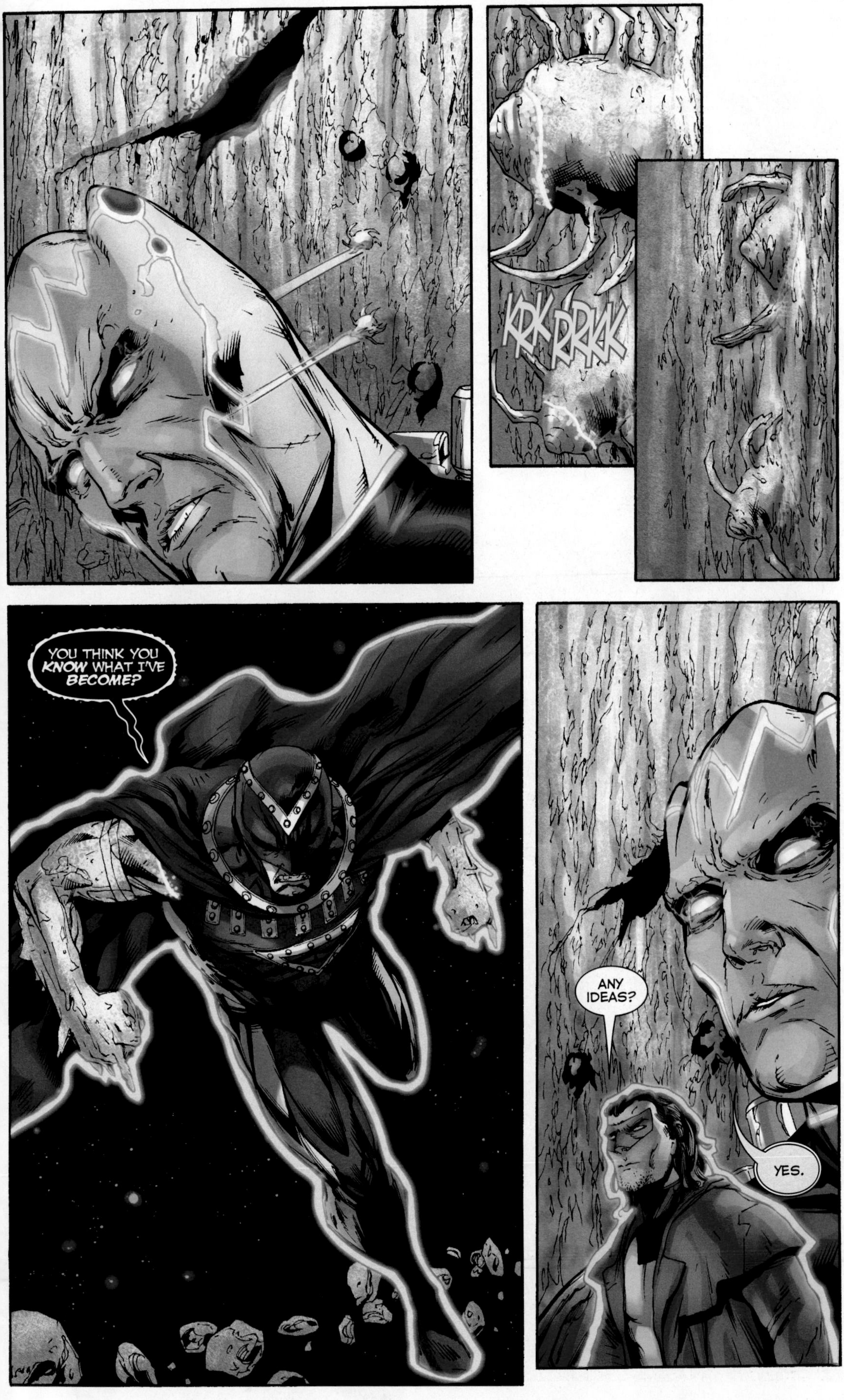
KRK KRRAK
YOU THINK YOU KNOW WHAT I'VE BECOME?
ANY IDEAS?
YES.

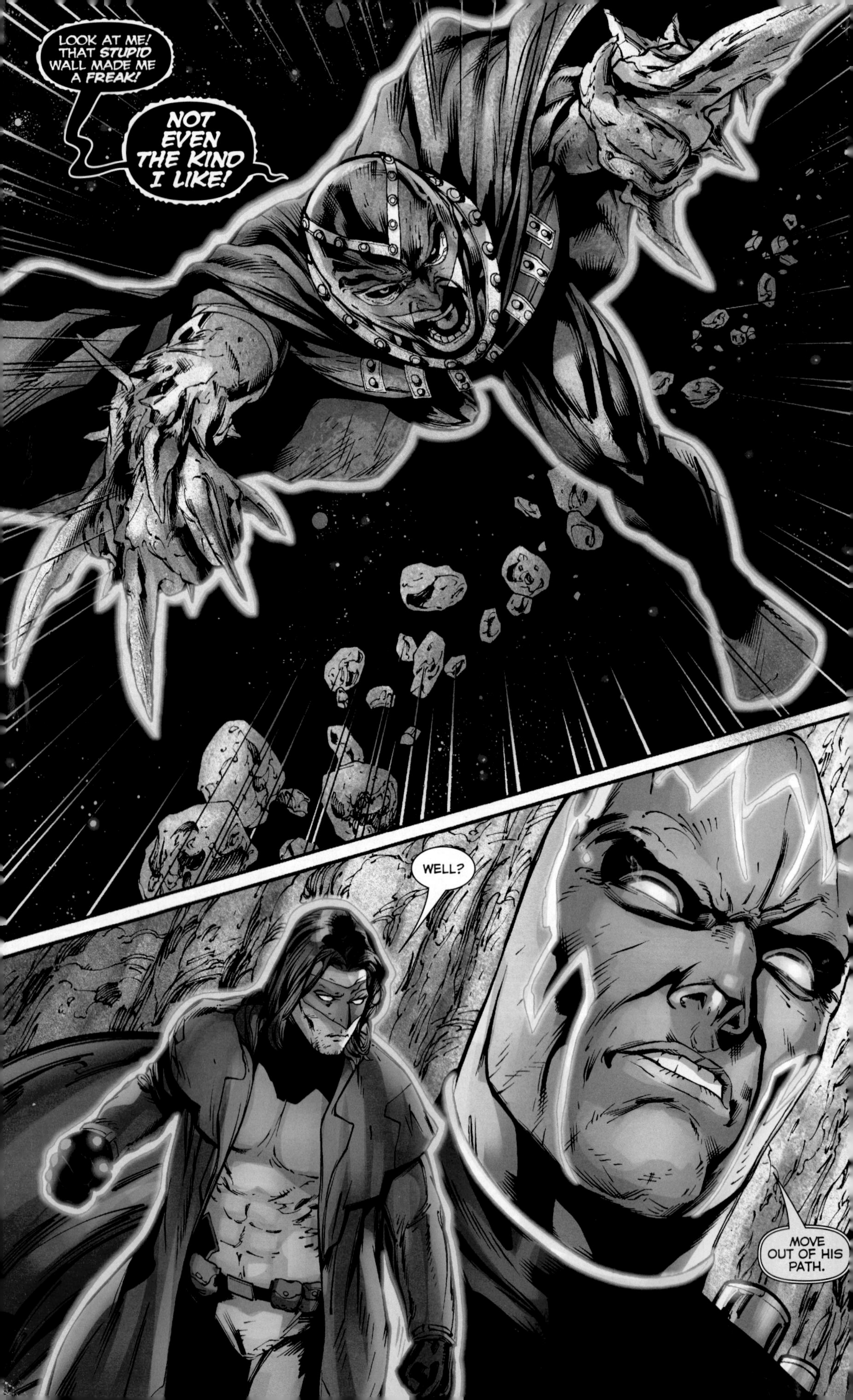
LOOK AT ME! THAT STUPID WALL MADE ME A FREAK!
NOT EVEN THE KIND I LIKE!
WELL?
MOVE OUT OF HIS PATH.

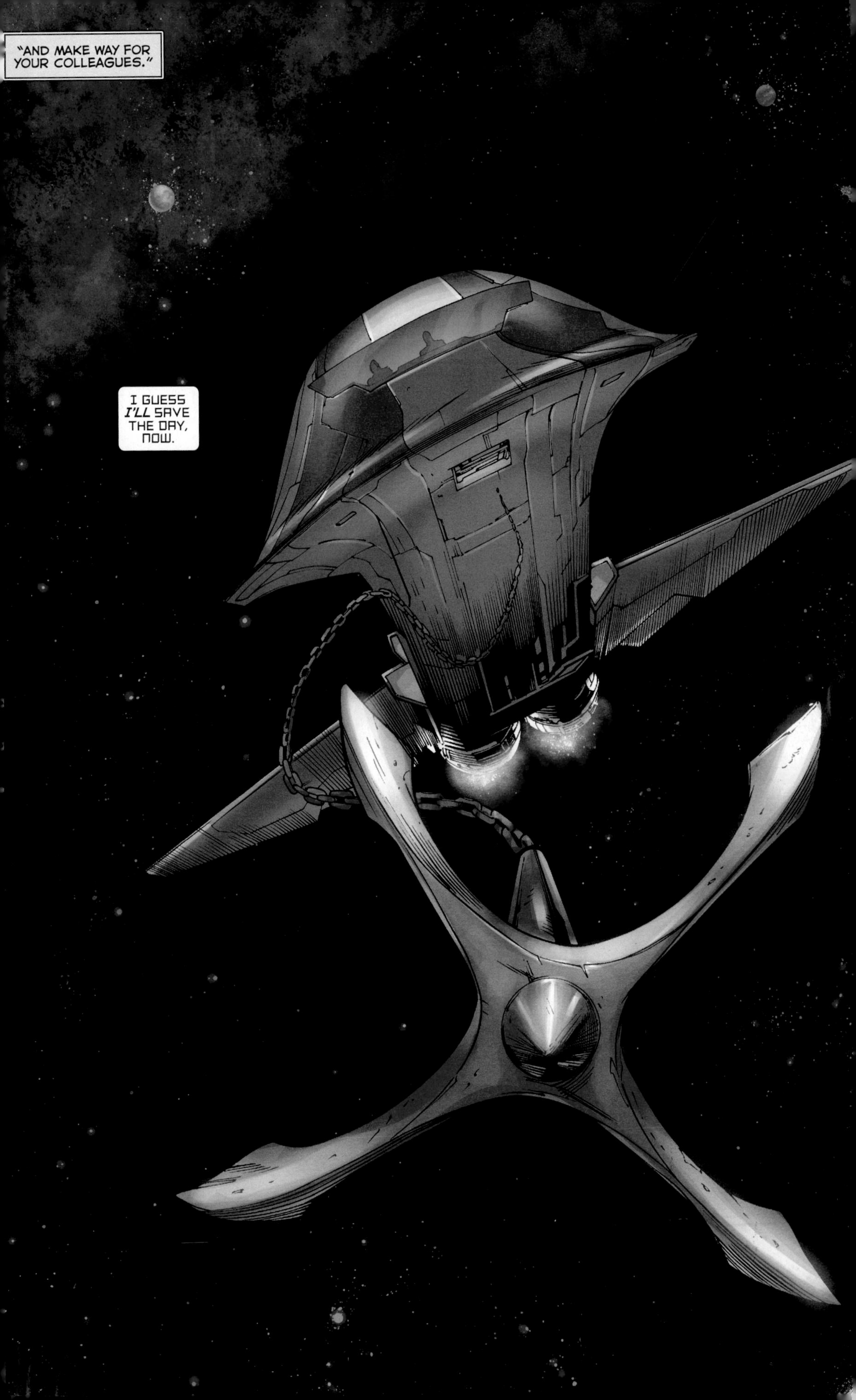
"AND MAKE WAY FOR YOUR COLLEAGUES."
I GUESS I'LL SAVE THE DAY, NOW.

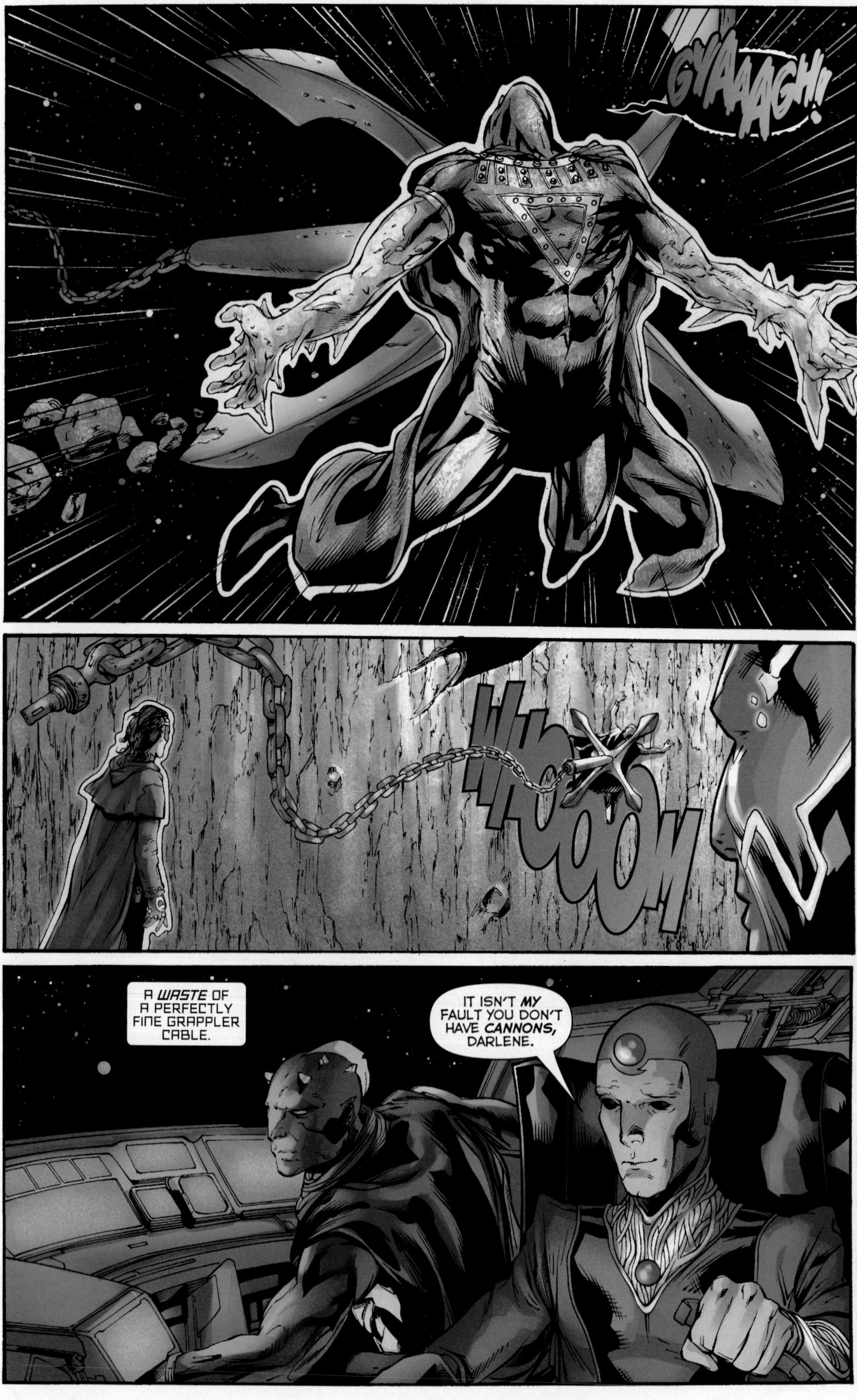
GYAAAAGH!!
WHOOOOM
A WASTE OF A PERFECTLY FINE GRAPPLER CABLE.
IT ISN'T MY FAULT YOU DON'T HAVE CANNONS, DARLENE.

:KOFF:

OKAY. HE'S CLOSE TO THE WALL. AND?

CURIOUS. I EXPECTED A DIFFERENT OUTCOME.

MEANING *WHAT*, EXACTLY?

YOU THINK YOU CAN *GANG UP* ON ME?

ON *ME?!*

I'LL *MURDER* YOU BOTH! OR AT LEAST MAKE YOU STOP *BOTHERING* ME!

WE HAVE TO *HELP.*

HAL IS ALONE AGAINST THE *GIANT* AND THAT *MANIAC!*

REMEMBER HOW *WELL* THAT WORKED OUT LAST TIME?

ALL THE MORE REASON: *NO.*

I THINK YOU SHOULD BOTH GO OUT THERE. I'LL *STAY* HERE.

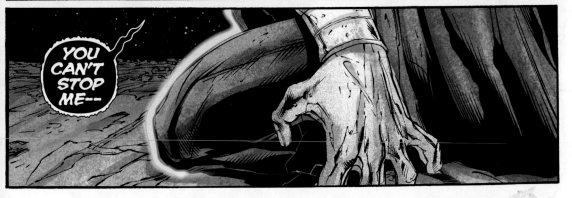

YOU CAN'T STOP ME--

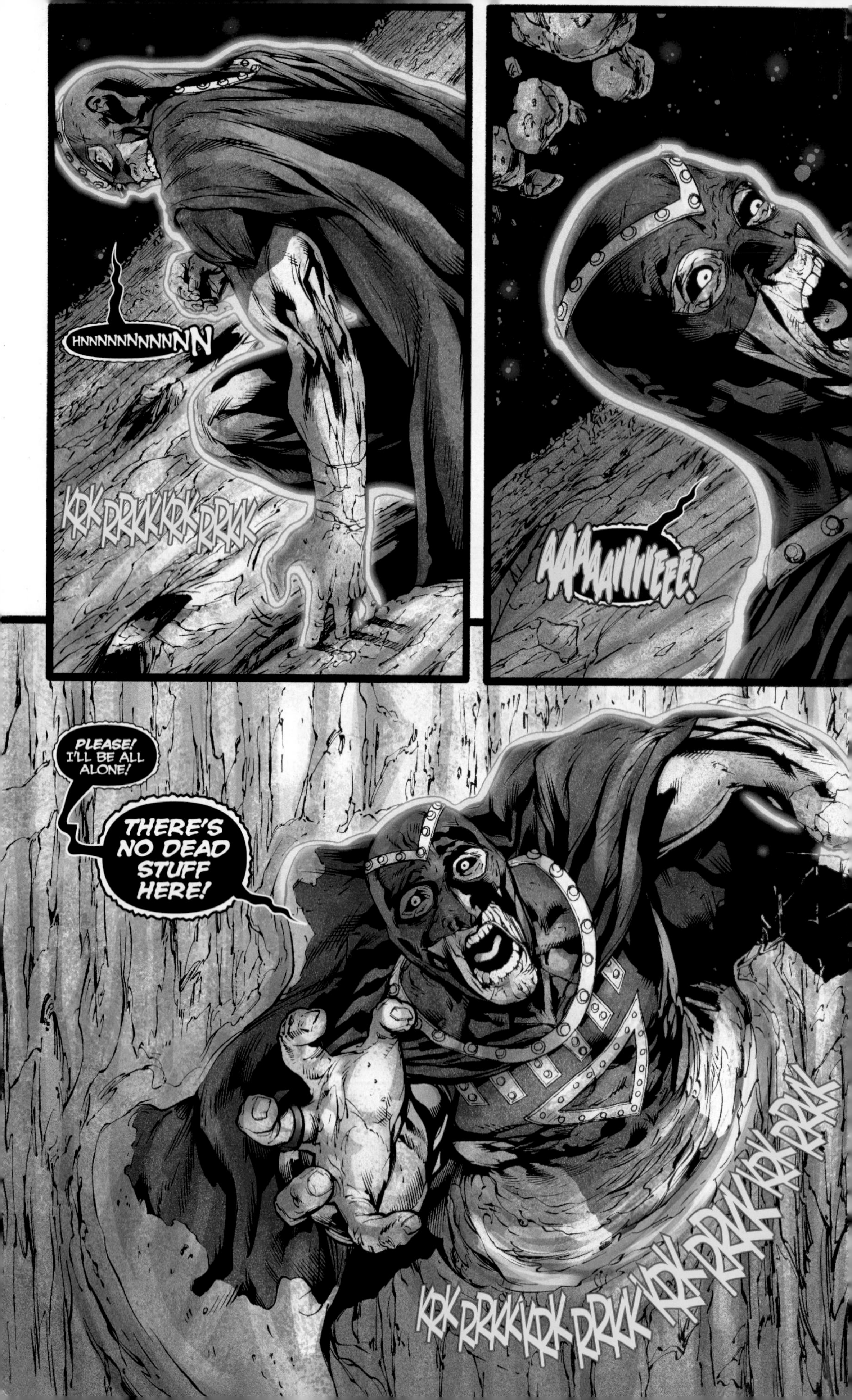
HNNNNNNNNNN
KRK RRKK KRK RRKK
AAAAAIIIIEEE!
PLEASE! I'LL BE ALL ALONE!
THERE'S NO DEAD STUFF HERE!
KRK RRKK KRK RRKK KRK RRKK KRK RRKK

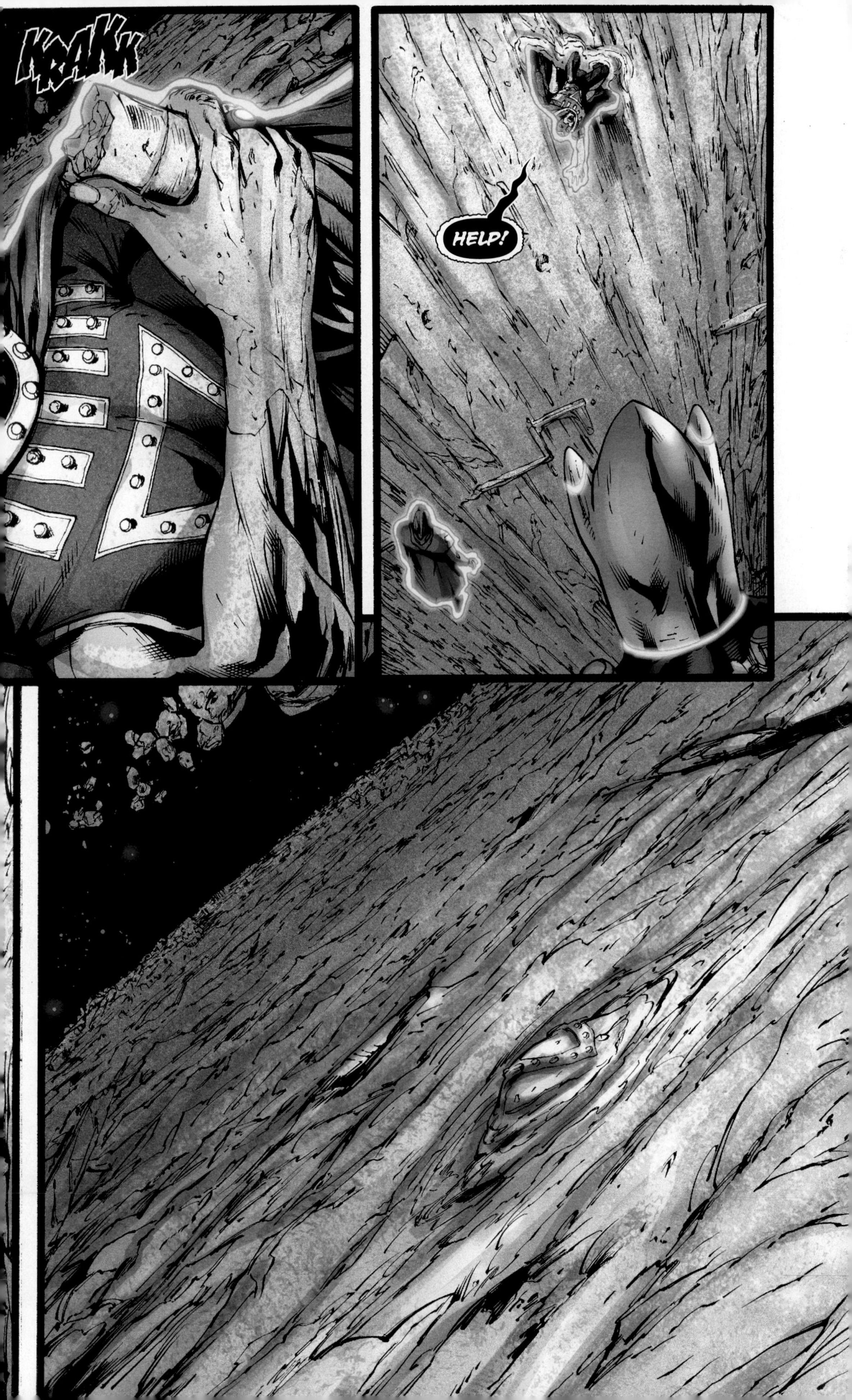
KRAKK
HELP!

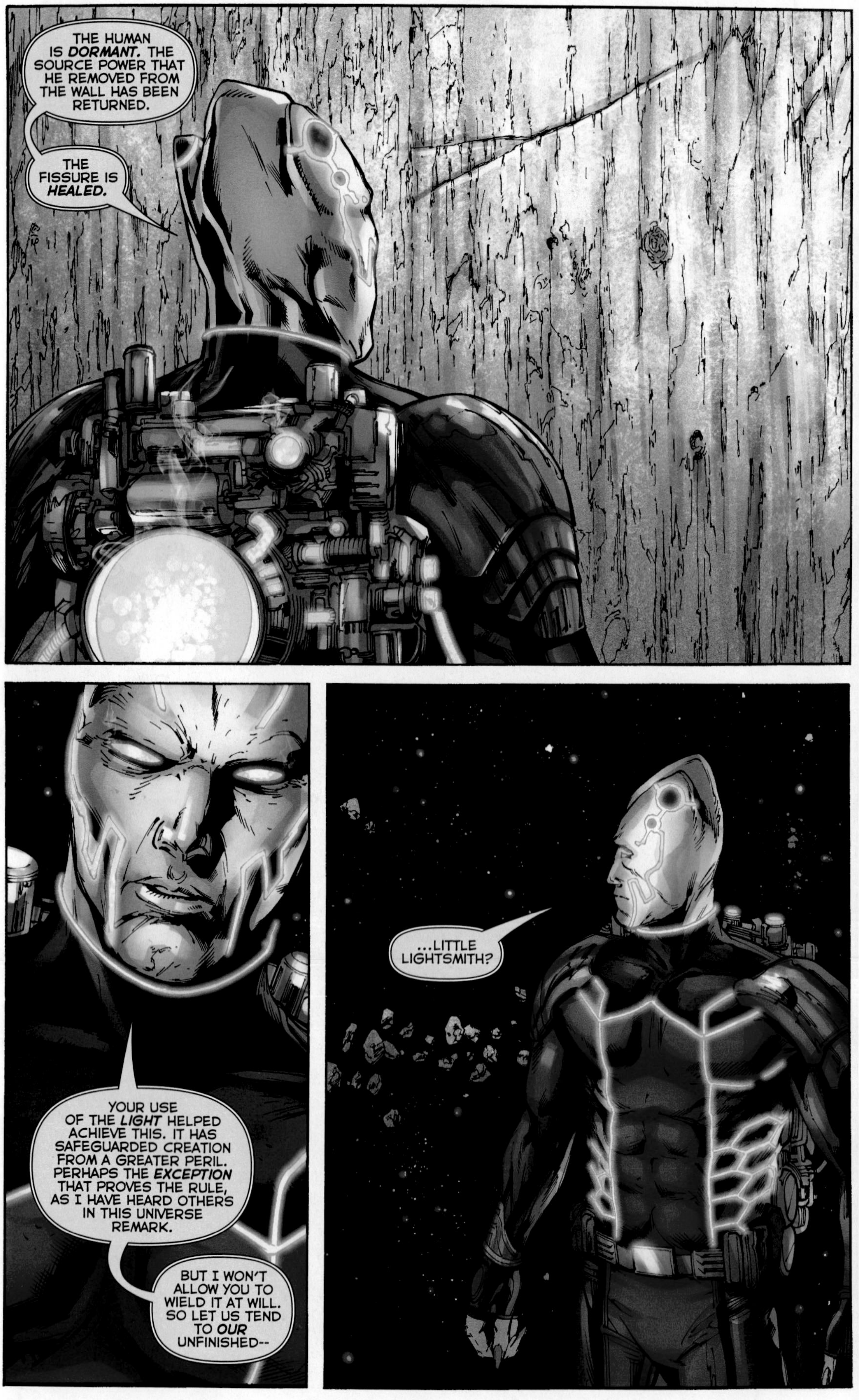
THE HUMAN IS DORMANT. THE SOURCE POWER THAT HE REMOVED FROM THE WALL HAS BEEN RETURNED.
THE FISSURE IS HEALED.
YOUR USE OF THE LIGHT HELPED ACHIEVE THIS. IT HAS SAFEGUARDED CREATION FROM A GREATER PERIL. PERHAPS THE EXCEPTION THAT PROVES THE RULE, AS I HAVE HEARD OTHERS IN THIS UNIVERSE REMARK.
BUT I WON'T ALLOW YOU TO WIELD IT AT WILL. SO LET US TEND TO OUR UNFINISHED--
...LITTLE LIGHTSMITH?

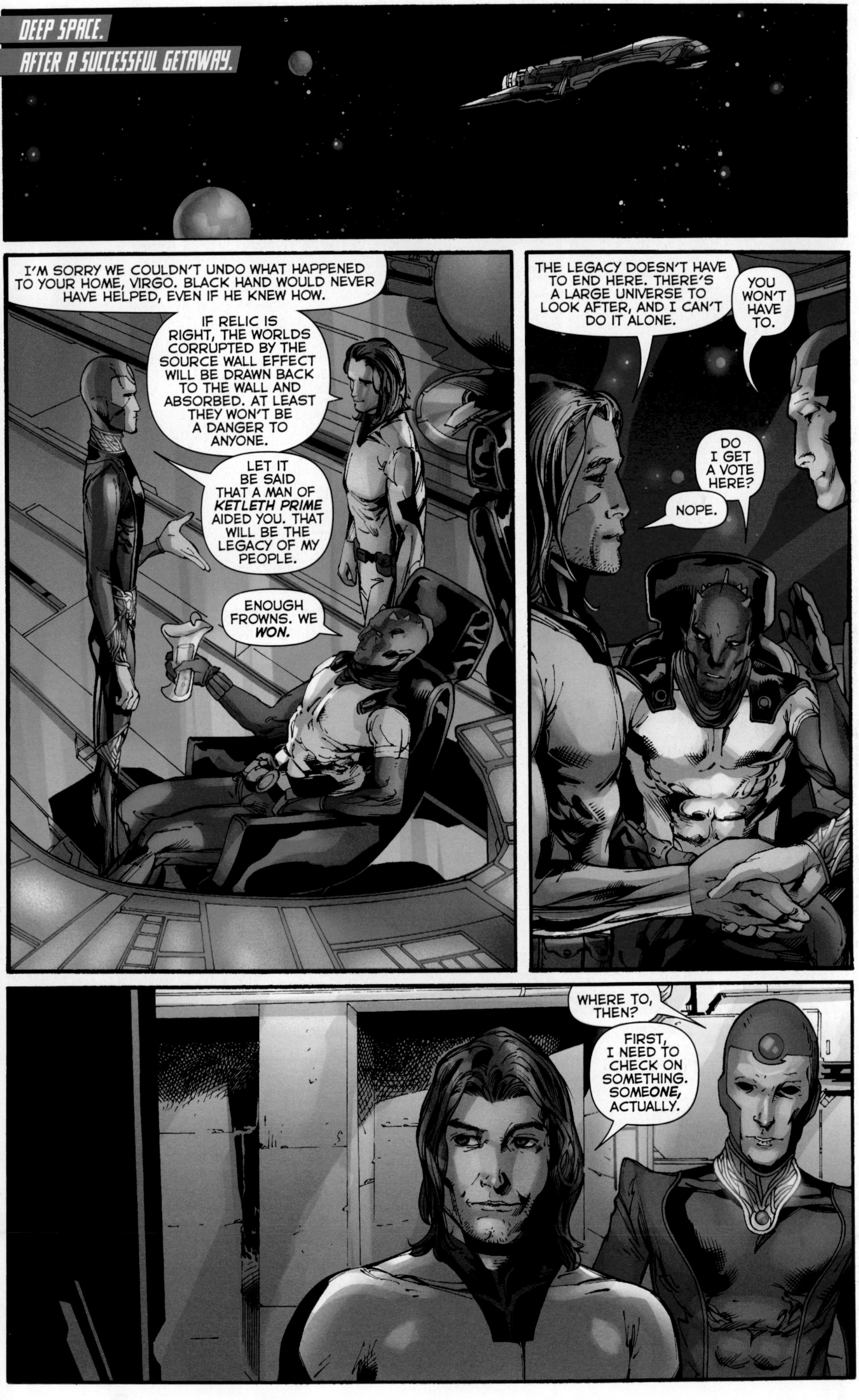
DEEP SPACE.
AFTER A SUCCESSFUL GETAWAY.
I'M SORRY WE COULDN'T UNDO WHAT HAPPENED TO YOUR HOME, VIRGO. BLACK HAND WOULD NEVER HAVE HELPED, EVEN IF HE KNEW HOW.
IF RELIC IS RIGHT, THE WORLDS CORRUPTED BY THE SOURCE WALL EFFECT WILL BE DRAWN BACK TO THE WALL AND ABSORBED. AT LEAST THEY WON'T BE A DANGER TO ANYONE.
LET IT BE SAID THAT A MAN OF KETLETH PRIME AIDED YOU. THAT WILL BE THE LEGACY OF MY PEOPLE.
ENOUGH FROWNS. WE WON.
THE LEGACY DOESN'T HAVE TO END HERE. THERE'S A LARGE UNIVERSE TO LOOK AFTER, AND I CAN'T DO IT ALONE.
YOU WON'T HAVE TO.
DO I GET A VOTE HERE?
NOPE.
WHERE TO, THEN?
FIRST, I NEED TO CHECK ON SOMETHING. SOMEONE, ACTUALLY.

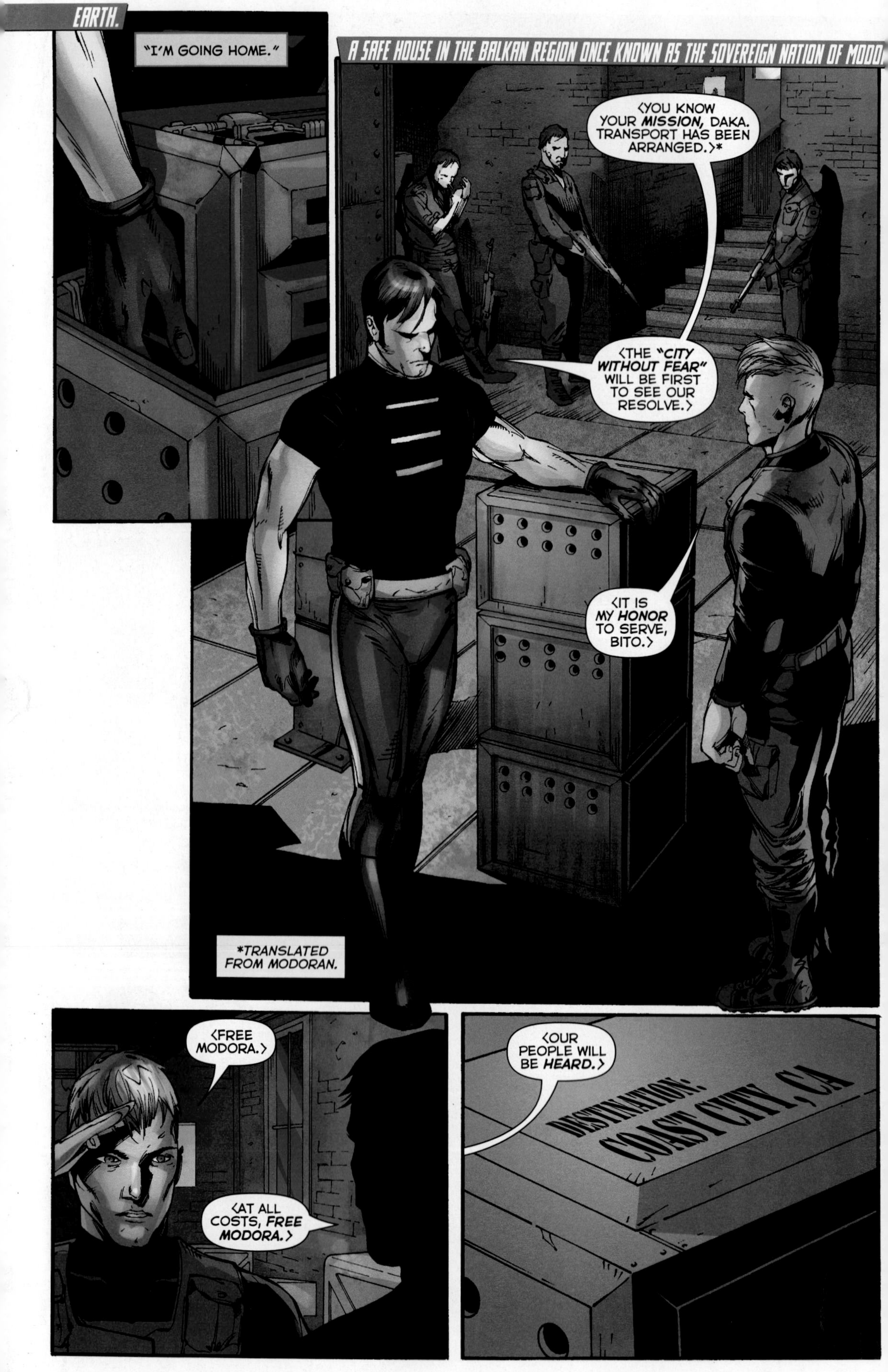
EARTH.
"I'M GOING HOME."
A SAFE HOUSE IN THE BALKAN REGION ONCE KNOWN AS THE SOVEREIGN NATION OF MODORA
<YOU KNOW YOUR MISSION, DAKA. TRANSPORT HAS BEEN ARRANGED.>*
<THE "CITY WITHOUT FEAR" WILL BE FIRST TO SEE OUR RESOLVE.>
<IT IS MY HONOR TO SERVE, BITO.>
*TRANSLATED FROM MODORAN.
<FREE MODORA.>
<AT ALL COSTS, FREE MODORA.>
<OUR PEOPLE WILL BE HEARD.>
DESTINATION: COAST CITY, CA

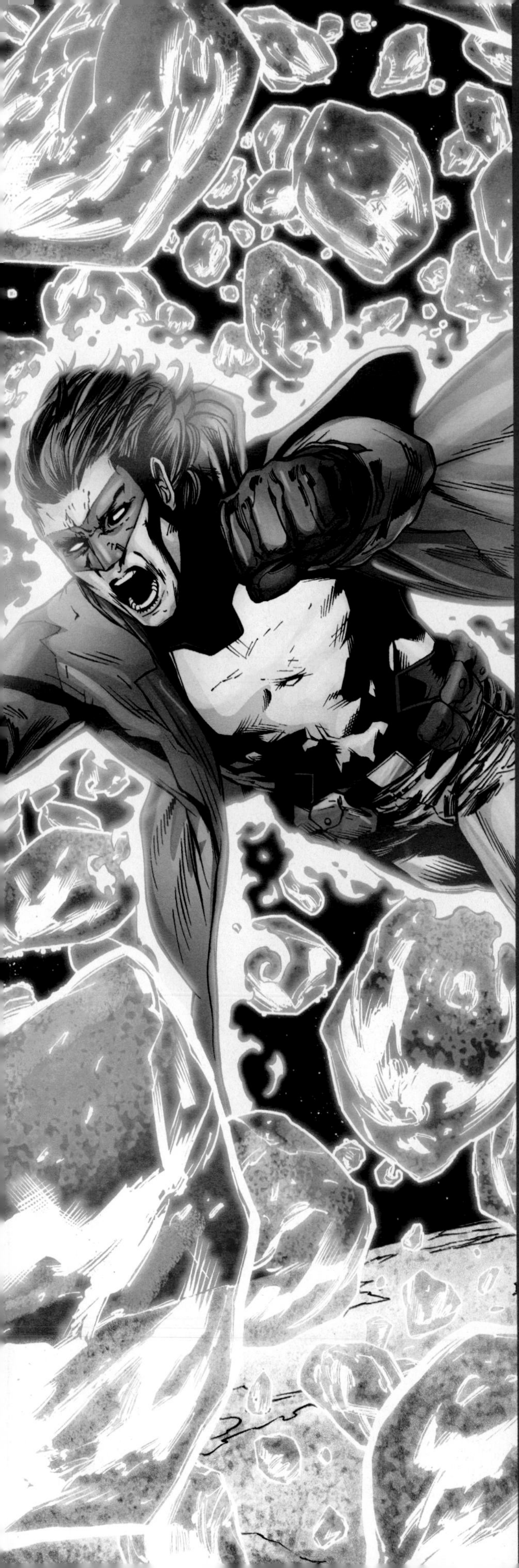

VARIANT COVER GALLERY

GREEN LANTERN #41
JOKER 75TH ANNIVERSARY
VARIANT BY BEN OLIVER

GREEN LANTERN #42
TEEN TITANS GO! VARIANT
BY JORGE CORONA

GREEN LANTERN #43
BOMBSHELLS VARIANT BY
EMANUELA LUPACCHINO
& TOMEU MOREY

GREEN LANTERN #44
GREEN LANTERN 75TH
ANNIVERSARY VARIANT
BY HOWARD CHAYKIN

GREEN LANTERN #45
MONSTER VARIANT
BY NEAL ADAMS
& ALEX SINCLAIR

GREEN LANTERN #46
LOONEY TUNES VARIANT
BY JORGE CORONA
& SPIKE BRANDT

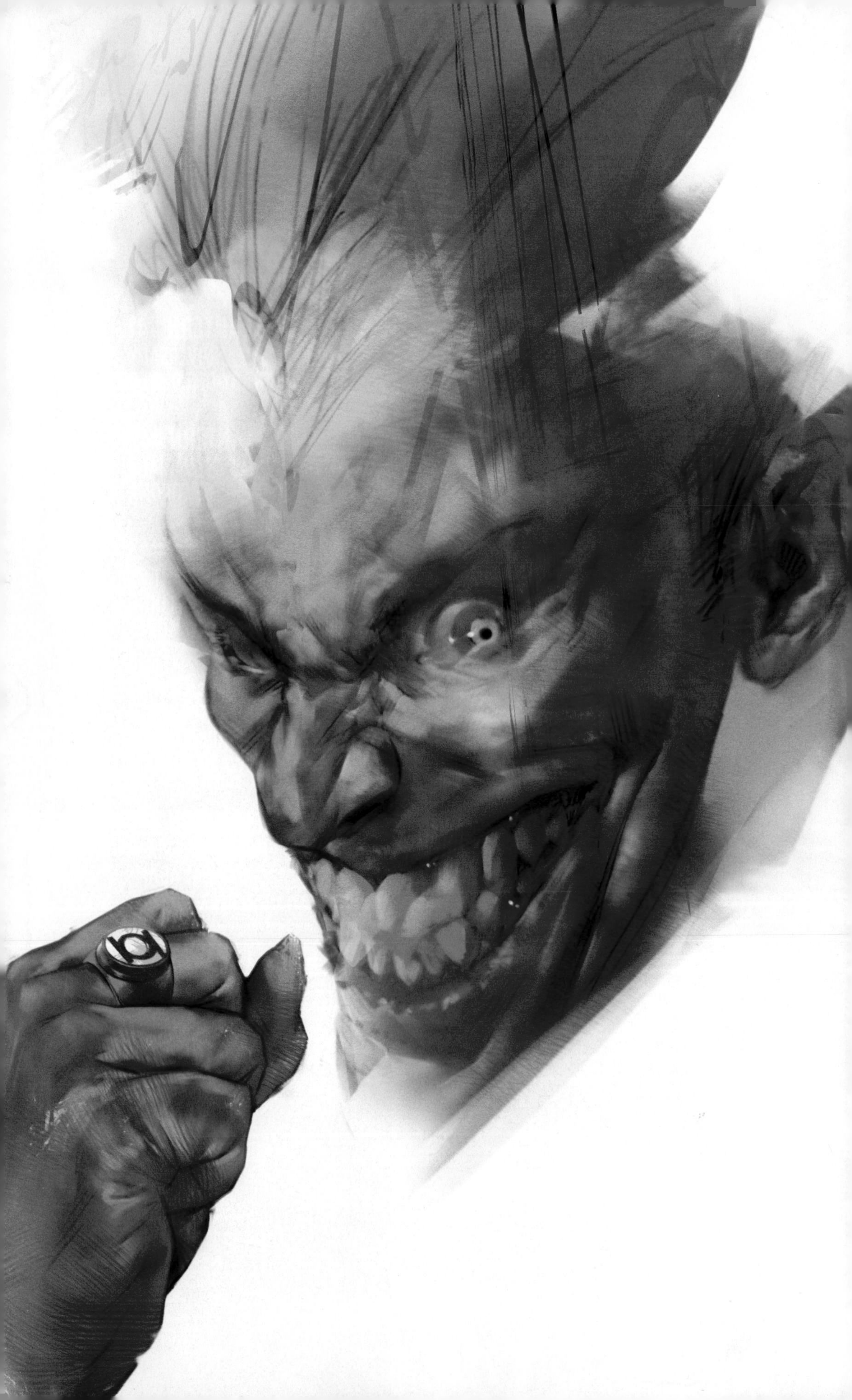

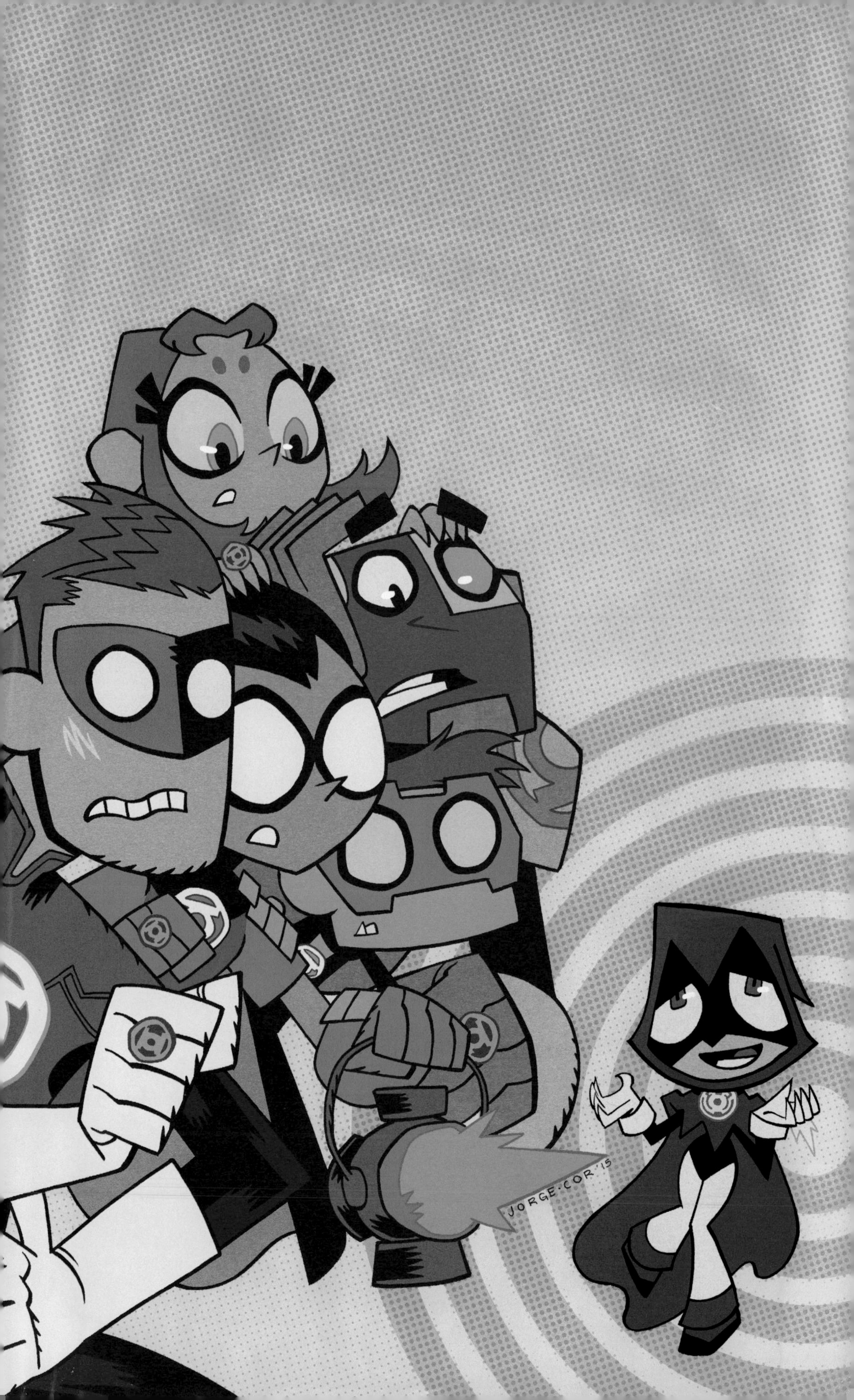
JORGE·COR '15

HAVE THE WILLPOWER?
JOIN THE CORPS
NO EVIL SHALL ESCAPE OUR SIGHT!

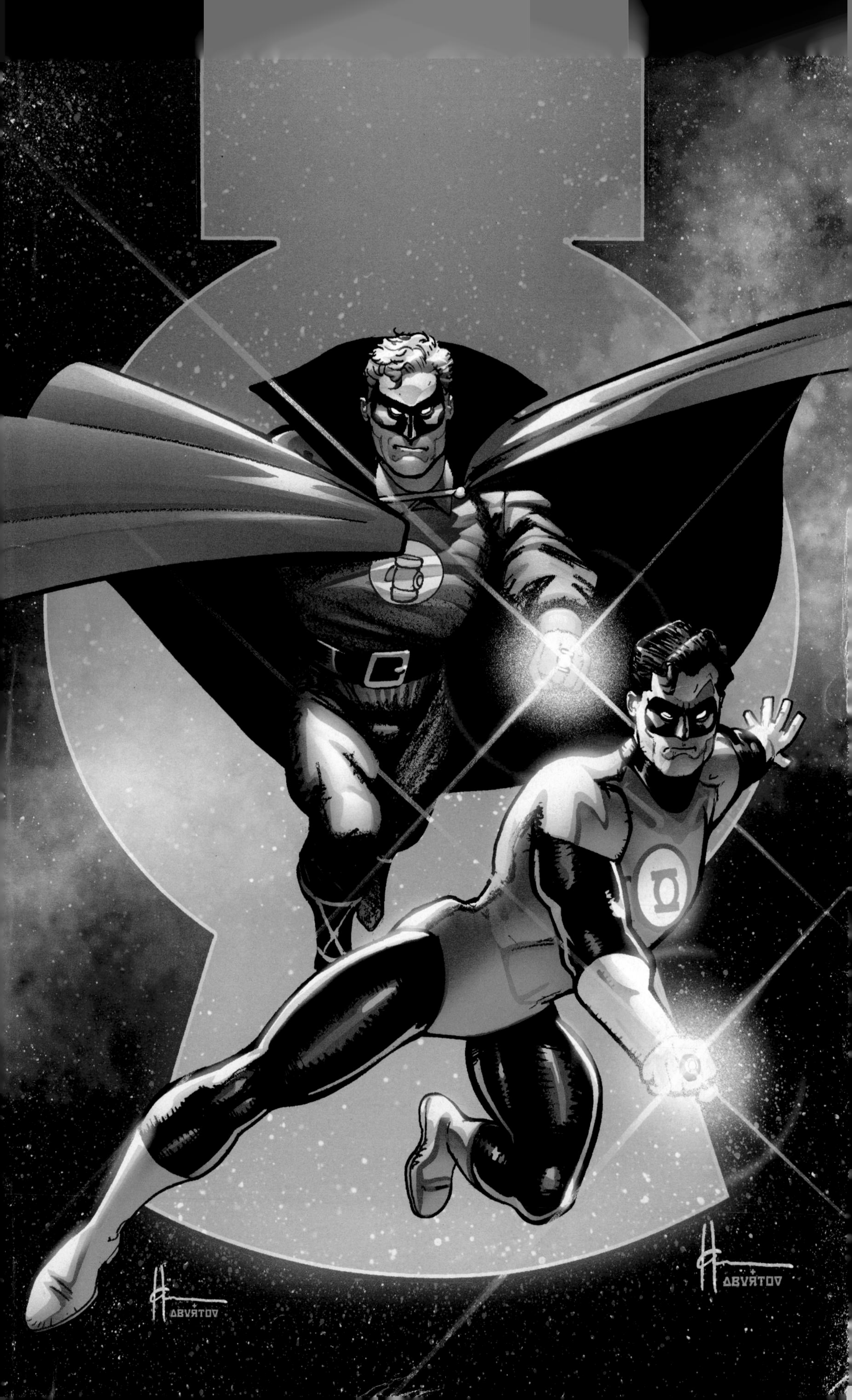

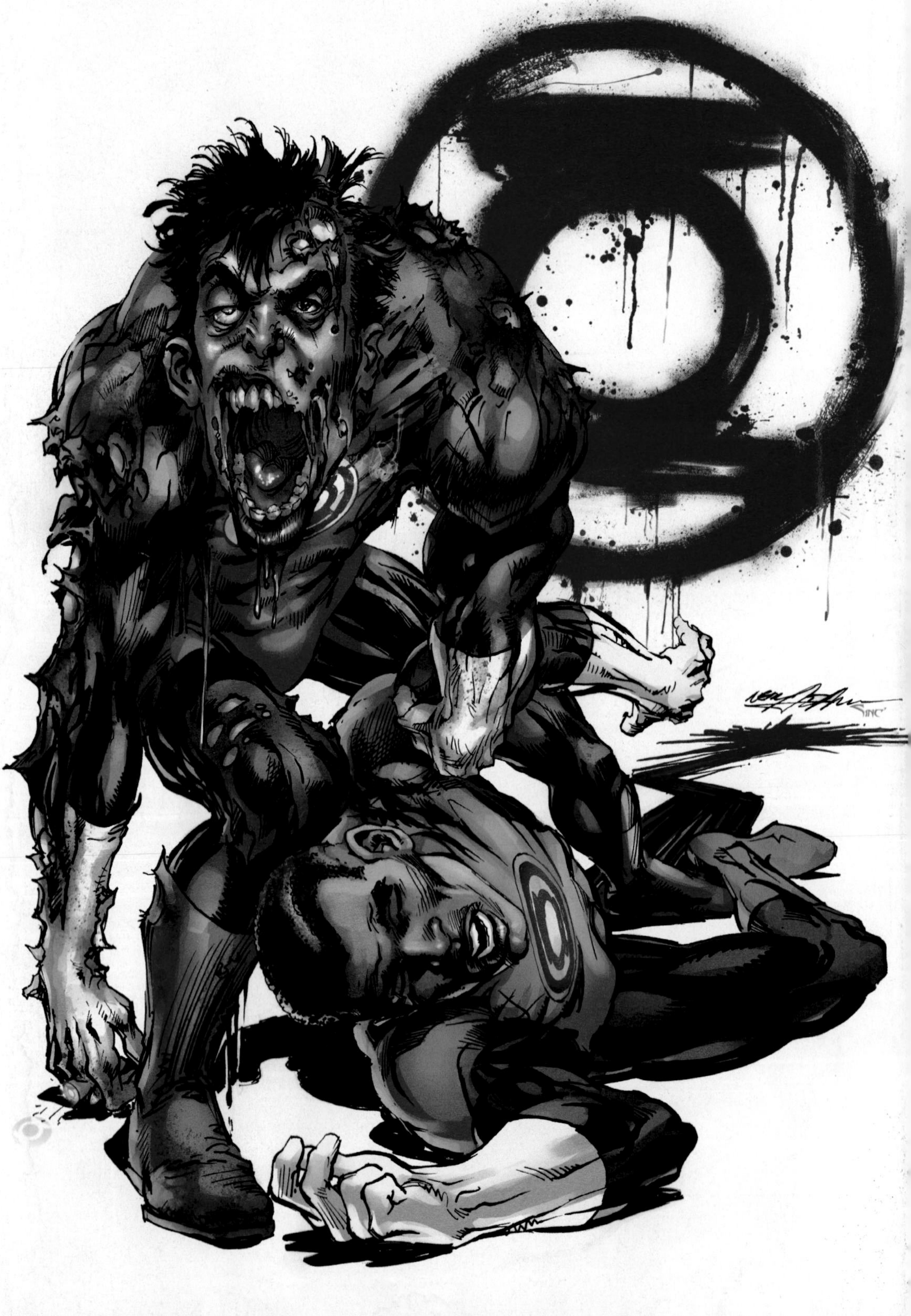

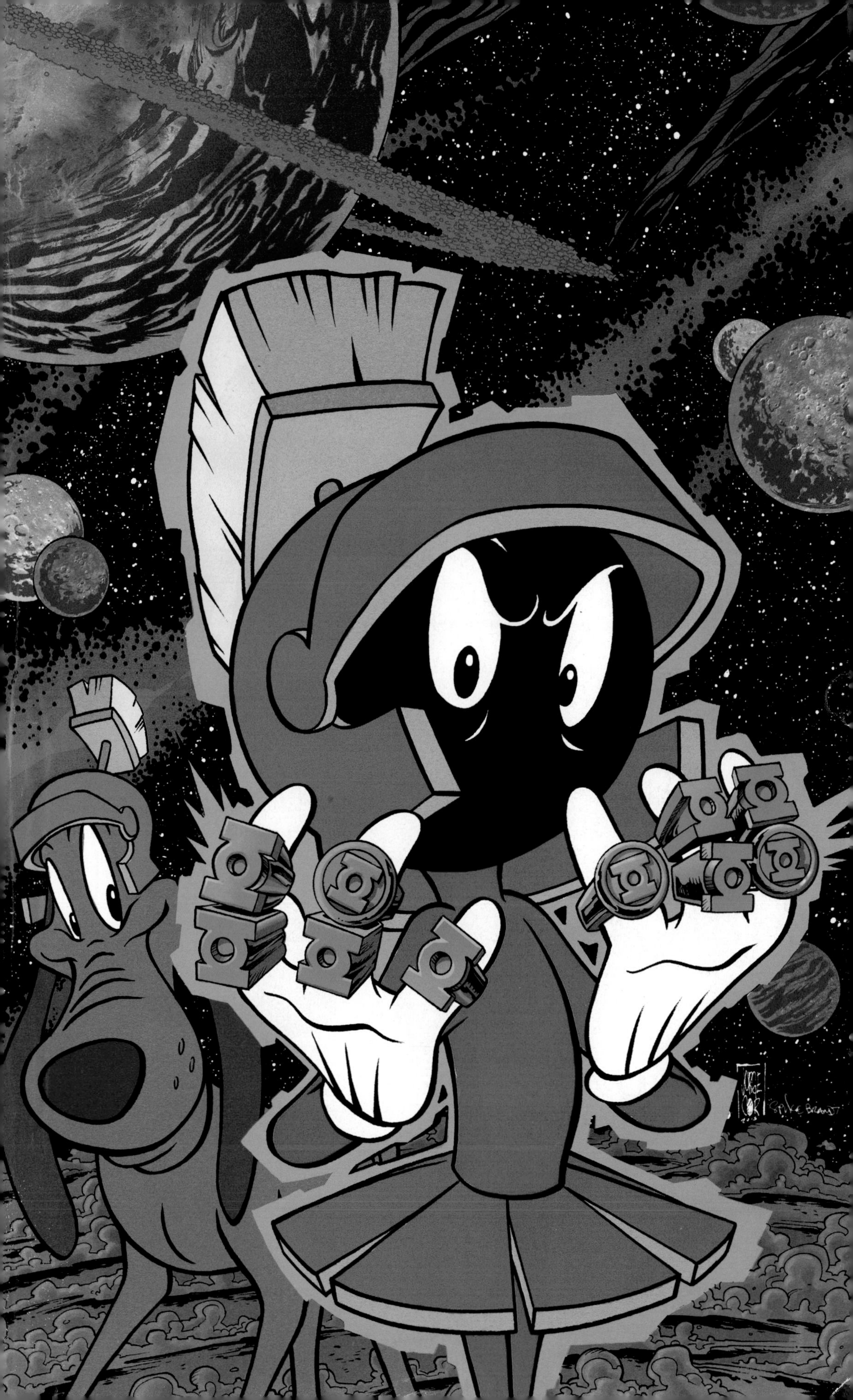

CHARACTER SKETCHES BY
BILLY TAN

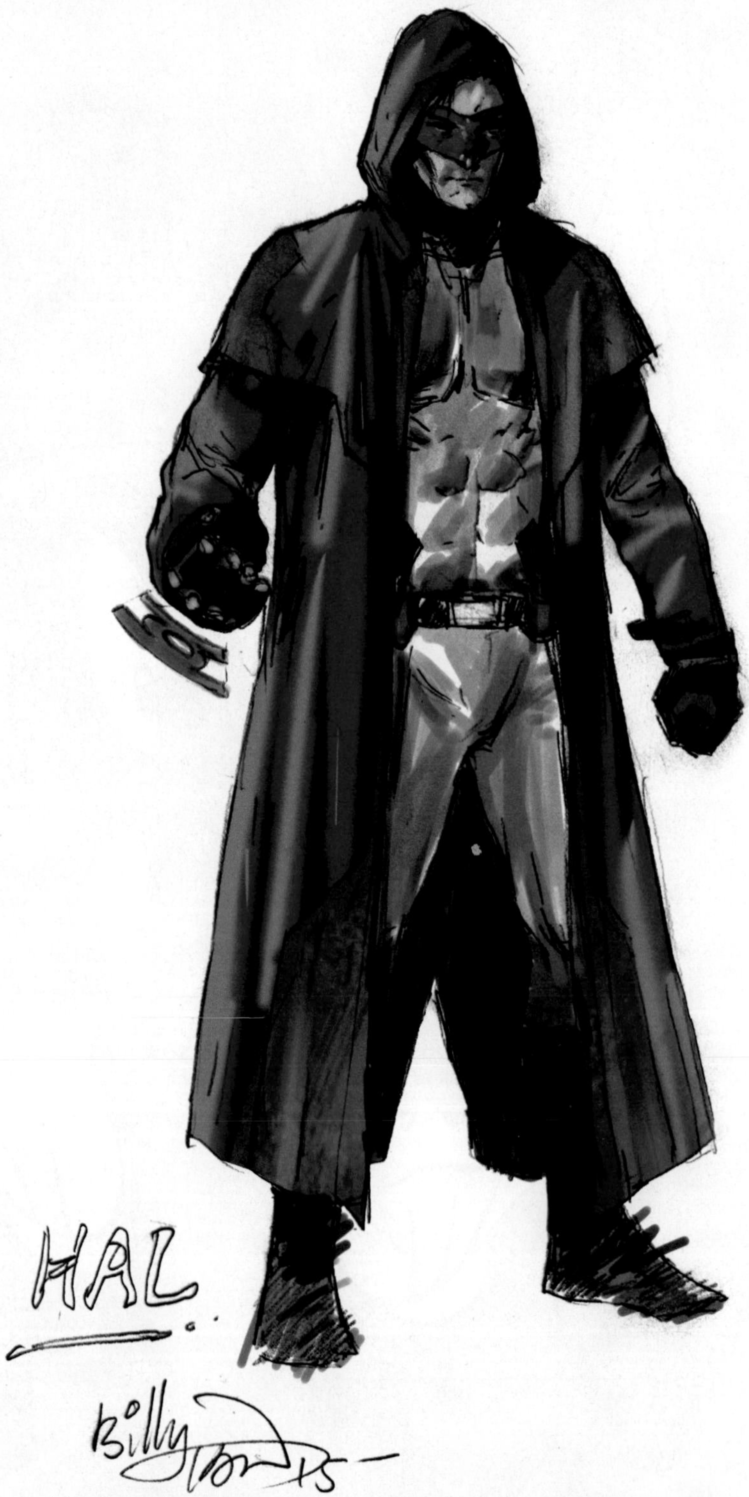
HAL

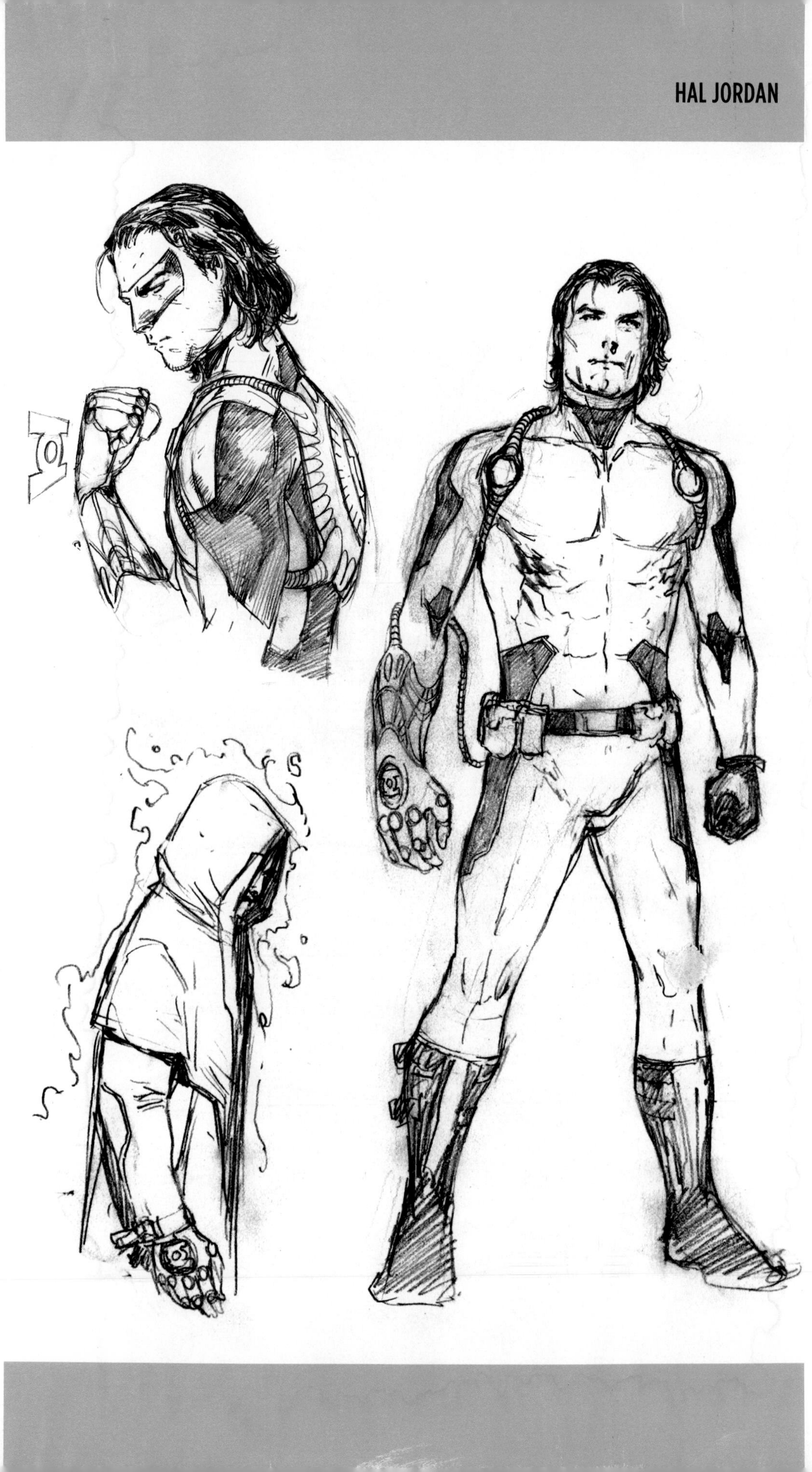

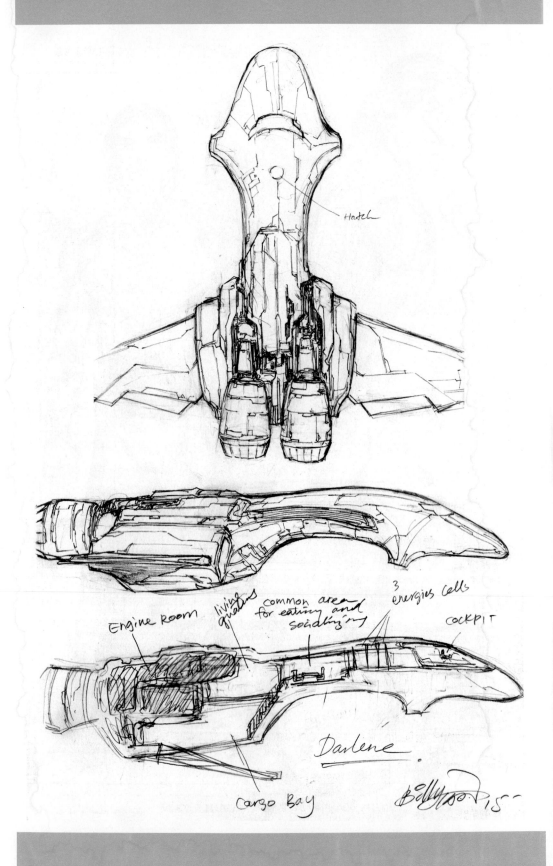

Hatch

Engine Room   living quarters   common area for eating and socializing   3 energies cells   COCKPIT

Darlene

Cargo Bay

PENCILS OF GREEN LANTERN #41, PAGE 8

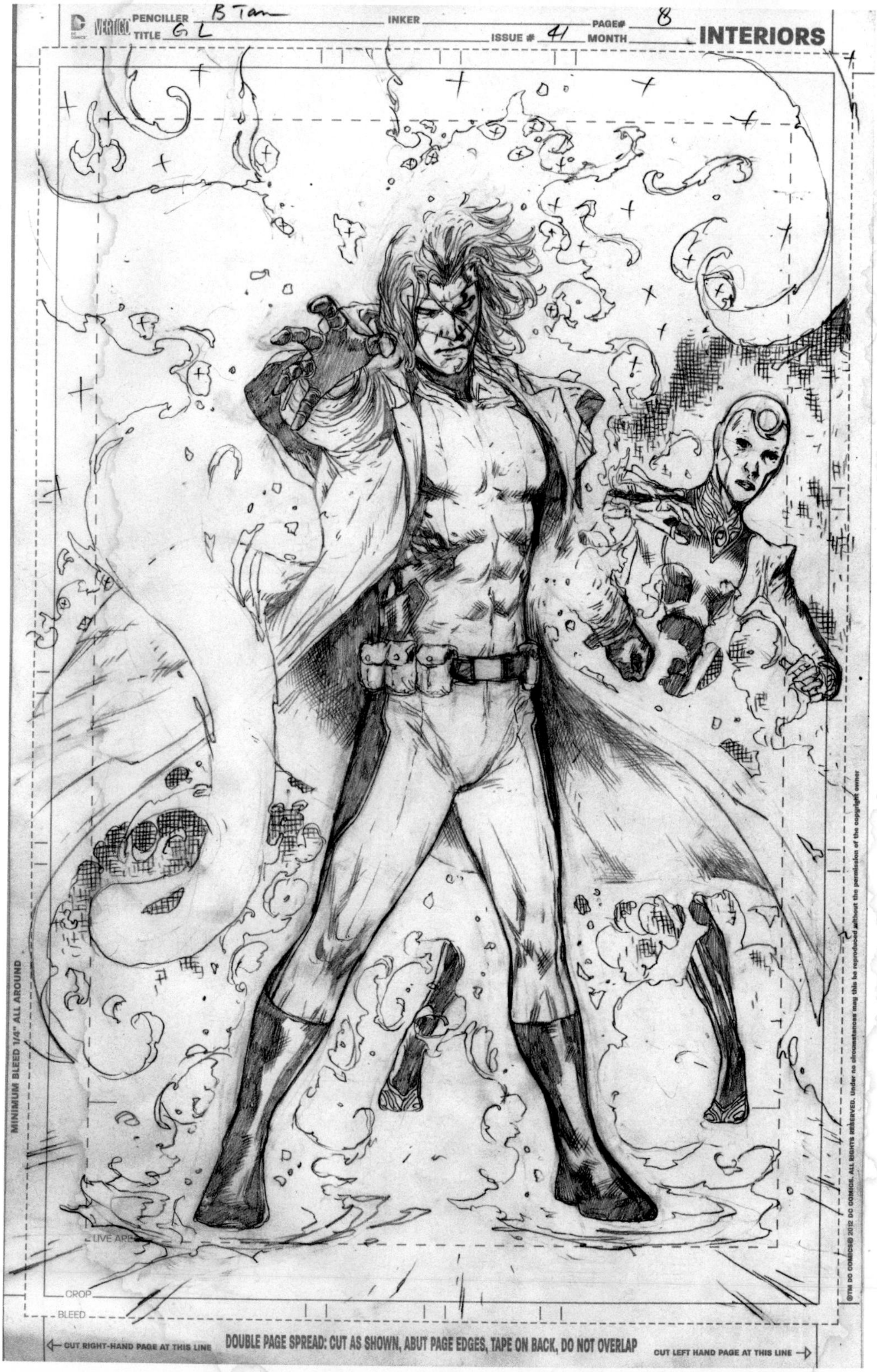

PENCILLER B Tan
INKER
PAGE# 8
TITLE G L
ISSUE # 41
MONTH
INTERIORS
LIVE AREA
CROP
BLEED
MINIMUM BLEED 1/4" ALL AROUND
CUT RIGHT-HAND PAGE AT THIS LINE
DOUBLE PAGE SPREAD: CUT AS SHOWN, ABUT PAGE EDGES, TAPE ON BACK, DO NOT OVERLAP
CUT LEFT HAND PAGE AT THIS LINE

EEN LANTERN #42, PAGE 22

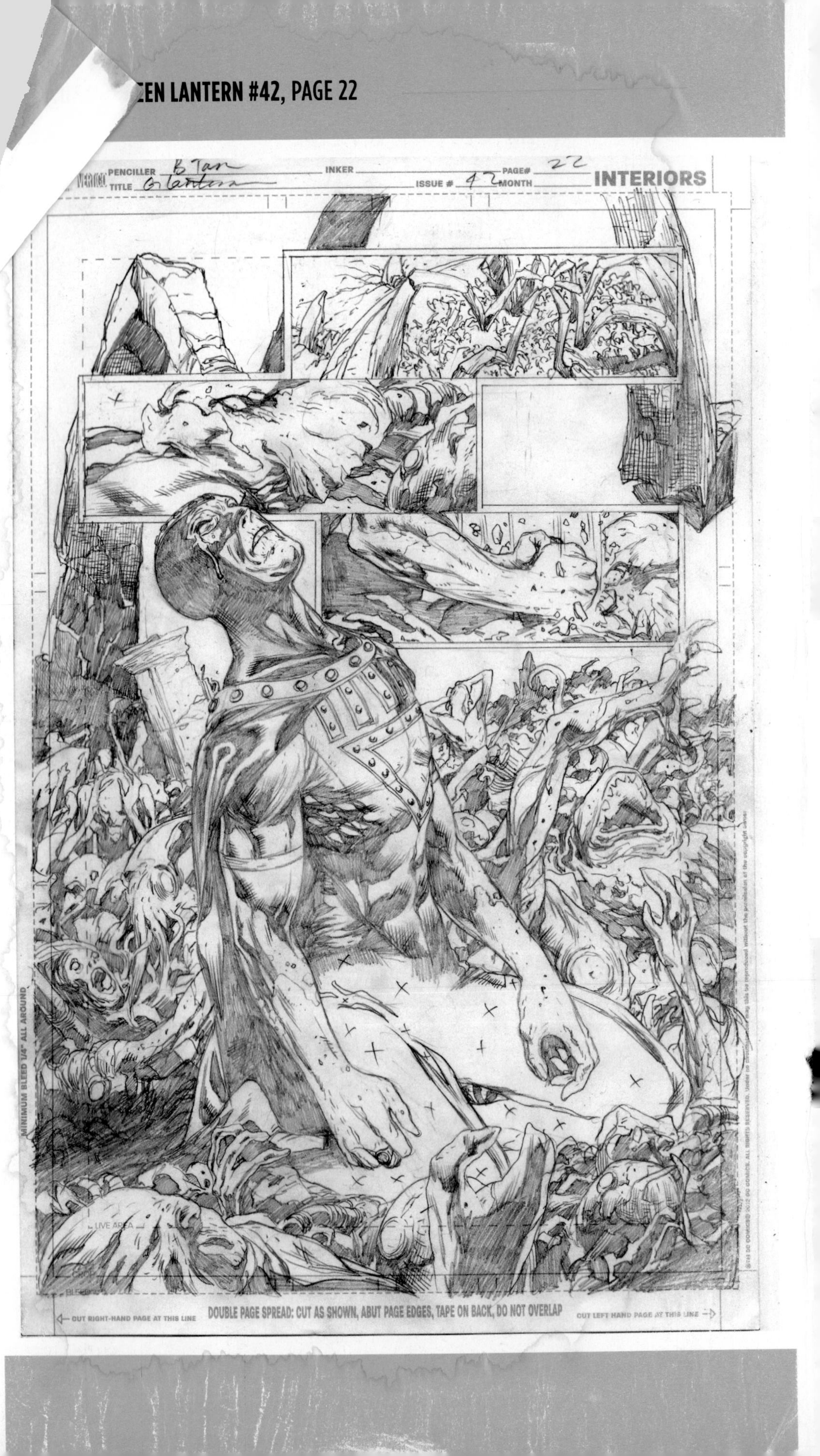

PENCILLER B Tan
TITLE G Lantern
INKER
ISSUE # 42
PAGE# 22
MONTH
INTERIORS
MINIMUM BLEED 1/4" ALL AROUND
LIVE AREA
CUT RIGHT-HAND PAGE AT THIS LINE
DOUBLE PAGE SPREAD: CUT AS SHOWN, ABUT PAGE EDGES, TAPE ON BACK, DO NOT OVERLAP
CUT LEFT HAND PAGE AT THIS LINE